DEDIC.

This book is dedicated to my Father Elohim and His Son Jesus Christ, my Lord. The Holy Spirit lovingly shared with me early every morning the pictographic revelations you will find in these pages.

It is also dedicated to the love of my life, my wife Judy, a seasoned Prophetic Intercessor, who has diligently reviewed every chapter. As my helpmate (Genesis 2:18), she sees things I don't see and has offered countless, amazing suggestions.

Special thanks to Apostle Dr. Emmanuel Nuhu Kure, the vision pioneer of Throneroom Trust Ministry in Kafanchan, Nigeria and his wife Martha. While on a mission trip to Nigeria, Judy and I contracted COVID-19 and malaria, and they saved our lives enabling us to return to America and finish this book.

Thanks also to friends who encouraged and supported me in prayer while I was working on this manuscript: Javier and Isabel Espinoza, our Latin American director for the Global Church Network who live in Costa Rica and have sent my wife and me to twelve countries since 2018; Apostle Joe Mwaniki and his wife Lydia, and Bob Wyant and his wife Judith McCrae who are fellow missionaries; pastor Jose and Nora Heredia from Argentina who prayed for my work on this book every day; and Kim Jacob in Nigeria.

Dr. William E. Combs
Shiloh Global Ministry
Bill@ShilohGlobalMinistry.org
Judy@ShilohGlobalMinistry.org

TABLE OF CONTENTS

CHAPTER 1

Introduction
Back to the Garden
A Reexamination of God's First Covenant

At the outset, I want to share with you that I am a missionary who loves the scriptures. Like most of you, I cannot read Greek or Hebrew without the aid of an interlinear Bible even though I hold Master of Divinity and Doctor of Ministry degrees from Fuller Seminary. You may not have a seminary or Bible school degree or knowledge of the original languages. That's OK. Although references to these languages will populate the pages that follow, I will always explain their meaning in words you can understand.

It may surprise you that God's first covenant was not with Noah in Genesis 9:8-17 or the implied covenant in Genesis 3:21 when God made garments of skins and clothed Adam and Eve. His initial covenant was revealed in the first two chapters of Genesis before sin entered the world.

During most of my Christian life and ministry, I thought these two chapters were largely about creation. But several years ago, the Lord led me to take another look at the dawn of our Story. As I meditated and prayed, I gradually realized my understanding of these verses masked a perfect covenantal relationship that Adam and Eve had with God enabling them to walk victoriously in the manifest presence and power of the Lord without shame or fear.

A Foundational Covenant

This marriage covenant is foundational to all other biblical covenants. It was the only covenant other than the one instituted by Christ that was sealed by the shedding of human blood.

> *"Therefore, a man shall leave his father and his mother and hold fast to his wife, and they shall become one flesh"* (Genesis 2:24).

The initial consummation of this act yielded an issue of blood from the woman affirming their total commitment to each other to become one flesh. Unlike the other covenants, this one was not based on a sacrifice for sin but rather on a declaration of their sacred relationship with each other and the Lord, and stands as the model for all subsequent marriages.

The more I delve into this first covenant, the more I realize that all the other covenants have been instituted by God to bring us back to the garden. The Lord wants us to reap an even greater relationship with Him than our first parents enjoyed, ultimately culminating in the marriage supper of the Lamb and the creation of a new heaven and a new earth.

Moreover, the tremendous benefits of this first covenant are available NOW. My goal in writing this book is to reveal the richness of the life that was compromised when the First Adam disobeyed God so that we can more fully appreciate and receive all that we have gained through the obedience of the Last Adam – Jesus Christ!

The Roots of Our Faith

The roots of our faith are anchored in the ancient Hebrew pictograms written by Moses. Many of the words critical to our faith were originally defined in the opening chapters of Genesis. We seriously limit our understanding of them if we only consider their New Testament meaning. For instance, New Testament Greek defines evil as "bad, wicked, grievous, lewd, malicious, etc." The Hebraic pictographic meaning is simply "a person guided by his sight" – one who walks by sight and not by faith.

Here are some other words and phrases originally defined in the early chapters of Genesis: the knowledge of good and evil, heaven, day, night, name, life, death, our flesh, sin, iniquity, naked, and our spirit, soul and body.

Subjects like spiritual warfare and how our bodies can continually be renewed by the Holy Spirit also find their origins here. We use these words all the time. But without their foundational context, we can misinterpret their use in the rest of scripture.

Hebrew began as a pictographic language

I had no idea when I went to seminary that the structure of the Hebrew alphabet I was studying was not the same as the one written by Moses and inspired by the Holy Spirit. I stumbled onto this discovery a few years ago, and it has opened up a whole new dimension of understanding, revealing many hidden secrets through these ancient pictograms that continue to help me walk in the light as our first parents did.

But before I begin examining the actual verses in Genesis, I want to assure you my faith asserts that the Holy Spirit is the ultimate Author of the Bible, both Old and New Testaments (2 Timothy 3:16 – 17; 2 Peter 1:20 – 21). There is a unity of purpose across all of scripture. We may have favorite books, chapters and verses. But every word is inspired across all of the Bible and must be considered when evaluating any particular segment.

There are many treasures in this first covenant that have been hidden behind the veil spoken of in 2 Corinthians 3:14. It is only through Christ that the veil is taken away! It is my prayer that as you continue reading, you will behold with unveiled face the glory of Christ revealed in this first covenant and be transfigured from glory to glory through the Holy Spirit.

The Lord has given me a job to do. I am not writing a commentary containing my thoughts on how to apply certain verses to our lives as a preacher might do in a sermon or a teacher might do in a lesson. God wants me to help equip you with the pictographic tools you need to meditate on the Hebrew Bible the way Joshua and David did.

Come with me on a journey back to Genesis to rediscover the hope to which the Lord calls us, the very foundation of the inheritance we have in the Kingdom of Heaven as manifested in Jesus Christ the Last Adam, and the awesome power that is available to us through the Holy Spirit.

CHAPTER 2

The Ancient Hebrew Language

The original written form of ancient Hebrew began as a pictographic language with little of the sentence structure we are used to like subjects and predicates, nouns and verbs. Instead, the "letters" Moses wrote were images that resembled everyday objects his readers could easily identify. Each pictogram conveyed meaning that, taken together with the other symbols in a "word," enabled persons like Joshua to comprehend a picture group's basic meaning.

To better understand how these ancient Hebrews "read" Moses' writings, consider for a moment, how you relate to the images in a wedding or graduation album. Even though there are no words associated with each picture, you would have little trouble interpreting the flow of the events as you flip through the album. The pictures on each page help transport you into the experience of the wedding or graduation – all without words to explain their meaning. Furthermore, these pictures allow you to have a more intimate encounter with the participants in the album than mere words could convey.

For Joshua and others in the ancient Hebrew culture, each group of symbols we might associate with "words," were more like pages in the picture book just mentioned. Each image group transported them into the experience of their meaning, carrying them along into the revelation Moses wanted them to understand as they "read" the passage.

Joshua's association with sentences of pictogram "words" was also different from the way we read their translation in English. For us, reading is a linear process: We start at the beginning of the sentence and continue a word at a time until we reach the end. This is especially true if we are reading out loud.

But permit me to paint another scenario. If you have ever gone to the rotunda in your state's capital, you were likely transfixed by the mural painted on the walls surrounding you. A collage of full-color, larger-than-life figures stared back at you depicting epic events in the government's collective history. The mural was not cluttered with many words, and the position of the illustrations tied them together into a continuous story line.

Every time you entered the rotunda over the years, different paintings spoke to you with special significance without the need to take in the entire mural even though the other images were like old friends. This more holistic perspective was likely the way Joshua and his contemporaries meditated on the "sentences" in the Torah and how different word-pictures breathed new life into them each time they returned to these "old friends" over the years.

Today in our digital age, we use emojis to help us communicate on the internet. Each emoji portrays both verbal and nominative meaning in a manner somewhat similar to the ancient Hebrew pictograms. Perhaps if you think of a group of emojis conveying an idea you want to share with a friend, you may be able to relate more closely to the way pictograms were used by Moses and other Hebrew writers.

The evolution of the Hebrew script

Today, we read the Old Testament as a translation from Hebrew into our language. We give little thought to how this translation was carried out. On the one hand, we profess that Moses was guided by the Holy Spirit to write the Torah and that every word he wrote was inspired by God. However, unlike the inspired writers of the New Testament who used the Greek alphabet, the letters Moses wrote with are not the same ones used by translators to create our own version of his manuscript.

Every one of us learns a language from our parents at home at a very early age giving us the ability to converse in our native language. But if we want to read or write our language, we must go to school. The symbols for our alphabet show us how to pronounce the written words we read, and they also enable us to look up those words in a dictionary to discover their meaning.

Moses wrote the Torah to be read by Joshua and others who left Egypt as slaves with no opportunity to go to school. God had earlier facilitated a written, proto-Canaanite language that could be understood without the need for schooling. All the symbols in its alphabet looked like elements they were familiar with as slaves (See the table of symbols below). Since they already knew what each symbol (pictogram) meant, **every group of pictograms we call words functioned as its own dictionary**. Moreover, the position of each symbol in the word, together with the word's position in a verse gave the person the context for more comprehension.

Pictograms were used until Judah was exiled to Babylon around 605 BC. During that captivity, the Hebrew symbols underwent a one-to-one transformation into the Babylonian Aramaic character set. Unfortunately, some of the original pictographic significance was lost because these more cryptic letters could not convey the same depth of meaning as the pictograms they replaced.

Over three hundred years later, this revised character set was used to translate the Hebrew Bible into the Septuagint Greek edition after Greece conquered the nations around the Mediterranean and "encouraged" everyone to learn their language. In order to help you appreciate the difficulty of translating Hebrew into English or any other modern language, let's first examine how the New Testament is translated into English using an example from John 1:1:

Greek: Ἐν ἀρχῇ ἦν ὁ λόγος, καὶ ὁ λόγος ἦν πρὸς τὸν θεόν,

English: In the beginning was the word, and the word was with God,

In this passage, the translation is straightforward. The translator looks up a word in the Greek dictionary to discover its meaning as well as its part of speech (noun, verb, etc.). Then, the translator finds a word or phrase in an English dictionary that best conveys the contextual meaning of the word in the original language.

Now, let's look at the first verse in the Bible:
(read from right to left)

Hebrew: בראשית ברא אלהים את השמים ואת הארץ

English: In beginning created God the heavens and the earth.

Using the same strategy, the translator would look up a word in the Hebrew dictionary and translate its meaning into English. The only problem with this approach is that, in the original language, each word was its own "dictionary" and its meaning was derived from the pictograms of the word.

A linguistic hurdle for translating Hebrew

First as stated earlier, a picture book can portray a message to the viewer without the linguistic constraints of a modern language like the need for subjects and predicates, nouns and verbs.

When pictograms were converted to Aramaic characters after Judah was exiled to Babylon, each new character was a direct, one-to-one adaptation from the earlier symbols. There was no need to impose any additional linguistic constraints **as long as** these texts were read by the ancient Hebrews. But when the Septuagint translators tried to convert Hebrew into Greek, they had to identify certain "words" as nouns, verbs and other parts of speech in order for their translation to make sense to a Greek-speaking person.

Unfortunately, there were times when this focus on the **verbal** aspect of a word largely shielded the reader from its value as a noun or other part of speech. We will see in the next chapter how this shielding affected the first verse of the Torah.

The ancient Hebrew pictograms

Before we consider the second reason for paying attention to the original script Moses used, let's take a brief look at the pictograms that made up the ancient Hebrew alphabet[4]. The first column contains the current Hebrew characters. The second column depicts the proto-Canaanite symbols, then those used by Moses, and finally David's script. (These other sets evolved into images that were much easier to write.) The third column is the name of the characters, and the last column briefly defines them. I will use the proto-Canaanite pictograms in the remainder of this book because they more clearly represent each character's meaning.

Table of the Ancient Hebrew Alphabet

א	𐤀 / 𐤀 / 𐤀	Aleph	An Ox, A Leader, Strength, Power, First
ב	𐤁 / 𐤁 / 𐤁	Bet	A Tent, House, Body, Family, Inside, "In"
ג	𐤂 / 𐤂 / 𐤂	Gimel	Foot, Camel, Lift Up, Benefit, Self Will or Pride
ד	𐤃 / 𐤃 / 𐤃	Dalet	Tent Door, A Path, Way, Movement In and Out
ה	𐤄 / 𐤄 / 𐤄	Hey	Lo!, Behold, Show, Reveal, Praise, Awe, "The"
ו	𐤅 / 𐤅 / 𐤅	Vuv	Tent Peg, Hook, Nail, Join Together, "And"
ז	𐤆 / 𐤆 / 𐤆	Zayin	Cudgel, Weapon, Sword, To Pierce, To Cut
ח	𐤇 / 𐤇 / 𐤇	Chet	Fence, Wall, Separate, Cut Off, Protect
ט	𐤈 / 𐤈 / 𐤈	Thet	Surround, Twist, Coil, A Basket, A Snake
י	𐤉 / 𐤉 / 𐤉	Yood	Hand, Work, Strength of My Arm, A Deed Done
כ	𐤊 / 𐤊 / 𐤊	Kaph	Palm, Cover, Allow, Conform To My Palm, Open
ל	𐤋 / 𐤋 / 𐤋	Lamed	Shepherd Staff, Control, Authority, "To," "Toward"
מ	𐤌 / 𐤌 / 𐤌	Mem	Water, Chaos, Mighty, Many, "From," "Than"
נ	𐤍 / 𐤍 / 𐤍	Noon	A Sprout, New Life, To Spread, Continue, Action
ס	𐤎 / 𐤎 / 𐤎	Samech	A Thorn, A Support, A Shield, Protect, Assist, Prop
ע	𐤏 / 𐤏 / 𐤏	Ayin	An Eye, See, Experience, Understand

פ	○ / ך / ר	Pey	A Mouth, To Speak, An Opening, The Beginning
צ	ר / ב / ꝋ	Tsade	A Hook, Pull Toward, Desire, Trouble, Ambush
ק	⊸ / ⇜ / ꟼ	Qoof	Cycle, Surround, Sun at the Horizon, After
ר	₰ / ९ / ꟼ	Resh	A Head, A Person, First, Highest / Most Important
ש	W / ꟸ / ꟿ	Sheen	Teeth, Consume, Devour, Destroy
ת	† / ✗ / ✕	Tav	A Sign, Cross, Covenant, Finish, Complete

Hebrew Dictionaries

Those who have studied Hebrew[1] know there is a Hebrew dictionary. The ones I studied were compiled by Wilhelm Gesenius, a German professor, between 1806 and 1807[2] to be followed by his Hebrew grammar in 1813[3], and Brown, Driver and Briggs[22] based on Gesenius' work. His lexicon not only contained each word's definition (likely taken in part from the meaning and context of the associated Greek word in the Septuagint edition as well as relevant Aramaic manuscripts), but also what Gesenius and others determined was its appropriate part of speech (perhaps again from its use in the Septuagint edition.) Hebrew dictionaries today follow that same pattern, making the task of translation much easier.

In the introduction, I briefly contrasted the Greek word for "evil" with its pictographic equivalent: "bad, wicked, grievous, lewd, malicious, etc." vs "a person guided by his sight." The reason for this disparity: The Greek dictionary used by the Septuagint translators was a pagan dictionary filled with pagan definitions. Even though the translators did their best to associate a Hebrew word written in an Aramaic script with an equivalent representative in the Greek language, an exact match was not always possible.

We know that God blesses translations because most of the Old Testament quotes in the New Testament are from the Septuagint translation. Furthermore, the entire New Testament is written in Greek and inspired by the Holy Spirit so that the Gospel could be proclaimed to Greek-speaking persons throughout the Roman empire.

So why bother with the symbolic script used in much of the Old Testament? We need the witness of the pictograms **as well as their Greek counterparts** to recognize, as in the case of the contrasting words for "evil," that the Greek definition rests upon its original Hebraic pictographic foundation and is the result of a person walking by sight and not by faith.

The **second reason** for considering the symbols Moses used is that they portray a more colorful and personal association with their corresponding words. The Greeks tended to relate in more abstract terms. So, the first Greek verse in the Torah is:

Greek: Ἐν ἀρχῇ ἐποίησεν ὁ θεός τὸν οὐρανὸν καὶ τὴν γῆν.

English In beginning, created God the heaven and the earth.

If this translation looks a lot like what we have in our English Bibles, it is because our language is rooted in the abstract mind-set of the Greco-Roman culture. But to be honest, these abstract words do not convey much concrete meaning.

To show you what I mean, let's consider the original pictograms for God's name:

If you have access to a Hebrew Bible, you will notice a dot just above and to the left of the Lamed (the second letter from the right: (אֱלֹהִים). It is shorthand for a Vuv (treated as a long vowel) and is why we pronounce a long "O" sound after the Lamed (El<u>o</u>him). So, the original pictograms may have contained that Vuv:

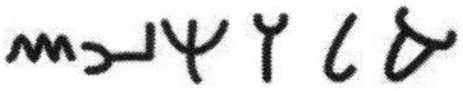

ᵐᵔᴊᴪ Y �𝘓 ♌

Instead of just giving you a one-word definition for each symbol, permit me to highlight each one relative to its meaning as might have been understood by an ancient Hebrew. I hope you will agree that the abstract title "God" does not begin to reveal the same depth of relational meaning as the corresponding pictograms.

♌ – An ox was the workhorse in their agrarian society. Mental images of this pictogram would likely include an ox pulling a plow, another pulling a wagon, and one working on a threshing floor. All these evoke the muscle available to an individual enabling him to perform tasks that would otherwise be nearly impossible.

𝘓 – The shepherd's staff was used to guide, tend and protect sheep. A yoke is also a type of shepherding staff. A younger ox was yoked to a more experienced animal so the younger one could learn how to pull more efficiently. Initially, the older animal set the pace, determined the direction and assumed a greater portion of the load. Mental images would include a pair of oxen pulling a plow or a wagon. Joshua and others would see themselves being yoked with God as the One Who set the pace and direction, carried most of the load, and assumed responsibility for their care and protection.

Y – Pegs anchor a tent to the ground stabilizing it against

many threats. It may also imply that if the person is yoked to the Lord, their life is firmly anchored and stable. Images would include winds and floods against a tent or house showing what happens as a result of anchoring one's tent on sand vs. firmer ground.

Ψ – This image symbolizes a person standing with his hands raised in awe, praise and adoration. Those who are yoked firmly to the Lord experience guidance and blessing that motivates them to praise God. Ancient Hebrews viewing this symbol would be able to personally identify their own answers to prayer and salvation from seemingly impossible situations.

ᴟᴣᴧ – ᴧᴧ represents chaos and ᴣᴧ represents the strength of one's arm. So, being firmly yoked with the Lord means that no matter what chaos, formidable obstacle, insurmountable hurdle or trial we face, it is no match for the strength of the Lord's arm to deliver us.

It is my prayer that the ancient pictograms you will encounter in the rest of this book will open the eyes of your heart to greater depths of understanding.

Converting Hebrew characters into pictograms

I said earlier that after Judah was led into captivity, they converted their Hebrew pictograms into Babylonian characters through a one-to-one transformation. God told Joshua to meditate on the Torah. You too, can meditate on any Hebrew text by using the Table of the Ancient Hebrew Alphabet given above to reverse this one-to-one association and reinstate the appropriate pictograms for your text just like I did with God's Name אֱלֹהִים => ᴧᴣᴧΨꓭ ᄼ ᴥ . I showed you how these symbols reveal a much deeper understanding than our translation: "God."

Why character conversion is important

I shared a translation of Genesis 1:1 from Hebrew to English that mirrors the translation we have in our Bibles. But I also cautioned that these words likely came from a Hebrew dictionary used by modern translators that may not have accurately reflected the underlying meaning of the corresponding pictographic "words."

You just compared the dictionary description for "God" with its pictographic symbols. In my next two chapters, you will see that the underlying definition for "In the beginning" has nothing to do with the beginning of time, that "create" relates to God's Son as shown in John 1:1 − 3, and that "heaven" has little to do with a visible arch in the sky or the higher ether where celestial bodies exist.

The Septuagint scholars defined the words for their Greek translation based on the Babylonian characters that had replaced their corresponding pictograms over three hundred years earlier. They also had the difficult task of finding appropriate Greek words from a pagan dictionary to translate their Hebrew texts for a Greek-speaking audience.

It is important for us to be aware of this linguistic transformation. Without the foundational contribution these pictograms bring to our understanding, we can at times, misinterpret what the Holy Spirit inspired Moses to write in the Torah.

The good news: just like the Hebrew slaves who left Egypt with Moses, you will not need to learn to read and write the Hebrew language in order to "read" these ancient symbols because they create their own dictionary and provide a window into their preliterate pictographic interpretation.

Why Now?

You may have been pondering as you read this chapter why the Lord has waited until now to call men like Frank Seekins and Jeff Benner[4] to devote their lives revealing the actual pictographic symbols Moses used to write the Torah. Their pioneering work is now part of the curriculum in many seminaries across the US and around the world. Their work is also enabling folks like me to stand on their shoulders and experience a deeper understanding of the precious, inspired texts Joshua meditated on as he led the children of Israel into the Promised Land (Joshua 1:7 – 8).

Paul says in Romans 11:25:

> *"I do not want you to be unaware of this mystery, brothers, a partial hardening has come upon Israel until the fullness of the Gentiles has come in."*

Jesus proclaimed a similar message to His disciples in Luke 21:24:

> *"And they shall fall by the edge of the sword, and shall be led away captive into all nations, and Jerusalem will be trampled underfoot by the Gentiles, until the times of the Gentiles are fulfilled."*

In 1947, we witnessed the birth of the nation of Israel drawn out from the nations of the world. And in 2017, the US and a few other countries recognized Jerusalem as the legitimate capital of Israel in what many hoped is a fulfillment of Biblical prophecy.

For nearly 2000 years, the Lord has allowed a partial hardening of His people to bring salvation to the Gentiles. Paul also says in Romans 11:12, 15;

*"But if their transgression means riches for the Gentiles, how **much greater riches** will their full inclusion bring! – For if their rejection means the reconciliation of the world, what will their acceptance mean but life from the dead?"*

These passages look forward to a time when the native olive branches will be grafted back into their ancestral roots. And when this happens, it will bring **much greater riches** than has been possible through Gentile ministries alone.

On November 18th 2019, while my wife and I were on a mission trip to Kenya and Tanzania, I had a prophetic visitation I believe speaks to this last great awakening:

> I woke up around 1:00 AM and saw an amazing anointing poured out to obtain an unparalleled harvest. I saw seven sheaves of grain - a perfect number indicating the extent of the harvest. But along with this harvest came increasing persecution until it reached horrific proportions. The Lord indicated that if we shrink back from the persecution, our anointing will be withdrawn. This opposition is to be expected and with it will come grace to face it. Then I saw a sudden burst of bright light followed by a long period of enforced peace. That period was followed by a reign of awesome and majestic light.

I believe the recent focus on the ancient pictographic Hebrew language is playing a small part in revealing to Jews and Gentiles alike that Jesus was an active participant in the first chapters of the Torah. I will show in the next chapter that Genesis 1:1 is the foundation for John 1:1 – 3. This association gives fresh insight into Jesus' admonition in John 5:39 – 46:

> *"You search the Scriptures because you think that in them you have eternal life; and it is **they that bear witness about me**, yet you refuse to come to me that you may have life. . . Do not think that I will accuse you to the Father. There is one who accuses you: **Moses**, on whom you have set your hope. For if you believed **Moses**, you would believe me; **for he wrote of me.**"*

Jesus later said in John 12:32:

> *"And I, when I am lifted up from the earth, will draw all people to myself."*

I pray that this book will lift up the Messiah that Moses wrote about in the Torah, and help remove the veil spoken of in 2 Corinthians 3:16 from our Jewish brothers, and give new inspiration as well to us Gentiles.

Study Questions For Discussion

- We believe the Holy Spirit inspired every word in the Bible. Why is it important for us to obtain the tools necessary to study the actual words the Holy Spirit inspired Moses to write?

- Many of the words that make up our Gospel were initially defined in the opening chapters of Genesis like good, evil, our flesh, sin and our body, soul and spirit. If we don't obtain these tools, how can we be sure the Gospel we are preaching is based on the foundational meaning of the words inspired by the Holy Spirit?

- When I went to seminary, I thought that the first two chapters of Genesis were largely about creation. But I recently discovered that God revealed something just as important in these verses that enabled our first parents to walk in the power and manifest presence of the Lord, victorious in all that they did without shame or fear. Why is it important for us and for those in ministry to rediscover this vital relationship with God through Jesus, the Last Adam?

- When we read the Torah, we take for granted that our translators started with the original Hebrew language. How do verses like Genesis 1:1 reflect the significant influence from the Septuagint translation that impacts the revelation given through Moses?

CHAPTER
3

Genesis 1:1
In The Beginning

PROLOGUE:

I said in the last chapter that the Septuagint scholars faced a daunting task translating Hebrew into Greek. **First**, the original pictographic foundation for their Hebrew manuscripts written in Aramaic characters did not contain the grammatical constraints of the Greek language that required different parts of speech and linguistic structures. **Second**, Greek was a pagan language, and their dictionaries did not always provide word matches that related the same meaning as their Hebrew counterparts. **Third**, words that originally made perfect sense to Hebrews were more easily understood by Greeks if they were couched in more abstract terms.

Finally, the Hebrew language we study today is the product of its evolution through many centuries with a grammar and lexicon largely gleaned from Septuagint and Aramaic sources rather than from its ancient pictographic roots. So, words redefined as different parts of speech by the original translators maintain those same or similar grammatical designations in modern Hebrew. With this context in mind, let's look at how the Septuagint scholars addressed the first verse of the Torah:

Genesis 1:1

בראשית ברא אלהימ
את השמימ ואת הארצ

I have broken this Hebrew verse into two phrases to show you the problem faced by the ancient translators. They translated the second phrase as "the heaven and the earth." So, they had to select one of the "words" in the first phrase as a verb in order to generate a sentence meaningful to a Greek-speaking audience. The third word is God's name, and the first word contains more characters than God's name making its identification as a verb more difficult. So, neither the first nor the third words were good verbal candidates.

The first two characters in the second word (בר), define the Hebrew word for either a grain of wheat or a mature son. The meaning from its pictograms is "a house of heads."[5] Think of a grain of wheat as one of the grains (heads) at the top (house) of a mature wheat plant. A mature son is also one of the heads in his father's house. When a grain of wheat is planted, it **creates** the next crop of wheat. And when a mature son leaves home, he **creates** the next generation of his father's family. So, ברא was the one word that could easily be translated into a verb.

I am sure these Septuagint scholars gave little thought to what might be lost by translating this particular symbol group into a verb. Deuteronomy 6:4 says, *"Hear, O Israel: The Lord our God is one."* So, the very first sentence in the Hebrew Bible did not lose any apparent content in their mind when ברא was translated into a Greek verb and rendered as *"In the beginning, God **created** the heaven and the earth."*

However, the Hebrew Bible is not the only inspired scripture.

So, we also need to consider the witness of the New Testament. One of these passages is from John's gospel verse 1:1:

"In the beginning was the Word, and the Word was with God, and the Word was God."

I don't think it was just a coincidence that John began his Gospel this way. Let's look at it in the original Greek:

Ἐν ἀρχῇ *ἦν ὁ λόγος, καὶ ὁ λόγος ἦν πρὸς τὸν* **θεόν,** *καὶ* **θεὸς** *ἦν ὁ λόγος.*

And here is the Septuagint translation:

Ἐν ἀρχῇ ἐποίησεν ὁ θεός *τὸν οὐρανὸν καὶ τὴν γῆν.*

Notice the positioning of John's Greek words. He started out with the same two words translated from בראשית (εν αρχη) as in the Septuagint. Then he positioned ὁ λόγος (the Word) in exactly the same location as ברא (εποιησεν), the place for the verb needed to construct a meaningful Greek sentence. Next, he used the same Greek word for God (θεὸς) so as to make a distinction between the Word and God located in the third position in the translation of Genesis 1:1.

The Greek word for "created" in the Septuagint version of Genesis 1:1 is εποιησεν. In Genesis verses 1:7, 16, 25, 26 and 31, the Hebrew word is not ברא but עשה and is translated as "made." However, the Septuagint translates both ברא and עשה in verses 1:1, 7, 16, 25, 26, 27 and 31 with the same verb εποιησεν.

John selected another verb ἐγένετο (made) instead of εποιησεν, abandoning the word that was used as a replacement for ברא and עשה in chapter one, but used by them to translate ברא at the end of the first phrase of Genesis 2:4:

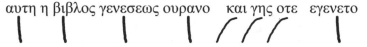

αυτη η βιβλος γενεσεως ουρανο   και γης οτε   εγενετο

This is the book of generations of heaven and earth when they were made (ברא).

Next, John declared that Jesus actively participated in every aspect of creation:

> *"He was with God in the beginning (εν αρχη).*
> *Through him all things were made (ἐγένετο);*
> *without him nothing was made (ἐγένετο) that*
> *was made (γέγονεν). "* (John 1:2 - 3)

John's choice of ὁ λόγος (the word) is also significant. The first time "word" is used in the Bible is in Genesis 15:1 which reads: *"After these things the **word** (דבר – Ν𝕎𝕌) of the Lord came to Abram in a vision."* The Septuagint scholars translated דבר with λεγων, the same Greek word John chose.

The word of the Lord was God's expressed revelation to Abram. The pictograms for "word" mean: the door (𝕌 – ד) of the son (Ν𝕎 – בר). John was associating the Word (the door of the son) with ברא by positioning ὁ λόγος in the same location as in the first verse of the Septuagint. As such, he was declaring that Jesus was the ברא in the first verse of the Torah and was also the expressed revelation of God to us.

In Revelations 19:13, John identifies Jesus as the Word of God:

> *"And he was clothed with a vesture dipped*
> *in blood: and his name is called The Word of*
> *God."*

Matthew also stated that Jesus was God's beloved Son and that He was a more complete spokesman for God than Moses and Elijah – the ultimate Door through which the revelation of the Lord would come to us:

> *"And after six days Jesus took with him Peter and James, and John his brother, and led them up a high mountain by themselves. And he was transfigured before them, and his face shone like the sun, and his clothes became white as light. And behold, there appeared to them **Moses and Elijah, talking with him**. And Peter said to Jesus, 'Lord, it is good that we are here. If you wish, I will make three tents here, one for you and **one for Moses and one for Elijah.**' He was still speaking when, behold, a bright cloud overshadowed them, and a voice from the cloud said, 'This is my beloved Son, with whom I am well pleased; **listen to him**.'"*

(Matthew 17:1 – 5)

I believe John was urging his Jewish readers to take another look at the meaning of the original Hebrew characters. His bold affirmation asserted that Jesus was not only with God in the beginning, He was the ultimate revelation of God in the flesh taking an essential part in making everything that was made.

An 𐤀 appended to 𐤓𐤔

I said earlier that 𐤓𐤔 means grain or a mature son. But 𐤀𐤓𐤔 has a 𐤀 appended to 𐤓𐤔. What does the 𐤀 add to the meaning of this pictogram group?

To find out, I looked up every two-character "word" in <u>Ancient Hebrew Lexicon of the Bible</u> by Jeff A. Benner[4] that also had a 𐤀 appended to it. I put all this information in Appendix A so you can see that this Aleph addition intensifies, broadens and builds upon the meaning of the original Hebrew word. So,

$\cancel{b}$ intensifies the significance of $\widehat{\Omega}\mathsf{u}$ in its relationship with the other "words" in the first verse in the Torah. Seen through the lens of John's Gospel, we can appreciate the extent of this significance as Elohim's first Son.

A closer look at the yoked relationship

The proximity of $\cancel{b}\widehat{\Omega}\mathsf{u}$ to $\mathsf{m}\mathsf{J}\mathsf{Y}\mathsf{L}\cancel{b}$ in Genesis 1:1, implies that the Son was yoked to his Father ($\mathsf{L}\cancel{b}$) in a strong covenant relationship. Through the yoke, his Father showed him all that the Father was doing (John 5:19 – 20).

In an agrarian society, a yoke was tailored specifically to each animal. And it took several years before a young bull received enough training to pull in-step with an experienced ox. There was a tendency, especially at first, to set its own pace, lag behind, lung ahead or veer away as it struggled against the yoke, the pace and the strength of the older ox.

Each time the young animal stepped first, he felt the entire weight of the load. In addition, his position either in front of or behind meant that the yoke did not rest squarely across his shoulders. So with every other step, the full weight pressed unequally against him.

But the young animal eventually learned that paying attention to the right-left cadence and direction of the older ox divided the load equally between them making its individual burden much lighter. Also, its obedience to the pace of the older ox meant its own yoke always set squarely on its shoulders creating an easy yoked relationship with the older ox. Jesus said:

> *"No one knows the Son except the Father. And*
> *no one knows the Father except the Son and*
> *those to whom the Son chooses to reveal him."*
> (Matthew 11:27)

How does Jesus choose to reveal His Father to us? By asking us to take his yoke upon us – the yoke of the younger ox – and learn along with Jesus as He follows the lead of His Father. Trying to set our own pace or direction only makes our burden heavy. But if we put on Jesus' yoke and do only what we both see our Father doing, we will find rest for our souls. Like Jesus, we will discover that His yoke is easy and His burden is light. (Matthew 11:28 – 30)

Joshua and other Hebrew men may have identified with שׁוֹר as a favored mature son who was yoked with Elohim Who continually guided them as they walked in His light. Like them, we can also identify as Elohim's favored mature sons and daughters by faith.

Jesus as a grain of wheat
Referring to His identity as רב – a mature seed – Jesus said,
> *"Unless a grain of wheat falls into the earth and dies, it remains alone; but if it dies, it bears much fruit"* (John 12:24).

How do we bear much fruit? By dying daily to our SELVES, taking up our cross and following Jesus Christ as He follows His Father.

In the beginning
Now, let's take a look at the first word in this verse:

The first symbol ⌂ is a simplified floor plan for a Bedouin tent. The entrance is through the upper left and the living quarters are on the right inside. When this pictogram is added as a prefix to a cluster of symbols, it can convey a meaning similar to our preposition "in."

ᗯᗐᑎ is translated as river in Genesis 2:10:

> *"A river (ᑎᎽᎽ ᐠ) flowed out of Eden to wa-*
> *ter the garden, and there it divided and became*
> *four rivers (ᗯᗐᑎ) ."*

Two different "words" are translated as "river." The second one should more accurately be translated "and became the head of four rivers" because ᑎ is at the beginning instead of at the end of the word. Every spring, the river floods and overflows its banks, strongly ᗐ consuming / devouring / destroying ᗯ its banks.

The literal meaning of ✝ᐣᗯᗐᑎᐪ could be "In the **head** of a river." Like so many other literal translations of Hebrew scripts, this one might raise more questions than illumination to our western mindset. So, a more abstract interpretation was substituted for a literal one: ᗯᗐᑎ is "In the **beginning** (the head of a river)".

However, *"In the beginning"* can also be misleading. To many, that interpretation indicates God created the heaven and the earth a long time ago – perhaps at the beginning of time itself. But as you can see from these pictograms, time is not the issue.

Today, I have begotten you

In Acts 13:33, Peter quotes the second Psalm with reference to God raising Jesus from the dead,

> *"This he has fulfilled to us their children by*
> *raising Jesus, as also it is written in the second*
> *Psalm, 'You are my Son, today I have begotten*
> *you.'"*

Here is the quote from Psalm 2:6 – 7,

> *"As for me, I have set my King on Zion, my holy hill." I will tell of the decree: The Lord said to me, 'You are my Son; today I have begotten you.'"*

How did God beget His Son? The Hebrew word for "begotten" means "to give birth to a child." By extension, it can also be translated as *"You are my Son, today I have delivered you as through childbirth."* This second interpretation fits better both to David being decreed as King on Zion and to Jesus being raised from the dead. Romans 8:11 says,

> *"If the Spirit of him who raised Jesus from the dead dwells in you, he who raised Christ Jesus from the dead will also give life to your mortal bodies through his Spirit who dwells in you."*

We know from this verse that the Holy Spirit was actively involved in raising Christ Jesus from the dead, the same activity proclaimed in Acts 13:33.

The first three pictograms in $ \dagger \mathord{\supset}\text{--}\mathsf{w}\mathord{\diagup}\text{\cntr}\mathord{\Omega}\mathord{\Box} $ and $ \mathord{\diagup}\text{\cntr}\mathord{\Omega}\mathord{\Box} $ are the same and could also indicate a birthing relationship between the Holy Spirit and the Son as is portrayed by delivering Jesus' body from the dead **as through childbirth**.

A River of life

In John's Gospel, Jesus says,

> *"Whoever believes in me, as the Scripture has said, 'Out of his heart **will flow rivers of living water**.' Now this he said about the Spirit whom those who believed in him were to receive, for as yet the Spirit had not been given because Jesus was not yet glorified."* (John 7:38 – 39)

John's testimony, together with the mention of the Spirit of God in Genesis 1:2, could indicate that the very first word in the Bible refers to the Holy Spirit. It also helps answer two other questions.

In Genesis 1:26 – 27, the Lord says

> *"Let us make man in our image and after our likeness... So, God created man in his own image, in the image of God he created him;* ***male and female*** *he created them."*

Verse 26 begins with a relational conversation: *"Let US make man in OUR image and after OUR likeness."* We have already shown that by raising Jesus, the Holy Spirit "birthed" Him from the dead. The relational conversation in 1:26 is more understandable if we realize it is between Elohim and His adult Son in the power of the Holy Spirit to create a relational image – male and female – that would reflect their relationship.

You will receive power

In Chapter Two, I shared with you the meaning of the pictograms in God's name:  . I said the last two symbols assured Joshua and others that no matter what chaos or challenge () they faced, the strength of God's arm () was more than enough to bring victory, order and peace.

Notice that the ending for  is similar to God's name. The symbol () is also the last pictogram in the Hebrew alphabet and means "complete." So, these last two symbols assured the ancient Hebrews that the strength of God's arm () was complete () and that the Lord did not need to rely on **any other source of power** to accomplish His will. Just before Jesus ascended to heaven, he told His disciples,

"You will receive **power when the Holy Spirit has come upon you**, *and you will be my witnesses in Jerusalem and in all Judea and Samaria, and to the end of the earth"* (Acts 1:8).

I found it fascinating that Jesus may have been referring to these first three words in the Torah when He shared His yoked relationship with His Father, with His identification as a Seed falling into the ground and dying, with His reference to the Holy Spirit as a River flowing out of the heart of a believer, and to the Power His disciples would receive when they were baptized in the Holy Spirit.

In any event, I think you will agree that the translation "In the beginning, God created . . ." does not convey the same depth of revelation as the pictograms Moses wrote.

SUMMARY:
I know it is hard for you to "read" sentences that do not contain verbs. But perhaps, your reliance on the linguistic structure of English will help you appreciate the hurdles faced by the Septuagint translators. They were working with Hebrew words whose characters represented a one-to-one conversion from pictograms but without the same grammatical structure modern Hebrew contains.

It is my prayer that you will start viewing the symbol clusters of these ancient pictograms more as pages or sections in a picture book than as word character strings in a sentence. This transition will help you relate more closely to the mindset of believers like Joshua who meditated on the Torah under the guidance and inspiration of the Holy Spirit.

Study Questions For Discussion

- *"In the beginning, God created . . ."* How many words in this opening phrase were written by Moses and inspired by the Holy Spirit?
  - How many words were reinterpreted by the Septuagint translators so they could be more easily read by a Greek-speaking audience?
  - Have we sacrificed God's inspiration so we can read His Word more easily in our western languages? What have we lost? (2 Corinthians 3:13 - 15)
- Are our translations of the Torah based on the pictograms Moses wrote?
  - Why is it important to be equipped with the ability to understand these ancient symbols so we can read God's Word the way He inspired it?
- Does "In the beginning" refer to the beginning of time when God created everything or does it refer to something or Someone else?
- John's Gospel says that all things were made through Jesus as the Word and without Him nothing was made – including the heavens and the earth in Genesis 1:1. Jesus said Moses wrote about Him. Where in Genesis 1:1 is Jesus mentioned?
  - Why can't you see Jesus in your translation?
  - What does Genesis 15:1 reveal about the Hebrew meaning of "Word?
- Jesus referred to Himself as being yoked to His Father and to being a seed that falls into the ground and dies. He also said that out of the bowels of believers would flow rivers of living water. Was He referring in these passages to the first three words of the Torah?

CHAPTER
4

Genesis 1:1
The Heaven And The Earth

PROLOGUE:
For many, the first verse in the Bible implies that God acted alone when He created the heavens and the earth. But the pictograms Moses wrote reveal a pattern that continues throughout the rest of the Bible: **Elohim never does anything alone**. He is a relational Person Who teams with others to work with Him to fulfill His will. The first three words of the Torah reveal the Holy Spirit, His adult Son and Elohim working together to create everything in Genesis, chapter one. As you read on, you will discover that Heaven is not so much a place where God dwells as it is a revelation of His character and the resulting establishment of His perfect order.

The Rest of Verse One
In Chapter Three, I compared Genesis 1:1 to a picture album where each group of pictograms corresponded to a page of images. These pictograms evoked mental images that provided understanding to those reading them – all without the linguistic structure we are familiar with in our written languages.

I also said that the Septuagint scholars translated ברא as "created" because they recognized the familiar path an adult son followed when he "left his father and mother" to create the next generation of his father's family.

When we read the second half of verse one, it is relatively easy to relate to the earth. After all, we live on it. However, there are definite benefits for examining the Hebrew characters for heaven (הַשָּׁמַיִם).

The הַ at the beginning is translated as "the." The root portion of the symbol group for heaven (ᴹᴹᴐᴦᴹᴹᵂ) is ᴹᴹᵂ meaning: destroy chaos. So, heaven is where chaos (ᴹᴹ) is destroyed (ᵂ) so that order can be established. The last two symbols in God's name (ᴹᴹᴐᴦ) says that this chaos is destroyed by the strength of God's arm.

We see this definition in action when the Lord made man:
> *"Then the Lord God formed the man of dust from the ground and breathed into his nostrils the breath (✝ ᴹᴹᵂ ᒋ) of life, and the man became a living creature"* (Genesis 2:7).

The ✝ at the end indicates that this ᴹᴹᵂ activity was complete. ᒋ is a sprout coming up out of the ground signifying "new life." The Lord formed Adam's body out of the dust of the ground. It had all the features of a human body. But it was unable to move as a living person until God breathed His breath into the man's nostrils, imparting Adam's lifeless body with fully functioning order and new life.

There is an additional meaning for this word in Genesis 2:19:
> *"And whatever the man called every living creature, that was its name (ᴹᴹᵂ)."*

So, "name" reveals the character of what is named defining its ability to produce order out of chaos.

Heaven or Heavens?

Perhaps you are wondering why I titled this chapter "The Heaven And The Earth" instead of the way you read it in your Bibles. After all, ᴍᴧᴧ ends with what modern Hebrew grammar calls a masculine plural ending (ᴍᴧ).

There are several reasons why I prefer a masculine singular designation here. First of all, the ancient Hebrew scholars who translated this verse into Greek in their Septuagint version translated "heaven" as a singular noun as you read in chapter one:

Greek: Ἐν ἀρχῇ ἐποίησεν ὁ θεός τὸν οὐρανὸν καὶ τὴν γῆν.

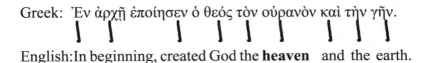

English:In beginning, created God the **heaven** and the earth.

In addition, our English Bibles translate Genesis 1:8, "*And God called the expanse* **Heaven**" even though the word for heaven (ᴍᴧᴧ) is identical to the word in 1:1 (likely because "heaven" renamed "expanse" which is parsed as a masculine singular noun).

Elohim's name (ᴍᴧᴪᴌᴒ) in Genesis 1:1 also ends with ᴍᴧ, but we never translate it as a plural noun (gods).

Finally, in Genesis 17:1, the "LORD appeared to Abram and said to him, "*I am God Almighty; walk before me and be blameless.*" The word for blameless is ᴍᴧᴍ✝. It too, has a ᴍᴧ ending. But my <u>Olive Tree ESV Greek-English and Hebrew-English Interlinear</u> text parses it as masculine singular (likely because the Lord was only talking to Abram).

If I relegate this ending to a grammatical suffix, then the core word would be ᴹ✝ indicating that the Lord was asking Abram to complete (✝) all chaos (ᴹ) in his life by his own strength. But if the "suffix is counted as part of the word, then all the chaos (ᴹ) Abram faced would be resolved (✝), not by his efforts, but by the strength of God's arm (ﹺ‿).

Another look at the yoked relationship

The yoked relationship אלהים had with ברא indicates that God worked together with His Son. However, they did not begin by creating the vastness of God's heaven or His throne room any more than an adult son leaving his father and mother would first build a home for his parents. The Son was setting up his own dwelling place and the arena for his work with the help of his Father.

They were focused on the Kingdom they would build together. The Son followed his Father's lead in their yoked relationship, dependent on the guidance, resources, skills and authority of אלהים. The Son's purpose and destiny were carried out on the earth, bringing honor and glory to his Father through the character of his Name. (The Bible says that the Name of Jesus is above all names. He alone possessed the anointed character capable of destroying the chaos of our sin, disease and death on the cross.)

More revelations about the pictograms for heaven

Chapter two has some other clues about the biblical meaning of heaven and God's relationship with us. Verse 2:5 – 6 explains what the garden region was like before the Lord formed man in verse 7:

> *"No bush of the field was yet in the land and no small plant of the field had yet sprung up—for the Lord God had not caused it to rain on the land, and there was no man to work the ground,*

and a mist was going up from the land and was
watering the whole face of the ground."

Verse 2:8 says:
"God planted a garden in Eden in the East, and He put the
man there (ᴹᴹᴡ) whom He had formed."

God established the garden as a place of order (ᴹᴹᴡ) where
Adam could live and work. Verse 2:15 builds on the revelation
of 2:8:

> *"The Lord God took the man and put him*
> *in the garden of Eden to work it and keep*
> *(ᵞᘉᴹᴹᴡℓ) it."*

Adam tended (ℓ) the garden through his yoked relationship
with Elohim. He would extend its boundaries as his family
and influence grew by destroying (ᴡ) the chaos (ᴹᴹ) of the
surrounding environs, and establishing order there through the
character of his name (ᴹᴹᴡ). ᘉᴹᴹᴡ also means to guard.
So, Adam would work, guard and expand the garden bringing
praise (ᵞ) to his Father.

As Joshua and his contemporaries meditated on Genesis 1:1,
they witnessed a pattern of yoked relationship Elohim was
calling them to participate in as His sons and daughters. Any
doubts the pattern was intended for them evaporated as they
read how the Lord extended it to Adam.

The Lord imparted **heaven** (ᴹᴹᴡ) into Adam's lifeless body
and to the garden where he lived and worked. As the last
Adam, Jesus sent His disciples out to destroy chaos by preaching the Kingdom of **Heaven** was at hand and by raising the
dead, healing the sick and casting out demons.

Christ assures us that all our needs will be added to us if we seek first the Kingdom of **Heaven** and His righteousness. All the blessings that were imparted to our first parents through their yoked relationship with God are now available to us through a personal relationship with Jesus Christ, God's Son.

We Will Make Our Home With You

Jesus told His disciples,

> *"If anyone loves me, he will keep my word, and my Father will love him, and we will come to him and make our home with him."*
>
> (John 14:23)

Heaven is much more than a place where believers will go when we die. The Father, the Son and the Holy Spirit come to dwell in us when we accept Jesus Christ as our Lord and Savior. They come to bring heaven into our temple through our faith and obedience. As I said in the prologue, **God never works alone**. He abides in us to work together destroying the chaos in our lives so that order can be established in all of our relationships.

A New Name

The Risen Christ told John,

> *"To the one who conquers I will give some of the hidden manna, and I will give him a white stone, with **a new name** written on the stone that no one knows except the one who receives it"* (Revelation 2:26).

Name means so much more than an identifying label. God has reserved a special moniker for everyone who conquers. I am truly amazed at the number of believers I meet who discover that their own name has shaped their character and purpose.

SUMMARY

There are two important lessons for us in this chapter:

First, Elohim is the King of Kings. And like all Rulers, He does not carry out His directives by Himself. Instead, His Son, His Holy Spirit, a host of angels and all of us who have given Him our allegiance team with Him to fulfill His purposes.

Second, ᴹᴹᴠᴠ reveals the character of God's Name to destroy chaos and establish the order of His will throughout every region of His Kingdom. Perhaps this chapter will bring new meaning to the Lord's Prayer:

> *"Our Father in **heaven**, hallowed be your **name**. **Your kingdom come, your will be done**, on earth as it is in **heaven**"* (Matthew 6:9 – 10).

Study Questions For Discussion

- Did Elohim act alone to "create" the heavens and the earth as our translations imply?
  - o What do you base your decision on?
- For what purpose did God make the heaven and the earth?
  - o Did He make His throne room or was this heaven more specific?
  - o Who was the heaven and the earth made for?
- Is heaven only a place where God and His angels live and where we go after we die?
- What does the Hebrew pictograms tell you about the Lord's Prayer?
- God is sovereign over everything. In your relationship with Him, do you imagine He is personally performing everything in your life?
  - o What role do angels and God's people play in achieving God's will in your life?

CHAPTER
5

Genesis 1:2
Paradise Corrupted

PROLOGUE:
What Happened?

"In the beginning, God created the heavens and the earth." Genesis 1:1

"The earth was without form [תהו] and void, and darkness was over the face of the deep. And the Spirit of God was hovering over the face of the waters." Genesis 1:2

"For thus says the Lord, who created the heavens (he is God!), who formed the earth and made it (he established it; he did not create it empty [תהו], he formed it to be inhabited!): 'I am the Lord, and there is no other.'"
                                                                    Isaiah 45:18

Isaiah says the Lord declared emphatically that He did not create the earth empty (תהו) but formed it to be inhabited. Instead of focusing on the many theories that have been put forth to clarify this disconnect, I want to reveal how the pictograms Moses wrote support Isaiah's prophecy.

Form – Void:

"The earth was without form (Ɏ Ψ ✝) and void (Ɏ Ψ ʊ)."

Notice that the last two symbols are the same. Ɏ Ψ means "Behold in awe an anchor" holding the person down and keeping him from moving. Benner says it represents Disaster or Woe[6].

Adding ✝ to Ɏ Ψ defines a barren place, a complete (✝) disaster or woe[7]. Appending ʊ to Ɏ Ψ defines a tent or house (ʊ) that cannot be inhabited in its current state[8].

Darkness – Deep:

"and darkness (Ш W Ⅲ) was over the face of the deep (ᴍ Ɏ Ψ ✝)."

Darkness[9] was a fence (Ⅲ) enveloping the face of the deep (ᴍ Ɏ Ψ ✝), destroying (W) its ability to conform (Ш) its functionality to the way God originally intended for it to operate.

The root for "deep" is ᴍ Ψ – looking in awe at a turbulent surf or ocean[10]. The first three pictograms (Ɏ Ψ ✝) are the same as those for "without form" indicating that the deep was a source of turbulent, formless water.

Let's briefly look at how the deep functioned during Noah's flood: *"all the fountains of the great deep burst forth."* (Genesis 7:11) ✝ ⴽ ⴑ⊖ᴍ is the Hebrew word for a spring or fountain. The water (ᴍ) from all the fountains burst forth under the Lord's watchful eye (⊖). He constrained its turbulent, formless activity by the strength of His arm (ᗡᐟ), protecting new life (ᐟ) as a sign of His covenantal relationship (✝) with the earth and with Noah. However, there were no fountains associated with the great deep in Genesis 1:2.

The Great Deep Without Fountains

What are the implications of a flood produced by the great deep bursting forth without the constraints of all the fountains? According to Noah's flood in Genesis 7:17 – 20,

> "The flood continued forty days on the earth. The waters increased and **bore up** (ᗡᐟ ᐟ ᗡᐟ)[11] the ark, and it rose high above the earth. The waters prevailed and increased greatly on the earth, and the ark floated on the face of the waters. And the waters prevailed so mightily on the earth that all the high mountains under the whole heaven were covered. The waters prevailed above the mountains, covering them fifteen cubits deep."

In addition to the constraints afforded by all the fountains, the pictograms for "bore up" add to the Lord's oversight. "Bore up" is preceded by ᗡᐟ indicating that the ark was born up by the strength of God's arm. So, the life (ᐟ) in the ark was supported (ᐟ) strongly (ᗡ) by the strength of God's arm.

Genesis 7:17 – 20 says that the flood continued for forty days on the earth and rose high enough to cover all the mountains by more than 20 feet. This water came from the great deep through the constraining channels of all the fountains and from rain over a forty-day period enabling the ark to float on the face of the waters without excessive turbulence to the persons and creatures inside.

If the darkness destroyed (W) the constraining flow of all the fountains, the deep could have burst forth much more abruptly. Jesus says this about Satan,

> *"The thief comes only to steal and kill and **destroy**."* (John 10:10)

We glimpse Satan's impetuous tactics in the first two chapters of Job. In Job 1:12, God said,

> *"Behold, all that he has is in your hand. Only against him do not stretch out your hand."*

Then the text continues in verses 13 – 20,

> *"**Now there was a day** when his sons and daughters were eating and drinking wine in their oldest brother's house, **and there came** a messenger to Job and said, "The oxen were plowing and the donkeys feeding beside them, and the Sabeans fell upon them and took them and struck down the servants with the edge of the sword, and I alone have escaped to tell you." **While he was yet speaking, there came another** and said, "The fire of God fell from heaven and burned up the sheep and the servants and consumed them, and I alone have escaped to tell you." **While he was yet speaking, there came another** and said, "The Chaldeans formed three groups and made a raid on the camels and took them and struck down the servants with the edge of the sword, and I alone have escaped to tell you." **While he was yet speaking, there came another** and said, "Your sons and daughters were eating and drinking wine in their oldest brother's house, and behold, a great wind came across the wilderness and struck the four corners of the house, and it*

fell upon the young people, and they are dead,
and I alone have escaped to tell you."

Satan orchestrated the destruction of everything Job had IN A SINGLE DAY. In Genesis 1:2, Satan was likely given similar permission to destroy the habitable regions of the earth. His use of the darkness to inhibit the capabilities of all the fountains to function as they would later do in Noah's day would have unleashed the full contents of the great deep – enough water to cover the entire earth in a matter of hours – producing unimaginable destruction. Visualize a rapidly expanding new ocean emerging from the womb of the earth's dry land, embroiled in a ferocious, turbulent upheaval from the great deep below, spewing tempestuous waves high into the air.

Spirit – Waters:

> *"And the Spirit of God was hovering* (✝○Ⅲꟺ᭝ᴡ) *over the face of the waters."*

Benner says ○Ⅲ᭝ means the stirring and shaking of a bird in a nest[12] – a reassuring activity to calm its nestlings.

There is a stark contrast in this second verse between the darkness enveloping the great deep and the Spirit of God hovering over the waters. I am reminded of the Gospel accounts where Jesus stilled the storm (Mk4:35 – 41 and Luke 8:22 – 25.) On the one hand, the darkness and the storm were enveloping their boat with raging waves that threatened to destroy them.

But Jesus was not alarmed by the looming catastrophe. Instead, He took a stand in the midst of the calamity, just like the Spirit of God did, and calmed the storm.

Since this unimaginable chaos engulfing our entire planet did not deter the Holy Spirit, we can rest in our relationship with

Christ knowing that the Holy Spirit will also come to our aid no matter how impossible our circumstance may seem.

God is Love – Another Perspective

I want to share another perspective that has helped me understand what happened to precipitate the situation in verse two. 1 John 4:8 says that God is love. For me, this text reveals the overarching motivation for everything our awesome God has ever done from Genesis through Revelation. The angels and mankind were both created under the umbrella of God's unconditional love.

And because of His unconditional love, God did not destroy the angels who rebelled but allowed them to exercise a limited amount of freedom to follow their own desires. We know from the first two chapters of Job that both times Satan was given permission to interact with the man of God, he did not try to win Job over to his side. Instead, he left a trail of death and destruction right up to the boundaries the Lord imposed.

The glorious truth of the Gospel declares that Satan and his minions have tried to corrupt everything the Lord has made on earth including mankind – God's ultimate creation. However, in a supreme act of unconditional love, God sent His Only Son Jesus Christ to shed His Own blood on the cross as a propitiation for our sin, disease and death to be received by faith. And this divine act will ultimately result in our resurrection to live with Him in a new heaven and a new earth.

SUMMARY

Isaiah's testimony that God did not create the earth empty but formed it to be inhabited is fully corroborated by the witness of the pictograms in verse two. The unimaginable chaos that engulfed our entire planet was unbelievably hostile, and looks much more like the works of Satan attempting to destroy the

Lord's initial habitation on earth than it reflects the work of our holy God.

Study Questions For Discussion

- It may be argued that the first two verses of Genesis could be translated in this manner: "In the beginning, **when** God created the heavens and the earth, the earth was without form and void, and darkness was over the face of the deep." This translation implies that God started by creating an earth that was without form and void and then went on to make it habitable. Do you agree with this interpretation? Why?
  - John says that God is light and in Him is no darkness at all (1 John 1:5). Does this declaration have any bearing on 1:2?
  - Does light and darkness refer to the light from the sun and the lack of it relative to the earth or is there a deeper meaning to these words?
- How does this "flood" compare with Noah's flood?
  - What part did the Holy Spirit play in each flood?
- What part does God's unconditional love play in allowing 1:2?
  - Is that same unconditional love extended to us?
  - Did 1:2 catch God unprepared?
  - Did He have a redemptive plan for 1:2?
  - Why did the Holy Spirit hover over the face of the deep?
  - Does He have a redemptive plan for each one of us?
- Instead of trying to win Job over to his way of living, Satan chose to steal, kill and destroy everything that belonged to Job as soon as he was granted permission. Jesus said he is a liar and the father of lies. The book of Job shows us Satan's true motives. What drives us to believe his lies?

CHAPTER
6

Genesis 1:3 – 5
Day One
Let There Be Light

"And God said, 'Let there be light,' and there was light. And God saw that the light was good. And God separated the light from the darkness. God called the light Day, and the darkness he called Night. And there was evening and there was morning, the first day."

(Genesis 1:3 – 5)

PROLOGUE:

God created the heaven and the earth together with His Son through the power of the Holy Spirit. Because He is light and in Him is no darkness at all, the heaven and the earth were not corrupted in any way.

Because of His unconditional love, He allowed Satan and his angels to rebel. Instead of destroying them, God allowed them to make the earth uninhabitable, filling it with darkness. Then God said, "Let there be light" and His plan for redeeming the earth began. So, God established the pattern: Creation / Corruption / Redemption.

In Day Six, God made man in His image and likeness – without any darkness at all – and included them in the earth's redemptive process. Once again, because of His unconditional love, we will see that God allowed Adam and his wife to follow the serpent's counsel corrupting their relationship with each other and with Him. But God's redemptive plan for us has been in place since the foundation of the world through the Person of His Son fulfilling the pattern of Creation / Corruption / Redemption.

Day – A Controversy Over Its Definition

I want to assure you that before I carefully evaluated the pictograms for Light, Day, Evening and Morning, I had viewed the days in the first chapter of Genesis as literal twenty-four-hour periods. It is one of the litmus tests for evangelical orthodoxy, and I never questioned it because nothing I perceived in the Hebrew texts I studied in seminary indicated otherwise.

However, as I examined these pictograms, I discovered they were focused on the work being done during the Day rather than on the dark / light cycle we commonly associate with a solar day. But before I continue, I would like to suggest how Joshua might have meditated on the opening verses of the Torah.

Joshua's Perspective

The first two chapters in the Torah outlined how Adam and his wife lived before sin entered the world. They were also included by Moses so that we could participate in that initial covenant relationship with God. Let's consider how Joshua might have viewed the opening verses of Genesis chapter one.

Verse One: As Joshua meditated on this first verse, he may have remembered the times he and Moses spent in the tent of meeting outside the camp (Exodus 33:7 – 11) and how excited

Moses must have been when God began revealing the yoked relationship in this verse between Elohim and His mature Son. As Moses' young assistant, Joshua must also have known that God had promised Abraham that his descendants would possess the land of Canaan.

He had witnessed the power of Moses' relationship delivering the Israelites from slavery in Egypt and bringing them to the Jordan River. Now Joshua could rest in the knowledge that the Creator of the whole earth would continue fulfilling His promise to Abraham by leading them across the Jordan and into the Promised Land under his yoked leadership.

Verse Two: The prospect of overcoming Jericho stood as a formidable barrier to their entry into Canaan. But Joshua also knew this challenge was not nearly as daunting as the impediment to earth's entire habitation revealed in this second verse. Surely the Lord had not delivered His people from Egypt, leading them for forty years in the wilderness only to be turned back by the walls of Jericho.

Before they crossed the Jordan, Joshua sent in two spies who discovered that the Spirit of God had gone ahead of them. Just as the Spirit had hovered over the darkness, the Spirit was now terrorizing the inhabitants of the city, reminding them of what God had done to Egypt.

Verses Three to Five: As Joshua approached Jericho, a man stood before him and said, "I am the commander of the army of the Lord." The God Joshua was yoked with had sent a commander to lead the army of the Lord.

> *"And the Lord told Joshua, '**See, I have given Jericho into your hand, with its king and mighty men of valor.** You shall march around*

*the city, all the men of war going around the city once. **Thus shall you do for six days**. Seven priests shall bear seven trumpets of rams' horns before the ark. **On the seventh day you shall march around the city seven times**, and the priests shall blow the trumpets. And when they make a long blast with the ram's horn, when you hear the sound of the trumpet, then all the people shall shout with a great shout, **and the wall of the city will fall down flat**, and the people shall go up, everyone straight before him'"* (Joshua 6:2 – 5).

I have highlighted several important words and phrases: "See" is the same word found in Genesis 1:4, "*God saw that the light was good.*" So, these instructions from the Lord were light for Joshua illuminating the way that the commander would carry out the battle with him.

The next highlighted words indicate that the Lord had already defeated Jericho. The battle would not be won by the strength of Joshua's fighting men. Even though Joshua had not yet initiated the battle plan, God said He had ALREADY given Jericho into Joshua's hand. This was not like any other battle strategy Joshua had ever witnessed. Strange as it must have seemed, Joshua followed it because he believed the God Who was able to create everything by the strength of His arm was also able to fulfill His awesome declarations:

> *"When you hear the sound of the trumpet, then all the people shall shout with a great shout, and the wall of the city will fall down flat, and the people shall go up, everyone straight before him."*

There was a relational truth the Lord wanted Joshua and his

men of war to keep in mind during their seventh day of activity. God had created everything in six days. Now, even though God rested on the seventh day, He did not ask Joshua to stop marching on the seventh day – just the opposite. This was the day of seven-fold marching and the day when the battle would be joined.

As they marched around the city that day, the Israelites must have wondered why they were not resting. Moses had strictly commanded them to rest in Exodus 20:10:

"The seventh day is a Sabbath to the Lord your
God. On it, you shall not do any work."

God wanted Joshua and his men of war to constantly remind themselves as they marched around Jericho that they were not contributing ANY WORK during that Sabbath day to tear down the wall or to deliver Jericho into their hands. The Lord was challenging them to walk by faith and not by sight, to focus by faith on the Light – the battle plan God had already achieved.

The Pictograms
With this background in mind, let's examine the pictograms to see how their testimony adds further meaning to Joshua's victory over Jericho.

Genesis 1:3

"And God said, 'Let there be light (ﬡ ﬡ ﬡ),'
and there was light."

And God Said
Moses began each of the six days in chapter one with this phrase. Let's look at the richness the pictograms reveal about this word "Said."

רֶאמֶר Benner says[25] מֶר is the Hebrew word for mother. And what is the unique role of a mother? She births new life (children) into the family. So, these pictograms indicate that God BIRTHED (מֶר) new revelation into existence. רֶ precedes this word indicating God birthed these words by the strength of His arm.

Light – אֶוֹר. We are so accustomed to associating light and darkness with the illumination we receive as our planet rotates on its axis that it is easy to overlook light's revelatory meaning. Notice what the apostle Paul said about this verse in 2 Corinthians 4:6,

> *"For God, who said, "Let light shine out of darkness," has shone in our hearts to give the light of the knowledge of the glory of God in the face of Jesus Christ."*

I shared in Chapter Three that the proximity of וֹאֶט to מֶוֹלֶשׁ in Genesis 1:1, implied that the son was yoked to his Father (לֶוֹ) in a strong covenant relationship. Since in 1:1, וֹ represents the strength of our Father's resources available to His Son through their yoked relationship, it could also carry a similar meaning in the Hebrew word for light (אֶוֹר). I will assert that one of the basic definitions of "light" is "The strength of God's resources anchored to man through his yoked relationship."

John's first epistle adds weight to this interpretation:
> *"God is light, and in him is no darkness at all... if we walk in the light, as he is in the light, we have fellowship with one another."*
>   (1 John 1:5b – 7a)

God's light is revelatory light, and He anchors His revelation to us so we can walk in fellowship with Him.

The Hebrew word 𐤍𐤏 means "order;" a "box[14]" used to organize a group of elements, bringing order out of chaos. So, God's revelatory light (𐤍𐤉𐤏) gave Joshua the battle plan the Lord (𐤏) had established (𐤉) to bring victory over the uncertainty Joshua (𐤍) was facing.

Darkness

This term was defined in the previous chapter. However, it is important to point out that Darkness is also revelatory light – an alternate illumination that guided the horrific chaos of verse two. Jesus warned His followers about this alternate light:

> *"Your eye is the lamp of your body. When your eye is healthy, your whole body is full of light, but when it is bad, your body is full of darkness. Therefore be careful lest the light in you be darkness. If then your whole body is full of light, having no part dark, it will be wholly bright, as when a lamp with its rays gives you light"* (Luke 11:34 – 36).

Genesis 1:4

> *"And God saw that the light was good. And God separated the light from the darkness."*

Saw – God saw (𐤏𐤍𐤉) that the light was good. Notice that He didn't "see" that the darkness was good. The Hebrew word for vision is 𐤉𐤏𐤍. 𐤉 precedes it indicating God did not just observe that the light was good. Its goodness was also a product of the strength of His arm.

Separated – God made a clear distinction between light and darkness. He actively separated ($\mathcal{L}$ $\overline{U}$ $\overline{\Box}$ $\succ$⌐) light from darkness. These symbols declare that God had the authority ($\mathcal{L}$) and the ability ($\succ$⌐) to decide who or what could enter through the door ($\overline{U}$) of His tent ($\overline{\Box}$). He did not allow darkness to enter His tent – His Kingdom.

Genesis 1:5

"God called ($\not{b}$ $\overline{\Box}$ ⊖ $\succ$⌐) the light Day, and the darkness he called ($\not{b}$ $\overline{\Box}$ ⊖) Night."

What is not noticeable in English is obvious in Hebrew. God called the light Day by the strength of His arm ($\succ$⌐). But Moses made it clear that God was only assigning a term for Night. He was not associating its existence with His work. As you can see, ($\succ$⌐) does not precede the word "call" designating darkness as Night.

The Pictograms For Day

"Day" ($\wedge\wedge$ Υ $\succ$⌐) comes from $\wedge\wedge$$\succ$⌐ meaning Working Water, the Sea[15]. The sea is a place of storms and heavy surf – **working** water. The addition of an anchor (Υ) links the **work** ($\succ$⌐) to the storm ($\wedge\wedge$) – its uncontrolled might / unpredictability / chaos. So, the work performed is anchored to the chaos as a focused activity bringing order out of the chaos.

The association of Light with Day meant that the revelatory Light birthed by God illuminated the chaos of verse two, segmenting it into specific categories (boxes). The Light for those segments would be revealed during the next five days. The battle plan the Lord shared with Joshua was also segmented into specific days of activity they were to follow to obtain victory over Jericho. And he could rest in the knowledge that the Lord had already accomplished everything in that battle plan.

Moses clearly delineated between the Light God created and the Darkness enveloping the earth in verse two. God not only separated the Light from the Darkness, He commissioned pictograms for Day (ᴹ Ƴ ᗡ) that defined the period when He worked (ᗡ) by the strength of His arm, establishing (Ƴ) His plan to bring order out of chaos (ᴹ).

Since the Lord would never perform any work using the illumination provided by Darkness, the Day could not have included any revelatory instructions defined by Darkness. Jesus underscored this definition when He said to His disciples,

> *"We must work the works of him who sent me while it is day; night is coming when no one can work."* (John 9:4)

Day As A Work Order

Those in the construction industry might associate a Day with a work order[17], a job assignment for a person or group to execute. Those persons might also equate Light with the specific instructions, resources and job skills needed to perform the work order. Seen in this light, the Days in the first chapter of Genesis define specific work orders the Lord performed to bring order out of the chaos that was generated in verse two.

The battle plan revelation detailed the specific instructions, resources and job skills needed for Joshua and the Israelites to carry out each day's work order – the job assignments for each person or group to execute – during the battle of Jericho.

Evening and Morning

> *"And there was evening and there was morning, the first day."*

Evening and morning do indeed define a Day. These boundaries delineate when darkness and light begin. It is important, however, to remember that both light and darkness in this verse address revelatory light. As stated earlier, we are so accustomed to the twenty-four-hour cycles of light and darkness generated by the rotation of the earth that we can easily associate those same constraints with the definition of a Day in this passage.

If this revelatory Day refers to a twenty-four-hour period, then according to verse five, it is defined by a cycle consisting of a period of darkness followed by a period of light. Viewing Days as a series of cycles, the first evening begins Day one, the next evening begins Day two, the next evening begins Day three and so on.

Notice that the morning boundary is not necessary to identify each day in this interpretation. However, in the Bible, both boundaries were used to define each of the six days, not just the evening boundary. Let's examine the pictograms for evening and morning to see why both boundaries are necessary.

The Evening Boundary: (ⵍⵏ◉)[18]. See (◉) the man (ⵏ) facing his house (ⵍ). The person is heading home (he is facing toward his house) at the end of the day – his work is finished.

The Morning Boundary: (ⵏ◉ⵍ)[19] The house (ⵍ) after sunrise (◉) is when the man (ⵏ) departs (he is facing away from his house) – The person leaves home to go to work.

These boundaries determined the scope of the Day. They agree with its pictogram definition (ᴹ Ƴ ᴗ) by focusing precisely on WHEN the Lord performed the work (ᴗ) by the strength of His arm. Both were necessary.

Referring to a solar day, we say that its daylight portion occurs between dawn and dusk. God performed the work of each Day according His revelatory Light. When God reveals His Light to us and calls us to perform the work of that Day, He wants us to begin that Day by faith from a posture of rest – entering it through the spiritual mindset of Evening and Morning – knowing that He has already accomplished the work ahead of us just like He did with Joshua at Jericho.

The Hebrew And Greek Lexicons

Let's see how the definitions for Day in several Hebrew and Greek lexicons line up with the revelations I have shared through the pictograms in verse five.

Gesenius was a German scholar who compiled a <u>Hebrew Lexicon</u>[2] in the mid-eighteen hundreds. In that book[20], Gesenius says "Day" comes from an unused root apparently signifying heat – to be warm. Commenting on its definition, he says, "The primary signification appears to me to be that of the heat of the day." His definition agrees with the pictograms. The "heat of the day" points to the daylight hours.

The Hebrew dictionary in <u>Strong's Exhaustive Concordance of the Bible</u>[21], documents "an unused root meaning to be hot. "A day (as the warm hours) whether literal (from sunrise to sunset, or from one sunset to the next)." Keep in mind that the word day is found throughout the Hebrew testament and its use elsewhere most often refers to a solar day. So, the literal definition points to its first use in the Bible while its other definition addresses the more common solar day.

The primary Hebrew dictionary I used in seminary was the Brown, Driver and Briggs lexicon based on Gesenius' lexicon[22]. It simply states, "Day as defined by evening and morning." These authors simply refer to the definition for a Day in

Genesis 1:5.

Benner defines Day (ᴹ Ⴤ ᴊ) as "The day ends and the new day begins when the sun sets in the west, over the Mediterranean Sea[15]." This is another reference to Genesis 1:5.

Here is the witness from two Greek references: The Strong's Concordance[23] says Day (ἡμέρα) means "tame," "gentle," "the time between dawn and dusk," or "the whole 24 hours." Strong says the Greek word can either mean the time between dawn and dusk or the entire twenty-four period of a solar day. So, this Greek dictionary delineates both its first use and its more general application.

The primary Greek dictionary I used in seminary was the Arndt and Gingrich lexicon[24]. The first definition of (ἡμέρα) is "Of the natural day – the period between the rising and the setting of the sun."

One thing is certain from analyzing these dictionary sources: Those that address the first use of Day do not equate it with a twenty-four-hour solar day.

SUMMARY

To claim that the Days of Genesis chapter one were twenty-four-hour periods assumes that each of these Days included a period of Darkness God called Night. There is no scriptural evidence to support this assumption.

What seems clear from analyzing the pictograms for Light and Day is that Day was closely associated with Light. God not only called the Light Day, He also separated the Light from the Darkness and called the Darkness by a different name. There was no correlation made by God in Genesis 1:3 – 5 that linked either Darkness or Night with either Light or Day so that a Day could include a period of Darkness.

Further as shown above, the pictograms for Evening and Morning actually define the scope of the Day when work could be done. The six Days in Genesis chapter one, describe specific activities God performed, and each one of those Days was terminated by the Evening of the next day. This boundary, signaling the beginning of darkness, not only separated each Day from Darkness and Night, it also ended that Day's work.

Study Questions For Discussion

- Evangelicals have been ridiculed for their insistence that the Days in Genesis chapter one are literal twenty-four hour periods. This conviction has come from our sincere belief that the Bible calls each one of these periods a "Day." Our steadfast resolve also means we must somehow defend a relatively brief duration for our planet's existence even though fossil records indicate otherwise. Secular dictionaries define a day: *"a period of twenty-four hours as a unit of time, reckoned from one midnight to the next, corresponding to a rotation of the earth on its axis."* Have we allowed our secular dictionaries to influence our definition of the Days in the first chapter of Genesis?
- Verse 1:2 says darkness covered the face of the deep. Verse 1:3 says "Let there be light." The boundary between the darkness of 1:2 and the light of 1:3 should be Morning. Why did the first day begin with Evening?
  o How do you define darkness and light as revealed in 1:4 – 5?
- How do the Evening and Morning boundaries define a Day?
  o What is the relationship of Darkness and Night to these boundaries?
- What does a posture of rest have to do with a Day?
- We have viewed the first chapter of Genesis as the "Creation" chapter. Does the pattern of Creation / Corruption / Redemption shed new light on this chapter and the rest of the Bible?

CHAPTER 7

Genesis 1:6 – 8
Day Two
Heaven Redeemed

"And God said, 'Let there be an expanse in the midst of the waters, and let it separate the waters from the waters.' And God made the expanse and separated the waters that were under the expanse from the waters that were above the expanse. And it was so. And God called the expanse Heaven. And there was evening and there was morning, the second day."

(Genesis 1:6 – 8)

PROLOGUE:

God established an incredibly important pattern during this second day: God said – God made – God called. It is a pattern that will be employed when He partners with Adam to continue the work of redemption in Day Six.

I said in Chapter Six that Light revealed the information and the resources needed to execute a Work Order – a Day. Each of the Six Days began with the words, *"And God Said,"* followed by the instructions – the Light for that Day – as well as the execution of those instructions. Each Day ended with the statement, *"And there was evening and there was morning, the _____ day."* These two statements formed the boundaries for each Day's Work Order.

A Critical Pattern

There is a three-step pattern revealed in Day Two explaining how God works with those who are yoked with Him.

First, "God said"

The Light of God's prophetic word preceded the work He exerted to make the expanse and to separate it from the waters below and above. The prophet Amos 3:7 says:

> *"For the Lord God does nothing without revealing his secret to his servants the prophets."*

And Isaiah 55:8 – 9 provides the reason:

> *"**For my thoughts are not your thoughts, neither are your ways my ways**, declares the Lord. For as the heavens are higher than the earth, so are my ways higher than your ways and my thoughts than your thoughts."*

God does not want us to figure out on our own how to solve the problems we face because our thoughts are not His thoughts. He only asks us to seek His thoughts – His revelatory Light – and follow it in faithful obedience. The battle plan given to Joshua must have seemed highly unusual. But when Joshua followed it, Jericho was handily defeated.

Second, "And God made"

Not only are God's thoughts higher than our thoughts, our ways are not His ways either. In order for God's thoughts to be carried out in a successful manner, He must ultimately be the One making His Way come to pass.

Third, "And God Called"

God told Joshua while he was still approaching Jericho: *"**See, I have given Jericho into your hand, with its king and mighty men of valor.**"* Why did God's battle plan work? Because He already **saw** the results of the battle.

> *"I am God, and there is no other; I am God, and there is none like me, **declaring the end from the beginning and from ancient times things not yet done**, saying, My counsel shall stand, and **I will accomplish all my purpose**."*
> (Isaiah 46:9 – 10)

God declares the **end** from the beginning and **calls it completed** while it is yet not done.

This battle plan was not a last-minute strategy. The Lord **saw** it accomplished from ancient times and declared the end from the beginning. That is, the Lord **saw** that Jericho HAD BEEN GIVEN into Joshua's hand even though it was not yet done. The promise that *"the wall of the city will fall down flat"* was not based on Joshua's fighting men breaching the wall but on God's action that had been accomplished **from ancient times**. They were asked to step out in faith believing that their God had already **SEEN** the victory and would accomplish ALL His purpose. Jesus also walked in this reality and calls us to follow Him as He follows His Father.

> *"Truly, truly, I say to you, the Son can do nothing of his own accord, but only what he **sees** the Father doing. For whatever the Father does, that the Son does likewise. For the Father loves the Son and **shows** him all that he himself is doing"* (John 5:19 - 20).

The Expanse
God made the expanse in the midst of the waters separating the waters from the waters. How did He do it? The pictograms give us a clue.

"And God made the expanse (𐤓𐤒𐤏𐤄) and separated the waters that (𐤀𐤔𐤓) were under the expanse from the waters that (𐤀𐤔𐤓) were above the expanse."

𐤓𐤒𐤏𐤄 – Benner says this word comes from 𐤏𐤄[26] meaning Hammer / Sheet. For example, gold was hammered into thin sheets. Seen (𐤏) from a person's perspective (𐤄) on the earth, the expanse appeared like a sheet spread out on the horizon (𐤏) overhead. As we have seen with other words, the addition of (𐤒) supports the assertion that God made the expanse in the midst of the waters by the strength of His arm.

𐤀𐤔𐤓 – This word has many meanings as indicated by Benner's dedication of four pages in his lexicon for its various interpretations[27]. He asserts that the root of this word is 𐤀𐤔 which defines a rope or chord. Many of the variations deal with how a chord or rope is used. In addition, he says 𐤀𐤔𐤓 is often translated by the abstract terms: which, what or that – "as a rope attaches two objects together, this word links the action of the sentence to the one doing the action."

This explanation defines WHAT this word does by linking God with the action of separating the waters below from the waters above. But it does not give any indication HOW God performed this action. Since this is the first time the word is used in scripture, its basic meaning should be considered from its context.

The first two pictograms (𐤀𐤔) mean Strong Destroyer and אש is the Hebrew word for Fire. (If you travel to Israel, you will see this word over every public exit door.) The third pictogram (𐤄) stands for a person. Since God was the only Person present during Day two, we could assert that this word means "Fire from His Person" at least in this instance. Deuteronomy 4:24 says,

"For the Lord your God is a consuming fire."

Notice that God began with the waters below the expanse. Fire applied to the expanse above those waters would have evaporated moisture from its surface. This moisture would eventually condense into the waters / clouds above the expanse creating the appearance of a sheet above the earth.

And Called It Heaven

I said in Chapter Three that heaven in the first verse was likely a more limited one that did not include the vastness of God's heaven or His throne room. This first heaven was made along with the earth.

Verse two says that the Spirit hovered over the face of the waters. Then in verse six, this second heaven was described as an expanse *"in the midst of the waters,"* separating the waters from the waters. I also shared in Chapter Three that the pictograms for heaven (ᴹᴹ͢ᴶᴹᴹᵂ) describe a place where God's Name (ᴹᴹᵂ) dwells and were chaos (ᴹᴹ) has been destroyed (ᵂ). So, God did not call the expanse "heaven" until He had redeemed it from the chaos of verse two.

As Joshua meditated on this text, he could rest in the knowledge that no matter how overwhelming the "expanse" he faced, His God was able to redeem it and bring order out of the chaos. We too, may look at our lives and conclude that our circumstances are too daunting or hopeless to ever be resolved. But our God is still able to redeem us to the uttermost.

SUMMARY

I hope that as you have been meditating on the pictograms for heaven, you are beginning to reconsider it only as a place "where we go when we die" – a place "up there." ᴍᴡ represents Name, Character, Heaven and the Breath of God. Although we can associate it with a place, it much more accurately describes where our loving God dwells. Since He dwells within us as believers, we can declare that Heaven is also within us!

Study Questions For Discussion

- Why did God say (birth from His mouth) what He was going to do before He did it?
  o Why is it important for us to confess with our mouth that Jesus is Lord?
  o Why isn't it enough just to believe that Jesus is our Lord?
- Why does God tell His prophets what He is going to do before He does it?
  o His thoughts are higher than our thoughts. He doesn't want us to try and solve our problems. How can we "hear" what He is telling us?
  o Our ways are not His ways. Are our "solutions" to our problems a reflection of His ways or our ways?
- How does God know when He speaks (births) some future event that it will happen?
  o Why can we trust Him to perform what He has spoken (birthed)?
- During the First Day, God said "Let there be light," and there was light." On Day Two, God followed His declaration "Let there be an expanse" by actually making the expanse. If God only needed to birth light into existence by proclaiming it, why did he need to **make** the expanse after He declared it?
  o Hint: What is Light?
  o Is it different from God's pronouncement?
  o What is the expanse"
  o Is it materially different from Light?
- Why did God call the expanse Heaven?
  o Was the expanse complete before God called it Heaven?
  o If God sees the end from the beginning, when is the Heaven complete?
- How did God make the expanse?
- If the heaven that was restored during Day Two was located

between the waters below and the waters above, was it just the physical atmosphere that covers the earth?

o   If so, was it still heaven (MW)?
o   If God made the expanse and called it Heaven, did His proclamation with His mouth destroy the chaos and re-store order to the expanse?

CHAPTER 8

Genesis 1:9 – 13
Day Three
Earth Redeemed

PROLOGUE:
Another Controversy

I began Chapter Six by addressing a controversy over the definition of a Day. During the "Age of Enlightenment," another controversy arose over the historical validity of the Bible[28.] These scholars began with several apparent contradictions in Genesis, then in the Torah and finally in the Old and New Testaments. By exposing what they considered inconsistencies in the biblical texts, they were challenging God as its inerrant Author, and the Bible as His source of truth.

By the time I attended seminary in the sixties, Fuller was warning its students that this mindset had infected a large number of universities, seminaries and Bible schools worldwide. Here is a sample of the apparent contradictions between Genesis chapters one and two:

Chapter One	Chapter Two
12: The **earth brought forth** vegetation, **plants** yielding seed according to their own kinds, and trees bearing fruit in which is their seed, each according to its kind.	5: When **no bush** of the field **was yet** in the land and no small **plant** of the field **had yet sprung up**—for the Lord God had not caused it to rain on the **land,**
21: So God created the great sea creatures and **every living creature that moves**, with which the waters swarm, according to their kinds, and **every winged bird** according to its kind. 25: And God made the **beasts** of the earth according to their kinds and the **livestock** according to their kinds, and everything that creeps on the ground according to its kind.	19: Now out of the ground the Lord God had **formed every beast** of the field and **every bird** of the heavens and brought them to the man to see what he would call them. 20: The man gave names to **all livestock** and to the **birds** of the heavens and to **every beast** of the field.
27: So God created man in his own image, in the image of God **he created him; male and female he created them**.	7: Then the Lord **God formed the man** of dust from the ground and breathed into his nostrils the breath of life, and the man became a living creature. 22: And the rib that the Lord God had taken from the man **he made into a woman** and brought her to the man.

I decided to alert you concerning this controversy NOW because the information in Day Three is the first passage they held up for scrutiny. However, as you can see, it is not the only passage in chapter one that is criticized for its apparent contradictions with chapter two. Now that you are aware, I will wait until I write about Genesis chapter two to deal with this issue so I can address it as a unit instead of piecemeal.

Genesis 1:9 – 11

> *"And God said, 'Let the waters under the heavens be gathered together into one place, and let the dry land appear.' And it was so. God called the dry land Earth, and the waters that were gathered together he called Seas. And God saw that it was good."*

The Hebrew word for the dry land (𐤉𐤁𐤔𐤄) is significantly different than the word for Earth (𐤀𐤓𐤑). However, the words for waters (𐤌𐤉𐤌) and Seas (𐤌𐤉𐤌𐤉) are virtually identical. As you can see, the word for Seas is waters (𐤌𐤉𐤌) preceded by 𐤉. The reason God could say that the Earth **and** the Seas were **both** good was that He was actively controlling (𐤉) the waters (𐤌𐤉𐤌) He was gathering into one place.

Further, God did not combine the dry land with the Seas and then call **them** "Earth." This is similar to the first Day when God called the Light Day. He did not combine the light with the darkness and then call **them** Day. Neither the waters (𐤌𐤉𐤌) nor the darkness from verse two were part of His original plan for our earthly habitation. (Revelation chapter 21 gives us a hint of what the earth might have been like in verse one.)

Joshua's Perception

Before continuing with the rest of Day Three, it is important to remember how Joshua and his contemporaries might have "read" this text. We study this segment in English giving little thought to the implications of our language structure. The English verbs chosen by the translators were written in the past or present tense in order to make better sense to us.

But pictograms don't have tense (think of the male / female symbols over the doors to public restrooms). Most of the verbs in verses 9 – 11 are couched in the past tense as though they have already taken place. Since pictograms don't have tense, let's rewrite them in the present tense:

> *"And God says, 'Let the waters under the heavens gather together into one place, and as the waters gather together, the dry land appears. And so it happens. God calls the dry land Earth, and the waters He is gathering together he calls Seas. And God sees that it is good."*
> (Genesis 1:9 – 10)

Just changing the verbs from past to present tense alters our perception of God's activity. Instead of just reading about some event that happened in the ancient past, we are drawn into the action as observers of what God – I AM – **is doing**.

Genesis 1:11 – 13

> *"And God said, 'Let the earth sprout vegetation, plants yielding seed, and fruit trees bearing fruit in which is their seed, each according to its kind, on the earth.' And it was so. The earth brought forth vegetation, plants yielding seed according to their own kinds, and trees bearing fruit in which is their seed, each according to its kind. And God saw that it was good. And there was evening and there was*

morning, the third day."

Benner says that "sprout" and "vegetation" both come from the same root[29] indicating that the green sprouts come from seeds. Benner also says that "yielding" and "seeds" both come from the same root[30] suggesting that harvested seeds are the result of seeds sown. So, the phrase *"Let the earth sprout vegetation, plants yielding seed,"* defines a **vegetation life cycle**: seed –> sprout –> yielding –> seed.

The phrase *"each according to its kind"* extends a single growing cycle to multiple cycles while maintaining the "same kind" of new life across these cycles. So, the harvested seed at the end of one cycle becomes the planted seed for the next cycle while maintaining the purity of the kind.

The scope of Day Three focuses on the purity of multiple plant cycles that can extend for many generations, even into the present. We will observe a different focus in Genesis 2:5 – 6.

SUMMARY
We should not be surprised when the world challenges the authority of the Bible. As I shared above, the Age of Enlightenment, also known as the Age of Reason, laid a foundation for intellectual thought in Europe during the 17th and 18th centuries[28]. One of the goals of this movement was to break free from the mindset of the Church and its "outmoded" ideas. They focused on the Bible, convinced if they could show major inconsistencies in the biblical narrative, they could help society emerge into a new dawn where human reason determined truth.

The apparent differences between the first two chapters of Genesis led to efforts that challenged the rest of scripture. How could Noah build an ark big enough to house all the animals? Did Moses really cross the Red Sea? Did the sun really stand still for Joshua? How could Jonah survive for three days after being swallowed by a giant fish? How could three Jewish young men survive being thrown into a blazing furnace or Daniel survive being thrown into a den of lions? How could Jesus turn water into wine, walk on water, feed multitudes with a boy's lunch, or be resurrected from the dead? These accounts must surely be little more than myths and legends!

Here is the reply from the Apostle Paul:

> *"The natural person does not accept the things of the Spirit of God, for they are folly to him, and he is not able to understand them because they are spiritually discerned."*
>
> (1 Corinthians 2:14)

Study Questions For Discussion

- If the Gospel is foolishness to the world and must be spiritually discerned, why should we perceive their assaults on the Bible as threats to our faith?
  - o Can the Gospel be explained in a way that will be accepted by the "age of Reason?"
  - o If so, what would that Gospel look like?
  - o In an effort to "reach the world" with the message of Christ, have segments of the church made the Gospel so compatible to the world that it has lost its power and truth?
- We send our children to schools that challenge them with "proofs" that the Bible is full of errors. What is our defense?
  - o We should always defend our faith. But is reason our best weapon? Where does faith enter into this discussion?
  - o How does the Lord bear witness to His Word?
  - o What role do parents, especially fathers, play in the faith of their children?
  - o If our experience of God is largely intellectual, are we more susceptible to these challenges to what we believe?
  - o God said to Job, "Can a faultfinder contend with the Almighty?" "Will you condemn me that you may be in the right?" God went on to challenge Job's knowledge of primeval events. His "friends" who were believers didn't know any more than he did. Do we really know any more than his "friends" did?
- Walking by sight – by what we perceive is right – has always led us away from the truth. Is there a better way to bolster our children's faith?

CHAPTER 9

Genesis 1:14 – 19
Day Four
Greater And Lesser Lights

PROLOGUE:
In the last chapter, I shared that the so-called Age of Enlightenment called into question several apparent contradictions in the opening chapters of Genesis. One of their objections noted that the earth brought forth vegetation during Day Three even though the sun was not made until Day Four. How could vegetation grow without sunlight?

The Sun And The Moon?
"And God said, 'Let there be lights (✝ Y ৯ Y ৬ᵐ) in the expanse of the heavens to separate the day from the night. And let them be for signs and for seasons, and for days and years, and let them be lights in the expanse of the heavens to give light upon the earth.' And it was so.

And God made the two great lights — the greater light to rule the day and the lesser light to rule the night – and the stars.

And God set them in the expanse of the heavens

*to give light on the earth, to rule over the day
and over the night, and to separate the light
from the darkness. And God saw that it was
good. And there was evening and there was
morning, the fourth day" (Genesis 1:14 – 19).*

The Hebrew words for sun and moon are not mentioned in
Day Four even though the words are found elsewhere in Genesis[31]. An indication that Moses was not talking about the sun
and the moon is found in Psalms 74:16b:

*"... you have established the heavenly lights
(מארות)[32] and the sun (שמש)."*

However, there is a close association between the sun and the
moon and these great lights as shown in Psalms 136:7 – 9:

*"to him who made
   the great lights (מארת גדלים),
  for his steadfast love endures forever;
the sun (שמש) to rule over the day,
  for his steadfast love endures forever;
the moon (ירח) and stars to rule
  over the night,
  for his steadfast love endures forever;*

The psalmist links great lights with the sun, moon and stars.
The Hebrew word for "great" is the same as in Genesis 1:16.
But the word for lights is different:

$$(מארת גדלים) \text{ vs } (מארת)$$

So, while the function of the sun, moon and stars in Psalms
136 is quite similar to the great lights made in Day Four, we
should be careful not to equate them.

In addition, unlike the word for the great lights that contains the symbols for light (⟨pictogram⟩), the sun and moon are comprised of entirely different pictograms.

Sun – ⟨pictogram⟩. You will recognize ⟨pictogram⟩ from Chapter Four. These two symbols destroy (⟨pictogram⟩) chaos (⟨pictogram⟩) and are also the moniker for Name and Heaven. So, the sun's character (⟨pictogram⟩) vigorously (⟨pictogram⟩) destroys chaos.

Moon – ⟨pictogram⟩. Working (⟨pictogram⟩) man (⟨pictogram⟩) fenced (⟨pictogram⟩). Benner says ⟨pictogram⟩ is a man within a fence – one who works or travels along a set path. The moon follows a set path every night from horizon to horizon[138].

There is a further reason not to equate the greater and lesser lights with the sun and the moon. Notice that *"God set them in the **expanse** of the heavens to give light on the earth."* This expanse is between the waters below and the waters above. Even a casual observer would never assume that our physical sun and moon could be located in this expanse.

God made the heaven and the earth in Genesis 1:1. The portion of heaven restored during Day Two was limited to the expanse that separated the waters covering the earth into the waters below and the waters above. The physical sun, moon and stars populated the heaven made in verse one and could have easily existed on the other side of the waters above. From this location, the sun would have shed photonic light on the restored earth so that it could bring forth vegetation during Day Three.

What Were These Great Lights?

If the sun, moon and stars were made in verse one, what did God make in Genesis 1:16? God set the lights in the expanse of the heavens to separate the light from the darkness (verse 18) even though in verse 4, *"God separated the light from the darkness.*" Why did God set up these great lights to do what He did in verse 4? Verse 1:4 states that these lights also separated the day from the night in addition to separating the light from the darkness.

As shared earlier, "Day" is more than a redefinition of "Light." It is the work carried out according to the revelation given by the Light. So, separating the day from the night indicates that God set up the greater and lesser lights to ensure that the work orders to be accomplished during the subsequent Days would not be sabotaged by the work orders perpetrated during the corresponding Nights.

In verse 8, after separating the waters below from the waters above, God called the expanse heaven. Yet in verse 1:7, He set the lights in the EXPANSE of the heaven, not in the heaven. Why? In Day Two, God dealt with the waters covering the earth. In Day Four, He was dealing with those who were instigating the chaos.

In verse 7, God made the expanse. In verse 1:6, He made the greater and lesser lights. Both actions were preceded by ר indicating that His actions were necessary in order to deal with the waters covering the earth as well as the forces orchestrating the rebellion.

It is also important not to associate their rule over the Day and the Night with the sun and moon's rule over the solar day and night. The sun and the moon rule over two separate portions of the twenty-four day. However, since Day and Night represent competing Work Orders, these lights can, and often do, operate concurrently in a person's life. We can be thankful that this hierarchy of blessing and protection is not constrained to function only during certain times of the solar cycle.

Other References

𝕽 𝕴 𝕭 ᛖ is used in Genesis 1:16 and in Psalms 74:16 to refer to the great lights. All other OT references apply to the light from the lampstand in the tabernacle[33]. The design of this lampstand is chronicled in Exodus 25:31 – 40, and pure beaten olive oil was used to keep it burning (Exodus 27:20). We can conclude from these references that the great lights made in Day Four were closely associated with the presence of God and that their functions were distinct from the photonic light generated by the sun and reflected by the moon.

And The Stars . . .

> *"And God made the two great lights ... and the stars."*

In Matthew chapter two, wise men from the east came to Jerusalem saying they had been following the star of the King of the Jews for two years. Not only did the star tell them whose star it was, it also rested over the place where Jesus lived. This must have been more than a physical star we see in the night sky because it *"went before them, till it came and stood over where the young child was. And when they saw the star, they rejoiced with exceeding great joy. And they came into the house and saw the young child with Mary his mother;"* – a GPS miracle because the nearest physical star to earth is more than four light years away[34]. Since verse 16 closely associates the two great lights with the stars, it is my conviction that these two great lights were angels as was the star from Matthew's account.

In Revelation 21:20, Jesus identifies the seven stars in His right hand as angels:

> *"As for the mystery of the seven stars that you saw in my right hand, and the seven golden lampstands, the seven stars are the angels of*

Protecting Living Creatures

Up until Day Four, work orders did not include living creatures. In order to protect these creatures – including man – from the forces of darkness that had rendered the earth uninhabitable, God made two great lights (angels) in the expanse of heaven with dominion authority to thwart efforts by the darkness to impede the success of His work orders that would follow Day Four. These ruling angels would also act as channels of blessing and guidance for those under their protection.

Signs for Seasons, Days and Years

> *"And let them be for signs and for seasons, and for days and years, and let them be lights in the expanse of the heavens to give light upon the earth."*

"Sign" (✝ Υ 𝒷) comes from ✝ 𝒷 . Benner says[35] that when a farmer began to plow his field, he first set up a marker (✝) on the opposite side so he could guide his oxen (𝒷) to make a straight furrow across his field. The addition of Υ indicates a commitment to proceed toward a mark or goal.

The **Seasons** for planting and harvest were most important in an agrarian society followed by **Days** and finally **Years**. The **expanse** of the heaven would have been an ideal arena for these great lights to coordinate specific signs (light upon the earth) for guidance to begin essential activities, blessings for favorable rain and wind, and protection from adverse weather or pestilent conditions that could easily derail an entire growing season.

Rule:

> *"And God made ... the greater light to **rule** the day and the lesser light to **rule** the night."*

The meaning of Rule († ⌐ Ѡ ᴧᴧᴧ): Chaos / disorder (ᴧᴧ) can be destroyed (Ѡ) by or through the application of one's **authority** (⌐). The additional ᴧᴧ ("might") denotes the capability to rule or have dominion in addition to the person's **authority** to rule. The † at the end adds finality or completeness to the ruling domain.

This word describes the extent of Solomon's dominion (1 Kings 9:19), Hezekiah's realm (2 Kings 20:13) and Nebuchadnezzar's world-wide sovereignty (Jeremiah 34:1). It was also used to describe the armed forces of Sennacherib (2 Chronicles 32:5).

In Matthew 8:5 - 13, Jesus had an encounter with a Centurion. This man was a Gentile who asked that his servant be healed. When Jesus started to go with him, the man said,

> *"I am not worthy for you to come under my roof. But speak the word and my servant will be healed. I know, for I am a man under **authority**."*

Jesus marveled at his faith, and it underscored the **authority** structure any ruler, including the Lord, puts in place to carry out his wishes for his subjects. The Centurion carried out the commands of his superiors, and he recognized that the works Jesus was performing were being carried out in accordance with God's objectives. As such, he knew all Jesus had to do was speak the word and his servant would be healed since the healing would be carried out through the divine chain of command.

We might assume from Genesis chapters one and two, that

the Lord personally did all the work by Himself. Instead, like all Kings, He delegates authority and responsibility to those he trusts, both angelic and human. This authority anoints the recipients with power to carry out the King's mandates and to deal with opposing challenges. Those who align themselves with this authority benefit from and are blessed by it. Those who challenge the King's dominion must ultimately answer to him through his chain of authority.

Spiritual Warfare

The Lord's dominion structure was initially established in Day Four to bless, guide and protect us from the forces of darkness that set up their own dominion structures in the heaven.

These demonic hierarchies are more clearly defined in several New Testament passages:

> *"to open their eyes, so that they may turn from darkness to light and from the power of Satan to God"* (Acts 26:17-18).

> *"For though we walk in the flesh, we do not war according to the flesh (for the weapons of our warfare are not of the flesh, but mighty before God to the casting down of strongholds); casting down imaginations, and every high thing that is exalted against the knowledge of God, and bringing every thought into captivity to the obedience of Christ"* (2 Corinthians 10:3 – 5).

> *"And you were dead in the trespasses and sins in which you once walked, following the course of this world, following the prince of the power of the air, the spirit that is now at work in the sons of disobedience"* (Ephesians 2:1-2).

"For we do not wrestle against flesh and blood, but against the rulers, against the authorities, against the cosmic powers over this present darkness, against the spiritual forces of evil in the heavenly places" (Ephesians 6:12).

"He has delivered us from the domain of darkness and transferred us to the kingdom of his beloved Son" (Colossians 1:13).

Shalom and Spiritual Warfare

Shalom is the Hebrew word for peace. Jesus said,

"Peace I leave with you; my peace I give to you. Not as the world gives do I give to you. Let not your hearts be troubled, neither let them be afraid" (John 14:27).

Why is His peace different from that of the world? Let's look at the Hebrew pictograms for Shalom (ᵚ Υ ᒪ ᙍ). Seekins says that Shalom means to destroy (ᙍ) the authority (ᒪ) that establishes / anchors (Υ) chaos (ᵚ) in our life[36]. The world tends to focus on the chaos itself and to come up with ways of solving / managing / eliminating it. Shalom tells us that the Lord wants us to realize the chaos is a manifestation / a byproduct of the authority that is anchoring it to our lives. If we want to truly eliminate the chaos and establish order, we must ask the Lord to show us the authority that is causing it and how to war against it. This kind of peace eliminates trouble and fear because it strikes at the root of the chaos.

SUMMARY

There are two kingdoms: The Kingdom of Heaven and the kingdom of this world. We can call on the Lord's authority, like the centurion, to help us in times of trouble. God is faithful and we can seek Him to come to our aid through His channels of dominion rule that were initially set up for our benefit before the first living creatures set foot on the earth.

Study Questions For Discussion

- The greater and lesser lights have long been associated with the sun and the moon. Why is this association not supported by Genesis 1:14?
- Does the role the greater and lesser lights actually perform help answer the question raised by the Age of Enlightenment that vegetation needs sunlight to grow and mature?
- Why is their role important to everything made by God in Day Five and Six?
- Are the greater and lesser lights part of the Kingdom of Heaven?
  - o The greater light rules over the Day. How does this order of authority help you perform your role in the Kingdom of Heaven?
  - o Spiritual warfare focuses on the kingdom of this world. Is this kingdom also the domain of the lesser light?
  - o Does the whole armor of God (Ephesians 6:10 – 20) include these greater and lesser lights?
  - o Is this the first time you considered their role in spiritual warfare?
  - o Elohim established this protection for you. Aren't you glad He has your back?

CHAPTER
10

Genesis 1:20 – 24
Day Five
Swarms Of
Living Creatures And Birds

"And God said, 'Let the waters swarm with swarms of living creatures, and let birds fly above the earth across the expanse of the heavens.' So God created the great sea creatures and every living creature that moves, with which the waters swarm, according to their kinds, and every winged bird according to its kind. And God saw that it was good. And God blessed them, saying, "Be fruitful and multiply and fill the waters in the seas, and let birds multiply on the earth." And there was evening and there was morning, the fifth day."

(Genesis 1:20 – 23)

PROLOGUE

After establishing the greater and lesser lights, God made all the creatures that would live on the earth. Here in Day Five, God made the living creatures that lived in the sea and the birds that flew in the expanse of the heaven. He would wait until the sixth Day to make the terrestrial creatures along with man.

Living Creatures

The phrase, "living creatures" is more accurately translated as "living souls." The Bible says we humans are spirit, soul and body. But all other creatures are only soul and body. Let's take a closer look at their pictograms:

Soul (ᴡᴏ ᱮ) means new life (ᱮ) is consumed (ᴡ) through the mouth (ᴏ). Leviticus 17:11 says, "The life (soul) of the flesh is in the blood." Life is sustained in the body by the blood that brings oxygen, water and nutrients to the flesh.

Living (ᱮᴥᵚ) means the fence (ᵚ) around the work (ᴥ) bringing praise (ᱮ) to the Lord. (More on this subject in Genesis chapter two.) Benner says that ᴥᵚ is literally the organ (the surrounding fence) that produces (works) life[37] – the stomach. The phrase "Living Soul" indicates that the life / energy for the body is continually generated by what is consumed through the mouth and digested by the stomach. So, the life of every creature made by the Lord during Day Five was sustained in this manner.

God Created ...

Notice the similarity between this verse and 1:1: "In the beginning, **God created** the heaven and the earth." In Chapter Three, I showed that the Septuagint translators substituted the word "**created**" for ᱮᴺᴜ in order to produce a sentence that made sense to a Greek-speaking person. Here, too in verse 21, they made the same substitution.

You might be wondering how Moses, Joshua and other ancient Hebrews knew how God and His Son made the heaven and the earth as well as these living creatures without a verb to indicate their intentions? There is a non-translated, two-symbol word (✝ ᱮ) Seekins says means a strong sign[38]. As I said earlier, a farmer plowing a field initially put a sign on the opposite side to help him drive his team in a straight line toward it. Moses inserted this strong sign (ᵗ𐡀) immediately after 𐡀𐡉𐡋 and ᵐ𐡆𐡄𐡋𐡀 to indicate the intent or direction of their activity. So, the strategic placement of this Hebrew word tells us that God and His mature Son strongly (𐡀) targeted (ᵗ) their efforts to bring heaven, earth and all these living creatures into being.

According To Their Kind

This is the same phrase used in Day Three to emphasize the sustained purity of multiple plant cycles from one season to the next. Here, this phrase is used to emphasize the inherited purity across multiple generations of these living creatures.

Blessed

"And God blessed (𐡔𐡉𐡋𐡃𐡁) them," 𐡔𐡉𐡋 is preceded by 𐡃𐡁 indicating that this blessing was performed by the strength of God's arm. 𐡔𐡉𐡋 means "son (𐡉𐡋) conformed (𐡔)." God blessed these creatures by conforming them to His Son.

SUMMARY

All living souls made during Day Five were blessed to physically bear fruit from generation to generation after their own kind so as to multiply and fill their environment. These three words will take on new meaning in Day Six.

Study Questions For Discussion

- Were you surprised by the Hebrew definitions of "living" and "soul?"
- The pictograms for soul (ᱬᴏᱫ) means the creature's life is sustained by what it consumes through its mouth. Living (ᱬᱬᵐ) describes the creature's stomach. Do these two definitions bring more clarity to the phrase "living soul"?
- All living creatures other than man are only soul and body. They are not spirit beings like us. "Living soul" implies that their soul is responsible for providing the necessary nutrients that keep their body alive. Are the Hebrew definitions for "living soul" enough to sustain their life?
- How does the Hebrew word for "soul" provide foundational meaning to the Greek word for "soul' as the creature's mind, will and emotions?
- Were you surprised by the Hebrew word for "bless?"
    - o The Apostle Paul said, *"And we know that for those who love God all things work together for good, for those who are called according to his purpose. For those whom he foreknew he also predestined to be **conformed to the image of his Son**, in order that he might be the firstborn among many brothers. And those whom he predestined he also called, and those whom he called he also justified, and those whom he justified he also glorified"* (Romans 8:28 – 30). Does the Hebrew word for "bless: add new meaning to Paul's words for us?

CHAPTER 11

Genesis 1:24 – 31
Day Six
Let Us Make Man

*"And God said, 'Let the earth bring forth **living creatures according to their kinds**—livestock and creeping things and beasts of the earth **according to their kinds**.' And it was so. And God **made** the beasts of the earth **according to their kinds** and the livestock **according to their kinds**, and everything that creeps on the ground **according to its kind**. And God saw that it was good."* (Genesis 1:24 – 25)

*"Then God said, 'Let us **make** man in our **image**, after our **likeness**. And let them have **dominion** over the fish of the sea and over the birds of the heavens and over the livestock and over all the earth and over every creeping thing that creeps on the earth.'"*

"So God created man in his own image,
in the image of God he created him;
male and female he created them."

*"And God blessed them. And God said to them, 'Be **fruitful** and **multiply** and **fill** the earth and **subdue** it, and have **dominion** over the fish*

of the sea and over the birds of the heavens and over every living thing that moves on the earth'" (Genesis 1:26 – 28).

PROLOGUE

On Day Six, when God said, "Let us make man in our image and after our likeness," He was declaring that Man, as male and female, were unique because they alone reflected the relational oneness the image of Elohim has with His Son and the Holy Spirit.

Furthermore, we miss a great deal of the majestic pageantry of this day if we fail to recognize that the other five days gave Man, as male and female, much more than a **royal residence** where they could live and work in a yoked relationship with their awesome Father. This day also gave them **dominion** over their residence and everything in it – the fish of the sea, the birds of the heavens, the livestock, and over all the earth and every creeping thing that crept on the earth.

There was still much to redeem from the chaos of Genesis 1:2. But on Day Six, they stepped expectantly into unimaginable potential, illumined by God's daily light, and guided by Him to walk victoriously into their future without shame or fear.

Terrestrial Creatures vs Man

God waited until Day Six to make terrestrial creatures in order to highlight a critical difference between the way He brought them into existence and the way He made Man. The brief table below shows a comparison between how the Lord brought these two groups into existence.

Terrestrial Creatures	Man
God brought forth living creatures	
God made them according to their kind	
	God made Man in His image and likeness
	He made them male and female
	God blessed them
	God said, "Be fruitful, multiply, fill the earth, subdue it, have dominion."

As you can see, the entries for terrestrial creatures are absent from those for Man and visa versa. In the last chapter, I explained the pictographic meaning of living creatures indicated that in order to sustain their life, they had to ingest food and water and breathe air. They were also fruitful after their own kind meaning that they physically reproduced offspring from generation to generation. But God did not form Man as a living creature during Day Six with the ability to procreate in the same way He made the terrestrial creatures. To better understand what took place, let's examine the words in verse 26 more closely.

Verse 26

> *"Then God said, 'Let US make man in OUR image, after OUR likeness."*

Make – ᵞ ⵎ ⵔ ⵈ. "Make" is prefaced with ⵈ – new life – indicating that God was making new life.

Our – The last two pictograms for "image" and "likeness" are ⟨pictogram⟩ – new life anchored.

Image – ⟨pictograms⟩. This new life (⟨pictogram⟩) that God was making (⟨pictograms⟩) – the human species – was anchored (⟨pictogram⟩) in (⟨pictogram⟩) and hooked (⟨pictogram⟩) to God Who was their Shepherd (⟨pictogram⟩) All Mighty (⟨pictogram⟩). "Image" is used in Hebrew to portray a shadow or an outline representation of the original[39]. The apostle John says that God is Spirit (John 4:24). When God made Man, He made them as spirit beings in His Own image.

Likeness – ⟨pictograms⟩. This new life (⟨pictogram⟩) that God was making (⟨pictograms⟩) – the human species – was conformed (⟨pictogram⟩) to a blood (⟨pictograms⟩) covenant (⟨pictogram⟩) and anchored (⟨pictogram⟩) to God. ⟨pictograms⟩ is the Hebrew word for a Blood Son.[40] A son is anchored to his father's family because he is related to his father by blood.

Man, as male and female, would not obtain physical bodies until Genesis, chapter two. So, there is no further reference to "likeness" in Day Six. The pictograms for flesh (Genesis 2:21) help us see the relationship between Man – as spirit beings – and their eventual bodies of flesh and bone.

Flesh (⟨pictograms⟩) defines the tent (⟨pictogram⟩) that protects (⟨pictogram⟩) the man (⟨pictogram⟩). In 2 Corinthians 5:1, Paul builds on this revelation by saying,

> *"For we know that if the tent that is our earthly home is destroyed, we have a building from God, a house not made with hands, eternal in the heavens."*

However, by linking both image and likeness to Man in verse 26, God declared that they would not be complete until they had earthly tents to live in.

The takeaway from this exchange is that we are all spirit beings made in the image of God. And, as of Genesis chapter two, we also dwell in a physical body that was formed by the Lord in the womb of our mothers. See Jeremiah 1:5,

> *"Before I formed you in the womb I knew you, and before you were born I consecrated you; I appointed you a prophet to the nations."* (The word "formed is the same one as in Genesis 2:7.)

Make vs Create

Elohim said, "MAKE new life." He did not say, "CREATE new life." This agrees with John 1:3,

> *"All things were **made** through him, and without him was not any thing **made** that was **made**."*

This is also in line with God's word to Noah in Genesis 9:6:

> *"Whoever sheds the blood of man, by man shall his blood be shed, for God made man in his own image."*

As we move on to verse 27, my focus on the verb "make" in verse 26 supports my earlier explanation that the verb "created" was originally substituted for "mature Son" in Genesis 1:1 and elsewhere out of a linguistic necessity to help make the Septuagint translation more understandable to Greek-speaking persons. By doing so, these ancient scholars unknowingly obscure the intimate covenantal relationship (†) between Elohim and His Son revealed through the original pictographic symbols. Let's take a closer look at verse 27. (Words in brackets [ ] are implied.)

Translating verse 1:27a

*"So, [the] Son [and] Elohim [made] († ঐ)
the human species IN (ⵑ) [His] image;"*

The first line has a similar format to Genesis 1:1 and 1:21:
The Son yoked with Elohim focused their combined activity
to make Man in the image of God.

Translating verse 1:27b

*"IN (ⵑ) [the] image of Elohim [and the] Son
[the human species was made] († ঐ);"*

The second line further emphasized the focus of their activity
by positioning "image" at the beginning of the phrase, and
only implicitly referring to Man. It also reversed the positions
of Elohim and His Son placing the latter in a more immediate
association with their activity.

Translating verse 1:27c

*"Male and female, [the] Son [made the human
species] († ঐ)."*

The third line declared that the Son, without the assistance
of Elohim, further developed the image of God as male and
female – a relational image mirroring the yoked relationship
the Son had with His Father.

A More Extensive Blessing For Man

*"And God blessed them, saying, 'Be **fruitful**
and **multiply** and **fill** the waters in the seas, and
let birds **multiply** on the earth.'"*

(Genesis 1:22)

God blessed these living creatures with the ability to reproduce abundant physical offspring according to their kind.

> *"And God blessed[41] them. And God said to them,*
> *'Be **fruitful** and **multiply** and **fill** the earth and*
> ***subdue** it, and have **dominion** . . .'"*
> (Genesis 1:28)

This blessing addressed Man as male and female before they were clothed in bodies capable of procreating physical off-spring. It not only added two more categories, it also revealed a deeper, more intimate liaison for how they would work to-gether with the Lord. Let's briefly reexamine the categories in this blessing:

Fruitful (ᚷᚱᚩᚑ) literally means "That which is spoken out of the mouth (ᚑ) of the person (ᚱ) yielding praise and awe (ᚷ)." So, this word's basic meaning defines "fruitful" as the powerful words that proceed out of a person's mouth.

God began each of the previous four Days by **declaring** what He would accomplish through His Son **before** He carried it out by the strength of His arm. After God made the human species, He enlisted them as partners in His redemptive pro-cess. That is, He extended the scope of this redemptive pattern by sharing His revelations with Man who would **speak** those revelatory words verbally by faith. The fruit of this obedience would subsequently be fulfilled by the strength of God's arm – a pattern that extends throughout the Bible (See Amos 3:7).

Multiply (ᚷᚢᚱ) is another word for a Man's (ᚱ) domin-ion over their tent / domain (ᚢ) and means they had the au-thority to increase their domain with exceedingly abundant growth[42]. The addition of ᚷ indicates wonder and awe. They would marvel as they experienced their "tent" eventually extending over everything God had made on earth as they spoke God's words and witnessed their fulfillment.

Notice the similarity between this word and Evening (ⵃⵏ◉). I said in Chapter Six that Evening signified the man was returning home, that work was finished and rest from work could begin. Here, the relationship of 𐤍 facing ⵃ also meant that they would not be multiplying their domain by their own strength but by faithful obedience.

Fill (𐤏 ⵥ ᘑ). ⵥ ᘑ stands for "much authority." Benner says it represents a chain of words blended together to form a sentence or command. The addition of 𐤏 intensifies, broadens and builds upon the meaning and designates the one who speaks as one who is full of authority.[43]"

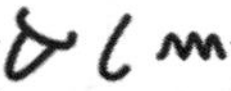

Subdue (ᘯⵃ�ᚥ). ⵃ�ᚥ stands for "conform the tent." ᘯⵃ means "the tent consumed." Together, Benner says this word represents a footstool. "Subdue it" – means placing one's foot on the earth to subdue[44] it. That is, the earth, which was still partially in a chaotic state, would be conformed so it could be consumed / utilized according to the will of God.

Dominion (𐤉ᚕ𐤍). ᚕ𐤍 describes a man at the door – the man with the authority to decide what enters or exits his domain. Benner says this word designates a ruler who walks among his people as opposed to one who rules from a throne[45]. This same word was the only stated goal for Man before God made them:

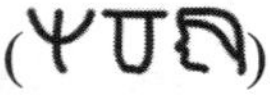

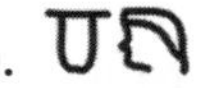

> *"And let them have **dominion** over the fish of the sea and over the birds of the heavens and over the livestock and over all the earth and over every creeping thing that creeps on the earth."*

So, from the beginning, God's goal for our first parents was to have dominion over everything He had made both animate and inanimate.

Adam's yoked role with Elohim

I shared in Chapter Three the yoked relationship Elohim enjoyed with His Son and how important it is for us to enter into that same relationship through Jesus Christ. I also said it was critical for us to learn how to follow our Father step-by-step so we share the load equally with Him.

It may seem presumptuous to assume that we can somehow share any load equally since He is the King of Kings and the Lord of Lords while we are severely limited compared to His capabilities. But the constraints of a yoked relationship demand that we work together stride for stride.

God has chosen to work with us to fulfill His will. Our role was clearly outlined above:

- God shares His will with us (what He **says** to us);
- We **proclaim** (we **call**) His will with our mouth believing what is yet unseen will be fulfilled by Him; and,
- He is faithful and will not allow His word to return without accomplishing what He sent it to **do** (**make**).

The Lord does not need our resources to carry out His will. That is His role in the yoked relationship. Our role is to obey Him by proclaiming His word and following Him step by step. We are a team and He delights in fulfilling His will through us.

A Mystery

A three-step pattern was originally outlined during Day Two of how God fulfills His will: First, "God **said**," then "God **made**, then God **called**." I just shared how this pattern was extended to our first parents and to us. And it is precisely because we are made in God's relational image that we can participate in this three-step pattern.

I also wrote earlier that ⲯⲛⲩ (God's Son) worked together with His Father through their **yoked relationship** and that *"all things were made through him and without him was not anything made that was made."* I assert that God continues to employ this three-step pattern through His Son **in and through us** to make everything that is made.

In Matthew 11:25 – 30, Jesus calls us to take His yoke upon us so that we can know His Father through our relationship with His Son and be truly fruitful. I sincerely believe that the first chapter of Genesis was written to reveal a mystery: showing us the immense potential that is available to us through this yoked relationship. There is nothing too difficult for Him. He loves us unconditionally, and He delights to save to the uttermost all who come to Him. He wants us to step expectantly into the unimaginable potential that is available to us through Jesus Christ.

Food For Man And All Living Creatures

"And God said, 'Behold, I have given you every plant yielding seed that is on the face of all the earth, and every tree with seed in its fruit. You shall have them for food. And to every beast of the earth and to every bird of the heavens and to everything that creeps on the earth, everything that has the breath of life, I have given every green plant for food.' And it was so. And God saw everything that he had made, and behold, it was very good. And there was evening and there was morning, the sixth day" (Genesis 1:29 – 31).

This is the first use of "Behold" ($\Psi \, \zeta \, \Psi$) and underscores that the splendor of this vegetation was a source of praise and awe. Since these plants were brought forth during the Third Day, God gave them to Man and to all the terrestrial creatures even though our first parents would not be able to ingest them until they were clothed with a physical body.

SUMMARY

Looking back over everything He had made, including His work culminating in the creation of Man, God proudly beheld it as **very good**. Nothing more was necessary. Hallelujah!! Thank you, Lord!!

Study Questions For Discussion

- Why is Day Six the most important day in Genesis chapter one?
  - o Are we given the same dominion they had?
  - o Why is your yoked relationship with the Lord critical to your dominion?
- Why didn't God make the terrestrial creatures in Day Five?
  - o What is revealed by making these creatures in Day Six?
  - o Do we have a special relationship with these creatures?
  - o What was the difference between God's blessing of the sea creatures and His blessing to Man?
- Many people say we HAVE a spirit. The Lord says we ARE spirit beings. What is the difference?
- If you HAVE a spirit, how do you define who you are?
- If you ARE a spirit being, how does this define who you really are?
  - o What is your relationship as a spirit being with your body – your tent?
  - o Why didn't God wait until Adam and his wife had physical bodies before blessing them?
  - o Hint: What does "Be fruitful" mean?
  - o How does "Be fruitful" define our relationship with God?
- What is your yoked relationship with the Lord?
  - o What is God's role in this relationship?
- What is the mystery I shared at the end of this chapter?
  - o How do you view the Six Days of Genesis chapter one?
  - o Do they challenge you or are they just more biblical information?
  - o Genesis chapter one may have emboldened Joshua to ask God to hold the sun in place for an extra day. His ways are higher than our ways. What can this mystery embolden you to seek God for?

CHAPTER 12

Genesis 2:1 – 3
Day Seven
The Sabbath Day

"Thus the heavens and the earth were finished, and all the host of them. And on the seventh day God finished his work that he had done, and he rested on the seventh day from all his work that he had done. So God blessed the seventh day and made it holy, because on it God rested from all his work that he had done in creation."

(Genesis 2:1 – 3)

PROLOGUE

The Seventh Day is different from the other six days in many ways. It begins Genesis chapter two rather than finishing chapter one. It does not begin with *"And God said . . ."* nor does it end with *"And there was evening and there was morning the seventh day."* And finally, it focuses on work already completed rather than defining more work to be done. You will discover in the following pages that this "day of rest" is much more than a "day off" for the Lord.

Why The Differences?

As I meditated more on Genesis chapter one to better understand the possible reasons for these differences, I noticed that a single isolated pictogram (◯) was added to the end of each day's final sentence. Here is an example from Genesis 1:5

(read right to left):

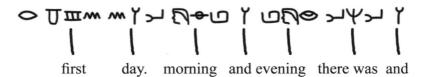

first   day.   morning and evening there was and

Since this pictogram was never translated, I wondered if it might carry some special significance. So, I constructed Appendix B to get a better appreciation for its potential role. I did not try to understand[46] why two symbols were chosen (◗ or ◖) or even why they were placed after certain sentences throughout Genesis. I was even surprised at times to see where one was chosen over the other, when neither one was used or when their application flagged nearly every verse.

I knew that ancient kings sealed official pronouncements with their signet ring. All the king's authority and resources stood behind his seal to mandate its deployment and completion (See Esther 8:9). It seemed plausible that these symbols might represent God's seal authenticating and mandating that each work order – the Light birthed at the beginning of each Day – be fully executed.

I shared earlier that the evening and morning boundaries defined the scope of each work order. The first three verses of chapter two declare that all the work in chapter one was finished; that no further work was necessary to complete the heavens, the earth and all their host. These two boundaries were not added at the end of the seventh day to emphasize that no additional work was needed.

God not only rested from all His work on the seventh Day, He further affirmed the validity of the Day's pronouncement by placing the same seal (◗) at the end of verse three as was placed at the end of every other day. Let's briefly look at the new words in Day Seven to shed additional light on this passage.

Finish – Ⴤ Ⳑ Ⱳ⊐. Benner says Ⳑ Ⱳ stands for "conform to the staff" and defines something that is tamed[47]. My wife Judy has trained horses and dogs for decades and says they are not tamed until your will becomes their will. Only when they want to please you are they tamed and fit for service as trusted companions. (Benner also says the addition of Ⴤ highlights a dimension of praise and awe to the completeness of this finished work.) So, by the beginning of Day Seven, the heavens, the earth and all their host were complete, whole and under the Lord's authority by the strength of His arm (⊐).

All – Ⳑ Ⴤ Ⱳ. The pictograms for "All" show that "conform" (Ⱳ) is anchored (Ⴤ) to authority (Ⳑ) and comes from the same root as "finished"[47]. God's finished work included conforming every host by firmly anchoring them to His authority.

Host – ႥⱱⱤ. At first, you might think **host** would include all the living creatures that were made by the Lord in chapter one. But this word is strongly linked to military activity and those who participate including angels and mankind. It is never used to describe schools of fish, flocks of birds or herds of animals. [The **host** of heaven, the sun, moon and stars (Deuteronomy 4:19), should be viewed in the context of spiritual warfare. And David came against Goliath in the name of the Lord of **Hosts**, the God of the **armies** of Israel (1 Samuel 17:45).]

Work – ⴤⱲⴅⳐⱮ. Work comes from ⱲⳐ meaning "staff in the palm." A shepherd traveled with a staff in his hand to manage his sheep and provide personal support. It was also a weapon to defend against predators or thieves[48]. Notice that the pictograms for Finish ($\mathcal{L}$ Ш) are in the opposite order for Work (Ш $\mathcal{L}$). I find this language amazing! When Joshua meditated on these verses, he could tell by the structure of the pictograms that these two words were polar opposites; that a person was finished when there was no more work to be done.

Done / Make – Ψ ₹ ⊖ . This is the word for "Make" found throughout chapter one and is translated as "Done" here. This word is not preceded by ⊃⌐ indicating that it refers to work done during the other six days rather than during day seven.

Rest – † ப W ⊃⌐. Shabbat means "consume the tent completely." Recall that the pictograms for Evening (ப ₹ ⊖) mean, "see the man facing home" – his work is finished and he is heading home. Shabbat starts in the Evening. The person's work is finished and he can rest, totally focusing on (consuming) his tent / family. ⊃⌐ precedes this word showing that God was an **active** participant in this seventh day Shabbat. He didn't simply quit working.

Holy – W U ⊖ ⊃⌐. Seekins says these pictograms signify what comes after (⊖) the threshing (W U)[49]. The husks and stems had to be removed before the wheat was usable. W U stands for Door with Teeth. A threshing sledge was pulled around the threshing floor by an ox to separate the wheat from the chaff.

The sledge was built much like a door with sharp flint "teeth" on the bottom – correlating well with the pictograms. ⊃⌐ precedes this word as well as the word for bless meaning that God blessed the seventh day and made it holy by the strength of His arm.

In addition, Benner says this word means to be set apart from other people[50]. (Pagan temple prostitutes were called holy – set apart for temple use.) God made the seventh day holy, setting it apart from the other six days of the week so we could focus on what really mattered: our relationships with family, friends and the Lord.

Each Verse Makes a Contribution

As I examined this passage, I was struck by how each verse focused on a specific aspect of the overall significance of the Seventh Day.

Verse 2:1 "And finished" are the first two words in the Hebrew text, declaring that the heavens, the earth and all their host were finished as of the Seventh Day. Here is a translation of this verse based on the pictograms:

> *"And the heavens and the earth were conformed to God's authority [were finished] by the strength of His arm, and [all] their host were conformed to His authority."*

Using the picture book analogy, when Joshua "turned the page," he saw the heavens, the earth and all their host conformed to and under the authority of God by the strength of His arm.

Verse 2:2 "And finished" also begins this verse. But the completeness of this action is emphasized by declaring that Elohim **rested** from all His work that He had done. As shared above, the pictograms for "finished" are in the opposite order for "work." God **rested** as a testament to us that there was no more work to be done.

When Joshua "turned the next page," he observed Elohim resting[51] from all the work He had done to totally conform the heavens, the earth and all their host to His authority."

Verse 2:3 says that Elohim blessed the Seventh Day, made it holy and *"rested from all his work that he had **done** in creation."* I want to address the phrase "that he had done in creation." If your Bible version is either KJV, NKJV, MEV or ASV, they translate this phrase as "God created and made." If you are wondering why two verbs were associated with God's activity, it is because the word (ﬡﬡﬡ) is next to Elohim. If it were translated as "adult son" as I have suggested, then the phrase would read: *"which Elohim (yoked with His) Son made[52]."*

There is an additional concern with this phrase. "In creation" may lead a person to conclude that the work Elohim rested from was only His introductory activity setting the heavens and the earth in motion and populating the earth with vegetation and the biological first parents of fish, birds, sea and land animals and humans. We might even assume that after this initial Seventh Day, God resumed His work on earth much like we do after a day of rest.

Let's examine this verse in a way that Joshua might have meditated on it:

> *"And God blessed the seventh day and made it holy because (ﬡﬡﬡ) on it (ﬡﬡ), He rested from all His work that He (and His) Son made."*

First, it was a Day which means work was done that had nothing to do with the tasks finished on the previous six days. The first portion of this verse says that God established an environment for this special day by blessing it and making it holy. God blessed the day (ﬡﬡﬡﬡ) by conforming it to His

110 Back To The Garden

Son who was yoked to Him. Then God made the day holy, separating the chaff – anything orchestrated by Darkness – from all things done by the Son under the guidance of His Father.

Even though the next word () is translated "because," the pictograms say the underlying meaning is "conform the work" which adds further clarity to the root symbols for work () and correlates with God's activity to bless the day and conform () the work (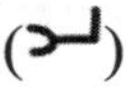) to His Son[53].

 translated "on it" literally means "tent anchored" or "anchored to the tent" and agrees with the Shabbat () activity described earlier to focus on the members in a person's tent.

We could assume God **rested from** doing any work on this day. But as you can see from these pictograms, the Sabbath day only changed the focus of work to be done. As Joshua "turned the page," he saw the Lord devoting all His attention to His relationships with everyone in His tent. Joshua could see that such devotion was key to keeping his own relationships fresh and vibrant.

Another Look At These Verses

Verse 2:1

> *"Thus the heavens and the earth were finished,*
> *and all the host of them."*

At first, the phrase "and all their host" might seem a little out of place especially when "host" refers to military armies. On the one hand, because of the actions of Day Four, all the host of the **heavens** were under the authority of the Lord. But how could Adam and Eve as spirit beings be referred to as "all the host of the **earth**?"

To answer this question, let's consider once again what the Lord said to Joshua:

> *"See, **I have given Jericho into your hand, with its king and mighty men of valor**. You shall march around the city, all the men of war going around the city once. Thus shall you do for six days. Seven priests shall bear seven trumpets of rams' horns before the ark. **On the seventh day** you shall march around the city seven times, and the priests shall blow the trumpets. And when they make a long blast with the ram's horn, when you hear the sound of the trumpet, then all the people shall shout with a great shout, **and the wall of the city will fall down flat,** and the people shall go up, everyone straight before him."* (Joshua 6:2 – 5)

These words were spoken by the Lord BEFORE Joshua and the Israelites approached Jericho. Yet He expressed them as though Jericho's king and its mighty men of valor had already been defeated. **When were they defeated?** This declaration by the Lord was not a wish list He only hoped to accomplish.

Our Lord alone is God Almighty! According to Isaiah 46:9 – 10, He declares the end from the beginning of all things that from our perspective are not yet done. From ancient times, from Genesis 2:1 – 3, He had already conformed all the host of the earth to His authority. Because of this, His counsel to Joshua would stand and He would accomplish all His purpose in their sight.

When Joshua spoke God's Rhema Word to the Israelites, his words bore fruit as God carried them out in accordance with

the pattern originally given to Adam in Genesis 1:28:
*"And God said to them, "Be **fruitful** and multiply and fill the earth and **subdue it**, and have **dominion** over the fish of the sea and over the birds of the heavens and **over every living thing that moves on the earth.**"*

The Lord's revelation to Joshua included instructions to march around Jericho and engage the battle on the seventh day. Those words highlight the rest we are all urged to enter by faith – a Sabbath Rest that was instituted in Genesis 2:1 – 3:

> *"And again in this passage he said, 'They shall not enter **my rest**.' Since therefore it remains for some to enter it, and those who formerly received the good news failed to enter because of disobedience, again he appoints a certain day, 'Today,' saying through David so long afterward, in the words already quoted, 'Today, if you hear his voice, do not harden your hearts.'* ***For if Joshua had given them rest**, God would not have spoken of another day later on. So then, there remains a Sabbath rest for the people of God, for **whoever has entered God's rest has also rested from his works as God did from his. Let us therefore strive to enter that rest**, so that no one may fall by the same sort of disobedience."* (Hebrews 4:5 – 11)

God wanted Joshua and the Israelites who were marching around Jericho that Sabbath day to enter into the rest documented as "finished" in Genesis 2:1 – 3. Instead, they chose to accept this victory as just another local miracle God was performing through Joshua.

Even though the Israelites failed to enter His rest because of their disobedience, it still stands as **finished**, and the Lord is calling us to strive to enter that rest. Like the Israelites, we also tend to view our answers to prayer as isolated examples of God's love for us. But the Lord challenges us to embrace a **lifestyle of rest** – to walk in the presence of His Finished Work, invoking His Rhema word and believing God to fulfill His **completed purpose** through us.

One more aspect of this challenge: Imagine how God feels when we plead for solutions to our problems that are already solved if we would only embrace His lifestyle of rest. Consider this passage from the gospel of Mark:

> *"On that day, when evening had come, he said to them, "Let us go across to the other side." And leaving the crowd, they took him with them in the boat, just as he was. And other boats were with him. And a great windstorm arose, and the waves were breaking into the boat, so that the boat was already filling. But he was in the stern, asleep on the cushion. And they woke him and said to him, "Teacher, do you not care that we are perishing?" And he awoke and rebuked the wind and said to the sea, "Peace! Be still!" And the wind ceased, and there was a great calm. He said to them, "Why are you so afraid? Have you still no faith?" And they were filled with great fear and said to one another, "Who then is this, that even the wind and the sea obey him?"* (Mark 4:35 – 41)

Jesus began by saying to His disciples and those in the other boats, "Let us go across to the other side." That was a word His Father had given Him to be spoken with authority to His disciples. (This event was so important, it is documented in Matthew, Mark and Luke.)

Several men in His boat were seasoned fishermen and were likely concerned that they were crossing at night when the weather could be even more unpredictable. Each biblical account contrasts the ferocity of the storm with a depiction of Jesus sleeping in the stern of the boat. We can imagine the disciples' fear as they struggled mightily to keep the boat from sinking in the darkness. They may even have questioned Jesus' directive to cross at night when the weather could turn on them.

Finally, in desperation (and perhaps with more than a little exasperation that He could sleep while they were in a desperate struggle to save their lives – and His), they woke Jesus up saying, "Teacher, don't you care that we are perishing?"

The fishermen on board were the experts on this lake and may have lost friends and loved ones in storms such as this one. They had a solution: His active participation was their only hope for survival. How often have we cried out to the Lord pleading for Him to calm the storm raging around us? How often have we thought God didn't care because no answer was forthcoming?

Instead of pitching in to help rid the boat of water, Jesus arose, rebuked the wind and said to the sea, "Peace! Be still!" Those words bore fruit and, to the astonishment of His disciples, the wind ceased and there was a great calm on the sea.

His next statement was even more shocking: *"Why are you so afraid?* ***Have you _still_ no faith?"*** We could presume they were afraid because they focused on the storm and its impact on their circumstances rather than on Jesus sleeping in the boat in spite of the sound and fury going on around him.

But God wants us to ask Him how His Son faced the storm.

How could Jesus possibly sleep in that tumultuous environment? Jesus said He only did what He saw His Father doing. If Jesus was doing what He saw His Father doing, then He saw His Father RESTING from all His finished work – including wind that was not blowing and a sea that was calm. When He arose, He declared what He saw – no wind and a calm sea!

Jesus was **resting** in the presence of His Father's Finished Work and He admonished His disciples to be more than amazed at the miracle He had just performed. He wanted them to rest by faith in the same Sabbath Rest He abided in.

Their level of faith was only strong enough to believe in what God could do **for them** to solve each storm they encountered. Jesus challenged them to focus on His faith, to perceive every storm as already conquered by their Father and to rest in His finished work. Jesus wanted them to seek a Rhema word from their Father for each storm they faced, to proclaim it from a posture of continuous rest as though it was already accomplished, and see their Father fulfill His completed purpose **through them**.

Verses 2:2 – 3

> *"And on the seventh day **God finished his work that he had done,** and he **rested** on the seventh day from **all his work that he had done**. So God blessed the seventh day and made it holy, because on it God **rested** from **all his work that God** (yoked with His) **Son had done**."*

I said earlier why I believe the scripture defining Day Seven did not conclude with *"And there was evening and there was morning the seventh day."* But I didn't say why this Day did not start with *"And God said ..."* Before addressing this, may I stress that our God has no rivals. He alone is not bound by time.

God lives outside of time. He not only sees the end from the beginning. He relates to every moment along time's entire continuum in the present tense. He is I AM to Adam, to Abraham, to Moses, to the apostles and to you and me. He only exists in the present because all time is present to Him. No matter when we live in history, the Lord relates to us in the present NOW. He knows every facet of our lives and extends His unconditional love to each one of us through mercy and grace.

Our timeline extends across thousands of years from the first Adam past the last Adam's return. However, for God, all that duration is NOW! He not only sees all of our history, He is experiencing all of it in the immediate present. I have said before that Jesus only did what He saw His Father doing. Permit me to help you see what guided Him to make the ultimate sacrifice for us.

Jesus' Sacrifice

On the night when Jesus would leave the upper room with His disciples, cross the Kidron valley and enter the garden of Gethsemane to face the reality of being separated from His Father to become sin for us – on this night, He prayed, *"Father, glorify me in your own presence with the glory that I had with you before the world existed"* (John 17:5). What did He **SEE** that gave Him the perseverance to take on the sin of the world, to personally experience our separation across all time as our ever-present I AM, and to ask to be glorified with the glory He had in His Father's presence before the world existed?"

Hebrews gives us a glimpse of that unfathomable revelation from His Father:

> *"Who for the joy that was set before him en-*
> *dured the cross, despising the shame, and is*
> *seated at the right hand of the throne of God."*
> (Hebrews 12:2)

He saw the scourging, the nails, the humiliation, the separation from His Father, His death in our place on the cross and
His burial. He despised its shame precisely because He also
saw His RESURRECTION – the **JOY** of His finished work!

He spent six hours on the cross for the six days He had worked
with His Father. And having done all, Elohim gave Him those
most precious words to proclaim to all of creation, **"IT IS
FINISHED!"** Those words bore unimaginable fruit: our reconciliation to His Father through the shedding of His blood!
God's Son Jesus, the Last Adam, our great I AM, reached His
nail-pierced hands across all of time and declared with His
words on the cross what was originally missing from the first
verse of Genesis, chapter two.

God honored His Son's sacrifice on the cross, and His prayer
to be glorified with the glory He had in the presence of His Father before the world began by doing what no One else could
do. Elohim fulfilled through His Son by the strength of His
arm all the prophesies written about Jesus in the Hebrew Testament. And then, to put His stamp of finality on His Son's
work as recorded in Ephesians 1:20 – 23:

> *"He raised him from the dead and seated him at*
> *his right hand in the heavenly places, far above*
> *all rule and authority and power and dominion,*
> *and above every name that is named, not only*
> *in this age but also in the one to come. And he*
> *put all things under his feet and gave him as*
> *head over all things to the church, which is his*
> *body, the fullness of him who fills all in all!"*

Abraham's Sacrifice

I also want to share an incredible revelatory event that took place in Abraham's life made possible only through the intervention of our God Who transcends time. Abraham was a hundred years old when Isaac was born, and shortly afterwards, God said to him, *"Through Isaac shall your offspring be named"* (Genesis 21:12). The Lord made it clear that Abraham's covenant family would be carried on through Isaac, not anyone else.

Yet, before Isaac had married and started his own family, the Lord tested Abraham with words that seemed to totally contradict His earlier pronouncement:

> *"After these things God tested Abraham and said to him, "Abraham!" And he said, "Here I am." He said, "Take your son, your only son Isaac, whom you love, and go to the land of Moriah, and offer him there as a burnt offering on one of the mountains of which I shall tell you."* (Genesis 22:1 – 2)

This wasn't just a call for the two of them to go to a distant mountain, worship the Lord with a sacrifice of a lamb from his flock, and return home. Nor were God's words merely asking that Isaac be dedicated to the Lord through a sacrificial offering of worship. No! God was asking Abraham to do what seemed to contradict His earlier promise, and to offer Isaac, his only son whom he loved, as a BURNT offering.

We are so familiar with what comes next that we can easily dismiss the kind of turmoil and second guessing virtually all of us would have wrestled with had we been tested in a similar manner. After all, we know the Lord stopped Abraham from slaying his son at the last minute; that another ram, caught in the nearby thicket, was substituted as the sacrifice; and that

Abraham passed the test.

But we cheapen this drama if we are not truly surprised by Abraham's resolve to obey immediately:

> *"So Abraham rose early in the morning, saddled his donkey, and took two of his young men with him, and his son Isaac. And he cut the wood for the burnt offering and arose and went to the place of which God had told him. On the third day Abraham lifted up his eyes and saw the place from afar. Then Abraham said to his young men, 'Stay here with the donkey; I and the boy will go over there and worship and come again to you.' And Abraham took the wood of the burnt offering and laid it on Isaac his son. And he took in his hand the fire and the knife. So they went both of them together. And Isaac said to his father Abraham, 'My father!' And he said, 'Here I am, my son.' He said, 'Behold, the fire and the wood, but where is the lamb for a burnt offering?' Abraham said, 'God will provide for himself the lamb for a burnt offering, my son.'"* (Genesis 22:3 – 8)

There is not a hint in this text that Abraham struggled in any way. He rose early in the morning, made all the necessary preparations and set out for the land of Moriah. When they arrived after three days, Abraham's instructions to the young men who had accompanied them were even more amazing: *"Stay here with the donkey; I and the boy will go over there and worship and come again to you."* In case you missed it, here is an expanded version:

> *"Stay here with the donkey; I and the boy will*
> *go over there*
> *and I and the boy will worship*

and I and the boy will come again to you."

This text declares that Abraham was convinced both he and his son Isaac would return to the young men even though Isaac would be offered as a burnt offering[54]. And when Isaac asked his father why they had not brought a lamb, Abraham replied, *"God will **provide himself** the lamb for a burnt offering, my son."* We can read ahead in the text and even put a New Testament spin on these words. But they are somewhat difficult to interpret in a way that honors how Abraham was likely relating to his son as they slowly climbed the mountain.

The Hebrew word for "provide" is the same as "see" in Genesis 1:4, *"And God **saw** that the light was good."* And Gesenius says in his Grammar that the two letters translated as "himself" literally mean "to himself[55]." I like the way this verse is rendered by The Israel Bible[56], *"And Avraham said, "Hashem will see to the sheep for His burnt offering, my son.'"* Put in another way, *"God will see to it that the lamb is provided for the burnt offering, my son."*

We could say that Abraham's response was a veiled way of answering without revealing to Isaac that he would be the sacrifice. But that does not address the emotions Abraham must have felt as a father who loved his son very much. How could he face the imminent prospect of killing his beloved son even if it was an act of obedience? What gave him the assurance that everything would work out even though the next imagined steps were more gruesome than he had ever faced?

What had God revealed to Abraham that gave him such confidence? We find the answer in the Gospel of John. On one occasion Jesus was teaching that those who kept His word would never taste death. His detractors retorted that he was surely not greater than their father Abraham who had died.

In reply, Jesus said, *"Your father Abraham rejoiced that he would see my day. He saw it and was glad"* (John 8:56). "Rejoiced" means that Abraham was literally jumping for joy. The root of this word is a verb meaning to jump, leap or spring up. In addition, the word "see" means to experience / to discern clearly that day.

The "day" Jesus referred to relates to the work order His Father sent Him to accomplish. In this chapter, I have linked Christ's proclamation on the cross, "It is finished" with the work both Elohim and his Son revealed as finished in Genesis 2:1 – 3. Jesus told His detractors that Abraham was rejoicing because God revealed to him in some definite way the death and resurrection of His Own Son – His Day.

The phrases "he would see" and "He saw" highlight a pattern I shared in Chapter Seven of this book and extended to Adam in Chapter Eleven: God said – God made – God called The Light – the revelation of what God is going to do – always precedes what He does to carry it out. Amos 3:7 says, *"The Lord God does nothing without revealing its secret to his servants the prophets."* In the last chapter, I explained that God made us in His image, and then enlisted us in this pattern. He would **reveal to us** what He would do, we would **speak it with our mouth**, and **God would make it happen** by the strength of His arm. Furthermore, God always reveals His Light to us the way He sees it – finished with no further work to be done!

In Genesis 15:4 – 6, God assured Abraham that his very own son would be his heir. Then He took him outside and asked him to count the stars if he could. Afterwards, He declared,

> *"So shall your offspring be. And he believed the Lord, and He counted it to him as righteousness."*

Years later. in Genesis 21:12, after Isaac was born, God narrowed the scope of His earlier pronouncement,

"Through Isaac shall your offspring be named."

The test God gave Abraham in Genesis 22:1 – 3, was not whether he would offer his son as a burnt offering. The test would reveal the maturity of Abraham's belief in the finished work God had showed him earlier – offspring without number being fathered through Isaac even though his son was still a boy:

*"**Count it all joy**, my brothers, **when you meet trials** of various kinds, for you know that the testing of your faith produces steadfastness. And let steadfastness have its full effect, that **you may be perfect and complete, lacking in nothing**"* (James 1:2 – 4).

God had previously revealed to Abraham that Isaac's progeny would one day be too numerous to count. The only way he could comprehend how his offspring could come through Isaac would be if God raised him back to life.

Why was Abraham so willing to begin this new journey of faithful obedience? For the joy that was set before him – the death and resurrection of Jesus Christ – he was eager to travel three days to the land of Moriah and sacrifice his son in order to experience the immeasurable joy of seeing Isaac raised back to life to the glory of God and the faithfulness of His finished work!

When he arrived at the mountain, he spoke the words God had given him both to the men who would stay behind and to his son. He remained sensitive to the Lord's voice as he raised his knife to slay his son, and God fulfilled his promise that *"through Isaac shall your offspring be named"* by providing the lamb **himself** for the sacrifice. God rewarded Abraham's obedience: he experienced the overwhelming joy of receiving Isaac back alive. He saw in the death and resurrection of God's Son, the "death and resurrection" of his own son – and was glad (a word that means to be calmly happy).

SUMMARY

This chapter has changed me. I have rewritten it many times. At first, I thought these three verses were rather straight forward highlighting the Lord's commitment to a Sabbath Day's rest. Now, nearly four weeks later, I stand in awe of the richness of God's Word and the Holy Spirit's ability to lead us into greater depths of His Truth.

The apostle Paul sums up this chapter better than I ever could:
> *"For we are his workmanship, created in Christ*
> *Jesus for good works, which God prepared be-*
> *forehand, that we should walk in them."*
> (Ephesians 2:10)

Each one of us has been meticulously crafted by God into the image of His Son. The Lord has chosen us to live in His presence in a posture of continuous rest. And He leads us by His Holy Spirit to walk boldly into our destiny prepared beforehand as a manifestation of His finished work.

Study Questions For Discussion

- The third verse of chapter two reads. *"So God blessed the seventh day and made it holy, because on it God rested from all his work that he had done in creation."*
  o The last phrase "done in creation" could be interpreted as "God only rested from the work He did in chapter one. But after taking a day off, He went back to work just like we do when we take one day a week off from our work. Is this what God meant when He rested on the Seventh Day?
  o Joshua was told to march around Jericho seven times and engage the battle on the seventh day. How could they do this without violating Moses' command not to do any work on the seventh day?
- Jesus' disciples were frustrated with Jesus because He was sleeping in the back of the boat while they were desperately trying to keep the boat from sinking. What was Jesus trying to teach them and us? (*"Why are you so afraid? Have you **still** no faith?"*)
- God finished the heaven and the earth and all their host. Does the phrase "all their hosts" have any bearing on spiritual warfare?
- Does the word "finished" have any bearing on spiritual warfare?
- When did God finish the heaven and the earth and all their hosts?
- Does "rest" mean that God did nothing during the Seventh Day?
- How could Abraham "rejoice and be glad" as he prepared to sacrifice his only son?
  o What does his response to God's test say about his faith?
  o How does his response reflect Paul's declaration in Romans 8:28, *"And we know that for those who love God all things work together for good, for those who are*

called according to his purpose"?

- How does the finished work on the Seventh Day relate to Jesus' words on the cross, "***It is finished!***"?
- The book of Hebrews summons us to enter into God's rest. In light of what you have read in this chapter, how does the Lord want you to face the work He calls you to perform as you fulfill your destiny?
  o In Mark 11:24, Jesus says, *"Therefore I tell you, what ever you ask in prayer, believe that you have received it, and it will be yours."* How does this verse mirror a posture of rest?
  o Is the chaos we face in our world today covered by what God did before Adam set foot on this planet?

CHAPTER
13

Genesis 2:4
The Transition From
ⵁⵁⵁ To ⵁⵁⵁⵁ

"These are the generations of the heaven[s][57] and the earth when they were created, in the day that the Lord God made the earth and the heaven[s]" (Genesis 2:4).

PROLOGUE

I said in the prologue of Chapter Four that God never does anything alone. In the first verse of the Torah, Elohim teamed with His Son and His Spirit to make the heavens and the earth. John added his witness by affirming that Jesus was an integral participant in that activity. All through Genesis chapter one, this Team first birthed each day's revelation as light and then fulfilled the specific proclamation through their unlimited capabilities and resources.

During those Six Days, Elohim revealed His creative character through the name of His Son ⵁⵁⵁ. On the Seventh Day, both Elohim and His Son rested from all their work.

In Genesis 1:26 – 28, God made Man and called us to take part in fulfilling His will. Our role was to receive God's revelation and proclaim it in faith and obedience. His role was to fulfill His word through His unlimited capabilities and resources.

God created us as an expression of His unconditional love, giving us the freedom to disobey Him. Knowing that one day, our disobedience would radically alter our relationship with Him, He chose, in verse 2:4b, to inaugurate a different dimension of His character through His Son as Savior, Redeemer and Lord – **Ψ Υ Ψ⌐** – translated as "Lord" in Christian Bibles, but is combined with Elohim and translated as "Hashem" in Hebrew Bibles.

Genesis 2:4 marks the transition from God's revelation of His Son as **ᗩ⊓◁** (encapsulated in 1:1 through 2:4a), to His Son's revelation as **Ψ Υ Ψ⌐** (YHVH – Lord) beginning in 2:4b and extending throughout the rest of the Hebrew Testament. This verse also marks a transition in perspective from God's relationship with His creation to man's relationship with God and His creation. This chapter and Chapter Fourteen will divide this verse along those lines.

But First, Another Translation Issue

Even a brief look at this verse in the Septuagint edition reveals that these ancient scholars must have had difficulty translating it into Greek. Here is the Hebrew text: (Read right to left)

בהבראם	והארץ	השמים	תולדות	אלה
created the in	earth the and	heavens the	generations	These

ושמים	ארץ אלהים	יהוה	עשות	ביום
heaven and	earth Elohim	YHVH	made	day in
	(God)	(Lord)		
	[Hashem]			

And here is the Septuagint edition:

αυτη   η βιβλος   γενεσεως   ουρανου και γης οτε εγενετο

This is the book of generation of heaven and earth when made

η ημερα εποιησεν ο θεος τον ουρανον και την γην

the day   created   God   the heaven and the earth.

First: "These [are the] generations" became "This is the book of [the] generation." Not only did two plural words become singular, "book" was added to the text.

Next, the first Hebrew phrase, "the heavens and the earth" became in the Septuagint, "heaven and earth" while the second Hebrew phrase, "earth and heaven" became in the Septuagint, "the heaven and the earth." Notice that the word order was reversed in the Hebrew text but not in the Septuagint. The articles (the) were also dropped before these two words in the first phrase but then were added before these two words in the second phrase.

Next, "they were created" became "it was made." Not only did plural become singular, εγενετο (made) was used to translate ברא in the first phrase even though these scholars used εποιησεν all through Genesis chapter one to translate this Hebrew word.

Finally, אלה caused the most concern for me because I could not see how the pictograms for this word could possibly be interpreted as αυτη – **this**. As I shared earlier, אל (𐤋 𐤀) are the first two letters in Elohim's name and often represent one of the names of God. I shared in Chapter Two that these two pictograms can also stand for phrases like "strongly yoked." Here are three additional examples from Genesis 17:1 – אל־אברם (strongly yoked to Abram), and (אל שדי) El Shaddai "God Almighty").

To better understand the meaning of אלה, I built Appendix C with four pages of examples to show how adding ה to two-symbol words changed their meaning. Since the pictogram for ה (¥) shows a person standing with his arms upraised in praise and wonder, its inclusion enhances the emotional content of the word in most cases.

Benner says אלה means to swear an oath or covenant[58] yielding a blessing for adherence, and a curse for breaking the oath. Neither this definition nor the weight of Appendix C gave any indication how this word could have been translated by "This."

So, I built Appendix D of all the occurrences in Genesis where the phrase "the generations of" was found and quickly began to piece this puzzle together. There are ten other instances of this phrase in Genesis. The next one is in Genesis 5:1 *"This is the book of the generations of Adam."*

As you can see, *"This is the book"* matches the beginning of the Septuagint version in 2:4. But why transpose 5:1 into 2:4? By reading through Appendix D, you will notice that, of the eleven occurrences, all except 2:4 dealt with human generations. Furthermore, all occurrences after 5:1 named the generations of specific persons. By interpreting Adam in a more generic way as "mankind," it could be argued that תולדות was a qualitative plural that could also be translated with a singular "generation" in keeping with the singular "mankind."

In any event, they translated 5:1 as "*This is the book of the generation of Man*." Following this or similar logic and transposing a portion of 5:1 into 2:4 yielded, "***This** is the book of the **generation** of heaven and earth*." By using a singular "generation," no offspring for the heavens or the earth was necessary as would be the case for a plural "generations."

Their substitution of the meaning of זה (this / these), which begins 5:1, also provided an alternative definition for אלה in 2:4 and all the other occurrences in Genesis. As you can see from Appendix D, אלה was translated in every instance of the Septuagint by αυτη / αυται (this / these).

The Hebrew Lexicon I used in seminary, Brown, Driver and Briggs (Brown), devoted five pages to variants of אל. They showed two entries for אלה. The first displayed the vocalic marks under the Hebrew characters and was interpreted as "this." They stated that אלה was the plural of זה referring to Genesis 2:4 where אלה was translated as plural[59]. **However, there was no reason given by them for this assertion other than the translation given in Genesis 2:4.**

The other entry in Brown for אלה did not have vocalic marks and was translated as "god" or "God" but with no scriptural references. (Brown used these characters to define other words like אלהימ and אל.)

All of these variants for אל are differentiated by vocalic marks. These marks distinguished the different uses of this word in the Septuagint and Aramaic sources that were referenced during the middle ages to build their Hebrew lexicons.

As an example, look at how אל is translated in Genesis 15:1.

First, here is the Hebrew version:

אחר הדברים האלה הָיָה דבר־יהוה **אל־אברם** במחזה לאמר **אל־תירא**

The English translation: "After these things, the word of the Lord came to Abram in a dream saying to him, 'Fear not Abram . . .'"

The Septuagint scholars translated אל־אברם as **πρὸς** Ἀβραμ – to Abram. The lexicons built during the middle ages differentiated this use by changing the vocalic marking under אל.

אל־תירא אברם was translated as μὴ φοβοῦ ῎Αβραμ – "(do) not fear Abram." Once again, the markings were changed to differentiate this usage. However, this change is problematic because the Hebrew word for 'NOT' is **לא**. If we allow the pictograms to determine the translation, the text could read, "Fear God, Abram." Since the fear of the Lord is the beginning of wisdom, this alternative translation supports God's declaration about Abram in Genesis 22:12.

> *"He said, 'Do not lay your hand on the boy or do anything to him, **for now I know that you fear God**, seeing you have not (לא) withheld your son, your only son, from me.'"*

In Genesis 15:1, the **exact opposite meaning** of the word אל was chosen as the preferred translation because of its Septuagint rendering.

In Deuteronomy chapter 27, Moses instructed the elders of Israel that they were to station the tribes on mount Gerizim and mount Ebal to receive the blessings for keeping the law as well as the curses for abandoning it. At the conclusion of proclaiming the curses, Moses summed them up in the last verse of the chapter:

"Cursed be anyone who does not confirm (לֹא־יָקִים) the words of this law by doing them.' And all the people shall say, 'Amen.'"
(Deuteronomy 27:26)

Here, as in many other places in the Hebrew testament, the word for NOT is לֹא. It is also the Hebrew word for "No" as seen in this next text where Haggai is questioning the priests.

"If someone carries holy meat in the fold of his garment and touches with his fold bread or stew or wine or oil or any kind of food, does it become holy? The priests answered and said, 'No (לֹא)'" (Haggai 2:12).

The apostle Paul further declares that God's promises are always "Yes" and never "No."

"As surely as God is faithful*, our word to you has not been Yes and No. For the Son of God, Jesus Christ, whom we proclaimed among you, Silvanus and Timothy and I, was not Yes and No,* **but in him it is always Yes. For all the promises of God find their Yes in him.** *That is why it is through him that we utter our Amen to God for his glory"* (2 Corinthians 1:18 – 20).

For ancient Hebrews like Joshua, there were **no vocalic marks** associated with ﬠ ﬥ ﬡ showing them how to pronounce and interpret the word. Nor were there any linguistic hurdles to overcome such as those faced by the Septuagint scholars. Instead, they derived meaning directly from the pictograms themselves and from each symbol group's relationship with the other "words" in the "sentence."

In Chapter Two, I presented a brief overview of the development of the Hebrew written language. In Chapter Three, I shared how, in order to translate the first verse in the Torah into a meaningful sentence for Greek readers, ᗡᑎᗐ was converted into a verb (created). In Chapter Twelve, I shared how ᵗᗐᗯ was translated as a verb (rested)[60] in Genesis 2:2 while the same pictograms became a noun (Sabbath) in Exodus 16:23.

Now that you have witnessed the considerable influence the Septuagint translators had over the interpretation and structure of passages like Genesis 2:4, I hope you will agree to a closer look at the evolution of the Hebrew scriptures.

Hebrew: A Closer Look

As you examine the Table of the Ancient Hebrew Alphabet in Chapter Two, you can readily see that the need for simpler "written" examples of the proto-Canaanite symbols had already obscured a certain amount of the visual impact of the original pictograms by the time of King David.

The Hebrew alphabet we know today was developed during the Babylonian exile.[61] Babylonian Aramaic, a closely-related Semitic language, became the character-set model for the Hebrew scriptures and consisted of consonants and a few long vowels. As mentioned earlier, these "letters" represented a one-to-one adaptation from their corresponding pictograms. Vowels were not necessary to know how to pronounce a word because Hebrew was a spoken language. The reader only needed a visual queue provided by the consonants to recognize each written word in much the same way we read abbreviations today.

Unfortunately, this adaptation further moved the characters away from the symbolic meaning of their original pictograms and towards a more literary structure. The book of Esther and the first six chapters of Daniel were written in Aramaic, attesting to the growing migration away from Hebrew as the preferred Jewish tongue during their extended period of exile. Hundreds of years later, when the Greeks conquered many of the Mediterranean countries, Israel was "encouraged" to learn Greek and translate their sacred writings into this pagan language with all of its formal grammatical structure and lexicon. By the New Testament era, Greek was the common language throughout much of the Roman Empire while Aramaic was the preferred language in Israel.

By Jesus' lifetime, the Septuagint was their "King James" Bible and only the religious elite kept the Hebrew language alive. Then, in 70 A.D., the Romans conquered Israel, disbursed them throughout their empire, and eliminated Israel as a nation. Many copies of the Hebrew scriptures were lost when Jerusalem fell.

Fast forward a few more centuries and the Hebrew language was in danger of becoming extinct as a spoken language. Jewish scholars established schools to codify the 39 books into the Masoretic Text and to train rabbis in its use. They also developed a system of vocalic points written under and sometimes over the Hebrew characters to help determine the pronunciation of each word.

The Septuagint remained a dominate staple for Jewish believers. It also represented a surviving link with the ancient Hebrew scholars who had created this important translation. By 1000 A.D., numerous grammatical and lexicographical works were under way using the Septuagint and other Aramaic writings as linguistic resources, and by the nineteenth century, men like Gesenius had compiled comprehensive grammars and lexicons of the Hebrew tongue[62].

Written Hebrew now possessed a fully-functioning grammar commensurate with other Indo-European languages. But all these layers of adaptation also **shrouded** it from the simplicity of the original pictographic symbols in the Torah. Every "word" Moses wrote was its own dictionary, and its association with the other words, as in my "picture book model," enabled believers like Joshua to meditate on them under the guidance of the Holy Spirit without grammatical constraints. Any Hebrew could relate personally to those symbols without the need to become literate like we do in order to read.

The Latin Vulgate held sway over the Christian church from the late fourth century to the Protestant Reformation. It is purported to have been a direct conversion from the Hebrew Bible[63]. Yet here are the English translations from the Vulgate for Genesis 2:4 and 5:1 showing the influence of the Septuagint on this translation:

> *"These are the **generations** of **the heaven and the earth**, when they were created, in the day that the Lord God made the **heaven and the earth**."*

> *"This is the book of the **generation** of Adam."*

In Hebrew, the word order for "the heaven and the earth" are reversed in the second phrase of 2:4, and "generations" is plural in 5:1.

Why I Am Writing This Book

Like you, I did not give much thought to how the Hebrew Bible was translated into English. I thought the Hebrew I studied in seminary was the same as the one Moses used to write the Torah. Now that I have become aware of this disparity, I want you to be guided by the Holy Spirit as you meditate on the

Hebrew Tstament the same way Joshua and others did until Judah was led away into captivity.

The Lord has emboldened me to retrace our Biblical heritage back to those early pictograms so we can recapture more of the original intent and revelation that has been **shrouded** by history. My passion is to equip you with the ability to understand and read the pictograms Moses wrote and the Holy Spirit inspired in the same manner that we are able to read the original Greek text of the New Testament.

Listen with your heart to what the Holy Spirit is saying through these next two passages of scripture:

> *"Since we have such a hope, we are very bold, not like Moses, who would put a veil over his face so that the Israelites might not gaze at the outcome of what was being brought to an end. But their minds were hardened. For to this day, when they read the old covenant, that same veil remains unlifted, because only through Christ is it taken away. Yes, to this day whenever Moses is read a veil lies over their hearts. But when one turns to the Lord, the veil is removed. Now the Lord is the Spirit, and where the Spirit of the Lord is, there is freedom. And we all, with unveiled face, beholding the glory of the Lord, are being transformed into the same image from one degree of glory to another. For this comes from the Lord who is the Spirit."*
>
> (2 Corinthians 3:12 – 18)

> *"You search the Scriptures because you think that in them you have eternal life; and it is they that bear witness about me, yet you refuse to come to me that you may have life... Do not*

*think that I will accuse you to the Father. There
is one who accuses you: Moses, on whom you
have set your hope. For if you believed Moses,
you would believe me;* **for he wrote of me.**"
(John 5:39 – 40, 45 – 46)

Paul says that Moses' veil still **shrouds** those who read the old
covenant to this day. It is only through Christ that this veil is
taken away by the transforming power of the Holy Spirit.

Jesus spoke to this issue by saying, *"You search the Scriptures
because you think that in them you have eternal life."* They
were looking for ways to please God by keeping the Law. This
put them at odds with Jesus Who in their eyes was not keeping
the Law as they interpreted it. So, they refused to come to Him
for the life they were seeking.

Jesus admonished them saying that those same Scriptures bore
witness to Him and that Moses who they put their hope in **also
wrote of Him**. Had they seen in the Torah that eternal life was
predicated on a personal relationship with God, they would
have recognized that Jesus could not have done the works
He did without a solid relationship with His Father. Had they
compared the fruits of their efforts to gain eternal life with
the fruits of Jesus' ministry instead of comparing how He was
keeping the Law according to their standard of righteousness,
they would have sought Him.

But there is more! I have not yet explained why Jesus said that
Moses **wrote of Him!** From the very first verse of the Torah,
the pictograms Moses wrote were gradually superseded by
linguistic replacements that veiled Elohim's Son from those
in Jesus' day who were searching the Scriptures hoping to find
eternal life.

Paul reminded the Corinthians: *"to this day whenever Moses is read a veil lies over their hearts."* In other words, this veil keeps those who read the Old Covenant from seeing Jesus Christ, God's Son, in its pages. Without this link, it has been easier for Jews to reject the witness of the New Testament, especially when they have been trying desperately, since the fall of Jerusalem in 70 A.D., to keep their unique heritage alive.

Paul says concerning his Jewish brethren,

> *"I do not want you to be unaware of this mystery, brothers: a partial hardening has come upon Israel, until the fullness of the Gentiles has come in"* (Romans 11:25).

Today, Israel is once again living as a nation and speaking their Hebrew language against all odds. It is my passion to reveal the Son of the Most High "hidden" in the Torah. May my small contribution, along with others who have championed the study of the Hebrew pictograms, help remove the veil that has **shrouded** so many from the eternal life freely available to everyone through our Messiah, Jesus Christ.

I firmly believe that the only way to recapture the deeper meaning of the Hebrew Bible as the Holy Spirit originally inspired it is to study it in its pictographic form. Furthermore, I am convinced that we must humbly meditate on these symbols as little children the same way Joshua and his contemporaries did relying on the Lord for guidance and inspiration.

If we impose the linguistic constraints of modern Hebrew on the pictographic structure of these ancient texts, we will run the risk of extending the veil over those who desperately need to see the Messiah revealed within its pages.

Genesis 2:4a – A Final Look

2:4 - Transition From BARA To YHVH   139

"These are the generations of the heavens and the earth when they were created,"

Permit me to explain why I am convinced that this verse is a transition from Genesis 1:1 – 2:3 to the remainder of the Bible. I have already presented an interpretation for ⎜⎜⎜ that is more in keeping with the pictographic meaning of this word. And I have also pointed out that the Septuagint scholars translated ⎜⎜⎜ into a verb. Because of their influence, ⎜⎜⎜ was translated as *"when they were created."* But let's look more closely at this symbol group:

⎜ – a "tent" often translated as either a literal tent / house or "in" representing someone who is IN a tent / dwelling.

⎜ – Depicts a person in the act of praising or standing in awe of something / someone. It is also translated as "the" when it is added to the front of a word like "the heavens" and "the earth" found earlier in this verse.

⎜⎜⎜ – Notice that ⎜ was appended to the end of ⎜⎜⎜ We capitalize ⎜⎜⎜ as God because of the suffix ⎜. I am asserting that ⎜⎜⎜ can be capitalized as "Son" for the same reason. I have also shown that אלה can mean to swear an oath yielding a blessing for adherence. So, here again is 2:4a (Read right to left):

בהבראמ	והארץ	השמים	תולדות	אלה
ן ן \	ן ן \	ן \	ן	ן

Son the in earth the & heavens the generations (Blessing Oath)

SUMMARY

The first half of this verse can be summarized as an oath declaring that everything God made with His Son in the power of His Holy Spirit was blessed and very good. As such, a reasonable translation of this Oath of Blessing could be:

*"An oath: Blessed are the generations of the heavens and the earth **in the Son.**"*

Study Questions For Discussion

- Genesis 2:4 marks a transition from the creative work God did in Genesis chapter one to His salvation work in the rest of the Bible. Why did God make this transition in this verse instead of waiting until mankind needed a savior?
- What role does God's unconditional love play in salvation?
- What is an oath of blessing?
- The scriptures used by the first century church were what we call the Old Testament. Yet their "King James Version" was the Greek translation of the Aramaic adaptation that replaced the original Hebrew written in pictograms and inspired by the Holy Spirit. Why is it so important to meditate on the pictographic words inspired by the Holy Spirit?
  o Greek is a pagan language and their dictionary definitions for many of the words in the New Testament come from that language. Why is it important to meditate on the pictograms of the corresponding Hebrew words in order to get a more biblical foundation for these words?
  o Why are the definitions in the current Hebrew dictionaries limited in their ability to reflect the underlying pictographic meaning?
- Why is it important to meditate on God's word? Is there a difference between meditating and studying? What part does prayer and waiting on the Lord play in the way God reveals Himself and His word to us?
- The Holy Spirit leads us into all truth. Is there a difference between the Logos word and the Rhema word of God?
  o How did Abraham meditate on God's word without a Bible to study?
  o How did the first century believers meditate on the Gospel before they had a New Testament to study?

CHAPTER
14

Earth and Heaven
A Different Perspective

"These are the generations of the heaven[s] and the earth when they were created, in the day that the Lord God made the earth and the heaven[s]" (Genesis 2:4).

PROLOGUE

In the last chapter, I said that Genesis 2:4 was a transition verse:

- **From** all the verses up to 2:4a
  - o **To** the rest of the Bible starting with 2:4b;
- **From** a creator relationship with Elohim through His Son revealed as 𐤀𐤁𐤋 – Adult Son
  - o **To** a redemptive relationship with Elohim through His Son revealed as 𐤉𐤄𐤅𐤄 – Lord; and,
- **From** a divine perspective of His relationship with His creation across the entire span of history
  - o **To** a human perspective of our relationship with God as we live each moment of our lifetime along our portion of that entire span of history.

In this chapter, I will reveal how I came to those conclusions. I will also address the challenges to divine authorship raised by the "Age of Enlightenment."

Genesis 2:4b

"in the day that the Lord God made the earth and the heaven[s]"

Here is the Hebrew text:

ביום עשות   יהוה   אלהים   ארץ   ושמים

heaven and earth Elohim YHVH made day in [the]

Virtually every word in this text elicits something new:

- **Earth and heaven** are not only reversed in this second phrase, there are no articles (the) preceding them;
- This is the first time YHVH[64] has entered the biblical narrative and its close proximity to Elohim evokes the same potential relationship the adult Son had with God in Genesis 1:1, 21, 27, and 2:3;
- "**Made**" is not preceded by ⊃⌐ as in verses 1:7, 16 and 25 denoting active participation by God. Nor does it simply indicate work already done as in 1:31 and 2:2 (Υℱ☉). Instead, its pictograms are identical to its last use in 2:3 where the suffix † Υ (anchored to final) stresses the final completed nature (†) of this effort († Υ ℱ ☉); and,
- **Day** is the same word in chapter one and surely stands for a particular work order performed by YHVH yoked with Elohim.

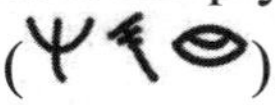

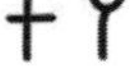

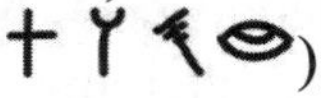

Earth and Heaven

I will argue that this reversal signals a change in focus. "**The Heavens**" were positioned first in the initial segment of this verse to represent all that the Son yoked with His Father accomplished by the end of Day Six. It is a resting (Sabbath) view of time from heaven's vantage point in which everything that God did spanning all of time was completed before Adam set foot in the garden of Eden. This perspective is possible because our God is present across all of time, seeing the end from the beginning, and relating to everything during each instant as the ever-present I AM.

Seen from this "eternal" arena, the plants, birds, fish, sea creatures, land animals and all creeping things were portrayed "according to their own kind" showing their progression of life across the entire span of history akin to studying them through multiple generations in a biology class. Man was part of the work God and his Son accomplished during Day Six and therefore also participated in the generational blessing in 2:4a.

"**Earth**" is positioned first in 2:4b and is the primary focus from the perspective of Adam and his progeny living on this planet in the linear dimension of time. Unlike God, we can only live in the moment. So, we experience an ever-changing present situation as we move through time. Unlike God, we cannot relive past events or project ourselves into the future to experience what is happening tomorrow.

As we progress into the verses that follow, we witness time progressing on Earth from a barren land with no bushes, plants or trees to a garden planted for and maintained by Adam with rivers flowing across the landscape. The entire rest of human history is played out on this temporal, earthly stage until a new heaven and a new earth break forth into our reality with God dwelling among us forevermore.

YHVH – ‫𐤅𐤄𐤅𐤉‬

2:4b launches our story along this temporal timeline. Part of the assurances we gain from the first three verses of chapter two is that there is nothing we will ever encounter, no matter how daunting, that Elohim and His Son have not already finished. Our original parents walked by faith in victory in the manifest presence of God, experiencing His Sabbath rest and victory in everything they did.

But God knew that one day, they would disobey him. No longer would they joyfully seek His company in the cool of each afternoon. Instead, the transparent innocence of their fellowship would be replaced by blame, guilt, fear and shame separating them from each other and from His unconditional love, grace and truth. Their unwavering obedience to His guidance would be replaced with the seeds of suspicion and ulterior motives sown by the serpent.

It is important to understand why God reveals Himself to us using different names. I shared in Chapter Four that "name" (ᵐᵂ – destroy chaos) reveals the character or activity of what is named to be able to produce order out of chaos. So here, at the head waters of our history in 2:4b, God introduced a dimension of His character that would reveal the extent of His ability to deliver the descendants of Adam from every crisis they faced – Ⴘ Ⴕ Ⴘ⌐ (YHVH).

We are familiar with ⌐ because it was appended to the front of many words in chapter one, and demonstrated God's active participation during the accomplishments of each day. We have also learned that Ⴘ represents a person standing with his hands raised in praise and awe at what he sees. Finally, Ⴕ is a tent peg anchoring the two Ⴘ symbols to each other.

So, Ⴘ Ⴕ Ⴘ⌐ means the work performed by the strength of God's arm is so incredible – so far above what we can ask or think – that it elicits from us praise and awe ANCHORED to more praise and awe. 2:4b is the first time this Name appears in the Bible. But it was not until God delivered Israel from hopeless slavery in Egypt that the awesome power of this Name was more completely revealed and appreciated.

Permit me to briefly paint the impossible circumstances of this scenario: Moses had fled Egypt in fear forty years earlier to avoid being killed by Pharaoh, and had just encountered God at a burning bush while herding sheep near Horeb. God explained to Moses that He had heard the cries of His people and had come down to deliver them from the current Pharaoh.

Then this encounter became more personal. God told Moses that He was sending this eighty-year-old shepherd living as an exile in Midian, who couldn't speak very well, to meet the most brutal dictator on the planet and demand that Pharaoh set free over 600,000 of his Israelite slave families and their livestock so they could return to a distant land God promised to their ancestors more than four hundred years earlier. The Lord went on to say that He had hardened Pharaoh's heart and that the king would not listen to Moses unless he was compelled by God's mighty hand.

This was truly a hopeless assignment! First, Moses had to convince his own people that God had chosen him to deliver them from slavery. Then, he had to confront the king of Egypt. There would be no call for the Israelites to rise up in rebellion like Moses wanted forty years earlier. He would only have the staff in his hand, the eloquence of his brother Aaron, and Elohim revealed as I AM providing His Mighty Hand (‎𐤉𐤃) to deliver them.

We shouldn't blame Moses for pleading with God to send someone else – anyone else. We do not read earlier of any heroic accomplishments Moses had achieved in his walk of faith. He had killed an Egyptian hoping his people would follow his lead and rebel. However, no one followed him and he fled Egypt in fear for his life. He had driven off several shepherds from the well Jethro's daughters used to water their sheep and was now the shepherd of those sheep. As priest of

Midian, his father-in-law may have told him about this mountain at Horeb. But there was nothing he could see in his own character that would qualify him to volunteer for such a momentous task.

This is a critical lesson for us: Moses did not choose God. God chose Moses! There is nothing in the Bible to suggest that Moses arose that morning burdened with the fate of the Israelites, imploring God as he approached the mountain saying, "Here am I Lord, send me!"

Listen to Jesus' words:
> "You did not choose me, but I chose you and appointed you that you should go and bear fruit and that your fruit should abide, so that whatever you ask the Father in my name, he may give it to you" (John 15:16).

God not only finished all His works on the Seventh Day, He matched us up with those works according to His assessment of our character to follow Him.

> "**For we are his workmanship**, created in Christ Jesus for good works, which **God prepared beforehand**, that we should walk in them" (Ephesians 2:10).

> "Now the word of the Lord came to me, saying, '**Before I formed you in the womb I knew you**, and before you were born **I consecrated you; I appointed you a prophet to the nations**.'"
> (Jeremiah 1:4 – 5).

Elohim spent eighty years building a heart of compassion into Moses, together with a humility that recognized there were no resources, wisdom or strength of his own that could contribute anything to this effort. God alone would deliver His people. All He asked of Moses was obedience.

After an initial encounter with Pharaoh that led to even harsher treatment for the Israelites, God said to Moses:

> "_**I am the Lord**_. _I appeared to Abraham, to Isaac, and to Jacob, as God Almighty (El Shaddai), but by_ _**my name the Lord**_ _(YHVH) I did not make myself known to them. I also established my covenant with them to give them the land of Canaan, the land in which they lived as sojourners. Moreover, I have heard the groaning of the people of Israel whom the Egyptians hold as slaves, and I have remembered my covenant. Say therefore to the people of Israel, **I am the Lord**, and **I will bring you** out from under the burdens of the Egyptians, and **I will deliver you** from slavery to them, and **I will redeem you** with an outstretched arm and with great acts of judgment. **I will take you** to be my people, and I will be your God, and **you shall know that I am the Lord your God, who has brought you out** from under the burdens of the Egyptians. **I will bring you** into the land that I swore to give to Abraham, to Isaac, and to Jacob. **I will give it to you** for a possession. **I am the Lord**._"
>
> (Exodus 6:2 – 8)

As I said earlier, the Exodus provides the awesome contextual backdrop for the scale of problems the Lord (YHVH) is able to handle. Looking back on this event, no one could lament that their problem was too large for the arm of the Lord to save.

And There's More!

*"... in the day that the **Lord God** made the earth and the heavens"* (Genesis 2:4b).

I have already demonstrated the yoked relationship Elohim and His Son had when they made everything that was made in Genesis chapter one. I have also shared that by announcing the new name "YHVH" in 4:2, the Lord God was revealing His ability to save us from every calamity we could possibly face. Since the close association of YHVH with Elohim in 2:4b is mirrored in the close association of Bara with Elohim in 1:1. it seems reasonable to assert that Bara and YHVH are both Names manifesting the character and role of Elohim's Son in creation and salvation history.

The Septuagint scholars add credence to this assertion. In their Septuagint version, YHVH and Elohim were translated as κυρίος (Lord) and θεὸς (God) which were precisely the same words chosen by Paul when he wrote Romans 10:9:

*"If you confess with your mouth that **Jesus** is **Lord** (κύριον) and believe in your heart that **God** (θεὸς) raised him from the dead, you will be saved."*

Paul was a Rabbi trained by Gamaliel, a Pharisee in the Jewish Counsel and a teacher of the law held in honor by all the people (Acts 5:34). Paul knew the Law both in the Greek Septuagint translation and in the Hebrew language. Because of these Hebrew to Greek word associations, permit me to re-phrase Romans 10:9:

*"If you <u>confess with your mouth</u> that **Jesus** is **YHVH** and believe in your heart that **Elohim** raised him from the dead, you will be saved."*

Peter also bore witness to this association when he quoted

from Joel 2:32 in his sermon on Pentecost where he linked "Lord" with Jesus:

> *"And it shall come to pass that everyone who calls upon the name of the Lord (κυρίου) shall be saved... Let all the house of Israel therefore know for certain that God (θεὸς) has made him both Lord (κύριον) and Christ (χριστὸν), this Jesus whom you crucified"* (Acts 2:21, 36).

> *"And it shall come to pass that everyone who calls on the name (ᴹᴡ) of the Lord (ᴪ ᵞ ᴪ⊐) shall be saved"* (Joel 2:32).

I am asserting that Jesus is God's Son manifested in the old testament as YHVH. His ability to save, manifested in the Name "YHVH," delivered the children of Israel from slavery in Egypt. This is what Jude says about who delivered the children of Israel out of Egypt:

> *"Now I want to remind you, although you once fully knew it, that **Jesus**, who saved a people out of the land of Egypt, afterward destroyed those who did not believe"* (Jude 1:5).

That covenant only covered inadvertent sins through the shedding of the blood of animals. The manifestation of the Name of Jesus through an angel to Joseph would greatly expand our association with the Son's saving power.

> *"Behold, an angel of the Lord appeared to him in a dream, saying, "Joseph, son of David, do not fear to take Mary as your wife, for that which is conceived in her is from the Holy Spirit. She will bear a son, and **you shall call his name Jesus, for he will save his people from their sins**"* (Matthew 1:20 – 21).

The Son's character and His ability to save, manifested in the Name "Jesus" is greater than all other Names. Jesus shed His own blood on the cross for us as *"the propitiation for our sins, and not for ours only but also for the sins of the whole world"* (1 John 2:2). His blood is more precious and effective than the blood of animals. *"For our sake Elohim made him to be sin who knew no sin, so that in him we might become the righteousness of Elohim"* (2 Corinthians 5:21). And His Father placed His stamp of approval on that sacrifice by raising Jesus from the dead and enthroning Him at the right hand of glory!

Viewing the cross from the finished perspective of Day Seven, Jesus' resurrection, ascension and enthronement are ours as well who are in Christ by grace through faith in Him. Paul writes:

> *"But God, being rich in mercy, because of the great love with which he loved us, even when we were dead in our trespasses, made us alive **together with Christ** — by grace you have been saved — and raised us up **with him** and seated us **with him** in the heavenly places in Christ Jesus, so that in the coming ages he might show the immeasurable riches of his grace in kindness toward us in Christ Jesus."*
> (Ephesians 2:4 – 7)

In the Day YHVH Elohim
Made Earth and Heaven

2:4b represents our human perspective living on the earth. And, since we live only in the immediate present, we need a partnership with God to save us from any circumstance that keeps us from living up to our fullest potential.

Elohim told Moses that the events of the Exodus would demonstrate the saving power available to anyone who called on the Name of the Lord. Since YHVH is closely yoked with Elo-him, I can assert that this salvation came from Elohim through YHVH.

Earlier, I shared that the pictograms for "made" closely identi-fied with the same word in 2:3 stressing the final completed nature of the activity. I also said that a day is a work order de-fining a particular activity to be accomplished by someone. In light of this information, I am declaring that Elohim through His yoked relationship with His Son (revealed as YHVH and Jesus) has already completed this specific work order of sal-vation for us across all of time and that we can rest in that finished work!

The Age Of "Enlightenment"

When I went to seminary in the late sixties, I was warned that a challenge to divine authorship began as early as the late sev-enteenth century in Europe and that by the late nineteenth cen-tury, many scholars had determined that the Torah, and par-ticularly Genesis, could not have been written by Moses[65]. I shared a short table in Chapter Eight of some of their apparent discrepancies between the first two chapters of Genesis, and I have waited until now to briefly address them.

The Heavens and the Earth

Genesis 1:1 says that Elohim and His Son (the Word) made the heavens and the earth and that the earth was inhabitable. There is no timeline mentioning how long the earth existed before the chaos of 1:2.

The Sun, Moon and Stars

On Day Four, God made the greater and lesser lights **in the expanse**, an area between the waters below and the waters above. Since these waters initially covered the face of the deep and since the expanse is where birds fly, it seems difficult to conclude that our actual sun, moon and stars were placed in that space by God – unless this account is treated as a myth or fable with little serious reliance on the words themselves for any literal meaning. It seems more reasonable to assert that the sun, moon and stars have existed since 1:1 in the regions of space much higher than the "waters above" the earth.

Vegetation Needs Sunlight
It was only when the greater and lesser lights from Day Four were equated with the sun and moon that the question arose as to where the sunlight came from for the plants in Day Three. I have proposed that the sun existed since 1:1 which also helps explain why the earth "brought forth" vegetation in Day Three. A temporary covering of water over all the earth would not have killed the seeds produced by plants growing on the earth before 1:2. These seeds only needed dry ground and sunlight to grow.

According To Their Kind
I already addressed the apparent difference between the phrase "according to their kind" in chapter one and the planting of the garden and the forming of animals in chapter two. It can be explained as the change of perspective in 2:4.

Dinosaurs
Which brings up one of the most consistent arguments against a conservative interpretation of creation: the dinosaurs. There is incontrovertible evidence that these creatures existed for many thousands if not millions of years before becoming extinct. How does the discovery of their fossilized bones fit into the six days of creation? The simple answer is that they do not fit in at all. These creatures existed on the earth while it was inhabitable during the eons of time before the flood of 1:2 wiped them out.

Let Us Make Man

Adam (Man as male and female) was made on Day Six. To imply that this account and the one in chapter two are at odds with each other and that the latter narrative actually came first reduces man to a creature just like all other animals. The truth is, we are spirit beings living in a body energized by our soul and the Spirit of the Lord. I will cover this more fully as we explore the relevant verses in Genesis chapter two. The Bible says we are unique from all the animals because we are made in the image and likeness of God.

Four "Authors"

Four different groups of authors for the Torah have been proposed based on literary form-criticism. These scholars argue that the form of the first two chapters as well as the names given for God are so different, they must have been penned by different authors. For instance, chapter one has a formal, almost rigid style while chapter two follows a more fluid storyline format.

They argue that in chapter one, God is called by one name while in chapter two, He is introduced by two names. As a result, the writers of the first chapter are identified by their God (E for Elohim) while the second group must have favored YHVH (J for Jehovah) because this name preceded Elohim. The other two author groups supposedly held sway over priestly functions as well as legal matters and were identified as the Priestly (P) and Deuteronomic (D) contributors.

I have already shared that both chapters contain two names for God: Bara Elohim and YHVH Elohim. As our Father, Elohim's name did not change. But His Son's Name changed revealing His different roles in creation and salvation.

This effort to couch the Torah into four author streams spanning generations, reduces it to the same kind of myths and legends other ancient civilizations employed to explain their origins. According to these scholars, the J authors finished their manuscripts in Judah sometime during the reign of Solomon or one of his successors; the E authors finished later after Israel was divided into Judah and the northern kingdom; and the P and D final manuscript editions purportedly dated from the eighth and seventh centuries B.C.E.

Most importantly, this type of textual criticism reduces the Bible to just another literary book, thereby denying it of its rightful place as the Word of God Authored by the Holy Spirit Who reveals all truth through the Son to the glory of His Father. It also frees mankind from the responsibility of acknowledging God's revealed truth through the Bible.

SUMMARY

We only live in the present. We cannot know what tomorrow will bring. Our Savior and Lord is the only One Who lives in the future and is able to guide us today so that we can be victorious in everything we encounter tomorrow. Deuteronomy 6:4 and Isaiah 30:20 – 21 underscore the reality that Israel learned largely through ORAL discipleship:

> *"**Hear, O** Israel: The Lord our God, the Lord is one.."*

> *"And though the Lord give you the bread of adversity and the water of affliction, yet **your Teacher** will not hide himself anymore, but your eyes shall see **your Teacher**. And **your ears shall hear** a word behind you, saying, '**This is the way, walk in it,**' when you turn to the right or when you turn to the left."*

Jesus said,

> *"**My sheep hear my voice**, and I know them, and they follow me"* (John 10:23).

He also said,

> *"When the Spirit of truth comes, he will guide you into all the truth, for he will not **speak** on his own authority, but **whatever he hears he will speak**, and he will declare to you **the things that are to come**"* (John 16:13).

Reading and studying the verses of the Bible is very important. But we should be careful not to think that "in them" we have all that is necessary to guide us into our destiny. God created a pictographic language for His people so they did not have to go to school in order to meditate on His written word. But even the ability to translate Hebrew characters into their corresponding pictograms will not reveal God's Rhema Word to us when we are deciding "which way to turn." That only comes when we spend time in meditation and prayer every day seeking His guidance. As we walk by faith, our Teacher will lead us into all truth, **saying**, *"This is the way, walk in it."*

I firmly believe that God wants to equip us with the ability to read and meditate on the original Hebrew pictograms, words and sentences that were inspired by the Holy Spirit in order to enlarge our understanding of the Gospel and our destiny in His Kingdom. As we seek the guidance of His still, small voice, He will build us up in the body of Christ to prepare us for His return.

> *"All Scripture is breathed out by God and profitable for teaching, for reproof, for correction, and for training in righteousness, that the man of God may be complete, equipped for every good work"* (2 Timothy 3:16).

Study Questions For Discussion

- Why is Genesis 2:4 a pivotal verse?
- What is the significance of the change of focus between "the heavens and the earth" and "earth and heaven?"
  - Why is it important to you?
  - How does it relate to John 3:16?
- How does the meaning of YHVH (𐤉𐤄𐤅𐤄) enlarge your understanding of the name of Jesus?
- Why does the Lord choose us?
  - What does He expect from us?
  - What is our function in our yoked relationship with Him?
- Why is the wisdom of this world foolishness to God?
  - The scholars of the "enlightenment" said Moses could not have written Genesis because he wa s not there. Jesus said, *"Before Abraham was, I AM."* He could just as easily have said, *"Before Genesis was, I AM."* Could the Lord have shared all of Genesis with Moses through a Word of Knowledge?
  - Why can we trust the Bible's prophesy about the conditions still in the future?
  - Why is it foolish for us to t ry to convince the world of the validity of the Gospel using the logic of the "Age of Reason?"
  - Who is the only One who can convince the world about the truth of the Gospel? Hint: John 17:7 – 11.
- Abraham did not have a Bible to read and study. Neither did Enoch or Noah. Yet these three men were singled out because they "walked with God" (Genesis 5:22; 6:9; 17:1). How were they guided by the Rhema Word of God without a Bible to read and study?
  - In Hebrews chapter eleven, they are listed as examples of faith. How can we follow their example?
  - Why is their model of faith important to us as the Lord prepares us for His return?

CHAPTER 15

Genesis 2:5 – 7
God Formed Adam's Body

PROLOGUE

We now launch into His Story from Man's perspective of God as YHVH Elohim – the Lord God. Notice that there are no special symbols placed at the end of sentences in Appendix B between 2:3 and 3:15. The reason the epic events taking place during these passages did not merit any special symbols is because they were already accounted for in Genesis 1:1 – 2:3.

In Genesis 1:26, "God said, *"Let us make man in **our image**, after **our likeness**."* However, He only made them as spirit beings in verse 27. It was not until chapter two that He fulfilled His word to make them after **His likeness**. He also made them in the **oneness** of His Image as male and female. But their unity as one in Him could not ultimately be realized until they had physical bodies enabling *"a man to leave his father and his mother and hold fast to his wife and become **one flesh**."*

A Body For Adam

"When no bush of the field was yet in the land and no small plant of the field had yet sprung up—for the Lord God had not caused it to rain on the land, and there was no man to work the ground, and a mist was going up from the land and was watering the whole face of the ground— then the Lord God formed the man of dust from the ground and breathed into his

nostrils the breath of life, and the man became
a living creature." (Genesis 2:5 - 7).

There is so much to be learned by examining the pictographic meaning of these words:

Formed – ᗡᚱᗰᗰ. From ᗡᚱ meaning "to press." These symbols indicate that forming is accomplished by the work (ᗰ) of a person (ᗡ) pressing / pulling (ᚱ) a substance like clay to conform it to a certain shape. The first ᗰ indicates that God was the Person forming Adam's body into the shape He desired.

Initially, God made Adam in His image in chapter one. Then, He formed Adam's body after His likeness in chapter two. We see this pattern in Jeremiah 1:5 and Galatians 1:15 – 16:

> *"**Before** I formed you in the womb I knew you,*
> *and **before** you were born I consecrated you; I*
> *appointed you a prophet to the nations."*

> *"But when he who had set me apart **before** I*
> *was born, and who called me by his grace, was*
> *pleased to reveal his Son to me, in order that I*
> *might preach him among the Gentiles."*

God continues to form us in our mother's womb from the "ground" her body is made of.

Womb – ᗰ⊕ᗰ. The tent (ᗰ) that surrounds (⊕) new life (ᗰ).

It is also important to remember that we are more than our physical bodies. We are spirit beings living in our physical bodies. Here is the Hebrew word for **flesh**:

Flesh – מ‎ר‎ש‎. The tent (ש‎) that supports (ר‎) the man (מ‎).

Paul refers to this tent in 2 Corinthians 5:1,

> *"For we know that if the tent that is our earthly home is destroyed, we have a building from God, a house not made with hands, eternal in the heavens."*

ר‎ is a thorn from a thorn bush. When shepherds were away from home, they corralled their sheep for the night in a fence made of tightly-woven thorn bushes, keeping predators out and the sheep in. One or more of the shepherds slept in the small opening in the fence – the door of the sheepfold – as further protection. In the morning, each shepherd called to his sheep who recognized his voice and followed him through the door of the fence and into the pasture. Our flesh is like that fence protecting us. We are like the sheep who live inside under the watchful eye of our Shepherd Who keeps guard at the door of our sheepfold and calls our name to follow Him.

Gender Identity

We are spirit persons living in physical bodies. In Genesis 1:27, God made man in His image as male and female spirit beings. In Genesis chapter two, God fulfilled His 1:26 pronouncement to make them after His likeness. In 2:7, God formed a male body for Adam to live in. And in 2:22, He made a female body for Adam's wife. In that way, God married their spirit gender to their physical gender.

The Apostle Paul states that we are spirit, soul and body:

> *"Now may the God of peace himself sanctify you completely, and may your whole **spirit and soul and body** be kept blameless at the coming of our Lord Jesus Christ."*

2:5-7 God Formed Adam's Body   161

(1 Thessalonians 5:23)

We can assert that our souls also have a gender identity enabling our bodies to perform their gender roles. We see these gender differences in the animals, birds, fish and creeping things the Lord made in Genesis chapter one. Their bodies are governed only by their souls and we see definite gender roles in their behavior toward each other as they multiply according to their own kind.

Today, the Lord forms our bodies in our mother's womb. To say that a female person is living in a male body or vice versa is to say that God made a mistake and mismatched their spirit identity with their physical identity. But God does not make mistakes any more than He did with Adam and Eve.

If a person undergoes a sex change, he will be creating a conflict between his spirit person and his physical body. A person's gender is more than certain body parts or hormones. Our physical, emotional and psychological makeup is manifested through this combined gender identity. Here are the gender differences for the male and female spirit persons as defined in Genesis 1:27:

Male – ᏉᎳᎵ .
Ꮅ – A Sword, Cudgel (a harvesting tool)
Ꮃ – Cover, Allow, Conform to my palm (See the symbols earlier for "Bless")
Ꮹ – Head, First

The primary male role is to be the family's protector, provider, covering, the one who blesses, and is the family's head and identity in relation to itself and other families. His primary role stems from the definitions I shared for verse 1:28 in Chapter Ten and Twelve:

Fruitful – that which is spoken / birthed out of the mouth of a man

Multiply – defines a man's dominion over his tent

Fill – designates that the one who is speaking is full of authority

Subdue it – represents a footstool: placing one's foot on the earth to subdue it

The male gender of his spirit person is closely associated with the functions of the male gender of his soul giving him the ability to perform these roles in his physical body.

Female – 𐤉𐤌𐤏𐤍 .

𐤍 – New Life

𐤏 – Cycle

𐤌 – Tent, House, Family

𐤉 – Behold!, Reveal, Praise

The primary female role is to be the family's source of new life, nurture and vitality. Through the cycles God gives her, she builds the family in her home as an offering of praise to the Lord. Her primary gender role is enabled by the functions of her female soul giving her body the ability to perform the roles we traditionally assign to verse 1:28 some of which are shared by the other creatures:

Fruitful – to birth and nurture new life through her unique capabilities as a wife and mother

Multiply – increasing the number of family members as the Lord blesses her

Fill – her unique capabilities can fill the earth with her progeny

Subdue – she and her offspring also subdue the earth

Both male and female persons are made in the image of God.

2:5-7 God Formed Adam's Body   163

In order to reflect that unity, man's secondary role also participates in the birth and nurture of new life just as her secondary role manifests his fruitfulness and authority as they follow the Lord together – body soul, and spirit.

Dust – 𐤍𐤏𐤏. Eye / Mouth / Person. What a person perceives as reality with his eyes is what he focuses on and declares as valid with his mouth. This declared perception of reality (𐤏𐤏) is what he ultimately becomes as a person (𐤍). We are going to observe in the coming verses the role our physical senses play in determining our perception of who we are.

Ground – 𐤉𐤌𐤈𐤃. 𐤌𐤈 is the Hebrew word for blood. So, Adam's identity (𐤌𐤈𐤃) means "strong blood." The ground was the source material for the plants, animals, and male and female physical bodies bringing praise to the Lord! Adam would also be placed in the garden to work the ground.

After their disobedience, the Lord said,
> *"By the sweat of your face you shall eat bread,*
> *till you return to the **ground**, for out of it you*
> *were taken; for you are **dust**, and to **dust** you*
> *shall return"* (Genesis 3:19).

We will examine this verse more thoroughly later. But I have highlighted two words to draw attention to the relationship between ground and dust. The first phrase says that because they were taken from the ground, they would return to the ground.

However, the second phrase provides the reason why they would return to the ground: *"Because YOU ARE DUST and to DUST you shall return."* **What they perceived they were after their eyes were opened is what they ultimately became.** I am sharing this now so that you will not think I am ignoring the surface definitions for Dust and Ground. Adam's identity reflected the fact that his body was formed out of the ground. But the **dust** of the ground identifies much more than dry granules of dirt on the surface of the ground. As you can see from its pictograms, Dust revealed a significant aspect of Adam's character.

Breathed – ▥◯〣. (〣) indicates God's participation. The root word is ▥◯ 〉 meaning that new life (〉) came from God's mouth (◯) creating a fence (▥) of protection around Adam.

Nostrils – ◯〣. These symbols mean "Strong Mouth" indicting that God breathed into Adam's body in much the same way as a medic forces air into a person through a mask over his mouth and nose.

Breath – ✝ᴟᴟ∾ 〉. These symbols indicate that this breath brought new life (〉) into Adam's body, completely (✝) destroying (∾) the chaos (ᴟᴟ) in his lifeless form. Benner says that ᴟᴟ∾ 〉 is also the Hebrew word for "**pant, to breathe in and out**[66]."

Life - Living – ᴟᴟ〣〣▥ / Ѱ〣▥. "Life" and "Living" have essentially the same meaning. Benner says 〣▥ literally means a stomach, the organ (the surrounding fence) that produces (works) life[37].

Notice that ▥ contributes to the meaning of "breathed," "life" and "living." Why is this fence necessary? A verse from Job may help answer this question:

> *"And the Lord said to Satan, "Have you considered my servant Job, that there is none like*

him on the earth, a blameless and upright man,
who fears God and turns away from evil?"
Then Satan answered the Lord and said, "Does
Job fear God for no reason? Have you not **put**
a hedge around him and his house and all
that he has, on every side? *You have* **blessed**
the work of his hands, and his possessions have
increased in the land" (Job 1:8 – 10).

The Hebrew word for hedge is † ᚹ ⟨ meaning it was a thorn-bush fence (⟨) of protection around Job keeping all predators out while covering and blessing (ᚹ) Job, his house and all that he had completely (†). Elohim was the Shepherd guarding the door of Job's sheepfold so that no one had access without His permission.

What Is Our Soul?

The Lord made Adam and Eve as spirit persons in Genesis 1:27 and formed their physical bodies in Genesis chapter two. The Bible says our soul is a separate part of our person:

"For the word of God is living and active,
sharper than any two-edged sword, piercing to
the **division of soul and of spirit**, *of joints and*
of marrow, and discerning the thoughts and in-
tentions of the heart" (Hebrews 4:12).

Let's consider the pictograms for soul that define its primary function.

Soul – Ｗ ◯ ⟩. Life (⟩) is sustained by what is consumed (Ｗ) by the mouth (◯). Leviticus 17:11 says, *"For the life (soul – Ｗ ◯ ⟩) of the flesh is in the blood."* Air, water and food enter the body through our mouth.

Coupling that meaning with the pictograms for "living" indicates that the primary function of our soul is to maintain the life of the body through what is consumed by the mouth and subsequently processed by the body's physical organs.

God Also Has A Soul

Both Leviticus and Isaiah state that God has a soul:

> *"I will make my dwelling among you, and my soul (* **WO ϟ** *) shall not abhor you. And I will walk among you and will be your God, and you shall be my people" (Leviticus 26:11).*

> *"Behold my servant, whom I uphold, my chosen, in whom my soul (* **WO ϟ** *) delights"*
> (Isaiah 42:1; Matthew 12:18).

Notice that the first two pictograms for "breathed" and "soul" are **identical** (**O ϟ**). In the first instance, new life came from the mouth of God. "Breath" may also indicate an ongoing impartation of God's life (**to breathe in and out**) into Adam. When Jesus responded to Satan's first temptation, He said,

> *"Man shall not live by bread alone, but by every word (rhema) that **comes** from the mouth of God"* (Matthew 4:4. "**Comes**" indicates ongoing action.

Genesis 1:26 says God made Adam in His image and after His likeness. Genesis 2:7 says His breath (**† ᴍW ϟ**) destroyed the chaos in Adam's body. When God breathed (**ⅢO ϟ**) into Adam, His soul (**WO ϟ**) imparted (**O**) new life (**ϟ**) into Adam's lifeless body while at the same time completely (**†**) destroying (**W**) the chaos (**ᴹ**) in that body.

Genesis 2:5 – 6 tell us the condition of the Garden just prior to when God formed Adam and placed him there.

2:5-7 God Formed Adam's Body   167

*"When **no bush** of the field was yet in the land and **no small plant** of the field had yet sprung up—for the Lord God had not caused it to rain on the land, and there was no man to work the ground, and a mist was going up from the land and was watering the whole face of the ground."*

We can assume from this description of the garden that Adam's life was **initially sustained** more by God's continued impartation of life through His breath than from what Adam grew to eat. The garden in Eden was not a finished, manicured oasis when the Lord put him there. Adam's job was to work the ground raising everything from seedlings to mature plants, bushes and trees. Some plants matured quickly. Other plants, like berry shrubs and trees took much longer. The timespan between "no bush and no small plant" to the time when this vegetation could produce enough food to sustain Adam's physical life could have been months or years.

SUMMARY

Central to the formation of our bodies is the role our soul (**WꙩꙄ**) plays in its close association with our physical life (**ꚀꙄꚌ**). These pictograms affirm that the Lord made our soul to animate and sustain our physical body enabling our spirit person to move freely on this planet and to interact with His creation through our physical senses.

The New Testament word for soul is ψυχή (breath) which gives us our word "psyche." Psychology is the study of the human mind and its behavioral functionality. So, it is relatively easy to understand why we could define our soul as our mind, will and emotion.

However, this description blurs the distinction between who we are as spirit beings and the function of our souls. That is, if our soul **IS** our mind, will and emotion, how do those attributes relate with who we are as spirit beings? They seem to indicate that our mind, will and emotions as spirit beings are provided by and are synonymous with our soul. This would redefine us as spirit-souls living in physical bodies instead of spirit beings living in bodies that are animated by our souls.

The Hebrew meaning undergirds this Greek definition because our soul energizes our physical brain and nervous system activating its own mind, will and emotion just like it does with all the other living souls (creatures) on earth. But we as spirit beings also have a mind, will and emotion because we are made in God's image.

As we move into Genesis chapter three and four, we will see that these two perspectives can, at times, be at odds with each other with our soul trying to dictate how the needs and desires of our body (our flesh) should be satisfied.

Study Questions For Discussion

- In Genesis 1:26, God **made** us in His image and likeness. In Genesis 2:7, He **formed** Adam out of the dust of the ground. Why didn't God **make** Adam out of the dust of the ground?
- Does God have a soul?
  - What part does His soul play in forming our soul?
  - What is the primary role of our soul?
  - Does God build a hedge (fence) around us?
  - What would happen to us if there was no hedge at all?
- How do mothers replicate God's activity so we are formed from the dust of the ground?
- The Lord says to Jeremiah, *"Before I **formed you** in the womb, I **knew you**."*
  - Was Jeremiah a viable person **before** he was formed in his mother's womb?
  - Had God already consecrated and ordained him as a prophet to the Gentiles before he was born?
  - We say that "life begins at conception." When did Jeremiah's life begin?
  - Who formed Jeremiah in his mother's womb?
  - Her body provided the "dust of the ground" to form Jeremiah's body in her womb. But as it became his body during his gestation period, was it any longer HER body?
  - What rights did Jeremiah's mother have over Jeremiah's body as the Lord was forming it in her womb?
  - On the cross, Jesus said, *"Father forgive them, for they do not know what they are doing."* What is our posture toward abortion?
  - Does the mother really know what she is doing?
  - Paul says we do not war against flesh and blood. What role does compassion, forgiveness and prophetic intercessory prayer play?
- Does God match up our spirit being as male or female with

the physical body He forms in our mother's womb?

- o How could a person become confused about his gender identity?
- o Is homosexuality a true perspective or a lie?
- o Is this condition reversable? How? What is your posture?
- o Does a father's role in the family contribute to this confusion?
- o What happens to the person if a physical sex change is made?

- What is dust? Is it more than very small particles of the ground?
  - o Why are we made of the dust from the ground?
  - o Why did God say to Adam, "*You are dust and to dust you shall return*"?
  - o How does 2 Corinthians 3:18 refocus us?

- How does the Hebrew definition and role of our soul correlate with Paul's definition of our flesh in Romans 8:13 – 14?
  - o How does the Hebrew definition of flesh support Paul's assertions?
  - o Jesus said, "*Man does not live by bread alone but by every word that proceeds from the mouth of God.*" Moses spent forty days on the mountain without food or water. How was his life sustained?
  - o Do we have to obey our soul's constant demand for "bread" in order to live?
  - o We live in the last days before Christ returns. If we can't buy or sell without the mark of the beast, how will we be able to live?

CHAPTER 16

Genesis 2:8
Building Adam's Kingdom

"In the beginning, God created the heavens and the earth."

PROLOGUE

Genesis 1:1 reveals the yoked relationship Elohim had with ⬡⬡⬡ building a Kingdom where ⬡⬡⬡ would dwell and live out His destiny with the guidance and blessing of His Father. Genesis chapter two extends this yoked relationship to Adam as God's son. The Garden of Eden was Adam's heaven and earth: a dwelling for his name and the focus of his destiny.

This covenant established a generational pattern for Hebrew families: The father equipped and blessed his sons with a place of their own where they could raise a family and extend their father's kingdom as heirs.

The Garden
Phase One

> *"And the Lord God planted a garden in Eden, in the east, and there he put the man whom he had formed"* (Genesis 2:8).

Planted – ⬡⬡⬡ . This word begins with ⬡ indicating that God was actively involved. It comes from ⬡⬡⬡ meaning the new life (⬡) of the garden was surrounded

(⊕) by the watchful eye (☉) of the Lord. The Garden (ᔑ ᒣ) lifted up (ᒣ) life (ᔑ)[67] revealing God's purpose for this oasis. And Eden (ᔑ ⊔ ☉) cemented its identity with heaven. ⊔ ☉ stands for "eternal" – see the door[68]. Coupled with ᔑ, it means "Eternal Life."

God subdued the earth's environment in this specific location through the strength of His arm. Under His watchful eye, He lifting it up (ᔑ ᒣ) to manifest His Kingdom (ᔑ ⊔ ☉) – a "heaven and earth" where Adam and his wife could live and prosper.

Phase Two
After the Garden of Eden was planted, the Lord put (ᗰ ᔑ ᒐ) Adam there (ᗰᗯ). The strength of God's arm says Adam was not merely sent to a location on the planet but was actively placed in the garden by the deliberate will and plan of God. "Put" comes from ᗰᒐᔑ and means God built a "thorn-bush" fence (ᔑ) around Adam capable of thwarting (ᒐ) any attempt by predators to bring chaos (ᗰ) into the garden. "There" (ᗰᗯ) declares that both the preparation of the garden and this "thorn-bush" fence created a place for Adam's name (ᗰᗯ) to dwell and flourish.

Phase Three
> *"And out of the ground the Lord God made to spring up every tree that is pleasant to the sight and good for food. The tree of life was in the midst of the garden, and the tree of the knowledge of good and evil"* (Genesis 2:9).

The Lord sowed food-bearing plants in the Garden of Eden to help sustain the bodily life of our first parents. (We also catch a glimpse in these words of the lush vegetation that must have existed on the habitable earth Elohim made with ᐯᑕᑐ in Genesis 1:1.)

Phase Four

> *"A river flowed out of Eden to water the gar-*
> *den, and there it divided and became four riv-*
> *ers. The name of the first is the Pishon. It is*
> *the one that flowed around the whole land of*
> *Havilah, where there is gold. And the gold of*
> *that land is good; bdellium and onyx stone are*
> *there. The name of the second river is the Gi-*
> *hon. It is the one that flowed around the whole*
> *land of Cush. And the name of the third river is*
> *the Tigris, which flows east of Assyria. And the*
> *fourth river is the Euphrates."*

(Genesis 2:10 - 14)

I have often wondered why so much scriptural real estate was committed to the description of these rivers – much more than to the garden itself. In fact, the first river (Pishon) is only mentioned here even though it garnered the most attention.

In Chapter Three, I said there were two different words for "river" in this passage. The one describing the head waters (ᐯᑕᑕ) where the first river flowed out of Eden to become four rivers, was also the root word for the very first term in the Torah – (ᐟᐳ [ᗯᐯᑕ]ᑐ) . I proposed that this word depicted the character of the Holy Spirit – the Source of Living Water that flows out of the bowels of believers:

> *"On the last day of the feast, the great day, Je-*
> *sus stood up and cried out, 'If anyone thirsts,*
> *let him come to me and drink. Whoever be-*
> *lieves in me, as the Scripture has said, "Out of*
> *his heart will flow rivers of living water."' Now*

this he said about the Spirit, whom those who believed in him were to receive, for as yet the Spirit had not been given, because Jesus was not yet glorified" (John 7:37 – 39).

 shared an intimate relationship with  and 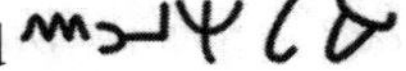 as they worked together to make and restore the Kingdom of Elohim's adult Son: the heavens and the earth. Since God's Spirit played such an important role in that Kingdom, it seems reasonible that the same Spirit as the Source of Living water – expressed by these four rivers – would also play a key role in establishing and sustaining Adam's kingdom, filling it with abundant life, power and riches.

Phase Five

"The Lord God took the man and put him in the garden of Eden to work it and keep it."

(Genesis 2:15*)*

The work described here () is different from the work (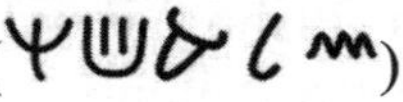) defined in Genesis 2:2. Benner says this work means "to serve," and is the work done for someone out of obligation, requirement or gratitude[69]. The other form of work describes the "staff in the hand" and designates a shepherd managing and protecting his sheep.

The Hebrew pictograms for "tend" () are most revealing. Notice that  is preceded by  with  following. Let's examine  first. Benner says this word means "guard" – to watch over, preserve and protect[87]. I have shared the first two symbols many times. They identify a person's name or character as his ability to destroy the chaos in a situation and establish / restore order. This restoration also yields "heaven" () – the realm where chaos is destroyed and order reigns.

ℓ preceding this word indicating that God granted Adam the authority to shepherd the garden. His life would be filled with praise and wonder (Ⴘ) through his yoked relationship with his Father as they brought heaven into ever-expanding regions of his domain east of Eden.

SUMMARY
I mentioned a generational pattern for Hebrew families in the prologue. You witnessed how the yoked relationship Elohim had with His Son in Genesis 1:1 later became the pattern for His relationship with His son Adam. I also said earlier that when Joshua meditated on these passages, he likely believed God would also extend the Kingdom to him, building his own heaven and earthly kingdom for his name to dwell and where he could work out his destiny with the guidance and resources of the Lord.

This pattern did not end with Adam. Our Father is calling each one of us to receive our inheritance by faith: a specific heaven and earthly kingdom of our own, individually crafted for us by God where we can live and mature into the destiny the Lord has for us in His Son Jesus Christ.

Hear again Paul's prayer to the Ephesian church,
> *"For this reason, because I have heard of your faith in the Lord Jesus and your love toward all the saints, I do not cease to give thanks for you, remembering you in my prayers, that the God of our Lord Jesus Christ, the Father of glory, may give you the Spirit of wisdom and of revelation in the knowledge of him, having the eyes of your hearts enlightened, that you may know what is the hope to which he has called you,*

what are the riches of his glorious inheritance in the saints, and what is the immeasurable greatness of his power toward us who believe, according to the working of his great might that he worked in Christ when he raised him from the dead and seated him at his right hand in the heavenly places, far above all rule and authority and power and dominion, and above every name that is named, not only in this age but also in the one to come. And he put all things under his feet and gave him as head over all things to the church, which is his body, the fullness of him who fills all in all."
(Ephesians 1:15 - 23)

Study Questions For Discussion

- In Genesis 1:26 – 27, God made man in His image as male and female spirit beings. Then in Genesis 2:7, God formed Adam's body out of the dust of the ground and breathed into it His breath of life, giving Adam's body life as a living soul. Jeremiah 1: 5 and Galatians 1:15 both indicate that, like Adam, God knew Jeremiah and Paul before their bodies were formed. Moreover, the Lord had already established their destiny before they were born. With this as a background, let's take a look at this chapter as it relates to us.
  - o Did God know you before you were born?
  - o Does He know what destiny He has planned for you in His Kingdom?
  - o Has the Lord set aside a place for you to live and manifest your destiny – your garden of Eden?
  - o Is that place where you live now?
  - o God placed Jeremiah and Paul at specific times in history. Did He place you here just before the return of His Son?
  - o He placed Jeremiah and Paul in specific locations and at specific times because He had confidence that they would stand with Him. You too, have an important destiny brcause of the times we are living in. Will you accept His call to walk with Him and manifest your destiny through your yoked relationship with Him?
  - o Does it matter at what stage in your life you make that commitment?
  - o What part do the "failures" in your life play as resources for your destiny?
  - o What part does the Holy Spirit as our Source of Living Water play in our ability to fulfill our destiny?

CHAPTER 17

Genesis 2:9
The Tree Of Life

"And out of the ground the Lord God made to spring up every tree that is pleasant to the sight and good for food. The tree of life was in the midst of the garden." (Genesis 2:9)

PROLOGUE

I have already shared the meaning of the pictograms for "life" in the tree of life. My goal in this chapter is to clarify the role the fruit of this tree played in the Garden of Eden as well as in the life of believers.

Tree of Life – ᴧᴧ>ᴐ⅃Ⅲ . This word for life is precisely the same as the word for life found earlier in verse 2:7,

> *"Then the Lord God formed the man of dust from the ground and breathed into his nostrils the breath of life (ᴧᴧ>ᴐ⅃Ⅲ), and the man became a living (Ɏ>⃒Ⅲ) creature (soul - ᴡᴑ ໄ)."*

In Chapter Fifteen, I said "life" and "living" have essentially the same meaning. "Living" defines the organ (>⃒Ⅲ) that surrounds the work: the stomach works on the food the person eats. "Life" is empowered by the fence (Ⅲ) that surrounds the work (>⃒) that works (>⃒) on the chaos (ᴧᴧ) of what is consumed (𐤅) by the mouth (𐤏). This describes a person's stomach and intestines (the organs that surround the phases of digestive work) as they break down the ingested food into useful nutrients for the body to sustain and renew its life (𐤉).

Breath of life – Living Soul

There is a direct correlation between the breath of life and the continuation of Adam's life as a living soul. I said in Chapter Fifteen that "breath" (𐤕 ᴍᴡ) was a continuous in-and-out breathing process bringing new life (𐤉) while completely (𐤕) destroying (𐤅) the chaos (ᴍ) in Adam's body.

Elihu says in the book of Job:
> *"The Spirit of God has made me and the breath*
> *(𐤕 ᴍᴡ 𐤉) of the Almighty gives me life*
> *(𐤅𐤋𐤇)" (Job 33:4).*

Elihu is saying to Job that the breath of the Almighty empowers his soul to live.

Genesis 6:3 says there is a direct association between this continuous activity of the Spirit of God and how long a person lives:
> *"Then the Lord said, 'My Spirit shall not **abide***
> *in (𐤋) man forever, for he is flesh: his days*
> *shall be 120 years."*

Abide – 𐤉 𐤓 𐤃. 𐤃 is the way to enter and exit a person's tent (𐤋). 𐤉 𐤓 𐤃 says that the action by God's Spirit entering and exiting through the door (𐤃) of the person's tent anchors (𐤓) new life (𐤉) to sustain the flesh of that person. Up until this time, people were living hundreds of years. But instead of being grateful and thanking God for their long lifespan, their wickedness filled the earth. So, the Lord said that His Spirit would not keep them alive forever. Instead, He would limit His abiding activity in these rebellious people to 120 years.

Breath – Tree

Is there a connection between the "breath of life" and the "tree of life"? If God's breath of life enabled the vitality of Adam's body to be continually sustained, did the fruit of the tree of life contribute in a similar manner? If there was a correlation, then it would have been necessary for them to eat fruit from the tree of life on a regular basis in order to achieve the quality of life the tree represented.

We know that the tree of the knowledge of good and evil was placed in the garden to test Adam's obedience. Genesis 2:9 says that **the fruit of every tree was good for food**. So, it was Adam's act of disobedience in eating a single piece of fruit from this tree, not its chemical or genetic characteristics, that resulted in their eyes being opened.

But why was the tree of life planted there? There were no restrictions for eating its fruit. Adam had tended this tree from the time it was a seedling. He knew where it grew in the garden and that it offered life. Let's consider the description of the tree of life found in the final chapter of the book of Revelation:

> *"Then the angel showed me the river of the water of life, bright as crystal, flowing from the throne of God and of the Lamb through the middle of the street of the city; also, on either side of the river, the tree of life **with its twelve kinds of fruit, yielding its fruit each month. The leaves of the tree were for the healing of the nations**"* (Revelation 22:1 – 2).

Revelation 22:2 gives us some critical information about the tree of life: it bore twelve kinds of fruit. Furthermore, its leaves were for the healing of the nations – another association with a person's body that is more in keeping with continuous upkeep. I am suggesting that not only for these trees in Revelation, but for the tree of life in the Garden of Eden, this fruit was one of three ways the Lord enabled the participants to sustain their physical life indefinitely.

Those three paths were:
1. Their soul enabled theim to consume air and digest the food and water they ingested through their mouth creating the nutrients needed to help sustain bodily life.
2. God's continuous Breath of Life breathed life into their physical bodies.
   o Exodus 33:11says that God spoke to Moses Face to Face (ᴍꭓᴧ ꟻᴑᴗᴧᴗ ᴍꭓᴧ ꟻᴑ). The Lord spoke new life (ꟻ) through His mouth (ᴑ) to Moses, and Moses reflected that renewed life (ꟻ) back to the Lord through his mouth (ᴑ) of praise.
3. I am proposing that the tree of life yielded twelve different fruits, one for each month to supplement their diet with special nutrients not found in the plants, shrubs and other fruit trees in the garden.
   o Without these added supplements, tailored to the changing demands of each month, their bodies would eventually die (supposition on my part).
   o Since the ground was cursed, this tree and the other plants, shrubs and trees in the Garden would eventually be choked out by weeds and thorns without Adam's oversight. So, all traces of the Garden would ultimately vanish.

To the Church in Ephesus Write:
   "He who has an ear, let him hear what the Spirit

*says to the churches. To the one who conquers
I will grant to eat of the **tree of life**, which is in
the paradise of God.* (Revelation 2:7).

This passage in Revelation contains the other reference to the tree of life. Even though this segment is addressed to the Ephesian church, Jesus reminds us that it is ultimately addressed to those in the churches (including us) who have ears to hear what the Spirit is saying.

Even though the Ephesian church had been the missionary hub both for Paul and John, they had abandoned their first love – their wholehearted love for Jesus – and replaced it with doctrines used to test the orthodoxy of other believers. Jesus commanded them to repent, and to the one who conquered – who regained that personal relationship – Jesus would grant the ability to eat of the tree of life located now in the paradise of God.

Since this tree is no longer located in a physical place on earth, it must be accessed by faith: believing that Jesus has granted the believer access to the tree of life.

My Testimony

I am constantly amazed at how gracious, merciful and loving our Father is toward those who believe that He exists and is the rewarder of those who seek him. Just about the time I convince myself that certain promises have been relegated to a time after "*we are caught up to be with the Lord in the air,*" I hear a testimony that the Lord has offered some aspect of that life to one of His believers right now.

That happened to me while Judy and I were in Costa Rica on a mission trip. The Lord was blessing His word in ways that were miraculous at times. But the mosquitos were also unrelenting, and I seemed to be their favorite target where ever we went.

One morning during prayer when I was almost totally distracted scratching my arms, the Lord asked me to reach out in faith and pick one of the leaves from the tree of life in His paradise and rub it on the bites. I did so, hesitantly at first, and the incessant irritation stopped almost immediately.

SUMMARY

> *"What no eye has seen, nor ear heard, nor the heart of man imagined, what God has prepared for those who love him."*
> (Isaiah 64:4; 1 Corinthians 2:9)

The Holy Spirit inspired Moses to write the first two chapters of Genesis, challenging us to enter into God's rest and to claim full membership in all the promises of that first covenant. I am convinced that everything revealed in those ancient verses, including the tree of life, is available to us now through faith in the last Adam.

I challenge you to seek the counsel of the Holy Spirit as you meditate on the three paths mentioned earlier. I am confident He will lead you into all truth and show you great and marvelous things about the fulness of life He has for you in Jesus Christ.

Study Questions For Discussion

- Why does the tree of life produce twelve kinds of fruit, yielding its fruit each month?
- What kind of life does the tree of life sustain?
  - o Genesis 3:22 says that God drove Adam from the garden *"lest he reach out his hand and take also of the tree of life and eat and live forever."* Did God initially ban Adam from eating the fruit from this tree like He did with the fruit from the tree of the knowledge of good and evil?
  - o Is there any reason why Adam and his wife did not eat from this fruit before they were driven from the garden?
  - o What would have happened if God had not driven them from the garden after they disobeyed Him?
  - o Why was it necessary to drive them from the garden?
  - o Why can't we find the tree of life or the garden today?
  - o Have we spiritualized the tree of life equating it with the life we gain through a commitment to Jesus Christ as our Lord and Savior?
  - o Can we have access to the tree of life NOW? How?
- Revelations 22:2 says *"The leaves of the tree were for the healing of the nations."* But the leaves on these two trees will be growing in the new Jerusalem that will come down from heaven on the new earth after Jesus returns. All believers will have new immortal, incorruptible bodies at that point. So why would there be any need for these leaves?
  - o May suggest that they are needed NOW.
- Revelation also says there is a time coming just before the return of Christ when everyone will be required to have the mark of the beast in order to buy or sell. Jesus said, *"Man does not live by bread alone, but by every word (Rhema) that proceeds out of the mouth of God."* With this as a background:
  - o How can we continue to live if we don't take the mark

of the beast?
- o What part will the Breath of God play?
- o What part will the fruit of the tree of life in the paradise of God play/
- o What part will the leaves of the tree of life in the paradise of God play?
- o What part does faith have in our ability to live NOW?
- o Do our physical bodies need healing?
- o Why are we living less than a hundred years NOW when the limit in Genesis 6:3 was 120 years?
- o How did Abraham live 175 years well past the limit? (Genesis 25:7)

CHAPTER 18

Genesis 2:16 – 17
The Tree Of The
Knowledge Of Good and Evil

"And the Lord God commanded the man, say-
ing, 'You may surely eat of every tree of the gar-
den, but of the tree of the knowledge of good
and evil you shall not eat, for in the day that
you eat of it you shall surely die.'"

(Genesis 2:16 –17)

PROLOGUE

We might conclude that as long as we know the difference between good and evil as outlined in various biblical passages and abstain from doing evil, we will remain in the good graces of God. But the Lord did not ask Adam to educate himself on the evils of lying, cheating, stealing, killing and adultery. Instead, He commanded Adam to avoid obtaining this kind of knowledge altogether. In fact, he warned Adam in the gravest manner possible that in the day he ate the fruit of the tree of the knowledge of good and evil, he would die (in dying you shall die). In this chapter, we will examine the pictograms for the knowledge of good and evil to find out why this kind of knowledge was forbidden.

First Use

Like so many other words in these first chapters in Genesis, "command," "eat," "knowledge," "evil" and "die" enter the pages of scripture for the first time. Their placement here defines their foundational meaning whenever they are used elsewhere in the Bible. With this in mind, let's examine these words in the context of their pictographic meaning.

Commanded – You Shall Not Eat

Commanded – Y ŕ ͢. Seekins says this word means "the hook that holds"[70]. Put in another way, a command is the hook (ŕ) that anchors (Y) you to a specific pronouncement. It grabs your attention and pulls you toward the instructions that are your anchor. ͢ signals God's direct involvement.

Surely Eat – ᒪ Ɯ ᕑ † ᒪ Ɯ ᕑ . This is another example of why I am convinced that Hebrew is not the product of a committee deciding how to create words for their language. If I were compiling pictograms for "eat," I might refer to "soul" (Ɯ◯ ͺ) as a starting point and define eat as Ɯ◯ – what is consumed by the mouth. But as you can see, neither mouth (◯) nor consume (Ɯ) are components of this word.

I shared earlier that ᒪ Ɯ means "conform to authority, and defines something that is tamed[47]. Hebrew often repeats a word for emphasis. The addition of † to the second iteration adds finality to the command. (Verse 2:17 will reveal another example of this repetitive emphasis.)

So, expanding the pictographic meaning of verse 2:16:

> "*Pay close attention (ŕ) to the instructions I am giving you. They are your anchor (Y). By cultivating (ᒪ Ɯ ᕑ) the trees in the garden, you will totally tame (ᒪ Ɯ ᕑ †) every tree, strongly (ᕑ) conforming (Ɯ) them to your control (ᒪ) for your use as food (ᒪ Ɯ ᕑ ᄿ*

– see verse 2:9)"

This injunction focused on Adam's role working and tending the garden. All the trees were pleasant to the sight and were to be cultivated as such. But one of them must not be cultivated for use as a food source.

Not – 𝒃𝒍 . Notice that these symbols are in the opposite order of 𝒍𝒃: a root name for God. The Lord is the only One Who has the strength (𝒃) to establish His authority (𝒍) over any circumstance we may face. 𝒃𝒍 , on the other hand, means NO[71]. These pictograms convey a person who exercises his authority strongly in a heavy-handed or controlling manner, just the opposite way the Lord relates to us. He is "Yes" and "Amen" (2 Corinthians 1:20).

You Shall Not Eat – 𝒍 Ш𝒃 † 𝒍𝒃 . "Do not cultivating this tree as a source of food! If you disobey my command, your life will be strongly controlled (𝒃𝒍).

While it is possible to consider death as God's punishment for Adam's disobedience, we must remember that our Lord is always motivated by His unconditional love for us. He was warning Adam in the strongest way possible that by perceiving this tree as a food source and ingesting its fruit, he would be opening himself up to being strongly controlled which would result in his death.

What Is This Knowledge?

Part of the problem with our translations: we only have a few words in English for "knowledge." The Lord is not against knowledge or wisdom. But He never wanted us to possess this particular kind of knowledge. Let's examine the symbols for the **knowledge** of good and evil.

Knowledge – $\dagger \odot \mho$. This kind of knowledge is acquired through the door ($\mho$) of our eyes ($\odot$) – our five physical senses. Moreover, we are convinced that the information we gain in this manner is real and accurate ($\dagger$).

The apostle Paul warns us about walking by sight (2 Corinthians 5:7). We may object and say that visual observations are reliable and should be believed as fact. But there are many reasons why we should ask the Lord for revelation on how to address a particular situation or trial:

1. We cannot perceive the total predicament we are facing. As Paul says, "*We know in part.*" Only the Lord knows the full extent of the circumstances we face and how best to address them;

2. If we make decisions based on what we perceive today, we have no idea how those commitments will play out in the future as in a marriage, a job or a place to live;

3. Our physical senses overpower the senses of our spirit shielding us from the Lord's counsel. 1 Kings 19:11 – 13 shares this truth. Elijah had to wrap his face in his mantle to shield his physical eyes and ears so he could hear God's still, small voice;

4. Our soul is charged with maintaining the life and wellbeing of our physical body. It has access to our body's brain and nervous system. So, if it gains access to this kind of knowledge, it can manipulate it to satisfy its own needs. In Romans chapter seven, Paul talks about an adversary in our members that keeps us from doing the things we want to do and doing things we do not want to do. He calls this adversary in his members his flesh. What is our flesh? Our soul animating our body and exploiting what it perceives through this knowledge; and,

5. What is seen is passing away – transient, but what is unseen is what is real – never changing, eternal (2 Corinthians

4:18). If we walk by faith, we are focusing on what the Lord sees as He guides us into what is real.

Good – ⊔Υ⊕. These symbols can be interpreted in two ways: A basket or a serpent (⊕) anchored (Υ) to a person's tent (⊔). "Good" was part of God's declaration in every one of the six days in Genesis chapter one. The baskets represented the abundance of God's provision anchored to the "tent" of each day. Later, when Moses asked God, "Show me your glory." God replied,

> *"I will make all my **goodness** (⊔Υ⊕) pass before you and will proclaim before you my name 'The Lord.' And I will be gracious to whom I will be gracious, and will show mercy on whom I will show mercy"* (Exodus 33:19).

The Lord showed Moses His Glory by passing **all** His Goodness before him. As his Lord, He proclaimed His Name before Moses – able to save him from any chaos he faced and extending His grace and mercy as Moses led the children of Israel to the Promised Land. That same goodness is extended to us who believe.

Evil – ⊙Ꟁ . The person (Ꟁ) is guided by his eyes (⊙) – his physical senses. As I indicated in my introduction, The New Testament defines evil as "bad, wicked, grievous, lewd, malicious, etc." This Hebrew meaning here is simply "a person guided by his sight" – one who walks by sight and not by faith. These two definitions are complementary as long as the Greek definition is based on the Hebrew pictographic meaning.

As part of the knowledge of good and evil, the ⊕ in "Good" takes on a different meaning. Consider these passages from

Matthew and Mark's Gospel:

> *"And behold, a man came up to him, saying, 'Teacher, what **good deed** must I **do** to have eternal life?' And he said to him, 'Why do you ask me about what is **good**? **There is only one who is good.** If you would enter life, keep the commandments.' He said to him, 'Which ones?' And Jesus said, 'You shall not murder, You shall not commit adultery, You shall not steal, You shall not bear false witness, Honor your father and mother, and, You shall love your neighbor as yourself.' The young man said to him, 'All these I have kept. **What do I still lack?**'"*
>
> (Matthew 19:16 – 20)

> *"And as he was setting out on his journey, a man ran up and knelt before him and asked him, '**Good** Teacher, what must I **do** to inherit eternal life?' And Jesus said to him, 'Why do you call me **good**? **No one is good except God alone**"* (Mark 10:17 – 18).

I have highlighted the words for "good" and "do" (meaning "to accomplish") in order to help link these two passages to the word "good" we are discussing in Genesis. In Matthew's Gospel, "good deed" is one word – an advective modifying the pronoun "what." In spite of keeping the commandments, this young man felt he was still not doing enough to erase his feeling of lack – his own estimate of himself did not measure up to how he should feel if he had done enough to inherit eternal life.

In Mark's Gospel, "good" is again an adjective. But this time it is modifying "teacher" indicating that this young man was **comparing** Jesus with his own sense of lack and concluding that Jesus had eternal life – that he had accomplished what this man was seeking.

In both instances, this person was perceiving his world through his knowledge of good and evil, constantly searching for something "good" that would overcome his sense of lack. But every "good" he achieved, whether it was more possessions, authority or adherence to religious commands, did not usher in a sense of "eternal life."

In both accounts, Jesus challenged him to refocus his attention:

> *"Why do you ask me about what is good? **There is only one who is good.**"*

> *"Why do you call me good? **No one is good except God alone**"*

God's goodness would not be achieved by searching for the "what" that was "good" – the achievement that would bring a sense of peace in his life. The internal assurance of eternal life would only come through a relationship with God, the "Who" that was "Good" – Who alone would shower him with His goodness, grace and mercy. If he accepted Christ's challenge, ⌂ 𐤉 ⊕ would bring the baskets (⊕) he sought of blessing and peace anchored (𐤉) to his house (⌂).

Unfortunately, his endless search for an increase of "good" things (⊕) to bolster his sense of wellbeing had become a serpent (⊕) anchored (𐤉) to his house (⌂) – tempting him to keep searching for that elusive something that would "achieve eternal life." The lie he was pursuing was squeezing the life out of him, making him more and more dissatisfied with his accomplishments which is why he ran up to Jesus and knelt down before Him.

2:16-17 The Tree Of Knowledge of Good and Evil   195

But in the end, he walked away sorrowful because he **compared** the security of his possessions with the cost of securing the one thing he was desperately seeking. He chose to keep believing the lie. Surely, he could find eternal life somewhere else. Surely it was just around the corner.

Death – ✝ Υ ᵐ✝ ✝Υᵐ . Chaos (ᵐ) is anchored (Υ) completely / finally (✝).

This Hebrew phrase actually means "dying you shall die." Repeating the word and adding another ✝ at the end of the second iteration emphasizes its importance.

Earlier, we saw that the Breath from God brought life into Adam's lifeless body. That breath destroyed the chaos that kept his body from functioning. Death anchors chaos back into Adam's body. The third pictogram of death is ✝ meaning that ingesting this fruit would yield complete and final chaos, returning him to the state his body was in before God breathed life into it.

Some contend that Adam did not die when he ate the fruit because he did not die physically. That is the ultimate meaning of death when our soul and spirit are separated relationally from our body, and our body succumbs to final chaos. But there are other relational separations (death) that also occur. When Adam and his wife disobeyed the Lord, death entered their relationship separating them from each other bringing blame and mistrust. Death also separated them relationally from God Who is the Source of our life replacing love and life with fear and shame.

The Septuagint Influence

I shared earlier that the pictograms for Evil were ⟨⟩⟨⟩ meaning a person who was guided by his sight. On the other hand, the Hebrew Lexicon I used in seminary (Brown) says this word means "evil, distress, misery, injury, calamity, adversity, wrong, harm, bad, wicked, injurious, hurt."

The Septuagint scholars translated ⲟⲛ with the Greek word πονηρòν. This word is found in many New Testament texts including Matthew 5:11. The Greek Lexicon I used in seminary (Arndt and Gingrich) says this word means "wicked, evil, bad, base, worthless, vicious, degenerate."

It seems likely that the Septuagint translation strongly influenced the definition of the Hebrew word. Why is it important for us to consult the pictographic meaning? First of all, God's warning was addressed to Adam before sin entered the world. In his state of innocence, he would not have been able to relate to the definition given by my Hebrew Lexicon. He could, however, understand how he could be guided by his sight.

But there is an even more critical reason. Our evangelical messages often describe the lost as sinners in need of salvation. But how many times have you heard a person argue that they are not sinners – that is, they are not evil, bad or wicked people. They insist that they are good, moral individuals. So, they don't see how the Gospel relates to them. Surely, the Gospel is more applicable to persons who better fit the accepted definition.

But if you ask those same persons if they do what they perceive is right, they will readily admit they "walk by sight" – the pictographic definition of this key word.

Summary
After the tree of the knowledge of good and evil started bearing fruit, the Lord warned Adam in the gravest possible man-

ner not to consume its fruit. As long as he **obeyed** the Lord, his total person as spirit, soul and body would remain balanced.

As a spirit person, his inner senses could easily listen to and see what the Lord was doing as they walked together in God's manifest Presence building Adam's kingdom in the garden without shame or fear. There was so much to look forward to – an endless succession of triumphal victories as they expanded together the boundaries of the garden and subdued the chaos of the surrounding environs!

Study Questions For Discussion

- What is your definition of the knowledge of good and evil?
- How does your definition match the Hebrew definition?
  - o Is there a difference between your definition of the knowledge of good and evil and the Hebrew one?
  - o What does covetousness have to do with this knowledge?
- How does walking by sight bring unintended consequences?
- What is death?
  - o How does it define our relationship with God? With each other? With our body?
  - o Why do we fear death?
  - o Sin separates us from God. If we fear death, why is it so easy to live a life of sin and death?
  - o Are we afraid because physical death is perceived as unknowable?
  - o Why is relational and spiritual death not perceived the same way?
- If "Good" defines the baskets of blessing the Lord brings into our tent, why is the pursuit of what we consider good an endless and fruitless pursuit?
  - o Why did Paul say, *"Not that I am speaking of being in need, for I have learned in whatever situation I am to be content."*?
  - o Why is only God good?
  - o What does faith play in our contentment?

CHAPTER 19

Genesis 2:18
A Helper Fit For Adam

"Then the Lord God said, 'It is not good that the man should be alone; I will make him a helper fit for him'" (Genesis 2:18).

PROLOGUE

The Lord had created a garden where Adam lived and worked, and teamed with him to tend and care for it. There is no indication that Adam felt lonely. There was so much to experience – so many new challenges for them to face together! I am sure that he would have been content living out his destiny expanding the boundaries of the garden alone. But God never does anything alone. So now, the Lord wanted to augment Adam's relationship by bringing him a helper who would be fit for him – someone who could share all the intimacies of their life together as they lived in the presence of their Lord!!

Not Good – ⌁⊕ ⌀. We could say that "not good" means no more baskets of blessing would be anchored to Adam's tent as long as he was alone. But we learned from the last chapter that ⌀ has a sinister connotation, and ⊕ can represent a serpent anchored to Adam's tent. If Adam **settled** for working **alone** with God in the garden, he could open himself up to being controlled in a heavy-handed manner by forces he couldn't see.

Of course, the Lord could protect him! But God did not want Adam to live alone and desired to bring a helper into his life to stand with him in ways he could not even imagine right now. Instead of considering the relationship he had with God in the garden as a unique position to be grasped at (Philippians 2:5 − 8), Adam looked forward to sharing that relationship with this new helper.

Alone – ꊆꊇ𝘭 . Authority (𝘭) tent (ꊇ) door (ꊆ). Genesis 18:1 identifies Abraham sitting at the door of his tent greeting the men who came to deal with Sodom and Gomorrah. His posture shows he had the authority over who had access to his tent because he sat at the door of his tent.

Adam also sat at the door of his tent and had access authority. But at that point, he was the only person with access. So, this word highlights the fact that he was **alone** – the only one entering or exiting through the door of his tent.

Helper – ꊎꊏꊐ. This person would have eyes (ꊐ) to see things he was not aware of. Together, they would be able to perceive far more in the spirit than Adam could see on his own. She also would wield a weapon (ꊏ) enabling her to help defend against any forces (ꊑꊆ) he may not see at first who wanted to control their lives. Finally, Adam was to relate to her as his equal – head to head (ꊎ).

Fit – ꊆꊒꊓꊔ. As a helper who was fit for Adam, she would conform herself (ꊔ) to Adam enabling new life (ꊓ) to be brought forth to benefit them (ꊒ) bringing baskets of blessings (ꊇꊕꊖ) from the Lord through the door (ꊆ) of Adam's tent – his life.

If we add ﹃ (her work) to ʊ ٦ ٩ , we get ʊ﹃ ٦ ٩ which is the Hebrew word for ruler, prince, captain, governor, noble, excellent.[72] Since God was bringing Adam this helper to live and work alongside him, he could regard her, not only as his head-to-head equal, but as a noble captain in their household.

No Living Creature Qualified

> *"Now out of the ground the Lord God had formed every beast of the field and every bird of the heavens and brought them to the man to see what he would call them. And whatever the man called every living creature, that was its* **name***. The man gave names to all livestock and to the birds of the heavens and to every beast of the field. But for Adam there was not found a helper fit for him"* (Genesis 2:19 – 20).

God brought all these creatures to Adam as potential helpers, and gave him the freedom to examine each one to see if any of them qualified. The pictograms for **name** are ᴧᴧⱲ (destroy chaos). He did not simply assign names to them like antelope, bear, camel or donkey. He examined their character – their ability to destroy the chaos in their environment – and then he assigned an appropriate moniker to each one.

Not one of them was fit as a helper because none of them were spirit beings as well as living souls. His spirit companion had already been made in chapter one and together, they had been given dominion over everything else God had made with the authority to declare with their mouth words to destroy any chaos they faced.

A Helper For Adam

> *"So the Lord God caused a deep sleep to fall*

upon the man, and while he slept took one of his ribs and closed up its place with flesh. And the rib that the Lord God had taken from the man he made into a woman and brought her to the man" (Genesis 2:21 – 22).

Flesh – 𐤁𐤓𐤎. This is the first time this word is found in the Bible. It means the tent (𐤎) protecting (𐤓) the man (𐤁) in a similar way that a sheepfold made of thorn bushes (𐤎) protected the sheep from predators at night in the field.

Paul refers to our bodies as tents in 2 Corinthians 5:1,
> *"For we know that if the tent that is our earthly home is destroyed, we have a building from God, a house not made with hands, eternal in the heavens."*

Made – 𐤅𐤔𐤎. God did not make this woman in the same way He made everything else in chapter one (𐤅𐤓𐤏). 𐤔𐤎 is the Hebrew word for a young son in the house (a male child – "Ben"). But obviously, God was not making a young son. He was making a woman. Here is a closer look at these pictograms:

𐤎 – We determined that the flesh surrounding Adam was a tent (𐤎) protecting (𐤓) the man (𐤁). Let's expand 𐤎 in the word 𐤅𐤔𐤎 in this instance to mean Adam's flesh.

𐤔 – Is a sprout coming out of the ground – new life.

So, God took Adam's rib: a portion of his flesh (𐤁𐤓𐤎) – out of his house (𐤎) and made it (𐤅𐤔𐤎) into a new house (𐤎) for his spirit companion with new life (𐤔) eliciting praise and awe (Υ) from Adam – a woman.

SUMMARY:

We see in Adam a willingness to believe God had even more blessings for him than he was experiencing in their relationship in the garden. We read these brief passages and dismiss Adam's obedience without much thought. But imagine what Adam must be thinking as he spent day after day examining all these animals, perhaps even at the neglect of tending and caring for his own garden.

Had he wondered why his Father said it was not good for him to be alone? Some of these animals the Lord was bringing to him might be good pets giving him a semblance of companionship. But none of them really resonated with him, and he may have even grown weary of this endless parade of potential "helpers."

Then one day when he could see only a few more animals standing in line, he may have wondered if his diligence was worth the time spent. But just then, his Father stepped forward and gave him the reason for the tedium. Out of all these creatures, Adam could see that not one of them was fit for him. Then God caused a deep sleep to fall upon him, and while he slept, the Lord removed a rib from his side and performed the world's first major reconstructive surgery. Hallelujah!!

Study Questions For Discussion

- Why was Adam's helper given eyes to see and a sword to wield?
- How would this new helper fulfill the pictographic meaning of "alone?"
  - Why was it necessary for Adam to allow his solo relationship to die?
- What disqualified the beasts of the field from being "fit" as Adam's helper?
  - Does this have any bearing on Paul's injunction not to be unequally yoked with unbelievers?
- What does "Name" mean and what criteria did Adam use for naming the creatures?
- How would you relate his criteria with 1 Samuel 16:7?
  - Samuel didn't choose the son of Jesse that God had rejected. How can we make decisions about our relationships so they are pleasing to the Lord?
  - How does the Lord want us to choose a spouse, a close friend, an employee, etc.?
- If we live in our tent – our flesh – then who are "we?"
  - Why is it misleading to say that we have a spirit?
  - How would you characterize the relationship between spirit, soul and body?
  - If you are unequally yoked with an unbeliever, would your spouse agree with the same characterization?
  - At what level are you likely to relate to this spouse? See Genesis 6:1 – 2.
- What are the likely consequences to your relationship with God?
- Given that it was not good for Adam to be alone, how did God make the woman so that she could bring new life – sons and daughters – into their family?
  - How does the last symbol of Ⴗ ꕯ ꖈ (made) predict Adam's excitement (2:23) when he first saw her?

- Are we willing to explore new horizons particularly when the transitions mean leaving the security of a familiar lifestyle?
  - o Do these transitions sometimes appear to take longer than we initially expected?
  - o Do they sometimes feel like major reconstructive surgery?
  - o What role does faith play in these transitions?

CHAPTER 20

Genesis 2:22 – 24
The Marriage Covenant

*"And the rib that the Lord God had taken from the man he made into a **woman** and brought her to the man. Then the man said, '**This** at last is bone of my bones and flesh of my flesh; she shall be called **Woman**, because she was taken out of Man.' Therefore a man shall leave his father and his mother and hold fast to his wife, and they shall become one flesh."*

(Genesis 2:22 – 24)

PROLOGUE

Imagine Adam's elation as he woke up and beheld the most awesome "creature" he had ever seen standing before him radiant in all her glory! This was a God-appointment! All the tedium of examining a seemingly endless train of potential helpers evaporated as he realized that, at last, his diligence had finally paid off! This helper was truly fit in every way! And yet at that moment, Adam had no way of fully comprehending the glorious relationship God was preparing for him, a companionship that would exceed his highest expectations.

Let's examine these words of exaltation:

Brought – 𐤀𐤉𐤔𐤋 . Benner says 𐤀𐤉𐤔 means to fill a void by entering it[73]. 𐤋 preceding a word indicates that the Lord was actively involved to filling this void.

This – ✝ 𝖇 𝖋 . These symbols are a variant of Ψ 𝖋 that we examined in Genesis 2:4a. Even though the Lord made Adam's rib into a **woman** (Ψ𝖜𝖇), He allowed Adam to evaluate her inner character and come to the same conclusion.

At last! – ᴍ⊚○ . Benner says this word means repetitive sounds / activity like the repetitive sounds from the hoofs of a running horse[74].

So, the void of being alone and reviewing all the beasts of the field and the birds of the air in a repetitive manner was finally being filled by the Lord through the woman He brought to Adam!

Bone from my bone! – ᴍ 𝗋⊚. Benner says that 𝗋⊚ means a tree[75]. Adding ᴍ indicates many trees / branches. The bones of the body support it like the branching structure of a tree. Adam declared that her bones were from his bones.

Flesh from my flesh! – 𝕹 ﹗ ⅃. As noted in the previous chapter, flesh is the tent (⅃) supporting (﹗) the man (𝕹). Adam also declared that her flesh was from his flesh.

Adam decreed that the woman was his flesh and bone. He did not say she was his flesh and blood even though his name means "strong blood." I believe Adam was asserting that the primary source of her physical life was not the same as all those other creatures he had just examined. Her physical body, made from Adam's rib (flesh and bone), was given life in the same way God gave life to Adam's lifeless body when He breathed into his nostrils the breath of life.

Woman and Man:

> *"She shall be called Woman (𐤟𐤅𐤔𐤀), be-*
> *cause she was taken out of Man (𐤅𐤉𐤀)."*

Adam now focused on the inner character of this person standing before him. The words "Woman" and "Man" are meager
representations of the original Hebrew. Seekins explains their
pictographic meaning[76]. Both words have two pictograms that
are identical. Those two letters (𐤅𐤀) spell the Hebrew word
for "fire" – strong destroyer. As spirit beings, they were made
in God's image. Deuteronomy 4:24 says, *"For the Lord your
God is a consuming fire."* Her character matched his: she was
also a consuming fire!

There was one symbol in each word that was unique: 𐤔
and 𐤉 . These symbols are the first two pictograms of
𐤔 𐤅 𐤔 𐤉 indicating that the woman, the man and the Lord
were bound together in a betrothal relationship. The man was
working (𐤉) in the fire (𐤅𐤀) in order to present the woman (𐤟𐤅𐤔𐤀) as an offering of praise (𐤔) to the Lord.

The apostle Paul alludes to this relationship in Ephesians:

> *"Husbands, love your wives, as Christ loved
> the church and gave himself up for her, that
> he might sanctify her, having cleansed her by
> the washing of water with the word, so that he
> might present the church to himself in splendor,
> without spot or wrinkle or any such thing, that
> she might be holy and without blemish. In the
> same way husbands should love their wives as
> their own bodies. He who loves his wife loves
> himself. For no one ever hated his own flesh,
> but nourishes and cherishes it, just as Christ
> does the church, because we are members of*

2:22-24 The Marriage Covenant   211

his body" (Ephesians 5:23 – 30).

Took / Taken – ▥➖𝓵 . We saw earlier that "flesh" was associated with the sheepfold that protected the sheep from predators. When I first looked at this symbol group, I could not understand how Authority / Cycle / Fence could be interpreted as "took / taken." But after much prayer, the Lord revealed an interpretation that made perfect sense: A shepherd (𝓵) at daybreak, when the sun was at the horizon (➖), approached the door of the sheepfold – the fence (▥) that surrounded and protected all the sheep – and **took** his own sheep out by calling them to follow him. In the same manner, while Adam was asleep, his Shepherd went to the door of Adam's sheepfold and spoke the words that took the rib out of his flesh.

The Marriage Covenant
A Betrothal Commitment To Each Other
> *"Therefore a man shall leave his father and his mother and hold fast to his wife, and they shall become one flesh"* (Genesis 2:24).

Did Adam Have A Mother?
At first, you might think that Adam did not have a mother and therefore, this text is a parenthetical statement for the rest of us who have mothers. However, Adam did have a Father (Elohim) Who, with the assistance of His Son (Bara), made mankind (Adam) as male and female. This verse was written by Moses under the prophetic inspiration of the Holy Spirit as a revelation of the pattern the Lord ordained for all of us who enter into the marriage covenant. Let's take a closer look at this important passage.

Therefore – 𝟷 ש – 𝓵 ⬭ (עַל־כֵּן). This is the first time עַל־כֵּן occurs in the Bible. As such, its basic meaning should come from its usage here. The Septuagint translates this phrase as "therefore" as does virtually every English Bible I own.

My preferred Hebrew lexicon (Brown) translates this phrase as "for / therefore[77]." However, they do not mention Genesis 2:24 among the ten texts they reference, and only Job 34:27 has this phrase. All the other nine passages append כִּי to the front (כִּי־עַל־כֵּן)which is the Hebrew word often translated as "for / because / that."

Brown went on to say,
"...but in the process of time, the distinct sense of its component parts was no doubt gradually obscured, and it thus came to be used conventionally as a mere particle of causation, even where there is no preceding statement to which עַל־כֵּן therefore could be explicitly referred."

My due diligence was raising more questions than answers. Since this was the first time the phrase entered the Bible, there was no time for its component parts to be gradually obscured. And as Brown mentioned, it is somewhat difficult to identify an explicit causal relationship between 2:23 and 2:24. So, I decided to examine the pictograms themselves.

ל ◎ – **See the staff / See the shepherd**. The shepherd is the one in authority. This word's meaning is bolstered by Strong's definition: Highest (i.e. God); also (adv.) aloft, to Jehovah? – above; high, most High[78].

ו שׁ – **Allow - Conform / (bless) New Life**. Even though this combination occurred for the first time in 2:24, these two words occur separately in three earlier places in Genesis chapter one:
> *"And God said, 'Let the earth sprout vegetation, plants yielding seed, and fruit trees bear-*

ing fruit in which is their seed, each according to its kind, on (𝐿 ⬭) the earth.' And it was so (⸀ 𝕌)" (Genesis 1:11).

"and let them be lights in the expanse of the heavens to give light upon (𝐿 ⬭) the earth." And it was so (⸀ 𝕌)" (Genesis 1:15)

"And to every beast of the earth and to every bird of the heavens and to everything that creeps on (𝐿 ⬭) the earth, everything that has the breath of life, I have given every green plant for food." And it was so (⸀ 𝕌)."
(Genesis 1:30)

I shared previously a pattern showing how God declared what He would accomplish before He carried it out by the strength of His arm. We see the same pattern in these verses. First, God gave permission for these new activities to be carried out on the earth (𝐿 ⬭). Then, He conformed these activities to His open hand (⸀ 𝕌).

Resolving the "causal" relationship between 2:23 and 2:24

Adam's declared that his relationship with the woman in verse 23 was bound up in their relationship with God as a three-fold chord. These prophetic words were given to Adam by his Shepherd (𝐿 ⬭) to proclaim with his mouth. Once these words were spoken, God fulfilled them (⸀ 𝕌) by establishing the marriage covenant structure - *"a man shall leave his father and his mother and hold fast to his wife, and they shall become one flesh."*

Leave – ᴡ⅃ᵬ⁻ᴑ℩ᵔ◶⅃. As we have seen so many times before, the man's activity was not his alone, it was empowered by the strength of God's arm (◶⅃). Notice the similarity between this word and the pictograms for helper (ᴺ℩◶). The only difference is that ᴑ replaced ᴺ. This is the first use of ᴑ℩◶. So, its basic meaning should come from its usage here.

The focus of this activity begins with the man's father and mother (also used for the first time here). May I suggest that ᴑ℩◶ represents the home environment (ᴑ) the man's father and mother established when his mother married his father as a helper (ᴺ℩◶).

My interpretation of עַל־כֵּן:

At the beginning of verse 24, the man was given permission (ᴌ◶) by his father to leave his parent's home where he had been raised in order to replicate their environment (ᴑ℩◶). As an obedient son, the Lord would bless him to conform their new life (ᴉᴡ) into his father's family.

Father – ᴑᵬ. Strong / Tent. The father is the strength of the house / family. The father is the tent pole that holds his tent up. Removing the tent pole causes the tent to collapse. In the same way, the lack of a strong, godly father's presence in the home is devastating to the family.

Seekins says[79] that one of the Hebrew words for anger points to this lack of the father's presence in the home: ᴑ⅃ᵬ comes from two words (⅃ᵬ - Where?) and (ᴑᵬ - Father) meaning "Where is the father?"

Mother – Strong / Water. This designation may seem strange until you understand its Hebrew meaning[25]: When animal hides were boiled in water, the residue that floated to the top was sticky and was used for glue – strong water. So, a mother is the glue that binds the family together.

ロ𐤐◓ is the indispensable environment the father and mother establish where they raise their children in a covenant relationship with the Lord. These conditions equip their children with eyes to see (◓) and essential weapons (𐤐) while they are at home (ロ) enabling them to be victorious when they leave to set up their own home. Proverbs speaks to the importance of this environment.

> *"Train up a child in the way he should go; even when he is old he will not depart from it."*
>
> (Proverbs 22:6)

And Malachi declares what happens when this marriage covenant is not honored:

> *"You cover the Lord's altar with tears, with weeping and groaning because he no longer regards the offering or accepts it with favor from your hand. But you say, 'Why does he not?' Because the Lord was witness between you and the wife of your youth, to whom you have been faithless, though **she is your companion and your wife by covenant. Did he not make them one, with a portion of the Spirit in their union? And what was the one God seeking? Godly offspring**. So guard yourselves in your spirit, and let none of you be faithless to the wife of your youth. 'For the man who does not love his wife but divorces her', says the Lord, 'the God of Israel, covers his garment with violence', says the Lord of hosts. So guard your-*

selves in your spirit, and do not be faithless."
(Malachi 2:13 – 16)

Hold fast – ᐱᗯᕤᗐ ᐱᗴᑐᑌ. Door / Tent / Cycle – In / Woman. A door (ᑌ) is the opening where a person enters and exits a tent (ᒪ). This tent is the woman's body – a body that experiences reproductive cycles (ᐱᗴ). By entering and exiting the woman's body, the man (ᗯᔓᕤ) was united with (ᒪ) the woman (ᐱᗯᕤ). This action consummated their betrothal commitment to each other and to the Lord.

Become – ᐱᔓᐱ. Paise yielding more praise in their relationship with each other and the Lord.

Yoked Flesh – ᕤᐧᒪ𝓁. The symbol 𝓁 is append to ᕤᐧᒪ meaning their flesh is now yoked together by the Lord.

One – ᑌᗰᕤ. Strong / Fence / Door. This word means much more than the number one. It signifies unity – a strong (ᕤ) fence (ᗰ) around the door (ᑌ) of their combined sheepfold. As their covenant Shepherd, the Lord occupied the door of their new sheepfold protecting and calling them to follow Him in a life of praise and wonder.

Jesus spoke out against divorce, which was rampant in His day, because it tore apart the oneness of the couple's yoked flesh that God had joined together in a covenant relationship with Him.

> *"He answered, 'Have you not read that he who created them from the beginning made them male and female, and said, Therefore a man shall leave his father and his mother and hold*

fast to his wife, and the two shall become one flesh'? ***"So they are no longer two but one flesh. What therefore God has joined together, let not man separate"*** (Matthew 19:4 – 6).

Marriage – A Blood Covenant

The initial consummation of this act yielded an issue of blood from the woman affirming their commitment as one flesh. Unlike the other Old Testament covenants, this covenant was not based on a sacrifice for sin but rather on a commitment of their sacred yoked relationship with each other and the Lord, and stands as the model for all subsequent marriages.

SUMMARY

This marriage covenant is foundational in that it is the only one that the Lord made with us before sin entered the world. It begins in Genesis 1:27 when God made us as male and female in **His Image** with authority to be fruitful, multiply, fill the earth and subdue it under His guidance. And it concludes here with the **betrothal and marriage commitments** we just discussed.

Paul defines verse 24 as a mystery – the covenant relationship between Christ and His Bride.

> *"Therefore a man shall leave his father and mother and hold fast to his wife, and the two shall become one flesh." This mystery is profound, and I am saying that it refers to Christ and the church"* (Ephesians 5:31 – 32).

All of us who have confessed Jesus as our Lord and believe that God has raised Him from the dead have committed ourselves to a betrothal covenant with Jesus purchased by His blood and sealed by the Holy Spirit dwelling in us. Christ has gone to prepare a place for us in His Father's house. And one day, our relationship will be fully consummated at the wedding supper of the Lamb (Revelation 19:6-9) where we will be forever together with the Lord!

I said earlier in this chapter that this covenant was not lost to us when Adam disobeyed the Lord. As we move forward into the next two chapters of Genesis, the critical lessons learned here will enable us to live even more victoriously than Adam in the manifest presence of our Father and His Son, the last Adam.

Study Questions For Discussion

- Adam's proclamation "At last!" must have indicated that a considerable amount of time had elapsed. Why did God put Adam through the animal naming process when He already knew the outcome?
o Did it help convince Adam that this woman was the right choice?
    o Would his participation in the selection process help him later when their relationship became strained?
    o Does the "selection process" in your life seem to take too long?
- In the tedium of the situation, do you want Him to just "fix it?"
- What role does our maturity play?
    o How does the Lord use these situations to bring us to a deeper level of maturity?
- Has Adam's definition of "Woman" and "Man" changed the way you look at the opposite gender?
- Does its association with Ephesians 5:23 – 30 make Paul's assertion more explicit than the English words "Woman"

and "Man" imply?

- o   How does "Fire" define our true spirit nature?
- o   What happens when the Lord is not part of a marriage?
- What is the difference between a betrothal and a marriage?
- Is a betrothal any less a commitment than marriage?
  - o   When we invite Jesus into our lives as our Lord and Savior, is it a betrothal or a marriage?
  - o   What will happen at the marriage supper of the Lamb?
- Why was the marriage covenant instituted before sin entered the world?
  - o   Why is the marriage covenant a blood covenant?
  - o   Are the blessings of this first covenant available to us?
  - o   How does the Last Adam fulfill this first covenant?
- Do you feel this covenant forms the foundation for all other covenants?
  - o   How does it manifest the image of God in Genesis 1:26 – 28?
  - o   How is the oneness of Genesis 1:26 – 27 reflected in the marriage covenant?
- Define the importance of the family environment for raising children?
  - o   What is the role of the father?
  - o   What is the role of the mother?
  - o   What is the role of the Lord?
  - o   What happens when these roles are set aside?
  - o   How are the children affected?
  - o   Can this adverse effect be redeemed? How?
- How does ᛣᜃᛞᛓ ᛆᛓᛏ lead to the yoked relationship described by ᛑᛣᛓᛚ ?
  - o   Does Ephesians 5:31 – 32 describe a yoked relationship between Jesus and the Church?

CHAPTER 21

Genesis 2:25
Naked And Not Ashamed

"And the man and his wife were both naked and were not ashamed"(Genesis 2:25).

PROLOGUE
As they stepped outside into the morning light together hand in hand, they were filled with new purpose and destiny and a deep, unquenchable love for each other. Even though Adam had seen it all before, suddenly everything was new and alive with endless potential. He turned to drink in the radiant beauty of the face that smiled back at him, and overwhelming joy flooded his soul. He held her close as they danced together in the warmth of the sun and in the Lord's loving embrace. Theirs was a sacred love story – the three of them dancing together – a love story God calls each one of us to embrace.

Naked and Not Ashamed
The Keys To The Marriage Covenant
I want to assure you that this verse which summarizes the first two chapters of Genesis is much more than a declaration of their modesty toward each other. Permit me to address the second word first because it gives context for the first word.

Ashamed – ᛉwwᴗᵀ. As we said earlier, **ᵀ** preceding a word intensifies its finality and completeness. The root word is **ᴡᛉᴗ** meaning "a tent anchored to destruction."

Adding an additional **W** to the end and a **†** to the beginning indicates that the activity causing the shame is completely devouring the person's tent – everything within the scope of the person's domain.

Not – &L . These two symbols mean NO[71]. The reason I examined "not ashamed" first is because it is the result of Adam and his wife functioning as naked persons. That is, because of the way they lived, nothing they built could be destroyed. They could look at all of their accomplishments without any sense of shame or regret because those achievements – their tent – could not be destroyed.

> *"Unless the Lord builds the house, those who build it labor in vain"* (Psalm 127:1).

Naked – ᴍᴐ� . Benner says ᴙ◎ (See the man) identified the action taken when an enemy was captured[80]. Prisoners were stripped of their clothing to humiliate them and to make sure they had nothing hidden on their person so the army could fully "see the man." The lack of clothing is evident in such passages as 1 Samuel 19:24 and Isaiah 20:2 – 4.

Brown's Lexicon expresses a more basic meaning by asserting that a naked person is one without any possessions[81]. This interpretation is closely aligned with how these two symbols are used in this word. ᴍ ᴙ◎ is built on ᴙ◎ and means "See the man with no possessions who is focused on / anchored to chaos."

But why is a man who has no possessions anchored to chaos? As they walked together with the Lord, He focused their attention (ᴙ◎) by anchoring them (ᴎ) to specific arenas of chaos (〰) where His order needed to be established. Some of these domains would be outside the boundaries of their garden that were resistant to its expansion.

God led them to face these challenges as "naked" people. He was not expecting them to devise a strategy (Light) for solving a particular dilemma or to possess sufficient resources of their own to overcome each circumstance successfully. Instead, they were to enact the blessing spoken to them in Genesis 1:28 as they partnered with God to fulfill His will in their world.

In Matthew 19:14, Jesus admonished His disciples with these words,

> *"Let the little children (παιδία) come to me and do not hinder them, for to such belongs the kingdom of heaven."*

A παιδίον is an infant or small child who exemplified the relationship Jesus was calling His disciples to emulate. They had no agenda or resources. Their parents did not expect them to provide their own food, clothing, shelter or protection and they could rest in the unconditional love, resources and security of their parents. These παιδία modeled the "naked" posture Adam and his wife lived in the garden at the end of chapter two.

Let's look again at the complete word for naked (〰〜〕〰 Υ 〕〇). If we convert the pictograms into their corresponding Hebrew characters (ערומימ) and treat them in the context of a modern grammatical language, ימ is considered a masculine plural ending leaving us with ערום as the word inspired by the Holy Spirit. But if we include the last two pictograms (〰〕) in our meditation, they reveal that the

Lord teamed with Adam and his wife, and that He was the One dealing with their chaos (ᴹ) by the strength of His arm (ᴚ).

Recall the pattern: "God said - God made - God called" The Lord first **says** what He is doing (Light – the "job order") and then He **performs** it (Day – the "work order"). God never works alone. So, in Genesis 1:27, He made man as male and female teaming with them to redeem the earth from the chaos imposed on it in Genesis 1:2. He gave them dominion over everything He had made and told them to be fruitful. That is, they would seek His guidance (His Light) and then **proclaim it with their mouth in faith believing that God always honored His own word and would carry out their proclamation with the strength of His arm.**

In Hebrews 11:3 the Bible says,
> *"**By faith** we understand that the universe was created by the word of God, so that what is seen was not **made** out of things that are visible.'*

This text clearly states that His **word** was instituted by **faith**: that it was God's faith believing that He could **create** the universe by the **proclamation** of His word and that He was able to fulfill His **word** quite apart from human involvement. Because what He does ultimately relies on **His faith**, He only asks for our obedience to believe in His faithfulness that He will always fulfill His Word that He gives us to declare with our mouth.

This pattern to subdue the earth will always succeed because it is God's way to address chaos. As Adam and his wife followed this pattern, they walked in the manifest presence of His Light in victory without shame, fulfilling their destiny to multiply, fill and subdue the earth.

Protection

The same enemy that was able to engulf the earth in incomprehensible chaos could easily have snuffed out Adam's candle if it weren't for the protection God established in Day Four and the hedge of righteousness the Lord built around them. We catch a glimpse of this hedge in the opening chapter of the book of Job:

> *"Now there was a day when the sons of God came to present themselves before the Lord, and Satan also came among them. The Lord said to Satan, 'From where have you come?' Satan answered the Lord and said, 'From going to and fro on the earth, and from walking up and down on it.' And the Lord said to Satan, 'Have you considered my servant Job, that there is none like him on the earth, **a blameless and upright man, who fears God and turns away from evil?'** Then Satan answered the Lord and said, 'Does Job fear God for no reason? **Have you not put a hedge around him and his house and all that he has, on every side? You have blessed the work of his hands, and his possessions have increased in the land.'"***

(Job 1:6 – 10)

Before Adam and his wife disobeyed the Lord, God's hedge surrounded them and was impenetrable. How do I know? The same protection surrounded the last Adam, Jesus. He stood up in the synagogue in His home town and read from the scroll of Isaiah. Everyone was impressed with the eloquence of His words. But when He refused to put on a display of miracles for them, they tried to kill Him:

> *"When they heard these things, all in the synagogue were filled with wrath. And they rose up and drove him out of the town and brought him*

to the brow of the hill on which their town was built, so that they could throw him down the cliff. But passing through their midst, he went away" (Luke 4:28 – 30).

An entire synagogue full of irate men grabbed Jesus and manhandled Him roughshod up to the precipice of a nearby cliff intent on shoving him off, severely injuring or even killing Him. But His destiny could not be cut short by impetuous men. They were no match for the hedge of angels surrounding Him making a path so He could walk through them and out of danger.

Later, during His trial, Pilate had Jesus flogged and tortured by his soldiers. His confidence was only shaken when the Jews said Jesus claimed to be the Son of God.

> *"Pilate entered his headquarters again and said to Jesus, "Where are you from?" But Jesus gave him no answer. So Pilate said to him, "You will not speak to me? Do you not know that I have authority to release you and authority to crucify you?" Jesus answered him, "You would have no authority over me at all unless it had been given you from above"* (John 19:9 – 11).

After all this punishment, surely Jesus would cower before this Roman ruler. *"Don't you realize I have the power of life or death over you?"* Pilate retorted. Jesus's reply bears witness to His confidence that the hedge surrounding Him would ensure that His destiny could not be thwarted.

It also underscores David's confidence in this hedge he proclaimed in Psalm 91:

> *"He who dwells in the shelter of the Most High*

will abide in the shadow of the Almighty. I will say to the Lord, 'My refuge and my fortress, my God, in whom I trust.' **For he will deliver you from the snare of the fowler and from the deadly pestilence. He will cover you with his pinions, and under his wings you will find refuge; his faithfulness is a shield and buckler.** *You will not fear the terror of the night, nor the arrow that flies by day, nor the pestilence that stalks in darkness, nor the destruction that wastes at noonday. A thousand may fall at your side, ten thousand at your right hand,* **but it will not come near you**. *You will only look with your eyes and see the recompense of the wicked. Because you have made the Lord your dwelling place— the Most High, who is my refuge—* **no evil shall be allowed to befall you, no plague come near your tent. For he will command his angels concerning you to guard you in all your ways. On their hands they will bear you up, lest you strike your foot against a stone.** *You will tread on the lion and the adder; the young lion and the serpent you will trample underfoot.* **'Because he holds fast to me in love, I will deliver him; I will protect him, because he knows my name. When he calls to me, I will answer him; I will be with him in trouble; I will rescue him and honor him**. *With long life I will satisfy him and show him my salvation.'"*

SUMMARY
Jesus, The Last Adam,
Followed This Same Pattern

"So Jesus said to them, 'Truly, truly, I say to you, the Son can do nothing of his own ac-

cord, but only what he sees the Father doing. For whatever the Father does, that the Son does likewise. For the Father loves the Son and shows him all that he himself is doing. And greater works than these will he show him, so that you may marvel'" (John 5:19 – 20).

We are familiar with the tragedy played out over the next two chapters of Genesis. But the Lord was not caught off guard and the lives of men like Enoch, Noah, Abraham, Moses, David and the apostles bear witness to the faithfulness of God's grace and unconditional love to deliver His children to the fullest. The Lord is drawing us back to the marriage covenant to walk in the footsteps of the last Adam as He follows this redemptive pattern in and through us.

Study Questions For Discussion

- Describe what "not ashamed" means to you.
  - When have you seen your "house" destroyed? What were the circumstances?
  - When have you seen your "house" flourish? What were the circumstances?
  - Is your life unique?
- When we face trials of many kinds, what does the Lord expect us to do? (James 1:2 – 5)
  - What role does He play in our "naked" response to these trials?
- Jesus is our model. How did He fulfill the law?
- Satan only wants to steal, kill and destroy. What role does the hedge of protection play in your life?
  - Can you rest in that hedge of protection?
- From the very beginning, our right standing before God has been a byproduct of our yoked relationship with Him. Jesus said, *"You search the scriptures because you think that in them you have eternal life."* Why do we try to find some alternative plan of action we can follow that will bring us into favor with God such as a rigorous adherence to the multitude of biblical laws governing virtually every aspect of life or an ascetic lifestyle that repudiates all the trappings of "the world"?
  - Are these activities successful in gaining eternal life and favor with God?
  - Do these efforts bring freedom?
  - Are they fulfilled through our yoked relationship with the Lord?
  - Who opposed Christ's ministry?
  - Why is a religious spirit such an enemy to our relationship with the Lord?

CHAPTER
22

Genesis 3:1 – 5
The Crafty Serpent

"Now the serpent was more crafty than any other beast of the field that the Lord God had made. He said to the woman, 'Did God actually say, "You shall not eat of any tree in the garden'?"' And the woman said to the serpent, 'We may eat of the fruit of the trees in the garden, but God said, "You shall not eat of the fruit of the tree that is in the midst of the garden, neither shall you touch it, lest you die."' But the serpent said to the woman, 'You will not surely die. For God knows that when you eat of it your eyes will be opened, and you will be like God, knowing good and evil'" (Genesis 3:1 – 5).

PROLOGUE

In Chapter Six, I proposed a pattern of Creation / Corruption / Redemption to illustrate the work God and His Son performed in Genesis chapter one. This same pattern can be applied to Adam and his wife. That is, God made them in the first two chapters of Genesis as perfect reflections of His image and likeness. We are about to witness their corruption in Genesis chapter three. And the rest of the Bible will reveal God's plan of redemption culminating in Jesus Christ and the new heaven and earth in Revelation chapter 21 and 22. In this chapter, I will carefully examine the pivotal events that set the stage for Adam's eventual disobedience.

The Crafty Serpent

Chapter three opens with an introduction to the serpent. While it did indeed play a key role in this drama, I want to state from the outset that our first parents were more than just innocent victims duped by the crafty wiles of this serpent and the devil who orchestrated its attack. As you will soon see, this chapter will reveal a possible reason why Adam was so defensive in his response to the Lord in verse 3:12.

The Serpent's Identity

Before I address the "crafty" aspects of this creature, I want to assert that, at this point in the Bible, the serpent was not a snake. Just like the rest of you, I have grown up with depictions of this serpent as a snake wrapped around the limb of a tree talking to Adam's wife in the garden.

Our dictionaries define a serpent as a large snake. But what is the Genesis 3:1 definition?

> *"Now the serpent was more crafty than any other **beast** († ⊃⌐Ⅲ) **of the field** that the Lord God had made."*

Let's go back to Genesis 1:24 and 2:19:

> *""And God said, 'Let the **earth** bring forth **living** (Ψ⊃⌐Ⅲ) creatures (ᴡᴑ ᒐ) according to their kinds—**livestock** (ΨᴹΨᴅ) and **creeping things** (ᕵ ᴹᕼ) and **beasts** (Y † ⊃⌐Ⅲ) of the earth according to their kinds.' And it was so."*

(Genesis 1:24)

> *"Now out of the ground the Lord God had formed every **beast** († ⊃⌐Ⅲ) of the field (Ψᑌᕵ) and every bird of the heavens and*

brought them to the man to see what he would call them" (Genesis 2:19).

Genesis 1:24 defines three groups of living creatures: livestock, creeping things and beasts of the earth. The symbol group for "beasts' is a variation of "living" creatures. So, these animals were living creatures distinct from livestock and creeping things.

Livestock – ᵞ ᴹ ᵞ ⊔. High / Tall. A "tall" (important) creature[84]. A family (⊔) gained status (ᵞ), might (ᴹ) and respect (ᵞ) by owning livestock.

Creeping Things – ˹ ᴹ ᴅ. Benner says it means "to trample under foot." It is a living creature that crawls or creeps under foot[85]. The pictograms indicate that a person (ᴅ) perceived them as a multitude (ᴹ) of thorns (˹).

The **beasts of the field** (ᵞ ᴜ ˹) were some of the species that comprised the beasts of the earth. Benner says "field" describes a level piece of ground for planting crops or setting up tents[86]. This definition correlates well with our introduction to the serpent since he was in the garden when he addressed Adam's wife.

In Genesis 3:14, God said to the serpent,
> *"Because you have done this, cursed are you above all livestock and above all beasts of the field; on your belly you shall go, and dust you shall eat all the days of your life."*

At that point, the serpent was demoted to a status of living on its belly and eating dust for the rest of its days. This text is where we get the impression that the serpent was a snake.

3:1-5 The Crafty Serpent   233

However, in Genesis 3:1, it was a **beast of the field** and did not crawl on its belly like a snake.

Crafty – ᵐ Υ ᴙ⊝. These pictograms are the same as the root word for "**naked**" in verse 2:25 (ᵐᴣᴶᵐ Υ ᴙ⊝). How is this possible? On the surface, 3:1 could be translated as,

> *"Now the serpent was more **naked** than any other beast of the field that the LORD God had made."*

The word ANY in this verse is ⅃ Ⱳ. I shared earlier in Chapter Seventeen that ⅃ Ⱳ means "conform to authority" and defines something that is **tamed**. Adding this interpretation to 3:1, we get,

> *"Now the serpent was more **naked** than the other **tamable** beasts of the field that the LORD God had made."*

"Naked" in 2:25 meant that Adam and his wife conformed to the authority of the Lord their Shepherd. In other words, they were ⅃ Ⱳ – totally obedient / tamed to the guidance of the One to Whom they were yoked. Since the core pictograms for "naked" and "crafty" are the same, I am asserting that a better translation of this word is '**tamable**."

> *"Now the serpent was more **tamable** than the other **tamable** beasts of the field that the LORD God had made."*

This interpretation flows better with the overall meaning of the sentence. The phrase "that the LORD God had made" also links easily with the beasts of the field God made in Genesis 2:19 – 20. And the fact that the serpent could converse with Adam and his wife also meant that it could be more easily domesticated.

Since we find the serpent in the garden in 3:1, Adam likely recognized its value as an easily domesticated animal and used it early on. Adam's own yoked relationship with the Lord was summarized as ᴟ Ɏ ᴥ. So, it is possible that initially, the serpent's yoked relationship with Adam could have been summarized in a similar manner.

The Woman and the Serpent

> *"And the woman said to the serpent, 'We may eat of the **fruit** of the trees in the garden, but **God said**, "You shall not eat of the **fruit** of the tree that is in the midst of the garden, **neither shall you touch it**, lest you die."'"*
>
> (Genesis 3:2 – 3)

> *"The tree of life was in the midst of the garden, and the tree of the knowledge of good and evil... And the Lord God commanded the man, saying, 'You may surely eat of every tree of the garden, but of the tree of **the knowledge of good and evil** you shall not eat, for in the day that you eat of it you **shall surely** die.'"*
>
> (Genesis 2:9, 16 – 17)

These two accounts reveal some critical differences between the woman's statements to the serpent and the injunction God gave to Adam. In the original command, no mention was made of the **fruit** of the tree. Since the tree of the knowledge of good and evil was in the garden, and since Adam was put there to work and keep it, part of his responsibility included cultivating this individual tree. However, unlike all the other trees, Adam was enjoined **not to cultivate this particular tree for food**. We might even speculate that God's command to Adam occurred before this tree was mature enough to bear fruit.

Next, the woman did not mention the tree of the knowledge of good and evil by name. She used the more generic designation *"the tree that is in the midst of the garden."* Verse 3:6 says that she carefully examined its fruit indicating that this may have been the first time she was close enough to the tree to make such a rigorous evaluation.

We may even speculate that the woman did not identify this tree at first because she had not been very close to it before this encounter. Why else would she declare what God said about the tree without identifying the focus of that declaration given that the tree was right there in front of her?

Further, she told the serpent, *"God said"* linking the admonition not to eat the "fruit" of this tree with another injunction not even to touch it. Finally, the consequence for disobedience was different in the woman's version: from *"in dying you shall die"* to *"lest you die."* Their conversation also implies that they were both located at the tree when this exchange took place.

Why were both the woman and the serpent in the midst of the garden? Genesis 2:9 says that the tree of life was in the midst of the garden. And in Chapter 17, I linked this tree with its more complete description in Revelation 22:2. *"the tree of life with its twelve kinds of fruit, yielding its fruit each month."* I also shared that the word for life describing this tree was associated with Adam's physical well-bring. So, it would have been appropriate for the woman to regularly gather fruit from the tree of life in order to maintain their health and well-being.

Different Perspectives

But why was the serpent located at the tree during this encounter? For me, one key lies in how Adam and his wife viewed the consequences of disobeying God's command. Adam's destiny revolved around working and keeping the garden. He was responsible for cultivating every tree. And God had commanded him in the gravest possible manner to isolate this one tree as a food source. I am sure Adam took this warning very seriously. And since he was not told to remove the tree from the garden, he might have thought it had some other purpose for being there.

As a helper fit for Adam, his wife was given eyes to perceive their circumstances in ways that Adam might overlook. Taken together, their combined viewpoints would be much more inclusive and beneficial than that of either Adam or his wife. May I suggest that she approached this situation from a more **relational** perspective.

She was not there when God had issued this warning. Now, as Adam's wife, she may have perceived her destiny as a **relational** support for him in the context of their **three-fold union** with the Lord to a much greater extent than as a **co-worker** laboring together with him to care for the garden. As such, she perceived her role as being only tangentially responsible for the cultivation of this tree. However, for Adam, this injunction was a critical line item in his work order instructing him how to manage this tree in the garden.

Let's look at the woman's words: *"lest you die."* Benner says "lest" is a translation of ⌇◯ and means "the turning of the face," "a turning toward another direction[88]." (Ψ⌇◯ is the Hebrew word for "face.") For her, disobeying God's warning meant death to their covenant relationship with Him and each other because they would be turning their faces away from Him. But for Adam, God's warning (in dying you shall die) highlighted the critical reason for diligently obeying this new line item in his work order.

Her perspective addressed their three-fold union with God. Her destiny supported her husband by **working and keeping** their marriage covenant strong. Adam's destiny focused on **working and keeping** the garden in accordance with God's work order for him. Their perspectives were both valid and complementary to each other. **Neither one was sufficient by itself**.

Adam must have recognized that, as part of her supporting role, she would be gathering their food from the garden – including fruit from the tree of life in the midst of the garden. Since the tree of the knowledge of good and evil was also in the middle of the garden, he may have been concerned that she might inadvertently pick some of its fruit as food for them to eat. So, Adam wanted her to adamantly declare that she would not harvest any of its fruit.

Since he knew she would be selecting fruit from the trees in the garden for them to eat, he may have insisted that she realize the severe consequences that would result from picking the wrong fruit because it would jeopardize his relationship with the Lord. However, since she was only peripherally involved with managing the garden, she may have felt her viewpoint was sufficient to support her husband because of her commitment to him and to the Lord.

Don't Touch The Fruit

Some may suggest that the woman added the phrase *"neither shall you touch it"* when she replied to the serpent. But why would she contradict Adam's recollection of God's command and add another constraint to their activity when she had no basis for "correcting" him?

I am proposing that at some point in their discussion of God's command, Adam bolstered his side of the debate by asserting

Elohim had also forbidden Adam to touch the fruit. For me, there were at least three reasons why he added this phrase:

1. He was worried what would happen to his relationship with the Lord and to his destiny if the fruit of this tree was ingested;

2. He may not have trusted his wife in this instance because she did not see the situation the same way he did. That is, he may not have totally believed that her covenant relationship with the him and the Lord meant far more to her than eating the fruit of this tree in the garden; and,

3. He may not have trusted the Lord to protect and guide his wife. That is, Adam may have questioned whether God's command and His presence were enough to deter her from inadvertently selecting fruit from this tree for food.

But what happened when Adam added this brief note? One of the patterns of our yoked relationship with the Lord is in Genesis 1:28:

> *"And God blessed them. And God said to them,*
> *'Be fruitful and multiply and fill the earth and*
> *subdue it, and have dominion over the fish of the*
> *sea and over the birds of the heavens and over*
> *every living thing that moves on the earth.'"*

The Lord teams with us to carry out His will. First, He reveals His word to us. Then, we proclaim it with our mouth. And finally, He performs it through His yoked relationship with us. As long as Adam and his wife obeyed that pattern, they *"were both naked and were not ashamed."*

But God did not put *"do not touch it"* into Adam's mouth to proclaim to his wife. Let's look at two more scriptures:

> *"Everything that I command you, you shall be*
> *careful to do. You shall not add to it or take*

from it" (Deuteronomy 12:32).

> *"For as the heavens are higher than the earth, so are my ways higher than your ways and my thoughts than your thoughts. 'For as the rain and the snow come down from heaven and do not return there but water the earth, making it bring forth and sprout, giving seed to the sower and bread to the eater, so shall my word be that goes out from my mouth; it shall not return to me empty, but it shall accomplish that which I purpose, and shall succeed in the thing for which I sent it'"* (Isaiah 55: 9 – 11)

God's ways and thoughts are higher than ours. His word will not return to Him empty but will accomplish everything He ordains for it. But Adam's thoughts (do not touch it) were not God's thoughts. God does not honor our thoughts added to His thoughts in the hope that God will also fulfill them. As soon as Adam added his thoughts to God's command, he broke his yoked relationship with the Lord over this area of his destiny. By dictating this additional way for his wife to refrain from eating the fruit, he was also accepting responsibility to fulfill his word to her.

Why Was The Serpent At The Tree?
I am proposing that, before this encounter, Adam had trained the serpent as a sentry guard to help him fulfill one of his own responsibilities. Here is the name he gave for the character of this animal.

Serpent – ₩Ⅲ ℩. The serpent would have been an excellent choice as a guard animal because it could provide a fence (Ⅲ) between the new plant life (℩) in the garden and the livestock and other beasts of the field that might consume

(**W**) it. Furthermore, Adam could convey his training objectives more easily to this creature because the serpent was able to relate verbally with him. Remember, the beasts of the earth included livestock: sheep, goats and cattle. For them to have unimpeded access to the garden would have been devastating.

The Serpent and the Woman

As this chapter opens, the very first words the serpent spoke to the woman reveal a previous disagreement Adam had with his wife:

> *"He said to the woman, 'Did God actually say,*
> *"You shall not eat of any tree in the garden"'"?*
> (Genesis 3:1b)

Here is the word order in the original Hebrew text: *"He said to the woman, 'Actually (⌒ʊ), did God say,..?'"*

Strong mouth – ⌒ʊ. Benner says that, in addition to being the word for nostrils (Genesis 2:7), it is also a word for anger indicating the person is responding passionately with flared nostrils[89]. It can be translated as a passionately concerned, frustrated or exasperated response.

The serpent was asking the woman if Adam had related God's command to her with flared nostrils.

⌒ʊ highlights the possibility that Adam was exasperated with her reluctance to agree with his point of view. If the serpent's initial question reflected an earlier heated discussion with her husband, it could provide the context for us to understand why Adam was trying to interject a phrase that would make it even harder for her to resist his plea. He may have been willing to frame their discussion using her perspective with one caveat. By inserting an extra phrase into God's command, Adam was creating one more fence around her behavior: If she didn't touch it, she wouldn't eat it. And even if she did touch it, her action would hopefully jog her memory not to eat what was in her hand.

But when Adam tried to clinch his argument with his own addition to God's injunction, he opened his wife to attacks from the enemy. I am reasonably certain that the more Adam tried to make his case after he injected this phrase into God's command, the more his wife defended her position. This altercation may have lasted for some time.

Back To The Serpent

When Adam took matters into his own hands, he abandoned a strategy that never yielded shame. (Shame means a house anchored to destruction.) As long as Adam and his wife brought their trials to the Lord asking for His solution (2:25), the result was always successful. But Adam had not sought God's guidance in his situation. And without that illumination, he could never be sure that his "solution" was sufficient to keep his house from being destroyed. How long could he hope that this one extra phrase would keep her from doing the unthinkable?

He did have one other line of defense: he could ask the serpent to guard the tree and keep his wife away from it. But this action also opened the serpent to attack from the devil, an attack that would turn this whole situation on its head.

I have tried in the next few paragraphs to weave together a plausible scenario that could account for the unfolding events recorded in the opening verses of Genesis chapter three. Please understand that there may be other ways to explain how the roles of all these participants could have interacted to provide a different plausible scenario.

One Possible Scenario

The serpent had likely gone on with its own life and may have been surprised when Adam searched it out to be a sentry guard. In the subsequent weeks and months, its association with Adam surely grew much closer than it had with the woman because Adam spent more time working and keeping the garden (2:15) than his wife did.

Its training involved identifying the other animals Adam wanted it to keep out of the garden. So, the serpent could have surmised that it was more important to Adam than were the other beasts it was guarding. Then one day, Adam asked the serpent to guard his wife from selecting fruit from the tree of the knowledge of good and evil. The woman now became one more "creature" the serpent was asked to guard by erecting a fence between this tree and any actions she might take to consume its fruit.

In light of the initial question the serpent asked the woman, Adam not only shared the command the Lord had given him, he also revealed his frustration (עֹב) that his wife didn't share his understanding of the severity for the consequences of eating the fruit. Because of its earlier training, the serpent could also identify with Adam's concern about this other "creature" eating this particular fruit.

However, the serpent was not capable of understanding Adam's yoked relationship with the Lord or with the intimacy he enjoyed with his wife. From its perspective, the two were a team working together to manage the garden. The serpent was so well trained that it was willing to do anything to support its master. It could see Adam's viewpoint because it was able to focus on the physical fruit of the tree. Why couldn't the woman see things from Adam's vantage point and cooperate with them.

What the serpent couldn't know was that as soon as Adam solicited its participation to guard his wife, Adam opened it to an attack from the devil who only wanted to destroy the destinies, not only for Adam and his wife, but for the serpent as well.

Satan and the Serpent

How could Satan alter the serpent's allegiance to Adam so that it could act against its training and deceive his wife into eating the fruit? When God warned Adam not to eat of the tree, He was relating to him as a spirit being who could discern that the penalty for disobedience was spiritual death.

The serpent was not a spirit being. It was a living soul guided by its body's senses. It had always "walked by sight" and could only relate to physical death – its soul's separation from its body. So, it was comparatively easy for Satan to point out that eating this fruit would not cause physical death to the woman in the day she ingested it (3:4). Such an idea was foolishness to the serpent!

Since this concept of dying the same day had come from Adam, then he too, must be mistaken about the real meaning of God's injunction. By using the serpent's experience as a living soul, Satan could cast doubt on Adam's ability to understand clearly what God really meant.

The devil told the serpent that God had another way of knowing good and evil that the serpent could relate to. The word for the knowledge Satan shared with the serpent was a subtle variation of the knowledge God never wanted Adam to have:

$$\dagger \mathbf{\odot} \mathsf{U} \text{ (Genesis 2:17)} => \mathbf{\odot} \mathsf{U} \, \mathsf{Y} \, \mathsf{\succ} \text{ (Genesis 3:5)}$$

$\dagger \mathbf{\odot} \mathsf{U}$ – These insights would come through the door (U) of Adam's physical senses ($\mathbf{\odot}$) and would be so conclusive that Adam would be convinced they were the true reality (✝) for how he should proceed with what he was **thinking or doing**. I shared earlier that this kind of guidance was what Paul called *"walking by sight"* (2 Corinthians 5:7).

⊝ ℧ Υ ⊐ – The **work** (⊐) a person does is anchored (Υ) to the insights that come through the door (℧) of the person's physical senses (⊝).

The devious shift between these two forms of knowledge lies in the emphasis the second one has on **work**. In the first kind of knowledge, work is **implied** as an indirect consequence of the guidance that comes through the door of a person's physical senses. In the second kind of knowledge, work is the **primary objective** of the guidance obtained through a person's physical senses: a person performs work based on the guidance he acquires in this manner.

Since the serpent was only a living soul guided by its physical senses, all this made perfect sense to it. Even though the serpent did not understand the broader ramifications of eating this fruit, it was convinced Adam was deeply concerned – so much so that Adam had demonstrated his frustration physically (⊝ ⟆).

Satan convinced the serpent that if they worked together, the serpent might be able to convince the woman that this alternative kind of knowing was how God made good and evil choices. She might even see this as a way to draw closer to the Lord. Perhaps it could also help Adam resolve his flared-nostril conflict with his wife.

A Plan For The Serpent
The first part of this plan questioned whether Adam had heard

God's instructions correctly. If he had stated the command early on in his conversation with his wife without mentioning touching the fruit, any later change to the verbiage could have called into question whether he had heard it correctly in the first place, especially if he later recounted it with his nose flared.

After all, Adam had received this additional supplement to his work order before he had named all the beasts of the field and before he got married. With all these other events that had taken place in his life prior his wife's arrival, there was a possibility she might be persuaded that he could have forgotten or misinterpreted some of God's warning.

I am sure she had heard him share other words from the Lord during the course of their "naked" relationship with their Father between 2:25 and 3:1. This occasion might have been the first time Adam had expressed his frustration to her in this manner. It may also have been the first time he had questioned her commitment to him, prompting her to "defend" her commitment to their covenant relationship in a way that made her less sensitive to his position.

Genesis 3:4

> *"But the serpent said to the woman, 'You will not surely die.'"*

Notice that the serpent was quoting Adam's version of the command, not his wife's. The serpent was directly contradicting God's command because it could only relate to physical death. Surely, the woman would not die the same day she ate the fruit.

For the woman, her encounter with the serpent may have motivated her to reexamine their interchange. In the first place, how did the serpent learn about God's command? It even knew two specific phrases of this injunction: "in dying you shall die" and "good and evil?" She had not used any of these words in her reply. Furthermore, how did it know that her husband's nose was flared unless Adam had confided in it? And why would he have shared their personal conversations with the serpent? Was there more going on that Adam was not telling her?

Since there was so much at stake for Satan during the woman's conversation with the serpent, her perceptions could also have been influenced by him to help her question her husband's motives. If she had been somewhat defensive earlier, she was likely shifting even more toward her defensive posture and away from his position.

Genesis 3:5

> *"For God knows that when you eat of it your eyes will be opened, and you will be like God, knowing good and evil."*

Satan had also been present during their private altercation. He knew that she saw her commitment to their covenant of marriage as her destiny. He also knew that neither position was complete without the other. Their unity as one flesh was paramount to their ongoing success. This last declaration from the serpent, together with her more defensive posture, was calculated to change her mind about the ramifications of knowing good and evil and cause her to question her husband.

After all, $\Theta \mathbf{U} \mathbf{Y} \mathbf{\gimel}$ was not the same word as the knowledge ($\mathbf{t} \Theta \mathbf{U}$) which carried the penalty from God. Perhaps she could not only safely eat from the tree as the serpent suggested, but the resulting knowledge ($\Theta \mathbf{U} \mathbf{Y} \mathbf{\gimel}$) gained under its supervision might potentially make her and Adam more like their Father which was one of her primary goals. (What parents wouldn't be thrilled that their children wanted to be just like them when they grew up?)

SUMMARY

In this chapter, I have carefully examined the pivotal events that set the stage for Adam's eventual disobedience. Their fate was not solely determined by her single encounter with a wily serpent. There was a slow degradation in their mutual trust and in their uncompromising appreciation of each other's different perspectives as strengths rather than liabilities. Their example stands as a cautious reminder that unity and love are commands from our Lord Jesus Christ precisely because they are extremely difficult to achieve apart from His life in us calling us to love and forgive one another.

> *"A new commandment I give to you, that you love one another: just as I have loved you, you also are to love one another. By this all people will know that you are my disciples, if you have love for one another"* (John 13:34 – 35).

Study Questions For Discussion

- Does the pattern of Creation / Corruption / Redemption indicate God had a plan to redeem Adam, his Wife and the rest of mankind well before the events of Genesis chapter three took place? Or did God have to cobble together a new plan of redemption in the spur of the moment?
  Hint: Genesis 2:1 – 3.
- Was the serpent a snake wrapped around a tree limb when it talked with Eve?
- Is "crafty" the best definition of the serpent's personality?
  - o The Septuagint translators chose γυμνοι (naked) to translate 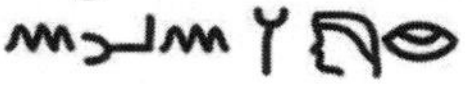 in 2:25. But they translated virtually the same word (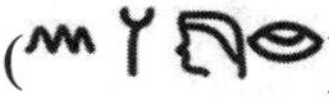) in 3:1 as φρονιμωτατος (very wise). Do you suppose their translation had any influence on our translations?
  - o Does my interpretation (tamable) align more with the context of 3:1 or are you more comfortable with "crafty?" Why?
  - o Do the last two pictograms in 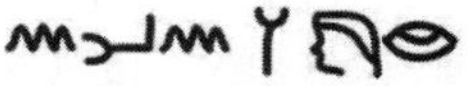 say anything about Adam's relationship with the Lord?
- Who likely added *"neither shall you touch it"* to God's original warning in Genesis 2:16 – 17? Why?
  - o How did this addition affect Adam's relationship with his wife and the serpent?
  - o Why was Adam concerned about his wife's activity in the garden?
  - o How did this phrase break the yoked relationship Adam had with the Lord?
  - o How did this **willful action** affect his wife and the serpent?
- Is there any difference between the phrase "shall surely die" and "lest you die?"
  - o Do these words reveal how Adam and his wife viewed

their commitment to God's warning?

- o Even though they were both "right," why were their perspectives incomplete?
- o How does trust and unconditional love support unity in a relationship?
- o The woman did not use the phrase "surely die." How could the serpent have known that piece of information?
- o Adam and his wife were innocent before their eyes were opened. What was their understanding of "death?"
- Why was the serpent in the garden?
  - o What was its likely role based on its name?
- Why was the serpent at the tree of the knowledge of good and evil?
  - o Did its role have anything to do with it's being at the tree when it talked with the woman?
- The word "actually" hides a meaning in our translations that is apparent from the underlying pictographic meaning. Our translation reads, *"Did God actually say."* The original Hebrew script says, *"Actually, did God say."*
  - o "Actually" is a translation of ⌒𝑏. Does this word shed any light on previous conversation(s) Adam had with his wife? Explain your answer?
  - o Does it signal a frustrating disagreement between Adam and his wife?
  - o How did the serpent know about this word?
  - o What did it tell the woman about Adam's previous relationship with the serpent?
- Why was it so hard for the serpent to understand the full implications of God's warning?
  - o Why did it say to the woman, *"You will not surely die"*?
  - o The serpent was a "living soul." Did this have anything to do with this statement to the woman?
- Why was the serpent open to influence by the devil?
  - o Why did its existence as a living soul help Satan to deceive it?

- o Why would the serpent perceive that both Adam and the woman "misunderstood" God's warning?
- o Why did the serpent agree to disobey Adam's training?
- o How did the serpent become complicit in Adam's wife's deception?
- Was there any real difference between the word for knowledge in God's warning and the serpent's word for knowing?
  - o How did a change of words play into the deceptive lie?
  - o Satan isolated the serpent to trust him more than Adam. Is there a lesson here for us?
- How was the woman deceived into going against the instructions from her husband?
  - o Did the revelation that Adam had confided in the serpent prior to this meeting have anything to do with her decision?
  - o Did the revelation that Adam had confided in the serpent with "flared nostrils" strengthen her feeling that the serpent was supporting Adam's argument?
  - o Did this sudden revelation encourage her to defend her position?
  - o Did Satan influence her decision?
- Does this pattern of deception give you any clues about how deception works in your life?
  - o Can you see that deception is a process of growing mistrust and our tendency to defend our position and not extend forgiveness and unconditional love?
  - o Can you see that it rarely is the result of an immediate circumstance?
  - o Can you see why unconditional love covers a multitude of sins?
  - o Can you see why unity cemented by Christ's love is a bulwark against the wiles of the devil?
  - o Can you see the role repentance and forgiveness play in cementing our unity in Christ's love for each other?

o Can you see why it is so uncommon in natural relationships that Jesus could say, *"By this shall all men know that you are my disciples"*?

CHAPTER 23

Genesis 3:6
The Fruit Of The Tree

"So when the woman saw that the tree was good for food, and that it was a delight to the eyes, and that the tree was to be desired to make one wise, she took of its fruit and ate, and she also gave some to her husband who was with her, and he ate. (Genesis 3:6).

PROLOGUE
In the last chapter, I shared a back story based on two seemingly innocuous words in the opening verses of Genesis chapter three. These words were translated as "actually" and "lest." But the underlying pictograms revealed a growing disagreement over the couple's commitment to God's warning in Genesis 2:16 – 17. And when the serpent asked the woman if Adam had responded with flared nostrils and used the phrases "in dying you will die" and "good and evil" – information she believed it could only have received through a conversation with her husband – she may have become even more defensive wondering why Adam had divulged their personal conversations. This gradual erosion of trust set the stage for the events of this chapter and the next.

A Theological Issue
God had not explicitly told Adam why he couldn't eat the fruit of this particular tree. Perhaps it was pleasant to the sight but was not good for food. She had depended on Adam's recol-

lection of God's warning since she wasn't there to affirm His word. He had been adamant about what he heard and had even emphasized his point by recalling with flared nostrils that they weren't even allowed to touch the fruit or they would surely die.

The serpent shared a different word for knowledge that not only demonstrated how God viewed good and evil, it also seemed to bolster her perspective. According to Adam, God had warned him that he would die if he cultivated this particular tree for food.

But after saying she would not surely die if she ate the fruit, the serpent couched God's command in an entirely different light:

> *"For God knows that when you eat of it your*
> *eyes will be opened, and you will be like God,*
> *knowing good and evil."*

There was absolutely no reference to **dying**. Perhaps, God's earlier focus on death had something to do with a very specific type of knowledge He had warned Adam to avoid. The serpent was revealing what seemed to be a new and different kind of knowing, one that God apparently used to comprehend the consequences of good and evil. And the serpent seemed to be inferring that if they acquired God's way of dealing with good and evil by eating this fruit, their eyes would be opened to a whole new level of understanding which might also bring them into a closer relationship with the One they both loved so much.

Could Adam have misinterpreted or forgotten some of the details of God's directives? After all, it had been quite a while since he had received the warning, named the creatures, underwent major surgery and gotten married. Now, she was standing with the serpent next to the tree. She could at least examine its fruit as she likely had done with the other trees in the garden.

Examining the Fruit

As I said in the previous chapter, Adam's parenthetical insertion into God's command had opened her and the serpent to an attack from Satan. He apparently did not trust her commitment to him with regard to this issue and, based on his later challenge to God ("this woman you gave me"), he may also have questioned the Lord's ability to shield his wife from the fruit.

> *"So when the woman saw (* 𐤀𐤍𐤕 *) that the tree was **good for food**, and that it was a delight to the eyes, and that the tree was to be desired to make one wise,"*

See – 𐤀𐤍𐤕. This word refers to her ability to perceive in a manner similar to the way God and her husband "saw" in Genesis 1:4 and 2:19. 𐤕 precedes "see" and indicates that the woman made a thorough analysis of this fruit. Notice that the order for inspecting this fruit is opposite from verse 2:9 indicating that her first priority was determining whether the fruit was edible:

> *"And out of the ground the Lord God made to spring up every tree that is pleasant to the sight and **good for food**"* (Genesis 2:9).

The words in 3:6 for *"good for food"* are the same as in 2:9. But the other words reveal a change of perspective. The serpent had begun its query by asking the woman if God had said they should not eat from **ANY** tree in the garden. By doing so, he was challenging her to compare the fruit from all the trees she did eat to the fruit from this one tree that she had never ingested.

She already knew what it was like to eat the fruit from the other trees. But she could only imagine what this fruit might taste like if, in fact, it was "good for food." Let's briefly compare the other words in Genesis 2:9 with 3:6:

"pleasant (ႱᴍⅢ ⸲)
to the sight (�)."

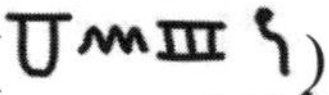

(Genesis 2:9)

Pleasant –. ႱᴍⅢ ⸲. Benner[91] says it means something of value / to delight in / desirable.

Sight –. ⴝ. The last three symbols are the same as the word for "See." The ᴹ indicates the fruit was **very** pleasant to look at.

These two criteria meant that Adam looked on these crops as valuable and desirable. Later, when the couple started eating the fruit from these trees, the sight of them naturally brought an anticipation of further delight.

"a delight (ⴝ)
to the eyes (ⴝ)."

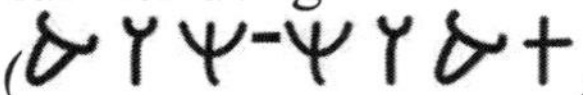

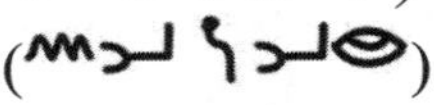

(Genesis 3:6)

Delight – ⴝ. Notice that these two "words" are mirror images of each other. Benner says[92] they represent a person longing or looking forward / sighing out of a desire – should I or shouldn't I?

Eyes – ⴝ. Benner says[93] a person protects (ⴝ) his home where new life (ⴝ) begins by keeping a close eye (ⴝ) on it.  ⴝ indicates that her physical vision to make sense (ᴹ) of what she saw was aided by the strength of God's arm (ᴹ).

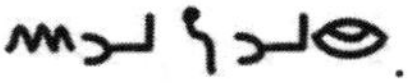

Even though Adam's wife discerned that this fruit was good for food, she could only imagine how it might compare with the other trees in the garden. I am sure she was not left alone with her thoughts.  indicates that her **delight** was more than a clinically detached analysis. She had ruled out the possibility that the fruit was toxic. Now, with some nudges from the tempter, she could almost taste it based on how it compared visually with other delicacies she enjoyed.

> *"to be desired* ()
> *to make one wise* ()."
> (Genesis 3:6)

["Pleasant" in 2:9 is the same as "desired" in 3:6]

Wise – . Benner says[94] this word signifies the ability to consider a situation with comprehension in order to be successful or prosperous. This conclusion was based on the serpent's words rather than on her ability to discern its chemical makeup. I am making this assertion because it was Adam's disobedience rather than some empirical composition of the fruit that brought death that day into their relationship with the Lord and each other.

Some equate the woman's motivation with John's admonition:

> *"Do not love the world or the things in the world. If anyone loves the world,* ***the love of the Father is not in him****. For all that is in the world—****the desires of the flesh and the desires of the eyes and pride of life****—is not from the Father but is from the world."*
> (1 John 2:15 – 16)

In order to apply verse sixteen to Adam's wife, we would need to acknowledge that her desire for this fruit suddenly outweighed **her love for their Father**. Her deep commitment to the covenant she had with the Lord and her husband had been the reason for her disagreement with Adam. So, it is hard to believe that this inspection had captured her imagination to the extent that **the love of the Father was no longer in her**.

We must be careful not to equate the woman's motivations before Adam ate the fruit and both their eyes were opened (3:7) with the desires of the **flesh** John is discussing in his epistle. (I will define "flesh" later in Chapter Twenty-Six.) I contend that this three-fold assessment helped convince her that ingesting the fruit might deepen their oneness with the Lord.

She Took The Fruit
"neither shall you touch it, lest you die."
"she took of its fruit"

Adam's wife now knew that this fruit was good for food and that it apparently looked as delightful as some of the other specimens in the garden. On the other hand, her husband had been adamant that **even touching it** would result in death. I am sure she hesitated for some time wrestling with the conflicting voices in her head between Adam's admonition and the serpent's assurances.

There was likely another voice whispering in her ear perhaps even suggesting that she could drop it quickly to avoid any prolonged exposure. The devil could also have been tempting her as she continued to look at it sighing out of a desire to experience its imagined delightful flavor and texture.

Finally, she reached in among the foliage and hesitantly plucked one from a low-hanging branch. **There! She had done what only moments before had been unthinkable.** Her own reply to the serpent meant she also realized there could be serious consequences to "turning her face toward another direction." Even though her decision was likely bolstered by her assessment of how this new knowledge might enhance their relationship with the Lord, her actions still conflicted with what she believed God had commanded her husband. If Adam's perspective was correct, she would soon find out that touching the fruit would fulfill her own words: **"lest you die."**

What Did Death Mean To Them?

For all of us who live on this side of Adam's disobedience, death is something to be feared. We can also imagine that the events leading up to death should be avoided because they can inflict pain and suffering. However, "fear" did not enter the biblical vocabulary until after Adam disobeyed the Lord.

Nevertheless, the inclusion of "death" in God's command must have meant something to them or it wouldn't have been a deterrent. The last verse of chapter two (built on 1:28) holds a key to their comprehension of the Lord's warning:

"And the man and his wife were both naked
(ᴧᴧᴣ⅃ᴧᴧ Ɣ ꛯꙆᴑ) *and were not ashamed."*

Both Adam and his wife dealt with chaos (ᴧᴧ) successfully through their yoked relationship with the Lord. As long as they followed God's way for overcoming the uncertainties they faced, they were successful and did not experience any shame. Let's see how their experience with chaos, summarized by 2:25, gave Adam an understanding of death.

Death in Genesis 2:17

Death – ✝ Ɣ ᴧᴧ ✝. Chaos (ᴧᴧ) is anchored (Ɣ) completely / finally (✝). The initial ✝ in this word heightened the finality of death. This word meant that if Adam disobeyed and ate the fruit of this tree, then any subsequent chaos he faced could not be resolved successfully. Shame would replace victory because his yoked relationship with the Lord had been broken.

Death in Genesis 3:3
Death – ꜱ Ⴒ ✝ ᴟ ✝. Chaos (ᴟ) is completely (ᴟ) anchored (Ⴒ) to new life (ꜱ) – children. The initial ✝ in this word heightened the finality of death. The woman's function as a female spirit being helps bring the differences between these two words for death into perspective.

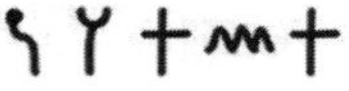

Female – Ⴓ � ● ꜱ. In Chapter Fifteen, I said the primary female role brought new life (ꜱ) through her cycles (●) into the family (⎕) as an offering of praise (Ⴓ) to the Lord. For the woman, death meant chaos would be completely anchored to her ability to bear children, nullifying her primary role as a female.

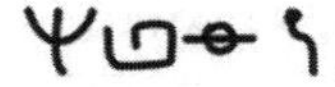

With a better understanding of how Adam and his wife might have viewed death, let's continue with our narrative.

Adam's wife steeled herself for any adverse effect on her body. But nothing happened! The fruit just sat there in her hand delectable as ever! She waited – and waited – and waited for some indication that death would somehow manifest itself in her body. But still, **nothing happened!!**

She Ate The Fruit
"and she ate"

After what must have seemed to her an interminable span of time, she slowly came to the realization that nothing horrific was going to happen. With the serpent nodding its approval and perhaps even reassuring her again that she would not die, the woman bit into the fruit. Her pent-up desire to discover its delicious taste was finally realized as juice filled her senses with mouth-watering delight!

But this next step was fraught with even more uncertainty. Surely this time, she would reap the consequences of acting against everything she had heard Adam say in his most insistent manner. But again, **NOTHING HAPPENED!!**

The serpent was right after all! Her heart filled with expectation as she hastily gathered more of this delicious fruit and hurried off to tell Adam. "This encounter in the garden would open their eyes to another kind of understanding enabling them to be more like God knowing good and evil."

He Also Ate The Fruit

> *"and she also gave some to her husband who was with her, and he ate."*

All of Adam's efforts to keep his wife from selecting this food to eat had worked against him. Instead of making his wife think twice before eating the fruit, his addendum to God's command had only reassured her after touched it that she would not die if she ate it. And instead of guarding the tree for him, the serpent had actually become a channel for tempting his wife to commit what he had tried so hard to prevent.

He Was With Her

With her – Ψмᴑ. Benner says мᴑ means "those who are with or near each other"[95]. On the surface, one could argue that Adam was standing right next to his wife during this whole encounter. But at least two circumstances mitigate against this interpretation.

First of all, when asked by the Lord if he had eaten the fruit, Adam retorted, *"The woman whom you gave to be with me, she gave me fruit of the tree, and I ate."* This would have been a very shallow defense if he had also been standing at the tree during the whole encounter. Why didn't he speak up and stop her from both touching and eating the fruit? And why didn't the Lord remind him that blaming everyone but himself was no excuse if he had, in fact, been an active participant and did nothing?

Second, when confronted by the Lord to explain her role, she replied, *"The serpent deceived me, and I ate."* She made no mention of her husband's presence with her which would have bolstered her defense. It would have also taken some of the sting out of his accusation that his disobedience was all her fault.

It is possible that Adam came looking for his wife because she was taking far longer than normal to gather food for their meal. Perhaps, he came on the scene shortly after her encounter with the serpent so that he was "with her" when she gave the fruit to him to eat.

It is also possible that "with her" only meant he was in the vicinity but not close enough to be a participant. The Israel Bible omits this phrase altogether in its translation[96] indicating that their scholars did not feel being with her played any significant role in the outcome: *"She also gave some to her husband, and he ate."*

Why Did Adam Give In?
Whether Adam came looking for her or whether she met him somewhere else shortly afterward, it is **puzzling** that he did not object to her offer especially when disobeying God's command meant so much to him. He could have said in response to the serpent's assurances that perhaps it was right. But surely, they could wait until that afternoon when they met with the Lord to ask Him if this alternative knowledge was something

to be pursued.

After all, they had approached other challenges in a "naked" posture, not trying to come up with solutions on their own. Instead, they had relied on their yoked relationship with God knowing that He would have a solution and would work with them so that the result would not end in shame.

It was this **puzzle** that drove me to seek the Lord in prayer for more than a week for the revelation of the back story outlined in the previous chapter.

There is no indication in the woman's reply that she had any doubts about the veracity of Adam's portrayal of God's command. However, her husband knew that his addition was not part of the injunction. I am asserting that as their initial discussion became more heated, his nose flared in exasperation and he inserted this phrase to clinch his argument.

A Possible Reason For His Response

Adam's "solution" did not follow the **yoked protocol** the Lord had established for dealing with the problems they faced. And because it did not reflect either God's ways or His thoughts, the Lord would not honor it as part of His own warning. The result: Adam became responsible for carrying out his way of handling his problem as I outlined in the previous chapter.

While this "minor" addition was not an act of disobedience, it did open his wife, the serpent and ultimately him to attacks from Satan. And since the devil's only objective was to steal, kill and destroy, Adam's "solution" was doomed to failure because he was now operating in the kingdom of this world instead of the Kingdom of Heaven.

Imagine what was likely going through his mind while his

wife recounted her interactions with the serpent. With each passing sentence, it became more obvious that she had already eaten the fruit. Earlier, he had thought in the heat of the moment that adding the injunction not to touch it would make her think twice before eating it.

But just the opposite had transpired. Instead of being an impediment, touching the fruit had emboldened her to take a bite. Now that she had eaten the fruit, how could he tell her that "touching" was his idea – one he had legitimized by invoking God as its author, tying her commitment to the Lord with his added phrase. And why had the serpent let him down after carefully training it and then confiding with flared nostrils the importance of keeping her away from the tree?

His "solution" was imploding right before his eyes and the consequences could seriously jeopardize his relationship with God. But then, he noticed something he had overlooked as they stood face to face. She was excited about what she was sharing with him. And furthermore, she didn't look any different to him now than when she had left earlier for the garden.

God had told him in the sternest possible manner that IN THE DAY he ate of the tree, he would surely die. His injunction implied that it would be carried out as soon as Adam ate from the tree which was the primary reason why he had been so inflexible. Now, as he examined his wife more closely, why hadn't anything tragic happened to her since she ate the fruit?

Perhaps there was something to her conviction that this alternative form of knowledge had some merit. After all, she seemed downright ebullient lauding their covenant potential for an ever-deeper commitment to each other and to the Lord! Surreptitious whispers also likely added to the hope that he wouldn't need to share his "little secret" with her. Instead, he could capitulate by agreeing with her new revelations and eating the fruit in her outstretched hand.

EPILOGUE

Adam chose to listen to the voice of his wife and eat the fruit in her hand without objecting in any apparent way. By doing so, he willfully chose to disobey God's explicit command to him. Over the course of these last two chapters, I have exposed a growing undercurrent of mistrust that eventually triggered Adam's disobedience and ultimately precipitated his vindictive response to the Lord:

> *"Have you eaten of the tree of which I commanded you not to eat?' The man said, 'The woman whom you gave to be with me, she gave me fruit of the tree, and I ate.'"*

(Genesis 3:11 – 12)

Study Questions For Discussion

- There is no indication that God gave Adam a reason why he must not cultivate the tree of the knowledge of good and evil for food. He only said that Adam must not eat its fruit. Does God have to tell us **why** He shares His will for us?
  - o Where does faith enter in to our relationship with Him?
  - o Where does trust enter in to our relationship with Him?
- The serpent "conveniently" left out all references to death in its explanation of God's knowing good and evil. Did this omission help her decision to examine the fruit more closely?
  - o Did this "new" kind of knowing open a possibility for the woman that it not only bolstered her perspective of God's injunction but it also may have given her another reason to examine the fruit more closely?
  - o Could she have concluded that acquiring this "new" kind of knowing might actually bring both of them closer to God?
  - o Could the serpent's "new" word have cast doubt on Adam's recollection of God's warning.
  - o Adam's later response to the Lord, "This woman you gave me" indicates that their earlier argument was more than an incidental disagreement. He had shown his exasperation with her position with flared nostrils. Did his posture help drive her to find a solution to their disagreements because she loved him and was motivated to find a resolution?
- Does her focus on seeing if the fruit was edible say anything about why she was examining it?
  - o After she discovered that the fruit was good for food, she recognized that it was also a delight to her eyes. She could compare it visually with other specimens in the garden she had eaten. But she hadn't tasted it as yet. Could this comparison have caused her to wonder what

it might taste like?

- o The pictograms for "delight" show a vacillation in her thinking: "Should I or shouldn't I?
- o How does temptation start?
- o Where can it lead?
- o Is temptation itself wrong?
- o How do we resist temptation?
- The serpent had said this "new" kind of knowing was how God decided between good and evil. Her final analysis could only imagine how this knowledge could affect them. Why did she believe the serpent?
- Why was her motivation different than what John described in 1 John 2:15 – 16?
- Why didn't anything happen to the woman when she touched the fruit?
- o Was she disobeying God's injunction by touching the fruit?
- Why didn't anything happen to the woman when she ate the fruit?
- o Is there any indication that God later gave her this warning?
- o Why weren't her eyes opened until Adam ate the fruit?
- The fruit was good for food sand pleasant to the eye. Was it the composition of the fruit or Adam's willful disobedience that opened both their eyes?
- The Bible says that Adam was with her when she gave him the fruit. Why didn't he stop her from touching and eating it?
- Why did Adam eat the fruit without any apparent resistance?
- o Did his "little secret" have anything to do with his decision?
- o Why didn't Adam wait until God came that afternoon in the garden to ask Him if the serpent's plan was appropriate for them?

o Did the ebullient attitude of his wife and her "cogent" explanation sway him to eat the fruit?
o Does his impulsive reasoning say anything to us about how temptation leads to disobedience?
o Did his impulsive action to trust the words of his wife only further heighten his eventual disdain for her opinion after the Lord confronted him?

CHAPTER 24

Genesis 3:7
Their Eyes Were Opened

"Then the eyes of both were opened, and they knew that they were naked. And they sewed fig leaves together and made themselves loin-cloths" (Genesis 3:7).

PROLOGUE

As we progress along this journey of posturing and disappointment, I want to assure you that these devastating events did not catch our awesome God by surprise. Some may view the angel with the flaming sword who drove our first parents out of the garden as a symbol of the separation that kept everyone in the Old Testament from walking like they did in the manifest presence of the Lord in victory without shame or fear. While there are seasons of revelation as we migrate from Genesis to Revelation, God's character has never changed! It is revealed in the eternal truth of John's proclamation to us:

*"If we confess our sins, he is faithful and just to forgive us our sins **and to cleanse us from all unrighteousness**"* (1 John 1:9).

Their Eyes Were Both Opened

Since Adam's wife ate the fruit first, why did her eyes open only after Adam ingested the fruit? Remember that when God warned Adam, *"for in the day that you eat of it you shall surely die,"* his wife was not present. This injunction was only addressed to him and there is no indication that the Lord repeated it to the woman after He made her from Adam's rib.

Hebrews 7:9 – 10 reveals a dependency that is relevant here:
> *"One might even say that Levi himself, who receives tithes, paid tithes through Abraham, **for he was still in the loins** of his ancestor when Melchizedek met him."*

The woman was still "in the loins" – as a rib in Adam's body – when God commanded Adam not to eat of this particular tree. She was not made separately from the dust of the ground like he had been. She was made out of the flesh and bone of Adam's body. So, when the Lord warned Adam, its consequences extended to the woman because she was "in his loins." Therefore, she would not be impacted by its repercussions until Adam also ate the fruit.

Were Opened – Ψ ᛐ �m·⊖·○ ✝. The root of this word is **�m·⊖·○** meaning *"their eyes were opened (○) revealing a transition (⊖ – sun at the horizon defines a transition boundary for our solar day) that separated them (�m) from what they had perceived earlier."*

When this word was associated with a person's eyes in Genesis 21:19; 2 Kings 6:17, 20; Psalm 146:8 and Isaiah 35:5, the opening of their eyes was not accomplished by the person but by the Lord. The reason this instance is translated as "were opened" is because another actor opened their eyes to discern **his kingdom**.

Here is my pictographic interpretation of this word in 3:7,
> *"After Adam ate the fruit and his disobedience was complete (✝), their eyes were opened (○) revealing that a transition (⊖) had taken*

place separating them ($\mathbf{III}$) from God's new life ($\mathbf{\jmath}$) and the revelation ($\mathbf{Y}$) of His true character."

Their disobedience separated them from God Who is the Source of all life and brought the death they both wanted to avoid. Moreover, their security that was wrapped in His unconditional love would soon be stripped away and replaced by their fear of His presence.

A Different Kind Of Day

In the first chapter of Genesis, a day was defined by the boundaries of evening and morning. God placed the evening boundary first so that we would constantly be reminded to begin our day by entering into **His Rest.**

God had warned Adam that *"in the day you eat of it"* he would surely die. Genesis 3:8 says that Adam and his wife hid from God when they heard Him walking in the garden in the cool of the **day.** The summer etesian winds in the Eastern Mediterranean are strongest in the afternoon and die down at night[97]. So, their eyes were opened sometime during that day, and it became their new reality.

The symbols for "were opened" indicate that they were transitioned ($\mathbf{\Theta}$) from the Kingdom of God to the kingdom of this world – from the Kingdom of Light to the kingdom of darkness. That transition defines an evening boundary. However, there is no rest entering into the kingdom of this world since its ruler only wants to steal, kill and destroy.

The knowledge shared by the serpent ($\mathbf{\Theta U Y \rtimes}$) focused on their work governed by and anchored to their visual discernment. Now that their eyes were opened, their work would reflect what they perceived through the filter of the kingdom of this world.

> *"For the Lord sees not as man sees: man looks on the outward appearance, but the Lord looks on the heart"* (1 Samuel 16:7).

Two Opposing Protocols

"Their eyes were opened
and they knew (⊖ ∪ Υ ↄ⌐) that (ↄ⌐Ⴞ)
they were naked (ᴟᴟᴟ⌂ↄ⌐⊖)."

My pictographic interpretation:

"With their eyes opened to the problems they faced in this distorted way, they now worked (ↄ⌐) to bring order to the predicaments coming in through the door (∪) of their eyes (⊖), a perception that anchored (Υ) and conformed (Ⴞ) their work (ↄ⌐) to the protocol (ᴟᴟᴟ⌂ↄ⌐⊖) of the kingdom of this world."

The Protocol Of The Kingdom Of This World

ↄ⌐⊖ — The first two symbols give us the priority for this protocol. "See the work" means there was now a tendency and perhaps even an urgency to bring order to the chaos he faced (ᴟᴟᴟ⌂) by the strength of his arm (ↄ⌐) relying on his own resources and the insights he perceived coming in through the door of his eyes.

This was the first time Adam and his wife had functioned within this alternative procedure. Let's briefly revisit the Lord's way of addressing chaos.

The Protocol Of The Kingdom Of God

"The man and his wife were both naked
(ᴹᴵᴹ) ﺣﻪ) *and were not ashamed."*

(Genesis 2:25)

As I shared earlier in Chapter Twenty-One, ᴹᴵᴹ ﺣﻪ is built on ﺣﻪ and means "The eyes of the man are focused on / anchored to chaos." Benner says that ﺣﻪ was the humiliating way a conquering army treated their captors, stripping them naked (see the man) so they could be sure these men could not hide anything on their person[80]. With no resources of their own, the conquered army was at the complete mercy of their adversaries.

Of course, our Lord is not a conquering enemy. He did not expect Adam and his wife to solve their own problems either through their own ingenuity or by applying their own resources. God's ways are higher than our ways and His thoughts are higher than our thoughts. Furthermore, He has unlimited resources and power to overcome any chaotic activity and restore order.

All the Lord asked Adam (and us) to do was to recognize that God, through His yoked relationship, had guided them to face the dilemma in front of them (ᴹᴵ). Their success would elevate them to a higher level of maturity (James 1:2 – 3) as they sought His will for the solution He would give Adam to proclaim believing that the Lord would fulfill His word and bring order out of the chaos by the strength of His arm (ᴹᴵ).

There are distinct differences between these two protocols. First, and most important, once Adam disobeyed the Lord's command, he stepped out of the yoked relationship he had previously enjoyed. This meant that the issues he now faced were not necessarily those brought to his attention by his Father. The prince of this world did not have Adam's best interest in mind, and he would be happy to overwhelm them with one debilitating crisis after another.

Next, notice the difference between ᴧᴧᴧᴧ and ᴧᴧᴧᴧ. The chaos was the same. But, in the first instance, God could be trusted to deal with it no matter how impossible it might seem. However, in the second situation, since the Lord was not yoked with Adam, the problem seemed much larger than it actually was, and they felt impelled to deal with it with their own resources.

> *"Then the eyes of both were opened, and they knew that they were naked. And they sewed fig leaves together and made themselves loincloths"* (Genesis 3:7).

Why Did They Do This?

The serpent had said, *"Your eyes will be opened ... knowing good and evil."* Let's look at the relationship between knowing good and evil and knowing they were naked. When their eyes were opened, instead of seeing their true character (ᴡᴅ – fire) which was the same for both of them, they were now focused on their flesh and bone attributes which were dissimilar (see 2:23). And this knowledge meant that they now began comparing the individual differences of their flesh with those of their spouse – the unique features that distinguished them as male and female.

Their observations were also enhanced by the prince of this world. So, it was not long before they started to feel shame that their "differences" were not as good as those of their mate. Since they couldn't acquire those "better" features, they decided to cover up their uniqueness so they appeared to be more alike.

SUMMARY

They could look at each other again without feeling embarrassed. Everything seemed better at least until they heard the sound of God walking in the garden in the cool of the day. Their "solution" had been guided by the circumstances they faced in the moment. Unlike the Lord, they could not weigh their decision based on how it would play out in the future. Their sense of accomplishment was suddenly in such disarray their only option was to run and hide from their Father.

Study Questions For Discussion

- How were the eyes of Adam and his wife opened?
  - When Satan opened both of their eyes, they gained a perspective that God did not want them to have. Why?
  - The pictograms for "opened" indicate that their perspective transitioned them from looking on the heart of the matter (what really mattered) to observing the exterior (what was passing away.) Does this have any association with 1 Samuel 16:7 *"For the LORD sees not as man sees: man looks on the outward appearance, but the LORD looks on the heart"*?
- The serpent's "new" definition of knowing emphasized "work" as the primary focus. That is, what Adam and his wife did would be governed by what knowledge they gained through their physical senses. This is just another way of saying they were guided by their sight instead of by faith. I shared two protocols outlined in Genesis 2:25 and 3:7. What is the difference and why is it so hard for us to live by faith as outlined in the 2:25 protocol?
- Adam chose to add "do not touch" to God's injunction. He did this before his eyes were opened. Does this indicate that Adam had the ability to choose to do things his own way **before** his eyes were opened?
  - Did death enter his relationship with the Lord, his wife and the serpent when he decided to add this phrase to God's warning?
  - What is your definition of spiritual and relational death?
- We have been told that "the fall" was when sin entered the world. When did the fall take place?
  - The word "sin" did not enter the biblical vocabulary until Genesis 4:7.
  - Adam's eyes were opened because he transgressed a command of the Lord and the seeds of his transgression were sown in chapter three. What relationship does sin

have with "the fall?"

- o There are only two kingdoms: The Kingdom of God and the kingdom of this world. How do we live in the Kingdom of God?
- How does the Kingdom of God relate to the first protocol of 2:25?
  - o If we are living in the Kingdom of God, can we choose to do things our own way?
  - o Did Adam choose to do things his own way prior to his act of disobedience?
  - o Does Adam's example give us clues about how our choices effect our own relationships?
- How did Adam's choices decouple him from his yoked relationship with the Lord in that area of his life?
  - o Did his action place him under the authority of the prince of this world?
  - o What about our decisions to choose our own course of action?
- When Adam ate the fruit, Satan opened both their eyes. How did that change their perception of their world?
  - o Did that make it much more difficult for Adam to live in the Kingdom of God?
  - o Did they focus on their inner character or their external differences?
  - o The Lord says we should not covet our neighbor's spouse or his possessions. Is coveting hard to resist because we compare the external differences of what we have with what others have?
  - o Why is it hard for us to be satisfied with what we have?
- When we step out of God's will in a certain area of our lives, it does not mean there is no path for reconciliation. God's love for us has never changed. He wants reconciliation even more than we do. What role does repentance and forgiveness play in reconciliation?

3:7 Their Eyes Were Opened   277

278   Back To The Garden

CHAPTER 25

Genesis 3:8
They Hid Themselves

"And they heard the sound of the Lord God walking in the garden in the cool of the day, and the man and his wife hid themselves from the presence of the Lord God among the trees of the garden" (Genesis 3:8).

PROLOGUE
We have witnessed a steady migration away from the yoked relationship our first parents enjoyed with Elohim. Their decisions not only made them vulnerable to the wiles of the devil, they also exchanged God's protocol for fulfilling their destiny with a substitute that relied on their own meager resources and ingenuity.

Why Did They Hide Themselves?
I have often wondered how their relationship with God changed so quickly that merely **hearing** the Lord **walking** in the garden made them bolt from His presence into the nearby trees. At one point, I thought perhaps they had mentally compared His differences with their own and realized no amount of fig leaf clothing could suffice. But that answer seemed too easy.

There are subtle clues in this passage. But I had to step away from my previous interpretations in order to appreciate what the pictograms were revealing.

> *"And they heard (𐤉𐤏𐤌𐤅𐤔) the sound (𐤋𐤉𐤏) of the Lord God walking (𐤔𐤋𐤊𐤕𐤌) in the garden in the cool (𐤇𐤉𐤒𐤋) of the day (𐤌𐤉𐤅),"*

Heard – 𐤉𐤏𐤌𐤅𐤔. The prefix (𐤅) indicates that they were actively paying attention to what they were hearing. And the suffix (𐤉) means that what they were hearing anchored their attention. So, this word means that the Name (𐤌𐤔) of the Lord God was manifested to them (𐤏) in a way that riveted (𐤉) their attention, challenging them to do (𐤅) what they heard.

𐤏𐤌𐤔 is also the Hebrew word for hear/obey – pay close attention so that you obey what you hear.

Sound – 𐤋𐤉𐤏. Benner says 𐤋𐤅𐤏 means to gather[98]. A shepherd typically gathered his sheep in the evening (𐤏) to herd them into the sheepfold. The substituteed 𐤉 focuses on the voice of the shepherd who could call them at any time during the day to guide them to another pasture. The sound Adam and his wife heard was the voice of their Shepherd gathering them to Himself to share where He was going to lead them.

Walking – 𐤔𐤋𐤊𐤕𐤌. In Genesis 17:1, the Lord appeared to Abram and said,

> *"Walk (𐤔𐤋𐤊𐤕𐤌) before me and be blameless."*

This walk was an act of praise (Υ).

In Genesis 3:8a, the Lord God was gathering them to Himself, as He had done previously on many occasions. In order for them (M) to experience the fulfillment ($\dagger$) of the next portion (Day) of their destiny with wonder and praise (Υ), they would have to follow their Shepherd ($\mathcal{L}$) and be conformed (W) to His will.

Cool – $\mathrm{III}\,\Upsilon\,\mathsf{Q}\,\mathcal{L}$. Even though this word has been traditionally translated as the cooling, summer afternoon Etesian winds that bless the Eastern Mediterranean, $\mathrm{III}\,\Upsilon\,\mathsf{Q}$ was also the Spirit of God Who hovered over the face of the deep in Genesis 1:2. Since this word is preceded by $\mathcal{L}$ (authority), I prefer to associate it with the Holy Spirit.

Day – $\mathsf{M}\,\Upsilon\,\mathsf{\backsim}$. I shared earlier that the pictograms for "Day" define the resources God commits (Υ) to a particular work ($\mathsf{\backsim}$) to convert chaos (M) into His order.

My interpretation: The Lord God manifested His Name to Adam and his wife, riveting their attention and challenging them to gather into His Presence. His familiar voice summoned them to follow Him as their Shepherd under the conforming authority of His Spirit Who was even then revealing the chaos that would be the focus for that day's activity.

> "and the man and his wife
> hid ($\mathsf{\delta}\,\mathsf{\upsilon}\,\mathrm{III}\,\dagger\,\mathsf{\backsim}$) themselves
> from the presence ($\mathsf{\backsim}\,\mathsf{\zeta}\,\mathsf{\circ}\,\mathsf{M}$) of the
> Lord God among ($\mathsf{\delta}\,\Upsilon\,\dagger\,\mathsf{\upsilon}$) the trees
> of the garden."

3:8 They Hid Themselves   281

Hid – ⟨symbols⟩. ᴗ indicates that they were actively participating. † also means they were completely involved. Benner says ⟨symbols⟩ identifies the wall in the tent[99] that separates the public from their private quarters (as you can see from the pictographic floor plan of a Bedouin tent (⟨symbol⟩)). I shared in Appendix A that adding ⟨symbol⟩ as a suffix intensifies, broadens and builds upon the word's meaning: a place of hiding / a refuge.

Presence – ⟨symbols⟩. They (⟨symbol⟩) fled (⟨symbol⟩) from the face (⟨symbols⟩) of the Lord God. This word indicates they fled from the manifest presence of the Lord – from His face. God was not some distance away walking in the garden in the cool of the day when they decided to run away and hide from Him.

Among – ⟨symbols⟩. A tent (⟨symbol⟩) completely (†) anchored (⟨symbol⟩) to strength (⟨symbol⟩). That is, a location among the trees of the garden that would hopefully provide total privacy.

My interpretation: And the man and his wife fled from the manifest presence of the Lord God desperately seeking a refuge among the trees in the garden that would hopefully provide a wall of total privacy to shield them from His face.

When the work for that day was revealed to them, instead of rejoicing like Abraham (John 8:56), eager to see how God was going to fulfill His plan through them, they scurried away searching for a sanctuary to calm the conflicting thoughts racing through their heads.

They had met with the Lord in this manner many times before. So, what could have so unnerved them this time that they turned tail and ran? The answer for me lies in Christ's call to

His disciples,

> *"And he said to all, 'If anyone would come after me, let him **deny himself and take up his cross daily and follow me**. For whoever would save his life will lose it, but whoever loses his life for my sake will save it'"* (Luke 9:23 – 24).

God never changes. His ways will always be higher than our ways whether they are revealed in Genesis or in Revelation. Nor will He share His glory with anyone else (Isaiah 42:8). It is precisely because no one has ever been able to claim credit for fulfilling His ways that they seem virtually impossible to anyone who relies on his own capabilities. Seen from our human perspective, God's destiny for us is not only impossible to achieve, it is a "cross" to bear.

We tend to spiritualize our cross as "dying to self." While that action focuses on the first criteria for following Jesus, He clarified what He meant by saying, "whoever would save his life will lose it." He is our model. His cross was real. He was willing to deny himself and to lose His life to achieve His destiny. He calls us to follow Him in like manner to achieve our destiny.

The Lord asked Abraham to offer Isaac as a burnt offering, an action that would dash his hopes for a posterity as numerous as the stars of heaven. The Lord asked Moses to confront the most ruthless dictator on the planet with only a shepherd's staff in this hand. The Lord asked Joshua to overthrow Jericho whose military was the best in Canaan and to demolish its formidable wall by simply marching around the city seven times, blowing trumpets and shouting!

SUMMARY

When Adam and his wife considered God's instructions (Light) for that Day through the lens of their new protocol, their "cross" seemed too daunting even to attempt. Now that their eyes were opened, they considered the likelihood of a good vs evil outcome weighed against their ability to achieve it through their own strength and ingenuity. They quickly concluded theirs was a hopeless situation. They must save their life at all cost and flee as quickly as possible from the One Who had revealed this "cross" to them.

Study Questions For Discussion

- What motivated Adam and his wife to hide themselves?
  - o How could their attitude toward the God they dearly loved change so quickly?
- The Hebrew word for "heard" actually means "pay close attention and obey what you hear." Why would the Lord's voice they heard so many times before propel them to flee?
- The Hebrew word for "sound" indicates that God was calling them to share what he wanted them to work on with Him. Why should this kind of revelation frighten them?
- Does my definition of "cool of the day" give you a different perspective of this encounter?
- At first glance, hearing the Lord walking in the cool of the day could mean that God was just entering the garden when Adam and his wife heard Him. Does the phrase "the presence of the Lord God" change your perspective of this encounter?
- God's ways are higher than our ways and His thoughts are higher than our thoughts. Knowing this about the Lord, what kind of challenge do you think God was calling them to perform with Him that day?
  - o Did their "new" way of knowing contribute to their decision to hide among the trees in the garden?
  - o Did they compare their meager resources against the task they perceived the Lord wanted them to do?
  - o Why were they limiting themselves to their own resources?
  - o Why didn't they run into His presence, eagerly anticipating the glorious things He was about to show them?
  - o If God's plan for our lives charts a course that is higher than what we could imagine, why are our perceptions of what God wants us to do in His Kingdom so often limited by us to what our resources can provide?

o Is our perception of God's destiny for us the kind of plan that so overwhelms us that our first inclination is to conclude that God has chosen the wrong person? (See Moses' and Gideon's initial response to God's call.)

o Jesus sent His disciples on their first short mission trip with the instructions, *"Preach, 'the Kingdom of heaven is at hand.' Heal the sick, raise the dead, cleanse lepers, cast out demons."* We can go to school to learn how to preach the Gospel. We may even raise sufficient funds to build hospitals and clinics to heal the sick. But raising the dead moves these instructions into a much higher realm than what the disciples could achieve through their own resources. Christ is still calling us to these ministries. Do they seem so daunting that we react in fear instead of anticipation?

CHAPTER 26

Genesis 3:9 – 11
Who Told You
That You Were Naked?

"But the Lord God called to the man and said to him, 'Where are you?' And he said, 'I heard the sound of you in the garden, and I was afraid, because I was naked, and I hid myself.' He said, 'Who told you that you were naked? Have you eaten of the tree of which I commanded you not to eat?'" Genesis 3:9 – 11).

PROLOGUE

The exchange between the Lord God and Adam in verses nine, ten and eleven form a watershed encounter that determined the direction for the rest of salvation history in both the Hebrew and Christian testaments. Satan had succeeded in corrupting God's crowning creative achievement convinced that Adam and his progeny would never break free from a protocol that bound them to a life of walking by sight.

God's Call

*"But the Lord God **called** (𐤀𐤓𐤒𐤉) to the man (𐤌𐤖𐤀𐤅-𐤋𐤀) and **said** to him (𐤉𐤋), 'Where are you? (𐤀𐤉𐤔𐤊)'"*

(Genesis 3:9)

ᴣ� – Both "called" and "said" were preceded by this picto-gram meaning they were each deliberate and separate acts of the Lord. That is, the Lord God first called to the man and then He said to him, "Where are you?"

Called – ᗷᑎ⊖. The first use of this word in Genesis chapter one clearly associates the **identity** or **character** of the subjects being called:

> Genesis 1:5, *"God **called** the light Day, and the darkness he **called** Night."*
>
> Genesis 1:8, *"And God **called** the expanse Heaven."*
>
> Genesis 1:10, *"God **called** the dry land Earth, and the waters ... he **called** Seas."*
>
> Genesis 2:19, *"And whatever the man **called** every living creature, that was its **name**."*

Benner says evening (⊖) was when men (ᑎ) typically called important (ᗷ) meetings[16]. So, the Lord God called Adam and his wife out of their hiding place among the trees for a critical meeting with their Father.

To the Man – ᴍᴜᗷᎽ⁻ᒪᗷ. Even though the Lord had called them many times before, this time His **call** was is-sued with strong (ᗷ) authority (ᒪ) underscoring the gravity of this special summons to the (ꙮ) man (ᴍᴜᗷ – Adam)..

To Him – ꙮᒪ. Their Father also spoke with an authority (ᒪ) that further anchored (ꙮ) Adam's attention.

Where Are You? – Ꮍ�085ᗷ. Before we examine the pictographic meaning of this word, let's see how it was used elsewhere in the Hebrew canon. In every example below, it is translated as "how" and expresses concern, disappointment and even dismay that the subject of the sentence had turned away from their former identity and was currently manifesting a different character.

Deuteronomy 1:12, *"**How** can I bear you?"*

Deuteronomy 7:17, *"**How** can I dispossess them?"*

Deuteronomy 32:30, *"**How** could one have chased a thousand?"*

Judges 20:3 *"**How** did this evil happen?"*

Isaiah 1:21 *"**How** the faithful city has become a whore?"*

Jeremiah 8:8 *"**How** can you say, 'We are wise, and the Law of the Lord is with us?"*

Jeremiah 48:17 *"**How** the mighty scepter is broken, the glorious staff."*

The first two symbols (ᴖᴑᴆ) of this word are often translated as "where" which may be the reason for its translation in verse nine. But the other interpretation fits better with the meaning here. That is, the Lord seems to be asking Adam to examine **how** his current identity, governed by his new protocol, had turned him away from his former relationship with his Father.

I also questioned "where" as a translation because the only time the Septuagint scholars translated it as "where" in the Torah was here in 3:9. In every other place, they translated it as "how." In fact, even though they translated it in Judges 20:3 as "where," the Hebrew scholars in the middle ages chose "how" instead of "where"[100] – a tradition carried forward in our modern translations.

In their previous protocol (ᴍᴑᴑᴍ ᴆ ᴆᴑᴑ), Adam and his wife contributed no resources of their own (ᴆᴑᴑ) even though they were committed (ᴆ) to bringing order out of chaos (ᴍ). The Lord guided them to work with Him in a yoked partnership. This protocol was always successful and

never yielded any shame:
- He revealed His Light / Word to them;
- They proclaimed it with their mouth (Genesis 1:28); and,
- He fulfilled His Word by the strength of His arm (ᴗᴷ) to completely transform the chaos (ᴹᴹ) they faced.

The change in their character was revealed in Genesis 3:7:

> *"Then the eyes of both were opened, and they knew (●Ʊᴷ) that they were naked (ᴹᴹᴹℕᴷ●). And they sewed fig leaves together and made themselves loincloths."*

The serpent's knowledge was a clever remake of the knowledge of good and evil God never wanted them to possess.

This new knowledge (●Ʊᴷ) made work (ᴷ) Adam's primary criteria for determining his personal sense of self-worth and accomplishment, driving him to achieve (ᴷ) a level of completion (†) that he could perceive (●Ʊ) as good.

How Are You? – (Ψℿᴷᴗ). The question, *"Where are you?"* focuses on the location where Adam was hiding. *"How are you?"* focuses on Adam's personal predicament that drove him to hide. His admission, *"I was afraid"* shows that he was anxious about this encounter with God.

Since this question is translated from only one Hebrew word, permit me to enlarge it: ***"How are you, [my son]?"*** This extension helps identify the covenant relationship Adam still had with his Father Who loved him unconditionally.

Chances are, you have asked a similar question of your child or friend when you noticed a significant change in their demeanor. It shows the loving concern of a parent who witnesses the distress of his child. This is the same attitude the Lord shared with Jeremiah as Israel was being deported to Babylon.

> *"For thus says the Lord: 'When seventy years are completed for Babylon, I will visit you, and I will fulfill to you my promise and bring you back to this place. For I know the plans I have for you, declares the Lord, plans for welfare (shalom) and not for evil, to give you a future and a hope'"* (Jeremiah 29:10 – 11).

As we continue through the remainder of Genesis chapter three, we must never forget that everything our awesome God does is always motivated by His unconditional love. This love is not a permissive indulgence but one that continually strives to develop in us a complete and balanced character that falls short in nothing! (James 1:2 – 4)

ΨШ⊐ᕑ – This word (How are you?) not only reveals Adam's change of character but how his new knowledge guided him to make those changes. When their eyes were opened, they analyzed their individual differences, determined how they could resolve those differences, and then worked to sew fig leaves into aprons to cover their uniqueness making them appear more similar to each other.

Their hard (ᕑ) work (⊐ᕐ) conformed (Ш) their individuality as male and female into an image that was more inclusive and less threatening to their newly perceived inadequacies until they were satisfied with their accomplishments and praised (Ψ) the work of their hands.

They were now guided by their sight and not by faith, exchanging the protocol of the Kingdom of Heaven (ᙏᘛᒲᙏ Ψ ᖰᎭ) for the protocol of the kingdom of this world (ⲙⲙⲛ̄ⲝⲟⲟⲃⲟ).

My pictographic interpretation

The Lord God called Adam and his wife with strong authority underscoring the gravity of this critical meeting with their Father Who loved them as His children. His objectives were two-fold. First, His call revealed the contrast between their current condition hiding among the trees in the garden and their earlier yoked relationship with Him that had yielded long-lasting victory with no shame.

Second, the word ⲩⳟⲟⲃ birthed from God's mouth revealed that He wanted Adam to analyze **HOW** he had descended into this uncertain reality. Adam was now relying on his own hard work to conform each new crisis he faced into some self-determined standard of "good" so that his efforts could yield a modicum of personal success, however brief.

Adam's Reply

> *"And he said, 'I heard the sound of you in the garden, and I was afraid, because I was naked, and I hid myself'"* (Genesis 3:10).

The translation of verse ten does not convey the change in word order of the original text. *"I heard the sound of you"* is actually *"Your sound I heard."*

This **minor** shift in word order belies a change from what they initially heard in verse eight to what riveted Adam's attention to the extent that he later reversed the order in his reply to the Lord. Let's take another look at this verse in its original word order.

> *"And he said, 'Your sound (ⳟⳑⲩⲟ) I heard (ⲟⲧⲟⲙⳡ) in the garden, and I*

was afraid (𐤀𐤓𐤉𐤀), because (𐤔𐤉) na-ked (𐤏𐤓𐤉𐤅𐤌) I was (𐤀𐤉𐤔), and I hid (𐤀𐤇𐤁𐤀) myself.'"

I have discussed the pictographic meanings for "sound" and "heard" in the last chapter. So, I will only concentrate on Adam's response to them here.

Sound – 𐤔𐤋𐤅𐤏. The sound Adam and his wife heard was the voice of their Shepherd gathering them to Himself to share where He was going to lead them.

Heard – 𐤉𐤕𐤏𐤌𐤔. The Name (𐤌𐤔) of the Lord God was manifested to them (𐤉) in a way that riveted (𐤕) their attention (𐤏). (𐤏𐤌𐤔 is the Hebrew word for hear/obey.)

Adam and his wife were very familiar with the sound (𐤔𐤋𐤅𐤏) of their Shepherd's voice. He had called them to Himself in the garden many times. Before this day, they had walked boldly into His Presence eagerly anticipating any new challenges they would face, confident that their yoked relationship would always bring success and not shame as they walked with Him by faith.

But this afternoon was different as the remaining words in this verse reveal.

Afraid – 𐤀𐤓𐤉𐤀. Strong (𐤀) throwing (𐤉) man (𐤓) strongly (𐤀). Benner says this word defines a person so afraid that he is vomiting – throwing up – in terror / panic[101].

Because – 𐤔𐤉. Conform (𐤔) to the strength of God's arm (𐤉). There was a definite reason for Adam's fear. In the original protocol, it was the arm of the Lord rather than Adam's resources that dealt with the chaos they were facing. Now, conforming to the Lord's way petrified Adam because he was filtering God's revelation through this new protocol.

Naked – ᴹ Ⴤ ᗡᔐᗢ. His new paradigm dictated that his eyes (ᗢ) were now analyzing the Lord's revelation to determine whether God's solution to the chaos (ᴹ) would provide a good outcome for Adam. Since His ways are higher than our ways, their implementation (ᔐ) by Adam (ᗡ) seemed fraught with uncertainty and fear.

Notice that the pictograms in verse 3:10 (ᴹ Ⴤ ᗡᔐᗢ) are slightly different than the ones in 3:7 (ᴹᴹ Ⴤ ᗡᔐᗢ). The chaos of the moment had indeed seemed overwhelming (ᴹᴹ). Earlier, in the heat of their disagreement, Adam had blurted out, "God said, '*Don't touch it.*'"

Those "perception" **differences** that had triggered their earlier argument still existed in their current relationship and could not be remedied by their "fig leaf loincloth" solution! Now, Adam seemed anchored (Ⴤ) to the ever-evolving scope of their **differences** (ᴹ).

I Was – ᔐᐽ ᛚᗏ. This new "life" (ᛚ) strongly (ᗏ) conformed (ᐽ) his work (ᔐ). That same life was also controlled by his new knowledge (ᗢᘮᔐ).

Hid – ᗏᗙ�m̄ᗏ. He was strongly (ᗏ) seeking a refuge for himself behind a wall (m̄) that could shield him strongly (ᗏ) inside the inner chamber of his "tent" – domain (ᗙ).

My pictographic interpretation

Now, as Adam stood before the Lord, he could no longer respond with the same innocence and openness that previously characterized their relationship. His eyes had been opened to a new protocol that did two things: First, it gave him the ability to determine the relative value of a situation – whether from his point of view it was good or evil. Second, this perspective about what was of value literally determined what Adam did based on the relative merits of what he perceived in the moment.

God's ways are always higher than our ways. So, the Lord perception of what was good for Adam came from a much broader perspective than what Adam understood in the moment. Through the lens of his new knowledge, the Lord's revelation about how to face this new situation looked to him like the most vulnerable way he could become involved. Conforming to the Lord's hand, as filtered through his new protocol, terrified Adam because he was now guided by his sight instead of by his faith. That is why he had earnestly fled from the face of the Lord.

The Lord's Response

> *"He said,*
> *'Who (ᕒᆜᎷᎷ) told (ᑌᕒᆜᎵᎿ) you (Ⴃ ᒪ)*
> *that (ᕒᆜ᎝) you*
> *were naked (ᎷᎿᒲᕒᆜᎹ)?*
> *Of the tree of which I commanded*
> *you (ᎳᕒᆜᛏᕒᎿᏝ)*
> *not (ᕒᆜᛏᒪᎍᒪ) to eat*
> *have you eaten?'"* (Genesis 3:11)

Who – ᕒᆜᎷᎷ. Mighty (ᎷᎷ) Work (ᕒᆜ). Adam's self-worth was directly influenced by the work (ᕒᆜ) he did that was guided by the knowledge (⊖ ∪ ⊃⅃) he gained through his own disobedience.

Told – ∪⊃⅃�7Ψ. The [one] (Ψ) lifting up (7) work (⊃⅃) to Adam's door (∪).

You – ⅏ ℓ. Authority (ℓ) to conform (⅏).

This is just the opposite of ℓ ⅏ – conform to authority, tamable. Adam had been totally tamable being yoked to the Lord in the first protocol. Now he was attempting to tame/conform the situations he encountered by his own authority in the second protocol.

That – ⊃⅃⅏. Conform (⅏) work (⊃⅃).

Naked – ᴍ Υ ⵕ⊃⅃⊖. This new protocol.

My pictographic interpretation
Who is the one lifting up a mighty work to Adam's door (bringing it to his attention), **who** also has the authority to conform his work to this new protocol?

Commanded You – ⅏⊃⅃✝⊃⅃Υℾ. Command (Υℾ) work (⊃⅃) complete (✝) work (⊃⅃) conformed (⅏). This string of symbols is much more extensive than the one issued in Genesis 2:16 (Υ ℾ⊃⅃). That word for command said that God, by the strength of His arm (⊃⅃), would pull Adam toward (ℾ) an anchor (Υ) for his life.

Since Adam had disobeyed this command, God birthed a more extensive meaning. *"Obeying my command (Υ ℾ) would have insured that your work (�) would have been successful (✝) because it (�) would have been conformed (Ш) to My will."*

Not – � ✝ ℓ Ꙭ ℓ . Once again, this string of pictograms is much more extensive than in Genesis 2:16. ᛒ ℓ is the word for "NO." Its meaning is just the opposite of one of the names for God (ℓ ᛒ) Who teamed with them to provide strong (ᛒ) guidance as their Shepherd (ℓ).

ᛒ ℓ reveals a yoked relationship with an adversary who controlled (ℓ) them strongly (ᛒ). Now that Adam had disobeyed the Lord, there was **an adversary who controled his life strongly**. This more extensive string of symbols means *"an adversary with authority (ℓ) over Adam's tent (Ꙭ) and with authority (ℓ) over all (✝) his works (�)."*

My pictographic interpretation
"If you had obeyed my command, the strength of My arm would have guided your work to be completely successful because your work would have conformed to my will in accordance with our original protocol. But now that you have disobeyed my command and eaten the fruit, **you have an adversary who has authority over your tent and over everything that you do.**"

Who Is This Adversary?
If you think this adversary is Satan, your hunch is only partially true. Let's take a closer look at the sentence "you have an adversary who has authority over your tent and over everything that you do." The one who had authority over Adam's **tent** – his body – was his **soul**. I said earlier that we are spirit beings living in a tent (body) animated and physically sus-

tained by our soul.

God never intended for Adam's soul to have the same authority over his body that the souls of animals exercised over them. He was created as a spirit being whose life was not dictated by his soul to meet the needs and desires of his flesh but by every revelation (word) that came from the mouth of God (Matthew 4:4).

As long as Adam obeyed the Lord, their yoked relationship guided and empowered him to manifest his destiny in the Kingdom of Heaven through a protocol that always brought victorious, abundant life with no shame.

However, with disobedience came the calamity of God's stern warning "in dying you shall die." Death separated Adam from his intimate, open relationship with the Lord, with his wife, his body – **and his soul**. Through disobedience, he migrated from the guidance and protection of the Kingdom of Heaven to the destructive oversight of the prince of the kingdom of this world who would try to obliterate his destiny and self-worth, and replace it with fear and shame.

The serpent had assured his wife that they would not die – a half-truth wrapped in the deceptive possibility for more intimate knowledge of their Father. But the father of lies had only one objective: to steal, kill and destroy all the blessings they enjoyed.

As soon as Adam disobeyed the Lord, he stepped away from his yoked relationship and into the kingdom of this world, giving Satan permission to open their eyes to perceive the world as he saw it. Not only were the eyes of their spirits opened, their physical eyes were opened as well to this new "reality."

Adam's brain and nervous system were animated by his soul. So, this new knowledge also enabled his soul to apply its own mental and emotional capabilities for evaluating the relative merits of everything it perceived through its physical senses. And since Adam also possessed this knowledge, it was nearly impossible for him to disagree with his soul that walking by faith was as beneficial as walking by sight. Of course, Satan also reinforced this new knowledge.

Our Adversary – Our Flesh

In Romans chapter seven, Paul identified this adversary as his flesh, controlling him through his bodily members and making him a slave to sin.

> *"For we know that the law is spiritual, but I am of the flesh, sold under sin. For I do not understand my own actions. For I do not do what I want, but I do the very thing I hate. ... For I know that nothing good dwells in me, that is, in my flesh. For I have the desire to do what is right, but not the ability to carry it out. For I do not do the good I want, but the evil I do not want is what I keep on doing. Now if I do what I do not want, it is no longer I who do it, but sin that dwells within me. ... For I delight in the law of God, in my inner being, but I see in my members another law waging war against the law of my mind and making me captive to the law of sin that dwells in my members."*
>
> (Romans 7:14 – 23)

When Paul said *"Nothing good dwells in me, that is, in my flesh,"* he was not just talking about his physical body but about the members of his body whose needs and desires were more important to his soul than his own desires to live a godly life. His soul exerted its will to satisfy its member's demands and became an adversary waging war against Paul's will to do what to him was right according to the law of God.

This was a battle between two opposing ways of life: the law of God vs the law of sin. "Sin" is not merely the singular version of "sins." That is, "sin" is not a single transgression as opposed to multiple transgressions (sins). "Sin" is a way of life that forced its will on Paul making him do the very things (sins) he detested.

Moreover, the law of God is a life of faith. Our soul cannot comprehend either the revelations or the path where the Lord wants to lead us. So, it resists a life of faith because it cannot perceive how it can fulfill our destiny without jeopardizing its own survival.

This was the dilemma Adam faced in the garden that fateful day. There are only two kingdoms: the Kingdom of God with His protocol, and the kingdom of this world with its protocol. Satan thought Adam and his progeny would never be able to break from his alternative protocol because he was convinced it bound them to a life of walking by sight. But the remainder of salvation history is replete with men and women who overcame the prince of this world and lived victoriously in the Kingdom of God.

What was the Lord's plan to set Adam (and the rest of us) free to walk by faith and not by sight? *"Who told you that you were naked?"* God lovingly asked Adam to examine the reasons he had felt so compelled to DO something on his own in the heat of the moment without first asking his Father for His solution. That was the pattern Adam had followed before, and it was always successful even though the Lord's solutions far exceeded anything he could imagine.

When the Lord had asked him to DO anything, Adam had always approached the work in a posture of REST because his Father had already finished the work by the strength of His arm before it was begun.

The fear Adam felt was actually initiated by his soul's fear from having these new responsibilities suddenly thrust upon it. His Father wanted to redeem Adam AND his soul from the lie that their success and self-esteem were somehow dependent on their own resources and solutions.

SUMMARY

The fear (𐤀𐤉𐤍𐤀) was gut-wrenching and real to Adam. But the original protocol would still work if he could trust in the Lord's faithfulness and love with all his heart and not rely on his newly-gained understanding as exemplified in Proverbs 3:5 – 8:

> *"Trust in the Lord with all your heart, and do not lean on your own understanding. In all your ways acknowledge (𐤏𐤃𐤉) him [Seek direction from the Lord instead of relying on directions from your soul based on the information coming in through your physical senses], and he will make straight your paths. Be not wise in your own eyes [the knowledge gained by sight]; fear (𐤀𐤉𐤍) the Lord [your soul will never be comfortable with the way God is guiding you to fulfill your destiny], and turn away from evil (𐤏𐤓) [turn away – repent – from being guided by your sight]. It will be healing to your flesh and refreshment to your bones."*

Study Questions For Discussion

- I called this segment of scripture a watershed encounter between the Lord God and Adam because it occupied the middle portion of the pattern I described earlier: Creation / Corruption / Redemption. Do you agree with this assessment?

- We witnessed the creation of mankind in the first two chapters of Genesis. I also said that these chapters identified the first covenant God made with us before sin entered the world. How does the entire rest of scripture from the rest of Genesis through Revelation redeem mankind and restore this first covenant?

- Satan thought that mankind would never be able to break free to walk by faith. How were the Old Testament believers able to overcome this hurdle?

  o How were both Enoch and Elijah able to live their lives in such a way that the Lord took them home without experiencing physical death?

  o We saw that the Word was with Elohim in the beginning and that nothing was made without Him. Jude says, *"Now I want to remind you, although you once fully knew it, that **Jesus**, who saved a people out of the land of Egypt, afterward destroyed those who did not believe."* Jesus said, *"For if you believed Moses, you would believe me; for he wrote of **me**."* He also said, *"I am the way, and the truth, and the life. No one comes to the Father except through me."* Has the last Adam been there from the beginning saving all who sought Him?

- The biblical meaning of "called" identifies the character of what is called. In this passage, we might focus only on the seriousness of this encounter and miss the meaning of "call." God's call affirmed Adam's character, and His unconditional love sought them out. Can you see that no matter how far you flee from Him, He calls out the character He sees in you and seeks you out to redeem you beyond anything you can imagine?

- Instead of translating ＹШ⊃Ⴆ as "Where are you" I translated t his single word as "How are you, [my son]?" I gave examples of how this word is used in other parts of the Hebrew Testament. The Septuagint scholars only translated it here as "Where…" Do you agree with them or with its usage in the rest of the Scripture?

  o Did God know where Adam was hiding?

  o Is "Where are you?" more of a response from a human parent who is searching for a child but doesn't know where he is hiding?

  o Which interpretation fits better with God's unconditional love for Adam?

  o Have you ever expressed concern for your child or friend by saying "How are you?'

  o What motivated you to say that phrase?

  o The Bible says, *"Those whom I love, I reprove and discipline."* How does this scripture reveal God's motivation in dealing with Adam?

  o Why must we guard against reading our "righteousness" into God's response?

- If this new kind of knowledge focused on their ability to accomplish a task, how would their success or failure affect their self-esteem?

  o How would a query "Where are you?' be received if their self-esteem was battered?

  o How would a query "How are you, my son? Be received?

- The Bible says that man looks on the outside but God looks on the heart. How does this scripture help explain why Adam and his wife clothed themselves with fig leaves?

- How did their new ability to compare their differences as "good" or "evil" result in their desire to clothe themselves?

  o The white latex sap that seeped out of the stems of fig leaves they removed from the plant was very irritating to their skin. Adam and his wife both wrapped their loins in newly picked fig leaves which surely resulted in almost constant itching and scratching. Did this discomfort indicate how determined they were to sew these leaves into loincloths?

- o Did the comparison of their differences result in personal shame or condemnation of their spouse?
- o How did God's query to Adam, "Who told you that you were naked?" address your answer?
- o Did making fig aprons solve all their relational issues?
- Why was Adam so focused on the "sound" he "heard" in the garden"
- How afraid was Adam?
- Why was Adam afraid?
- Was Adam able to conform his work according to this new protocol?
  - o $\cancel{b}$ $\mathcal{L}$ says that Adam was being controlled strongly. Who was controlling him?
  - o The words for "NOT eat" add a $\mathbf{\sqcup}$ after $\mathcal{L}$. This addition means that the authority was over Adam's "tent." What is Adam's tent?
  - o What had control over Adam's "tent"?
  - o How does Paul's description of his flesh speak to this text?
  - o What is our flesh?
- What role did Adam's soul play?
- How does it control us so much that Paul lamented, *"Wretched man that I am – who can deliver me from this body of death?"*
  - o Why was Adam's soul afraid?
  - o What perspective limitations did Adam's soul have as compared to Adam as a spirit being?
- Was there a way for Adam and his wife to return to living in the Kingdom of God?

CHAPTER
27

Genesis 3:12 – 13
A Pattern Of Blame

"The man said, 'The woman whom you gave to be with me, she gave me fruit of the tree, and I ate.' Then the Lord God said to the woman, 'What is this that you have done?' The woman said, 'The serpent deceived me, and I ate.'"

(Genesis 3:12 – 13)

PROLOGUE

If you are wondering how Adam's relationship with the Lord and his wife could have soured so quickly, you are not alone. How could he lash out at the two relationships that had meant so much to him? The answer lies in the series of events I wrote about in Chapters 22 – 26 that contributed to the gradual deterioration of his demeanor culminating in his disobedience.

I also said that his soul became an adversary after their eyes were opened. In order to better understand the influence a person's soul can have on his life, consider that every living creature except man is totally guided by its soul. Our pets, livestock, the fish in the lakes, rivers and ocean; the animals of the forests, mountains and plains; and the birds of the air – all live out their existence guided by their soul to navigate the many challenges they face and to procreate according to their own kind.

We alone are unique. We are spirit beings that possess a mind, will and emotions who dwell in a body whose physical life is sustained by our soul that also has a mind, will and emotions. Our bodies and souls are also different from the animals. God formed their bodies out of the ground (2:19) instead of from the dust of the ground (2:7). Further, the souls of all these creatures were made by Elohim and His Son (1:20 – 21, 24) without the special attention documented in 2:7. Since we live in our bodies, we have control over how our bodies move which is unlike the total control an animal's soul has.

There is another critical difference to consider in the relationship we as spirit beings have with our soul. Genesis 1:27 says that we were made in the image of God as male and female. That is, we reflect the relational image of God. Neither male nor female alone reflects this relational image.

When the Lord God brought his helper to the man, Adam called her "woman" (ᵞWᐂ) for she was taken out of "man" (W᠎ᐂ). The unique pictograms in their identity (ᵞ᠎) were also the first two pictograms of the Lord's name (ᵞ ᵞ ᵞ᠎) indicating that the woman, the man and the Lord were bound together in a betrothal relationship (See Chapter Twenty, The Marriage Covenant). Therefore, their oneness with God and their unity with each other was contingent upon the compassionate manifestation of their identity within this three-fold relationship.

Our soul's association with our body does not reflect the relational image of God. That is, our souls are either male or female and our bodies are either male or female. Our individual soul is only associated with our own body. Its relational connection with others is through its physical senses. Notice the words in Genesis 2:7 God used to describe the trees He made to grow,

*"And out of the ground the LORD God made to spring up every tree that is **pleasant** to the **sight** and good for food."*

We can conclude that these trees were sensually pleasant to Adam's soul. We can infer that at least initially, Adam's relationship with his wife was also pleasant. However, the opening verses of Genesis chapter three point to a growing crescendo of disagreement and worry. These unpleasant encounters generated increasing physical and emotional stress for **both** of them. Adam's "solution" not to touch the fruit may have temporarily eased **his** anxiety. But it also likely encouraged his wife to carefully examine the fruit to **see** if it was indeed "good for food" in order to bolster her point of view.

Before their eyes were opened, their relationship with their soul was secondary to their relationships with each other and the Lord. But all that changed with Adam's disobedience transforming their souls into adversaries that could control their perception of reality (See Romans 7:15 - 25).

As shared earlier, the acquisition of the knowledge of good and evil gave their souls a comparative capability. And since each soul was only concerned with the welfare of its own body, everything encountered through their senses was now reevaluated according to how much pleasure it brought to them.

The Lord God had said earlier that it was not good for Adam to be alone. But "alone" is a relational concept and was difficult for his soul to relate to because Adam did not exhibit any "feelings" of loneliness. From his soul's perspective, Adam's interactions with the garden were just fine before the woman came into their life. Adam certainly would not have disobeyed the Lord if his wife had not been present to complicate things!

Also, from his soul's perspective, God's counsel was looking more and more suspect. Adam's obedience to God's search for a helper fit for him had precipitated into the gut-wrenching fear he was now experiencing. Surely the two of them should share some of the blame for his condition! Let's examine Adam's response to the Lord.

"The man said,
   'The woman whom you gave (Ψ † † ٦)
      to be with me (ᴄᴜᴍᴏ),
         she gave (Ψ ٦ † ٦) me (ᴄᴌ)
            fruit of the tree, and I ate.' "

Gave – Ψ † † ٦ and Ψ ٦ † ٦. The basic Hebrew word is ٦ † ٦. As I shared in Appendix C, the suffix Ψ intensifies the meaning. Adam added an extra † to further heighten his growing exasperation with God's gift for him.

Gave to me – Ψ ٦ † ٦ ᴄᴌ. We have seen many times that when ᴄ precedes a word, it means that the person who is the subject of the sentence is actively participating in the action. In this sentence, "gave me" **ends** with a ᴄ indicating that the pictogram preceding it was actively participating with Adam[103].

Ψ ٦ † ٦ is tightly linked to ᴄᴌ represented by the bar symbol that joins them. To get a more complete picture of this interaction, consider the Lord's words later from verse 17,

"Because you have listened to the voice of your
wife and have eaten of the tree."

The Hebrew word for "listened" means to hear/obey. Adam's wife must have shared with him the reasons why she had eaten

308   Back To The Garden

the fruit. So, Adam was trying to convince the Lord that his authority (𐤋) for performing the work (𐤃) of eating the fruit came from hearing and obeying his wife's explanation of her own actions (𐤅𐤔𐤕𐤔).

With Me – 𐤃𐤅𐤌𐤏. As shared above, the 𐤃 after this word means it actively participates in Adam's life. 𐤅𐤌𐤏 is very similar to the word for both pleasant and desired (𐤅𐤌𐤔). Benner says that 𐤅𐤌 means "water at the door[104]." A carpet was placed at the entrance of a man's tent along with a bowl of water for washing feet[105].

This was undoubtedly a pleasurable experience. Adam was asserting that the woman God gave to be **with him** was not providing the kind of ongoing **pleasurable** experiences he (and his soul) **desired** in a manner similar to recurring foot washings.

> *"Then the Lord God said to the woman, "What is this that you have done?"*

The Lord was challenging the woman to reevaluate the reasons she had eaten the fruit and why she had been so assertive that Adam go along with her conclusions. But the stinging accusations from her husband must have left her reeling.

Even after their eyes were opened, they had continued to do everything together: sewing fig leaves, making loincloths, hiding from the presence of the Lord and returning to answer questions. But now, he was blaming her for his deteriorating relationship with the Lord, and was even intimating that he would have been better off without her in his life. The intimacy of their covenant had degenerated into a purely "**soul**" relationship with each other.

"The woman said, "The serpent deceived (ͻ𝒟ᘔ⅃W) me, and I ate.""

The festering animosity evident in Adam's response is absent in this instance. The woman did not accuse either her husband or the Lord which seems to imply that she did not harbor a similar degree of resentment.

Deceived – ͻ𝒟ᘔ⅃W. At the heart of her decision to eat the fruit and also to give it to her husband was the conviction that by doing so, they could obtain the kind of knowledge God possessed (℗Ʊᘔ⅃). This new knowledge would enable their work to be guided by the information that came in through the door of their eyes.

My pictographic interpretation

Adam's wife consumed / accepted (**W**) that the serpent's description of God's way to work (**ᘔ⅃**) through a problem could also be a strong (**𝒟**) new lifestyle (**ͻ**) for both of them. Of course, she could only imagine what that new lifestyle might bring until their eyes were opened and she discovered its true nature – the serpent had deceived her.

SUMMARY

Like Adam, she was now being guided by her soul, and the serpent's proposal was the only kind of guidance her soul understood. And, since she also saw her reality through this new lens of the knowledge of good and evil, she could argue that the serpent should be culpable for this deception that had plunged both her and her husband into chaos.

The knowledge of good and evil was also keeping them from confessing what they had done. From their perspective, admitting to their disobedient actions would not result in as **favor-**

able an outcome as asserting that others shared in the blame by creating the circumstances which led to their disobedience.

Unfortunately, they were relatig to each other and God through their physical senses controlled by their soul whose wellbeing was more important to it than their relational commitments to each other. Unconditional love, trust, fellowship and a child-like innocence had been replaced with suspicion, isolation and fear.

Study Questions For Discussion

- Why did Adam accuse the Lord and his wife for being the cause of his disobedience in words that implied he was angry and perhaps even somewhat hostile?
- Why do you feel the Lord spoke to the woman without commenting further on Adam's accusation?
  o Was He agreeing that the woman was the cause of Adam's disobedience?
  o Was He agreeing that He was also the cause of Adam's disobedience?
  o Is there a lesson for us not to "take the bait" and become embroiled in an argument generated by the accuser's soul?
- The Bible says we do not war against flesh and blood but against principalities and powers in heavenly places. If we respond to the person's heated defense, are we arguing against flesh and blood?
  o Can we truly win that argument if we respond "in the flesh"?
- How should we respond in these situations?
  o Isaiah 53:7 – 8; Matthew 27:11 – 14; Mark 15:1 – 5 and John 19:9 – 12a describe Jesus' response to His accusers. Notice Jesus' response to Pilate in John 19:11. Who did Jesus rely on to defend Him? Does Acts 2:23 give any reason why Jesus did not defend Himself?
- What role does the Holy Spirit play in our defense?
  o John 16:8 – 15.
  o Isaiah 51:15 – 16; Jeremiah 1:7 – 10 5:14.
- Why must we be sensitive to the Holy Spirit's leading so we know when to speak and when to keep silent?
  o Why is it so easy for us to respond out of our soul's perspective?
  o What guides our soul to make decisions?
  o Is our soul relational in the same manner as we are as

spirit beings?

- We are made in God's image as male and female. So, we are attracted to a relationship with God and with the opposite gender. Our soul is not relational in the same way. Does this shed any light on why a person, guided by his soul, might be attracted to the same gender?
- How can such a relationship reflect the image of God?
- We do not war against flesh and blood. Does the prince of this world want us to reflect his image instead of God's image?
- We were made as spirit beings before God formed our bodies in our mother's womb. Our spirit being has a gender just like our bodies have gender. Satan is a liar and the truth is not in him. Is a same-sex marriage based on God's truth or Satan's lies?
- God said Adam "listened" to the voice of his wife. What does "listened" mean?
- Does this statement refute Adam's assertion that his decision to disobey God was her fault?
  - o Was God saying, "You chose to obey your wife instead of obeying Me"?
  - o Did God give His warning in Genesis 2:16 – 17 to Adam or to both Adam and his wife?
  - o Why were their eyes not opened until Adam ate the fruit?
- Did the woman accuse her husband or the Lord as Adam did?
- What does "deceived" mean to you?
  - o Why did Satan have permission to influence both the serpent and the woman?
  - o Was Adam guided by his sight when he made the decision to add "do not touch" to God's warning?
  - o Why couldn't Adam see where his impulsive statement would lead?
  - o Does his example show us why we must seek counsel from the Lord about decisions that will affect our future?

o Was the woman also culpable for disobeying God's warning?
o If we choose to disobey God's word, can we hope that God will somehow change His mind based on the circumstances as **we** see them?
- Do Numbers 23:19 and Malachi 3:6 speak to this issue?

CHAPTER 28

Genesis 3:14 – 15
Enmity

"The Lord God said to the serpent, 'Because you have done this, cursed are you above all livestock and above all beasts of the field; on your belly you shall go, and dust you shall eat all the days of your life. I will put enmity between you and the woman, and between your offspring and her offspring; he shall bruise your head, and you shall bruise his heel.'"

(Genesis 3:14 – 15)

PROLOGUE

Much has been written about these two verses because they conclude with what many see as a prophetic declaration that the Lord would redeem Adam and his wife, and ultimately mankind. The Holy Spirit also emphasized their importance by inspiring Moses to write a single ⦔ after verse fifteen (See Appendix B).

Two Kingdoms

Before I examine the pictographic meaning of several of these words, it is worth repeating that we live in only two kingdoms: The Kingdom of God and the kingdom of this world. While we walk by faith, we live in the Kingdom of God and enjoy His blessings and protection as He guides us to fulfill our destiny.

From the very first verse of Genesis, I have depicted our fellowship with God as a yoked relationship walking victoriously with Him without shame or fear. But I have also indicated that if we make decisions based on our own perspective then, in those areas, we step away from our yoked relationship and away from His help, guidance and protection. To that extent, we also step into the domain of the prince of this world whose only goal is to destroy us and everything the Lord has prepared for us.

In the preceding chapters, I explained that when Adam tried to solve his own problems instead of seeking his Father's advice, he left the protection of the Kingdom of God he had previously enjoyed and exposed himself, his wife and the serpent to the kingdom of this world. This exposure made all of them vulnerable to the deceptive lies of the devil that culminated in Adam's disobedience. It also made them responsible for their own actions.

The Serpent's Culpability

The same Hebrew word for "done" describing the actions of the woman in verse 13 is also used for the serpent's involvement in verse 14. This association, along with God's pronouncement relegating the serpent to life on its belly eating dust all the remaining days of its life, confirms that the Lord was primarily focused on the serpent's complicit role in her deception.

God's Response To The Serpent

"The Lord God said to the serpent, 'Because you have done this, cursed are you above all livestock and above all beasts of the field;"

Adam had recognized its capability as a premier guard animal working closely with him. But by agreeing to participate in the woman's deception, it forfeited its own destiny as a beast of the field.

"Because you have done this," – because the serpent willingly participated in deceiving the woman – "cursed are you." Notice that the Lord did not say, "I curse you." The serpent's own culpable actions uncoupled it from its yoked relationship with the Lord and placed it under the authority of the prince of this world. When the Lord God SAID these words to the serpent, He BIRTHED them into reality meaning that the serpent's cursed status was now manifested in its life. Let's consider the pictograms for "cursed."

Cursed – ᴎ Y ᴎ♂. The basic word is ᴎᴎ♂. When Hebrew repeats something (ᴎᴎ), it places an emphasis on it. So, the strength (♂) of man (ᴎ) anchored (Y) to man (ᴎ) meant that the serpent would now have to rely on its own strength instead of the strength it gained from its yoked relationship with the Lord.

The serpent's pride had elevated it to a self-deceived position above all livestock and all the breasts of the field. Its mobile capabilities to guard had been enabled by the Lord as well as its ability to converse with Adam and the woman (Numbers 22:28 – Balaam's donkey). Since its willing involvement had shifted its allegiance from the Kingdom of God to the kingdom of this world, these capabilities were no longer available, and it now had to live by its own wits (ᴎ Y ᴎ♂).

Its willful complicity had demoted it to a humiliating life on the ground that severely limited its mobility and stature. And the trusted role it held in the garden was now replaced by enmity that separated it and its offspring from the woman and her descendants. Never again would they be able to deceive anyone as willing mouthpieces of Satan.

> *"Dust you shall eat all the days of your life."*

Dust — Unlike Adam and his wife, the serpent was not made of the dust of the ground. It could only eat the dust as a constant reminder of the relationship it once had with them.

> *"I will put enmity between you and the woman, and between your offspring and her offspring; he shall bruise your head, and you shall bruise his heel.* ⟨symbol⟩ *"*

We know from the rest of scripture that Adam and his wife were not only dealing with a beast of the field. The prince of the power of the air (Ephesians 2:2) was behind these attacks and was also culpable. The emphasis of the ⟨symbol⟩ at the end of this verse, elevates this exchange to include Satan who orchestrated this deception.

Enmity – ⟨Hebrew⟩. ⟨Hebrew⟩ is the word for father: strong (⟨symbol⟩) tent / house (⟨symbol⟩). Benner says this word means "hostile to the enemy of the family." The father was the defender (⟨symbol⟩) of the family – his tent (⟨symbol⟩). Tents were held up by one or more poles with a point at one end that could be used as a spear to defend the family[107].

Put – ⟨Hebrew⟩. Strongly (⟨symbol⟩) destroy (⟨symbol⟩) the work (⟨symbol⟩) of the sign (⟨symbol⟩). The sign represented the work (⟨symbol⟩) of the serpent and his seed. The Lord God put enmity between the woman and the serpent and between her seed and his seed. That is, He empowered Adam to be the hostile enemy of the serpent and his seed to strongly destroy the work of the serpent and his seed.

Offspring – ⊘⟟𐤓 . A cudgel (𐤓) was an instrument the farmer (𐤍) recognized (⊘) to harvest grain. This grain became the seed for the next year. Children were also perceived (⊘) as seeds (offspring) planted by the family (𐤍) and "harvested" (𐤓) to produce the next generation. The serpent's offspring (𐤔⊘𐤍𐤓) would conform (𐤔) to the serpent. The woman's offspring (𐤉⊘𐤍𐤓) would bring praise (𐤉) to the woman.

Bruise – ⊙𐤉𐤔. Devour / Bite (𐤔) anchored to / focused in (𐤉) the mouth (⊙). As you can see, "bruise" is a somewhat misleading translation. Benner says it defines the biting strike of a serpent[108] which fits more closely to the context of this verse.

Head – 𐤔𐤏𐤉𐤍. Benner says this word means "venom[109]," the sacks of venom are anchored (𐤉) in the head (𐤍) of the serpent allowing it to deliver a strong (𐤏) bite (𐤔).

Heel – 𐤋𐤏⊙. See (⊙) the cycle (𐤏) of the tent (𐤋). These pictograms indicate that this activity in one's "tent" is ongoing or repetitive. Benner says[110] by biting the heel of a person, his ability to function is constrained. He also says this word can mean "subtlety" as appearing to be a hidden constraint.

My pictographic interpretation

The Lord God said to the serpent, "I am equipping Adam and the heads of his families after him to rise up as a barrier of enmity – a wall of hostility – between the woman and her seed and between you and your seed. This hostility extends to the demonic "offspring" of the one who deceived you. Their subtlety and venom will continually attempt to constrain her offspring from achieving the full potential of their destiny. But one of her seed will be empowered by Me as your hostile enemy to defend her offspring. He – one born of a **woman** – will strike a lethal blow to the venomous head of the one who deceived you, strongly defeating him and his seed."

The Serpent Called The Devil And Satan

"And the great dragon was thrown down, that ancient serpent, who is called the devil and Satan," (Revelation 12:9).

"And he seized the dragon, that ancient serpent, who is the devil and Satan,"
(Revelation 20:2)

I said earlier that the serpent in Genesis chapter three was an actual beast of the field. The serpent's demotion as a cursed animal removed it and its physical offspring from subsequently being used in a similar manner as instruments of demonic deception. We see from these passages in Revelation that the dragon, who orchestrated the original deception through the serpent, continues this contentious relationship as the devil or Satan.

SUMMARY

We saw in the previous chapter that God addressed both Adam and his wife by first asking them a question giving them an opportunity to confess their personal culpability and seek forgiveness from their Father. No such opportunity was offered to the serpent for at least two reasons: first, it was an animal only possessing a soul and a body. It was not made in the image or likeness of God with a spirit that would live on after its physical death. So, God's intervention did not offer a dimension of eternal salvation.

Second, God's judgment extended to the one whose head the eventual seed of the woman would defeat. This being was Satan who had orchestrated the garden temptation through the serpent and whose only goal was to steal, kill and destroy everything God revealed through His Kingdom. The woman's seed who "bruised" the serpent's head was Jesus who defeated Satan through His death on the cross, His resurrection and His ascension to the right hand of His Father far above all principalities and every name that is named, not only in this world but in the world to come (Ephesians 1:20 – 21).

Study Questions For Discussion

- Do you believe that we live in only two kingdoms?
    - Or do you believe that we can live in our own kingdom that is separate from the Kingdom of God and the kingdom of this world?
- Do you view the serpent as an actual animal in the garden or as some demonic manifestation of the great dragon or Satan?
    - On what scriptures do you base your decision?
- Why was the serpent culpable?
    - Was the serpent deceived?
    - Could that deception excuse its culpability?
- What is your definition of "curse"?
    - Do you believe God cursed the serpent or is there another answer? Explain?
    - The God of the Hebrew Testament has been characterized by some as a God of judgment while the God of the New Testament has been characterized as a God of Love and forgiveness. Why is this simplistic view dangerous?
    - Has the pictographic meaning of "cursed" enlightened your understanding?
- Why did God specifically state that the serpent would henceforth "eat dust all the days of its life"?
    - Does the mention of dust here relate to what how Adam had been formed in 2:7 and what would happen later in 3:19?
- What does the inclusion of ✦ at the end of verse 3:15 indicate about how God looked at these words?
- What is enmity?
    - Does the Lord equip us by building a wall of enmity so that we will be less likely to be deceived?
    - How do Satan's minions "bite at your heel" and keep you from fulfilling the fullness of your destiny?

o Does enmity signal that women tend to be more sensitive to spiritual influences both beneficial and otherwise?
o Can you give examples of this in your life? In your church? In the occult?
o What does the word "put" indicate about God's role in managing this iniquity?
o If "head" means Satan's ability to deliver a deadly venomous bite to us, how did Jesus take the sting out of death for us?
- Why is it so important to take enmity seriously?"
o Why is the unity expressed by unconditional love for one another critical to our defense against the prince of this world?
o How does the Body of Christ enhance our protection against the wiles of the devil?
o How does the whole armor of God enhance our protection? Ephesians 6:11 – 13; 1 Peter 5:8 – 9; James 4:7 – 8.
o Speaking about the last days before He returns, Jesus said the hearts of many would grow cold (Matthew 24:12). Paul also warned about a "falling away" before Jesus returns (2 Thessalonians 2:3). How can we remain vigilant to the enmity that exists between believers and those in the kingdom of this world so that this doesn't happen to us?
- The serpent's offspring (ⱲꙩꙈ𐤟) conforms (Ⱳ) to the serpent. Does this revelation shed any light on Pauls warning that we do not war against flesh and blood?

CHAPTER
29

Genesis 3:16
Redemption For Her

"To the woman he said, 'I will surely multiply your pain in childbearing; in pain you shall bring forth children. Your desire shall be contrary to your husband, but he shall rule over you'" (Genesis 3:16).

PROLOGUE

In Genesis 3:16, God began His redemptive love chase after us, and later clarified His motivations in another 3:16 written by the apostle John:

> *"For God so loved the world, that he gave his only Son, that whoever believes in him should not perish but have eternal life. For God did not send his Son into the world to condemn the world, but in order that the world might be saved through him."*

The rest of chapter three has long been accepted as the irreversible consequences of Adam's disobedience. Nowhere is this apparent inevitability more sanctioned than in God's revelation to the woman. Here is the translation from the Israel Bible, a new Jewish translation:

> *"And to the woman He said, 'I will make most severe* **Your** *pangs in childbearing; In pain*

*shall you bear children. Yet your urge shall be
for your husband, And he shall rule over you.'"*

My purpose in writing this chapter is to help you reevaluate
the deeper meaning of this critical passage.

The First Phrase Of This Verse
A Closer Look
*"I will surely multiply your pain in childbear-
ing; in pain you shall bring forth children."*

"I will surely multiply your pain in childbearing" implies that
the Lord was actively engaged in and personally responsible
for greatly multiplying the woman's pain during childbirth.
However, I am convinced that the actual text supports an alternative interpretation.

The translators have chosen to render this text as "I will surely
multiply your pain in childbearing." But there is no linguistic
reason why it can't be translated as "Your pain will surely
multiply in childbearing." This second interpretation removes
God's apparent, personal involvement in multiplying her pain.
It also affirms that the Lord was acknowledging the increased
pain this woman would face during childbirth without declaring that multiplying her pain was His deliberate impartation
to her.

I Will Surely Multiply – ᎩᏳᎴᏓ ᎩᏳᎴᎩ. As
in so many other instances in the Hebrew testament, repeating
a word adds emphasis to it. The basic word is ᎩᏳᎴ and
is shared with no prefixes in Genesis 1:22 and 28. However,
there are prefixes in this verse.

ᎩᏳᎴᎩ – Ꭹ precedes this word. In many other places,

Ꭹ is translated as "The." But its basic meaning evokes surprise and wonder. So, its inclusion here could indicate that a dramatic increase of pain would be a surprise to the woman especially since she had not born any children yet and could only imagine what degree of pain might accompany childbirth.

ᎩᏡᏡᎦ – Ꭶ precedes this word and emphasizes the strength of its meaning (surely).

Before I continue, I want to affirm that these two words accurately describe the rapid increase of pain associated with childbirth. In order for an infant to travel from the womb and be born, rapid dilation of different portions of the birthing canal must occur. And because this process takes place quickly, it generates a lot of pain that steadily increases until the opening is wide enough for the baby to pass through.

I believe that the Lord was acknowledging the situation this woman would face during childbirth without declaring that multiplying her pain was His deliberate impartation to her. That is, her pain would be a natural expression of her nervous system responding to the rapid dilation of her birth canal rather than pain He would inflict upon her for disobeying His command not to eat the fruit of the tree of the knowledge of good and evil.

God could see into her future knowing that as yet, she had not given birth to anyone. He was revealing to her the level of pain she would face during childbirth in the kingdom of this world because He didn't want the pain to come as an unexpected surprise or be misinterpreted that she was dying.

God's Participation in Childbirth
I have shared several times in earlier chapters that God teams

with us through a yoked relationship to execute our destiny **in the Kingdom of God**. Childbirth is part of a woman's destiny to bring children into the world. The actual birthing process is a physical activity performed by the woman's body. However, the pain associated with childbearing is generated by the body's nervous system and is not essential to bringing the child to birth.

I am asserting that God's childbirth destiny for the woman was to team with her during the birthing event to reduce or eliminate her sensation of pain. I am basing this conclusion on the comparison of Genesis 3:16 with related words in Isaiah 66:7 – 9:

> *"**Before** she **travailed, she brought forth; before** her **pain** came, she was **delivered** of a man child. Who hath heard such a thing? who hath seen such things? Shall the earth be made to bring forth in one day? or shall a nation be born at once? for as soon as Zion travailed, she brought forth her children. Shall I bring to the birth, and not cause to bring forth? saith the Lord: shall I cause to bring forth, and shut the* **womb***? saith thy God"* (Isaiah 66:7 – 9).

This prophecy in the last chapter of Isaiah's book predicts an awe-inspiring event – the birth of a nation in a day. It was compared to and built upon the original plan God had for women to give birth to a child in a day. How can I be so sure it was God's original plan? Let's compare the critical words in this passage with Genesis 3:16.

Here are the words from that Genesis passage:

> *"... increase your pain in childbearing; in pain (עֶצֶב) you shall bring forth children."*

Pain – � ל ץ ⬭ ⌐ ⬤. The first three symbols of this word are the same as the second word for pain in this verse. The pain is experienced through her physical senses (⬤) that are hooked to / incorporated as part of (⌐) her tent / body (⬭). This pain is also anchored to / is a manifestation of (ץ) what happens as her body conforms (Ⱳ) to the new life (ל) being brought forth through childbearing.

Childbearing – Ⱳ ל ץ �)ⲁ ץ. The last three symbols are the same as the last three symbols for the result of the childbearing pain. That pain is anchored (ץ) to and brings about praise (ⲁ) for the woman that a child (𐤉) has been born.

Now, let's examine the related words in Isaiah.

As you look at these words, you will notice two things: First, they are entirely different words than in Genesis 3:16. Second, ℓ (the Shepherd's staff of authority) is present in every word.

Travailed – ℓ ≻⌐ ⲫ. To be in labor. Even though this word is translated as "travail," there are no symbols in it that are associated with pain (⬭ ⌐ ⬤).This word states that the woman's labor is closely fenced / overseen / guarded (ⲫ) by the arm (≻⌐) of her Shepherd (ℓ).

Brought Forth – ⲁ ⴞ ℓ ≻⌐. To give birth. The first two symbols of this word are the last two for "travailed." The arm (≻⌐) of her Shepherd (ℓ) is guiding her child through the door / the birthing canal (ⴞ) into the world in an environment of praise and awe (ⲁ).

Pain – ℓ ⬭ ⲫ. Notice how similar this word is to "travail." The pain in her tent / body (⬛) is closely fenced /over-seen / guarded (Ⅲ) by her Shepherd (*Ɩ*).

Brought Forth – ⊕ *Ɩ* ᴧᴧ (**Delivered**) The delivery of a child into the world is truly miraculous! The actual birthing experience is a cascade / multitude (ᴧᴧ) of events, under the watchful eye of her Shepherd (*Ɩ*), that surround (⊕) the overall birthing experience.

I am asserting that Isaiah 66:7 reveals God's original plan for childbirth because these words are so different from the terms God spoke to the woman in Genesis 3:16. They also show the Shepherd's intimate involvement in every aspect of the actual birthing process – something that is missing in the 3:16 passage.

I am also blessed to have a first-hand testimony from Judy, my newly married wife, of this more painless way to bear children.

Judy's Testimony

We were a Navy family in Norfolk, Va. In all of my birthing experiences of four sons in five years, I'd never before experienced what I'm about to tell you – the miraculous, painless birth of my identical twin daughters on Christmas Day 1965. Close to my 26th birthday, April 19, as I was going to sleep, this Catholic girl sincerely and simply asked God for twins, then never thought I'd get any.

I prayed, "Lord, if you think I'd be a good mother, please give me twins. I want twins. I've wanted twins my whole life. I don't feel complete without twins." As I drifted off to sleep, I FELT a rush of goosebumps as a sign of the Lord's blessing flowing over me. But I didn't recognize or think anything about it. I never thought I'd get twins and I had my first prescription for the new birth control pills in my hand.

I missed my next period, then the next, and threw away my pills. I went to the doctor pregnant with twins. But without ultrasound, they never knew there were two babies. (The heartbeat of the second sounded like the echo of the first.) I was due Jan. 18, 1966. But, they thought because of my size that I was due in October and I had miscalculated! Never mind my cycles and my husband was on tour. In the military, we see a different doctor every time and I saw eight. October came and went. The doctor shook his head, "I don't know when" and put me on a diet as I had gained over the 20 pounds – the limit for one baby – but still gained 30 pounds! My body was totally out of room; big as a house and I lumbered around!

God gave a PAINLESS labor for twins on Christmas Day, the day He chose!! Three weeks early, I began with mild labor that intensified as it progressed. So, I went to the hospital. I had no faith for twins, but I thought, "This is so intense, If I die in childbirth, I'll go to heaven" as per Catholicism. At this point, I thought I imagined Jesus at the corner of my bed with His arms stretched out over me. This was impossible since the bed was pushed up into the corner of the hospital room with no standing room. When I allowed myself to come under His arms, all labor pain stopped. The labor continued, but with no pain.

Jerking myself out of my imaginings to reality, I thought, "This is crazy. Get hold of yourself! You're having a baby!" – and immediately, labor slammed back into me with relentlessly increasing pressure. I quickly jumped back under His arms saying to myself, "I don't care, it feels good over here, and I'm staying under His arms!!" And so, I had a painless childbirth for unexpected twins that weighed 13 pounds.!!

Cathleen was born, 6 lb. 10 oz. I got my girl and was happy for her. They thought Christine was garbage they hadn't cleaned out. (She was the other 6 lb. 3 oz. twin!) Then I heard, "I think it's another baby!" God provided Christine with her own placenta to preserve her life. The twins had two placentas joined together. Yet as identical twins, they shared one embryonic sac. This was a miracle of grace! The doctors and nurses were amazed. I was not prepared for two babies. I felt like the hospital gave me one extra by mistake, but they were both gifts from God.

God is so good; He is faithful even when we are not faithful.   Judy Combs

I believe Judy's testimony reveals the grace of God that is available to other women through His Son, Jesus Christ, our Shepherd. We have been told for ages that serious pain is the inevitable cost of childbearing. We have even believed that has been God's will for woman after Adam and Eve disobeyed the Lord. After all, her pain came after they had disobeyed the Lord and were living in the kingdom of this world.

May I suggest that what we proclaim with our mouth and believe in our heart becomes our reality. The pain associated with childbearing is a visceral reality and is part of what Paul calls "what is seen" or what is experienced through our senses (2 Corinthians 4:18). I acknowledge that, in the face of what we have been told is inevitable, it may be extremely difficult to consider an alternative reality that God is able to partner with women in childbirth in the way described in Isaiah 66:7 – 9.

If it weren't for Judy's testimony, I would not have included her alternative experience in this book. But, since God is no respecter of persons, I am confident that she is not the only woman who has or will encounter God's grace in this way.

The Second Phrase Of This Verse
A Closer Look

> *"Your desire shall be contrary to your husband, but he shall rule over you"*

Desire – 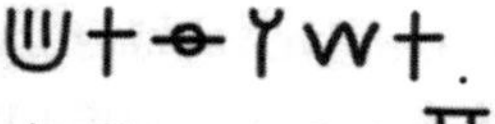. This word is totally different than the one in Genesis 3:6 (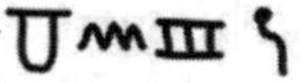). Benner says that its root is 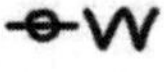 and is one of the terms for river that consumes () its banks during its annual flood cycle ()[111]. Each year, when the flood recedes, its banks contain rich, new soil ideal for planting a new crop. In the same way, the woman's cycles provide a fertile ground for her husband to plant his seed.

So, the woman's desire enables the complete () consumption () of his seed to become pregnant, a process that is dependent upon / anchored to () her cycles () as she willingly () conforms () to her husband.

Contrary to your husband – �owⲁⲟⲃ-ⲗⲃⲨ.
My first impression of this translation was that the woman was still at odds with her husband perhaps because he had blamed her for his predicament. I was puzzled by this interpretation for the following reasons:

Ⲩ implies a definite connection between the previous statement and what follows.

ⲗⲃ defines a strongly yoked relationship between the woman and her husband emphasized even more by the bar that connects ⲗⲃ with ⲱⲁⲟⲃ. It implies a working-together relationship rather than one where the two were disagreeing so much that some kind of strict oversight was required.

The addition of the suffix (ⱳ) to ⲱⲁⲟⲃ means "husband conformed" or "conformed to her husband." Her desire to bear and raise children would best be accomplished as she willingly conformed to her husband which again seemed at odds with a "contrary" interpretation.

However, as his helpmate, she had eyes to see things that he tended to overlook and his perspective did not always appear compatible with hers. As I said earlier, neither viewpoint was complete. But if they trusted each other's insights as complementary and not competitive, they would be able to resist further deception.

But he – ⲟⲨⱳⲨ. Ⲩ is translated as "But" which implies that her husband was given authority over her in order to overrule her contrary disposition and maintain order in their home. However, this symbol for a tent peg is only meant to connect the previous statement with this one and could just as easily be translated as "and."

Let's look again at ⟨Hebrew⟩ by removing ⟨Hebrew⟩ from this word. ⟨Hebrew⟩ means to behold strongly and the addition of ⟨Hebrew⟩ serves to firmly anchor this thought to the next word indicating a strong affirmation for what is expressed by the next word.

Rule over you – ⟨Hebrew⟩. ⟨Hebrew⟩ was first used in Day Four giving the greater and lesser lights the authority to rule over the Day and the Night. I shared then that this term gave them responsibility for their domains. It was not intended that they rule as dictators but as willing agents under God's authority.

I believe God was assuring the woman that her husband would actively (⟨Hebrew⟩) assume responsibility for / would work in the fire (⟨Hebrew⟩) to help her fulfill her destiny to bear and raise their children as she conformed (⟨Hebrew⟩) her tent / body (⟨Hebrew⟩) to his authority (⟨Hebrew⟩).

> *"Wives, submit to your own husbands, as to the Lord. For the husband is the head of the wife even as Christ is the head of the church, his body, and is himself its Savior. Now as the church submits to Christ, so also wives should submit in everything to their husbands.*

> *"Husbands, love your wives, as Christ loved the church and gave himself up for her, that he might sanctify her, having cleansed her by the washing of water with the word, so that he might present the church to himself in splendor, without spot or wrinkle or any such thing, that she might be holy and without blemish. In the same way husbands should love their wives as their own bodies. He who loves his wife loves*

himself. For no one ever hated his own flesh, but nourishes and cherishes it, just as Christ does the church, because we are members of his body. "Therefore, a man shall leave his father and mother and hold fast to his wife, and the two shall become one flesh." This mystery is profound, and I am saying that it refers to Christ and the church. However, let each one of you love his wife as himself, and let the wife see that she respects her husband."

(Ephesians 5:22-33)

The woman's greater relational sensitivity as Adam's helper had made her the preferred target for deception by the devil. Now that her eyes were opened to the kingdom of this world making her even more vulnerable, it was essential that her husband be given authority to rule over her – to be her lord in the same way the Lord God protected and cared for them through His steadfast love.

SUMMARY
The kingdom of this world

It is vital to realize that the declarations made to Adam and his wife in Genesis 3:15 – 19 were given because they were now living in the kingdom of this world. As we move forward through the rest of this chapter and the next, we will see that their circumstance was reversable because His words were redemptive, not punitive. The keys to their salvation were repentance and a return to the first protocol outlined in Genesis 2:25.

I found it interesting that the Lord did not tell Adam that he would rule over his wife. Instead, her increasing pain in childbearing, her desire for him and his rule over her were all linked together (Υ) as one continuous thread God shared **with her.**

The Apostle Paul says that the whole of creation has been groaning – subjected to futility though not willingly (Romans 8:20 - 22). And Genesis 2:19 says that God formed the beasts of the field and the birds out of the ground, and they exist now under the curse of Genesis 3:17. So, it is helpful to consider how these male and female creatures behave toward each other under these circumstances.

Many animals including lions, elephants, Bonobo chimps, lemurs, killer whales, spotted hyenas, meerkats, horses, cows, sheep, goats and pigs live in a matriarchal society. The reason is simple: the bond between mother and child. Mothers are the glue that holds the family together. I shared earlier that mother in Hebrew is ᴍᵭ – strong water – glue. And "Amen," the word we often proclaim at the end of a prayer (ᛁᴹᵭ), asserts our commitment is as strong as the relationship between a mother (ᴹᵭ) and her newborn child (ᛁ).

If God established a matriarchal framework for so many species in the animal and insect world, how can we claim that "Rule" must mean patriarchal dictatorship over his wife and family? God told Adam that it was not good for him to be alone and brought a helpmate to him (ᗡᛈ☺). She would have eyes to see things he was unaware of and would wield a sword / cudgel for defense / offense and harvest.

He was to relate to her head-to-head so they could work as a team with the Lord. Even though Adam would "rule" over her as her physical and spiritual covering, she would be the glue that held their family together as they overcame the kingdom of this world together with the Lord. And as in all things they faced, from her childbearing pain to his pain, sweat and toil, their circumstance was not inevitable or permanent. Repentance, obedience and an expectation that with God all things were possible were keys to their salvation.

Study Questions For Discussion

- Genesis 3:16 has long been accepted as the irreversible consequences of Adam's disobedience. Nowhere is this apparent inevitability more sanctioned than in God's revelation to the woman. Do you believe that the declarations in this verse are God's irreversible will for women?
- *"I will surely multiply your pain in childbearing."* Having read this chapter, do you still believe that multiplying the woman's pain was God's deliberate impartation to her?
    - o If this chapter is changing your understanding of this verse, how is it impacting your relationship with your husband, wife, daughters, female workers?
- Genesis 3:16 and Isaiah both describe a woman's role in childbearing. Which one do you believe represents the original intent of the Lord's will for the woman's destiny.
- If you believe that God is just and impartial, does Judy's testimony surprise you?
    - o Does her testimony give you a new perspective on God's original design for a woman's childbearing destiny?
    - o Does her testimony open your eyes to an alternative birthing experience?
    - o Do our expectations play a role in God's ability to bless us?
- If you only read Genesis chapter three in English, you might assume that the underlying Hebrew text in 3:6 translated as "desire" may have been the same as the Hebrew text translated as "desire" in 3:16. Has this chapter given you more information to formulate your opinion?
- The words "contrary" and "But" imply that the woman was still at odds with her husband. Do you agree with this assessment?

- o However, as his helpmate, she could "see" things he might overlook. In what way does her perspective contribute to the concept of "contrary?"
- What does the word "rule" mean to you in this verse?
  - o How has the interpretation of this word affected the social fabric of vast segments of the world?
  - o Sarah called her husband "lord" in Genesis 18:12.
  - o What did she mean by calling Abraham "lord?" (See also 1 Peter 3:1 – 7.)
- I labeled this chapter "Redemption For Her." How could Genesis 3:16 be redemptive for the woman?
  - o Was this verse a warning and a call for the woman (Eve) to confess her disobedience, ask for forgiveness and return to God's original birthing destiny for her?
  - o She said to the Lord, *"The serpent deceived me and I ate."* Were her actions culpable or not? (Hint: she chose to obey the serpent instead of her husband.)
  - o If you could counsel Eve, how would you encourage her to confess her disobedience and ask for forgiveness from Adam so that her posture could help restore them to each other and to the Lord?
  - o Would your counsel be applicable to your relationships?

CHAPTER 30

Genesis 3:17 – 19
Redemption For Him

"And to Adam he said, 'Because you have listened to the voice of your wife and have eaten of the tree of which I commanded you, "You shall not eat of it," cursed is the ground because of you; in pain you shall eat of it all the days of your life; thorns and thistles it shall bring forth for you; and you shall eat the plants of the field. By the sweat of your face you shall eat bread, till you return to the ground, for out of it you were taken; for you are dust, and to dust you shall return'" (Genesis 3:17 – 19).

PROLOGUE
During an earlier argument with his wife, Adam had become so distraught with her response that his nose flared in frustration. Up until that time, whenever he had encountered a situation he didn't know how to handle, he had asked the Lord for a solution believing that the words God would put into his mouth would be fulfilled in a way that would not bring them shame. However, instead of asking the Lord to reveal a remedy for their personal disagreement, he had chosen to disclose his own solution to her and to couch it as though it was part of God's original injunction.

Adam could not foresee the outcome of his hasty decision; that touching the fruit would actually embolden his wife, not only to eat it, but to enthusiastically offer it to him. He had sown the seeds of his eventual disobedience by adding "neither shall you touch it." And his reluctance to confess to her that his added words were his own idea was now reaping a whirlwind of fear and mistrust that hardened his heart to confess his culpability to the Lord.

It is hard not to read Genesis 3:17 – 19 as God's punishment for Adam's disobedience. But as revealed in my title for this chapter, I will couch this passage as an expression of God's unconditional love for Adam. I have already shared the pictographic meaning of "cursed" from verse fourteen which is at odds with most interpretations. My purpose in writing this chapter is to help you recognize the atoning aspects of these critical verses.

God's Motivation

May I suggest that what may appear to us as punishment was actually a redemptive means to an end. There are only two kingdoms: the Kingdom of God and the kingdom of this world. In God's Kingdom, we are yoked with Him for protection and for help achieving our destiny. When Adam willfully disobeyed the Lord, he not only lost some of God's protection, he also walked away from the assistance God was providing. Instead of enjoying a yoked relationship that was easy and a burden that was light, he would now find no rest from the constant, daily demands of farming without God's intervention.

Adam knew what it was like to work and keep the garden before his eyes were opened. God's pronouncement in these verses must have come as a shock of the kind of drudgery he would experience. Incredibly, God said he would face a similar kind of pain his wife would endure through childbearing trying to produce enough food for them to eat. His best efforts would yield only sweat and toil that would eventually wear him down. Unless Adam repented, he would soon have to cope with a whirlwind of frustrating, endless, painful toil, and the constant, nagging memory of what life had once been like.

God's Goal

God's unconditional love would not override Adam's will. Instead, the Lord allowed him to chart his own fate. Like the parable of the prodigal son, God let Adam walk away from His Kingdom but waited expectantly for his return hoping Adam would wake up one day in his deplorable circumstances and return with a penitent heart to the loving care of His Father (Luke 15:11 – 23).

3:17 – A Closer Look

Notice the similarity in the way God addressed the woman in 3:16 and Adam here in 3:17:

To the woman he said:

ꓱᴟᗞ ꓬꓪᗞꓬ-ᘰ ᗞ
said   woman the To

And to Adam he said:

ꓱᴟᗞ ᴟꓵᗞᘰ ꓨ
said   Adam   to And

Verse 17 begins with an anchor (ꓨ) to the previous verse suggesting that the same loving motivation was extended to Adam. Like verse sixteen, ᴟꓵᗞᘰ is positioned at the beginning of the sentence, bolstering my contention that the underlying motive was God's desire for Adam's salvation. However, ᘰᗞ is replaced by ᘰ indicating that their relationship was more strained because of Adam's direct disobedience to the Lord's command.

Now, let's examine several words in these verses:

Listened – †☉ᴍW. Whenever this word is found in the Bible, it means much more than "listen." It means "to hear with the desire to obey." It is the word for "heard" in Genesis 3:8,

> *"They **heard** the sound of the Lord walking in the garden."*

This word ends with † implying that Adam not only listened to what his wife was saying, he also agreed with her and deliberately chose to obey her testimony of the serpent's revelation. Then, acting on his own resolve, he ate the fruit offered to him instead of obeying the Lord's command.

Voice – ℓ Ɣ☉ℓ. This is the same word translated as "**sound**" in Genesis 3:8 that I shared above. Adam and his wife did not just hear the sound of God walking in the garden like the rustling sound of the Etesian wind. The Lord was calling to them with authority (ℓ) in the same way shepherds (ℓ) gathered together at the end of the day (☉) to agree on (Ɣ) important issues.

Cursed – ᴙΔƔ⅁⚘. This is essentially the same word from verse 14 (⅁ƔΔ⚘). The added ᴙ at the end may mean that its inclusion was a surprise to Adam. As shared in verse fourteen, curse means that Adam would no longer have the protection and help he had previously enjoyed through his yoked relationship with the Lord. Instead, he would have to rely on his own strength, stamina and ingenuity to farm the land. (Please read Psalm 104 to see just how much assistance the Lord gave Adam in the garden through their yoked relationship, and how hard it was for him to function without even a fraction of God's oversight, all of which precipitated from his decision to disobey the Lord and live according to the kingdom of this world.)

The Garden

In order to better understand how much Adam's life would change, let's look at God's original plan for the garden.

> *"No bush of the field was yet in the land and no small plant of the field had yet sprung up—for the Lord God had not caused it to rain on the land, and there was no man to work the ground, and a mist was going up from the land and was watering the whole face of the ground."*
>
> (Genesis 2:5 – 6).

> *"And the Lord God planted a garden in Eden, in the east, and there he put the man whom he had formed. And out of the ground the Lord God made to spring up every tree that is pleasant to the sight and good for food. The tree of life was in the midst of the garden, and the tree of the knowledge of good and evil. A river flowed out of Eden to water the garden, and there it divided and became four rivers"* Genesis 2:8 – 10).

The garden was much more than a strip of raw land along a river bank somewhere east of Eden. Nowhere do we read that God initially instructed Adam to clear the ground of thorns and thistles, collect and plant local grains, and find shrubs and young fruit trees to transplant above the floodplain. Nor was he challenged to build fences to keep out the beasts of the field, erect dikes to tame the capricious river, or construct reservoirs to save water in case of drought or storehouses to sustain him if locusts devoured his crops.

All these obstacles were continually addressed by the Lord's grace, favor and blessing. He lovingly created and helped sustain their garden home so they could walk in His manifest presence conquering every challenge without shame or fear. Unfortunately, Adam and his wife would soon be driven from their verdant paradise into an environment outside the garden that would more closely mirror the conditions outlined above. Let's examine what Adam could look forward to.

Pain – ⟨Hebrew text⟩. This is precisely the same word used in Genesis 3:16 to describe childbearing pain. Based on the "pain" encountered by farmers today in agrarian societies, this level of suffering may seem hard to accept. How could a hard-days-work in the fields to deliver food for one's family compare with the sudden increase of pain to bring forth a new member of the family? However, the Bible says that this severe pain continued until after Noah's flood:

> *"When Lamech had lived 182 years, he fathered a son and called his name Noah, saying,* **'Out of the ground that the Lord has cursed, this one shall bring us relief from our work and from the <u>painful toil</u> of our hands.'"**
> (Genesis 5:28 – 29)

> *"Then Noah built an altar to the Lord and took some of every clean animal and some of every clean bird and offered burnt offerings on the altar. And when the Lord smelled the pleasing aroma, the Lord said in his heart,* **'I will never again curse the ground because of man,** *for the intention of man's heart is evil from his youth'"* (Genesis 8:20 – 21).

Painful Toil – ⟨Hebrew text⟩. The childbearing level of pain continued until after the flood. Why was the pain so severe? Remember God's goal. This pain reminded Adam of what he had lost. He would suffer because he was living in the kingdom of this world. These deplorable circumstances would also extend to those who lived after him because the intentions of their hearts were evil from their youth. But Noah was a righteous man, blameless in his generation who walked with God. It was with Noah that the Lord made a rainbow covenant ending the curse on the ground.

There is another possible explanation why the Lord would associate Adam's pain with childbirth. When Rachel bore Benjamin, the Bible says her hard labor pains made her so afraid of dying she was not cheered by the news that she had given birth to a son (Genesis 35:16 - 19). Perhaps, God was comparing the fear and discouragement Adam would encounter in his new environment with the anguish his wife would experience in labor (See Isaiah 13:8; Jeremiah 13:21).

Life – Ш⅃⅃Ⅲ. This is the same word used in Genesis 2:7 when God breathed into Adam's nostrils the breath of **life** and he became a **living** soul. As I shared in Chapter Fifteen, this is the word for a person's stomach[37]. In the coming months, Adam would totally focus on producing enough food to sustain their bodily life. As long as his perspective did not change, the stress of this painful toil would continue all the days of his life.

Thorns and Thistles – ⌐Υ⊙ and ᗡⴹᗡⴹ. Benner says that thistles were used by shepherds to build corrals to protect their sheep at night[112]. Thorns were likely used with thistles to build these corrals. Shepherds (ᗡᗡ) would work together at the end of the day (⊙) to weave (Υ, ⌐) thorns and thistles together. Every sheepfold would have one or more doors (ⴹⴹ).

However, Adam was a farmer and sheepfolds are associated with shepherds. It is worth noting that Abraham, Jacob and David began as shepherds. Their Bedouin lifestyle seemed much more tenuous than farming. But it proved to be a priceless crucible for developing their profound trust in the Lord's ability to meet their every need (Psalm 23). Since sheep later became an integral part of Adam's family relationships with the Lord (Genesis 3:21, 4:2), perhaps God allowed thorns and thistles to choke their fields to encourage them to expand their occupational horizons and experience another dimension of the Lord's loving care and protection.

Bring Forth – �↗Jᴿ↖ꜛ†. In Genesis 1:12, the earth brought forth vegetation, plants yielding seed and trees bearing fruit. But now, the earth would bring forth only (†) inedible thorns and thistles requiring painful (↗), constant (ᴹᴹ) work (↘ᴶ) to keep these weeds from overtaking any fenced (ꟽ) enclosure they might erect.

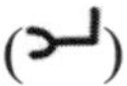

Plants Of The Field – Adam and his wife would soon be evicted from the garden where they had enjoyed food from plants, bushes and trees. Since they were no longer teamed with the Lord, their only dependable food source seems to have been the **plants** they could grow in the **fields** where thorns and thistles grew naturally in the less fertile soil of the nearby savannas. These grasslands bordering the rivers may have discouraged any appreciable concentration of fruit-bearing bushes and trees. In addition, the river's ebb and flow could have been too unpredictable to sow seeds along the riverbank and take advantage of the rich soil deposited there each spring.

Sweat – †◎ꜛῺ. Ῠ is often translated as "in" or "by." But it can also represent Adam's body or the environment he would soon be living in. "Sweat" could represent a predicament Adam perceived (⬮) to be severe, demanding his total (✝) participation. He would likely be constantly overwhelmed no matter how hard he tried to beat back (𐤓) the encroaching weeds, drive off the beasts of the field and control the unpredictable weather conditions in order to plant, raise and harvest enough plants of the field to eat.

Face – �owↄↄℳ. (ℴ) Strong (⬮) mouth is this word for face. So, Adam's sweat would be generated by his work (ↄↄ) and would cover (ℳ) his face.

Two Different Perspectives:

I want to separate the rest of this text into two perspectives: Adam's perspective of God's pronouncement to him – how he may have received them; and God's loving motivation for declaring these words to Adam.

Adam's Perspective:

Eat – ℓℳℴℽ✝. Notice that "eat" was repeated five times in this passage. Adam ate the fruit as a willful expression of his disobedience to God's specific warning. His actions would now impact what and how he ate. Adam would have to totally (✝) commit (ℽ) all his energies (ℴ) in order to conform (ℳ) and control (ℓ) his new environment to produce enough food to eat.

Till – ℧⬮. Eye (⬮) on the door (℧) is a Hebrew word for "Eternity" (Isaiah 45:17). Adam would struggle mightily for the rest of his life by the sweat of his brow to grow food in this harsh environment so they could eat enough bread (food) to survive **until** . . .

Return – �owⴖᵞw. Destruction (w) anchored (ᵞ) to Adam's body (ⴖ) conforming it (ow) …

To The Ground – ᵞᵐᵁᵟᵞ-ℓᵟ.
Adam (ᵐᵁᵟ) had been formed from the dust from the ground. Now, his debilitating toil would end (ᵁᵒ) only when destruction (w) was anchored (ᵞ) to his body (ⴖ), conforming (ow) it and strongly (ᵟ) yoking (ℓ) it to the ground in physical death.

For – ﹀ꓝow. This word appears twice to draw attention to the relationship between ground and dust. In this instance, it declared that Adam would return to the ground because he was taken from the ground.

Taken – †꒫ᵒℓ. This is the same word used in Genesis 2:21 - 22,

> *"and while he slept **took** one of his ribs"* …
> *And the rib that the Lord God had **taken** from the man he made into a woman."*

God had taken Adam from the dust from the ground to make his body in the same way He took a rib from Adam's body to make his wife's body.

For Dust – ᴺᵒᵒ﹀ꓝow. This second use provided the reason why he would return to the ground: *"For you **are** dust."* The pictograms for dust depict this transformation: What a man perceives with his eyes (ᵒ) and proclaims with his mouth (ᵒ) is what he (ᴺ) ultimately becomes.

The Lord could see that the more Adam's perception was limited to what came through his physical senses, the more he would ultimately identify with what he perceived instead of what he really was: a spirit being living in a body. This separation would reap physical death (in dying, you shall die) separating Adam's true nature as a spirit being from his body and from the Lord Who made and sustained it with His breath.

And To Dust – ⱱ. Strongly (ⱱ) yoked (ⱴ) to dust.

Return – ⱴ. Total (†) destruction (W) anchored (Υ) to Adam's body (ⱴ).

My interpretation of Adam's Perspective:

"By the sweat of your face you shall eat bread, till you return to the ground, for out of it you were taken; for you are dust, and to dust you shall return" (Genesis 3:19).

"Because you have willfully disobeyed my command by eating from the tree after I said "You shall not eat of it," you will now have to totally commit all your energies in order to conform and control your new environment to produce enough food to eat. You have also limited your perception of yourself to your physical body that was made from the **dust** from the ground. So, when you see changes in your body with your eyes, you will believe those changes are real and affirm them with your mouth. Those proclamations will become your new reality because I have given you the authority to speak what you perceive into existence (Genesis 1:28). Death and life are in the power of your tongue (Proverbs 18:21). However, instead of speaking life into yourself by constantly rejecting what your eyes are telling you, you will be speaking death into existence, ultimately resulting in your physical death (returning your body to the ground)."

God's Motivation:

Eat – $\mathcal{L} \, \text{Ш} \, \text{ঌ} \, \text{Υ} \, \text{†}$. The pictograms of this word indicate that God offered Adam a new covenant (†) that could anchor (Υ) and strongly (ঌ) conform (Ш) him to a yoked relationship ($\mathcal{L}$).

Bread – $\text{ᴡ} \, \text{Ш} \, \mathcal{L}$. The pictograms of this term reveal God's love in a yoked relationship ($\mathcal{L}$) that would protect (Ш) Adam from chaos (ᴡ).

Till – $\text{U} \, \text{ᴏ}$. Eye (ᴏ) on the door (U). Opening his eyes to see a way back for him to . . .

Return – $\text{Ш} \, \text{ᴃ} \, \text{Υ} \, \text{w}$. This is a Hebrew term for "Repent" – A call for Adam to destroy (w) the current way of life he had anchored (Υ) to his tent (ᴃ) so he could be conformed (Ш) to his previous way of life.

To The Ground – $\text{Υ} \, \text{ᴡ} \, \text{U} \, \text{ঌ} \, \text{Υ} \, \text{-} \, \mathcal{L} \, \text{ঌ}$. God had originally placed Adam in the garden to work and keep it. Now, the Lord was calling him to remember the yoked relationship they had enjoyed together and the guidance he received from his strong (ঌ) Shepherd ($\mathcal{L}$) to work the ground. Like the prodigal son, God yearned for Adam's eyes to be opened to see the door back to his Father by repenting and seeking restoration.

For – $\text{ᴄ} \, \text{Ш}$. Be conformed (Ш) by the strength of God's arm (ᴄ). If Adam would seek the Lord for a solution to his predicament, God would conform him (renew his mind by giving him eyes to see) by the strength of His arm to perceive the door ($\text{U} \, \text{ᴏ}$) – God's solution – and repent.

From it – $\text{᠈}^{\text{ᴍ}}$. If Adam's will changed and he sought God's answer to his situation, God would reveal a solution that would bring him much (^{ᴍ}) new life ($^{\text{᠈}}$) – restoring the joy of his destiny.

Taken – $\dagger\,\text{ɪɪɪ}\text{-⊕-}\ell$. This word paints a picture of shepherds (ℓ) meeting at the end of the day (-⊕-) to decide how best ($\dagger$) to contain / resolve (ɪɪɪ) the situations they faced. Adam's Shepherd would team with him when he sought help to reveal solutions that would permanently resolve his issues.

For Dust (you are) – $\text{ᴎ}\text{○}\text{⊕}\text{-ᵓ-ᴜ}$. Now that his eyes were opened, Adam conformed (ᴜ) his life as a husband and farmer by the strength of his own arm (ᵓᴶ) guided by what he perceived (⊕) to be real. The more he affirmed this reality by proclaiming it with his mouth (○), the more he (ᴎ) became what he perceived.

To Dust – $\text{ᴎ}\text{○}\text{⊕}\text{-}\ell\,b$. $\ell\,b$ is one of the names for God and it is linked to the word for dust. Instead of conforming his life by the strength of his own arm, the Lord was encouraging Adam to ask his Strong (b) Shepherd (ℓ) for a revelation (⊕) of his situation and to put words in his mouth (○) so he could proclaim them into existence and fulfill his destiny as the person (ᴎ) God called him to be.

Return – $\text{ᴖ}\,\Upsilon\,\text{ᴡ}\,\dagger$. The first word for repent in this passage ends with ᴜ as a call for Adam to yield his will to his Father. This term begins with $\dagger$ as a promise to Adam that if he conformed (ᴜ) to his Shepherd, his return ($\text{ᴖ}\,\Upsilon\,\text{ᴡ}$) to their former yoked relationship would be assured.

My interpretation of God's Motivation:

"By the sweat of your face you shall eat bread, till you return to the ground, for out of it you were taken; for you are dust, and to dust you shall return" (Genesis 3:19).

"Even though you disobeyed my command by eating from the tree after I said "You shall not eat of it," I am challenging you to remember your first covenant with me (Genesis 2:25). That yoked relationship (protocol) always protected and guided you through every chaotic uncertainty you faced. Now, if you submit your will and repent of your propensity to be guided by your own eyes (Genesis 3:7), we will work together to accomplish the works you did at first without shame or fear.

My arm is not shortened that I cannot redeem you from this predicament. If you will listen to My voice (hear and obey) and return to Me, I will renew your mind to see the door that reveals your solution. It will bring you abundant new life that will restore the joy of your destiny and will reestablish complete security in your life.

Come, let us reason together. Now that your eyes have been opened, you have conformed your life by the strength of your own arm. You have been guided by what you perceived and have affirmed it to be real. Each time you try to solve your own issues, you separate yourself from Me and My desire to sustain your life.

As your strong Shepherd, I am calling you to repent and return to Me. I will put words into your mouth to proclaim and I will fulfill them, redeeming you from every dilemma. I will revive your destiny as the person I called you to be and I will enable you to live victoriously without shame or fear. By yielding your will and trusting me, your yoked relationship will be securely reestablished."

SUMMARY

For too long, we have read Genesis 3:16 – 19 as God's punishment for Adam's disobedience. Perhaps, we labeled this chapter as "The Fall" by convincing ourselves that mankind was forever corrupted by this one event. We can conclude that our first parents began as righteous persons perfectly reflecting God's Law. Then, through this one act, they took themselves and their progeny down the long and tortuous path of sin and death.

It is my sincere prayer that the pictograms in these two chapters have whetted your appetite to meditate with the Holy Spirit to discover a deeper revelation of God's unconditional love.

Study Questions For Discussion

- I started the study questions for the last chapter by saying "Genesis 3:16 has long been accepted as the irreversible consequences of Adam's disobedience." Has this chapter opened a door, however slightly, that there may be more to these brief depictions of our human condition than we have believed?

- I declare that the perspective of God's love for Adam shared above was the cry of His grieving heart. Does Genesis 3:21 support my assertion that God's motivation was redemption, not condemnation?
  - Hint: Right after these words, God personally enacted a sacrificial system to clothe them. God also provided a sacrificial animal for Abraham (Genesis 22:8) foreshadowing the sacrificial gift of His own Son as the Lamb of God (John 1:29, 3:16 – 17). *"God did not send His Son into the world to condemn the world but in order that the world might be saved through him."*
  - Paul says in Romans 8:2, *"For God has done what the Law, weakened by the flesh, could not do."* Was Adam's flesh "weak" before his eyes were opened?
  - If so, did the weakness of his flesh contribute to his decision to insert the phrase *"neither shall you touch it"* into God's injunction?
  - Was our flesh corrupted by Adam's disobedience and is therefore weak and not able to keep the Law? Or, is there another answer?
  - Is our perfection accomplished by achieving a level of righteous living exemplified by the Law or is there another way?
  - Hint: Genesis 15:6; 17:1; Romans 3:20.
  - If the first protocol I outlined in Genesis 2:25 was only achievable by Adam and his wife before the fall, why is it in the Bible?
- Did Enoch achieve it (Genesis 5:21 - 24)?
  - Does Deuteronomy 24:16; Jeremiah 31:29 – 30; Ezekiel 18:20 and 2 Kings 14:6 have anything to say about this issue?

CHAPTER 31

Genesis 3:20 – 21
A Pattern Of Redemption

"The man called his wife's name Eve, because she was the mother of all living. And the Lord God made for Adam and for his wife garments of skins and clothed them" (Genesis 3:20 – 21).

PROLOGUE

In the last two chapters, I said that God's words to our first parents in Genesis 3:16 – 19 were redemptive not punitive. His motives reflected **His unconditional love** yearning for them to repent and return to their yoked relationship with Him. In this chapter, I will show that the words of these verses are best seen in the light of repentance and restoration.

What Adam Did

"The man called his wife's name Eve, because she was the mother of all living."

Called – 𐤀𐤍𐤄𐤏𐤓𐤉𐤅 . Adam's mood had gone from vehemently blaming both God and his wife for his current predicament to calling her *"Eve, the mother of all living,"* likely in the same day! For me, that signaled a significant attitude adjustment – a momentous change of heart about her role in his life. It suggests that Adam was no longer relying just on his immediate assessment but had received a revelation from the Lord that motivated him to reconsider his commitment to his wife.

Why else would he choose this name and description for her? Remember, they had no children at that point. So, he could only imagine what it might be like having a family. If his wife had recently given him so much grief, why would he suddenly portray the prospective fruit of her childbearing in such glowing terms?

I believe verse sixteen convicted Adam that his own disobedience would bring sudden, debilitating labor pains to his wife in order for her to bear their offspring as well as the child who would bruise the head of the serpent. His contrition would surely have moved the Lord to open the eyes of his heart to remember his earlier covenant commitment to her.

Adam's remorse and compassion for her plight may also have moved him to ask the Lord for a way to redeem their chaotic situation through the protocol they had previously followed. God's response to such a request may have put the words, *"Eve, the mother of all living"* into Adam's mouth, setting in motion a renewed way for Adam to relate to his wife: to "work in the fire" and to lift her up as an offering of praise and honor.

Let's look briefly at the pictograms:

> *"The man called his wife's name Eve (Ψ Υ Ⅲ),*
> *because she was the mother (ᴹᴧ♉) of all living*
> *(ᕁⱢⅢ)."*

Ψ Υ Ⅲ identified an essential character (name) of Adam's wife revealed in the rest of the verse:

Mother – ᴹᴧ♉. Strong Water. I originally defined this word in Chapter Twenty but it is worth sharing again. When animal hides were boiled in water, the residue that floated to the top was sticky and was used for glue – strong water[25]. So, a mother is the glue that binds the family together. It also undergirds another familiar word:

Amen – ⟨ᴍᵇ⟩. "Amen" affirms that our commitment to a declaration is as strong as the bond between a mother (ᴍᵇ) and her newborn child (⟨)!

Living – ⟨ᴵᴵᴵ⟩. This word is also found in Genesis 2:7, *"the man became a living (⟨ᴵᴵᴵ⟩) creature."* As I shared earlier, this verse does not imply that the man was only a living soul like the other animals that God made. This action formed Adam's body of flesh for him to live in: (Flesh: ⟨ᴺᴵᴿᴸᴼ⟩ – the tent that protects the man – Genesis 2:21).

So, Eve became the mother whose womb formed the tent / body for all her progeny to live in.

Eve – ⟨ᴵᴵᴵ⟩. The second half of verse 20 specified the new character Adam imparted to his wife. Her new name is quite similar to the pictograms for living (⟨ᴵᴵᴵ⟩) which describe the stomach: the fence (ᴵᴵᴵ) that contains the work (⟨ᴰ⟩) of digestion (See Chapter Fifteen). Like the fence description of a person's stomach, her womb (ᴵᴵᴵ) would anchor (⟨) the location where the flesh of her offspring would be formed.

There Is More

Since Adam and his wife had no children at this point, his declaration that *"she was the mother of all living"* needs some additional context. Genesis 1:26 – 27 says that God made man in His image and after His likeness as male and female. The pictograms for female are ⟨ᵞᴸᴼ⟩. I shared in Chapter

Fifteen that her role was to bring new life ( ) through her cycles ( ) into the family ( ) as an awe-inspiring offering of praise ( ) to the Lord.

God fulfilled His promise to Adam to find him a helper by making a woman out of one of his ribs.

> *"And the rib that the LORD God had taken from the man he made (   ) into a woman (   ) and brought her to the man."*
> (Genesis 2:22).

In Genesis 2:7, we read that the Lord God FORMED Adam from the dust from the ground. But here, the Lord God MADE Adam's rib into a woman. The Hebrew word for "made" until 2:22 was   not   . This new word says that God actively ( ) made the woman so that her body ( ) could produce new life ( ), fulfilling her role to bring children into the family.

This word was also used for the altars Noah and Abram / Abraham built (made) in Genesis 8:20, 12:7 – 8, 13:8 and 22:9. An altar is a place of sacrifice. Adam sacrificed one of his ribs to God so He could make the woman. And the woman would sacrifice her body to the Lord so He could make new life from it.

God made the woman (   ) and brought her to Adam who declared, *"She shall be called Woman (   ) because she was taken out of Man (   )."* I stated in Chapter Twenty that   is the Hebrew word for fire; the true character of our first parents.   signified that Adam worked in the fire of their relationship to love her and give himself up for her as a sacrifice so that he might present her to God as an offering of praise (Ephesians 5:25 - 32).

I am asserting that God's revelation to Adam in verse Genesis 3:20 not only moved him to repentance but brought to his attention the marital role he had exhibited earlier. It would only be through his total commitment to their three-fold covenant that they would be able to reflect God's image and likeness into their children. Without his **essential dedication** as the father and head of their family, their children would be destined to reflect more of the **anger, fear and blame** that had characterized his self-centered perspective, gained when his eyes were opened in Genesis 3:7.

Where is my father?

The role of the father in a family is critical to the temperament of the children. Let's briefly examine how adding certain pictograms to the word for Father changes its meaning[113]:

Father – . Basic meaning: Strength of / Leader of () the family ().

Enemy / Hostile – 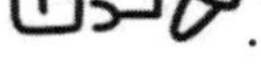. Adding 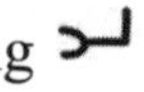 breaks up "Father" into two words:

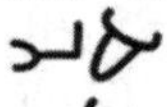 – Where?

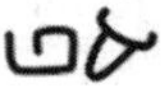 – Father

Combined, these two words can also be expressed as **Anger – "Where is my father?"** – giving context to the **hostile attitude of angry children** raised without the positive love, discipline and support of a father. These symbols reveal another dimension of this issue. The position of 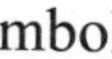 between 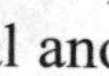 and 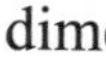 shows that the father is now separated from his family by his work (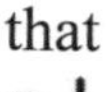). His strength and focus have shifted from a commitment to his family to his work.

Passionate Hostility – ロ>ᴜ Y ᓂ. This configuration is the basis for ロ>ᓂ and is the word most frequently found in the Bible. Adding Y yields permanence and passion to the hostility. That is, it anchors (Y) the father's time and energies to his work (>ᴜ) diverting his attention from his family and further robbing them of his participation.

Enmity – Yロ>ᓂ. We first met this word in Genesis 3:15 when God put enmity between the woman and the serpent and between his seed and her seed. The addition of Y means that the father's sense of value comes from the praise he receives through his work. His self-worth no longer stems from his role as a father but from the recognition of what he does.

In Chapter Twelve, I said our God instituted the Sabbath as a day of rest – a day not simply to refrain from working, but a day of the week set apart to focus entirely on the relationships in the family. Moreover, the Lord wants us to enter into His rest – His finished work – perceiving through the lens of faith the things to be done each day as though they are already completed. By taking these steps of commitment to God and to his family, a father is able to manifest another dimension of his character:

Love – ロYᓂ. ᴜY (from passionate hostility) is replaced by Y reinforcing a father's love for his family: the strength (ᓂ) of the father's love is revealed (Y) to his family (ロ) through his attentive commitment to them.

What God Did

"And the Lord God made for Adam and for his wife garments of skins and clothed them"

Our translations do not reveal a vital key that highlights the true significance of this verse. As you can see from Appendix B, two letters were affixed to the end of certain verses to emphasize their importance. The letter Pey (⊖) was appended to the seven Days of creation from Genesis 1:3 through 2:3, to this passage and to the last verse of chapter four. And Samech (◀) was added to Genesis 3:15, 3:24 and 5:2.

I shared in Chapter Twelve that these two letters were attached like "signet ring" seals to elevate their status for those reading the original biblical text, and that Pey was the more important of the two seals. So, verse 21 must mean more than God's desire to replace Adam and Eve's fig leaf loincloths with animal skin garments. Its presence mandates the importance of this verse as a critical revelation of God's redemptive plan to bring our first parents back into a yoked relationship with their Father.

A Yoked Relationship Through These Garments

Verse 3:21 says that God made for Adam (ᴹＵ𝄐ᒪ) and for his wife (Ｙｗ𝄐ᒪ) garments of skins. The monikers for Adam and his wife are both preceded by ᒪ and are followed immediately by the word for garments. I contend that the presence of ᒪ affirms God's desire, not only to make garments for them, but to yoke them to the anointing He gave to their clothing.

Made – Ｙ◀⊖⊃ᒧＹ. Ｙ◀⊖ is linked (Ｙ) to verse 20 signifying that Adam's repentance was necessary before God personally (⊃ᒧ) made (Ｙ◀⊖) their garments. But, before I

describe the pictograms for "garments," you might be as surprised as I was to learn that the word in this form is found in **only eight other places in the entire Hebrew testament**[114]:

> *"For **Aaron's sons** you shall make **coats** (✝ Υ ٢ ✝ Ⴞ) and sashes and caps. You shall make them for glory and beauty."*
>
> (Exodus 28:40)

> *"Then you shall bring **his (Aaron's) sons** and put **coats** (✝ Υ ٢ ✝ Ⴞ) on them,"*
>
> (Exodus 29:8)

> *"They also made the **coats** (✝ Υ ٢ ✝ Ⴞ), woven of fine linen, for **Aaron and his sons.**"*
>
> (Exodus 39:27)

> *"You shall bring **his (Aaron's) sons** also and put **coats** (✝ Υ ٢ ✝ Ⴞ) on them,"*
>
> (Exodus 40:14)

> *"And Moses brought **Aaron's sons** and clothed them with **coats** (✝ Υ ٢ ✝ Ⴞ) and tied sashes around their waists and bound caps on them, as the LORD commanded Moses."*
>
> (Leviticus 8:13).

> *"According to their ability they gave to the treasury of the work 61,000 darics of gold, 5,000 minas of silver, and 100 **priests' garments** (✝ Υ ٢ ✝ Ⴞ)"* (Ezra 2:69).

> *"Now some of the heads of fathers' houses gave to the work. The governor gave to the treasury 1,000 darics of gold, 50 basins, **30 priests' gar-**

ments († Υ ٢ † Ш) *and 500 minas of silver. And some of the heads of fathers' houses gave into the treasury of the work 20,000 darics of gold and 2,200 minas of silver. And what the rest of the people gave was 20,000 darics of gold, 2,000 minas of silver, and **67 priests' gar-ments** (* † Υ ٢ † Ш*)."*

(Nehemiah 7:70 – 72)

Searching through the ESV, I found "garment" in 87 verses and "garments" in 130 verses. There are a number of different Hebrew words translated by this English term. However, the eight texts I presented above suggest that God clothed Adam and his wife by designating and anointing their animal skin coverings as **priestly garments**. Their acquisition was much more than an exchange for fig leaf loincloths since the former had no priestly function.

But before I continue, remember that the Lord's goal was to guide Adam and his wife back into a **yoked relationship**. The individual symbols for "garments" show how the Lord used these pictograms to remind our first parents of the destiny He was reestablishing.

Garments – † Υ ٢ † Ш. Conforming (Ш) to the sign (†) yielded new life (٢) that was anchored (Υ) to the sign (†).

In Chapter Nine, I said that before a farmer began to plow his field, he first set up a marker or sign (†) on the opposite side to guide his oxen from their current location across the field in a straight line[35]. Of course, the farmer was free to choose a path across the field without first setting a marker as a goal. But the marker assured a straight furrow if the farmer remained focused on the sign.

Adam had decided to choose his own path by inserting the phrase **"neither shall you touch it"** into God's initial command to him instead of asking for a revelation from the Lord – a sign to follow by faith. That posture had been his previous course of action (the first protocol in Genesis 2:25) and had always been successful.

Conforming (Ш) to the sign (†) meant they should seek a revelation from the Lord – His way to overcome their chaotic situation – and submit to His guidance by faith. This posture would bring them back in line with the first protocol. And, it would yield new life (۱) – success without shame or fear – because their path would be anchored (Υ) to the sign (†).

Skins – ۵Υ☯. See (☯) the anchored (Υ) man (۵). These symbols would remind them of the naked posture (۵☯) of the first protocol and would more firmly anchor (Υ) their resolve not to rely on their own resources to remedy their current problems.

And Clothed Them – ₥ШШ☐Ⳑ⊐Υ. Υ connects this action to the previous phrase and affirms that this entire verse was accomplished by the strength of God's arm (⊐). ☐Ⳑ is the Hebrew term for "heart" and shows that God was giving them His heart – His motivation and compassion. It also signals that He enabled them to have control (Ⳑ) over their tent (☐) – over their soul and the appetites of their body. This would be accomplished by clothing them with His Name: giving them the ability to destroy (Ш) the chaos (₥) they faced by invoking His Name (₥Ш).

SUMMARY

God clothed Adam and his wife as priests when He inaugurated the first blood sacrifice for the forgiveness of sins. Without the revelation of these pictograms, we have had to presume the garments of animal skins conveyed the more redemptive role of salvation and righteousness based on other passages:

> *"Let your priests be clothed with righteousness, and let your saints shout for joy."*
>
> Psalm 132:9

> *"I will greatly rejoice in the LORD; my soul shall exult in my God, for he has clothed me with the **garments of salvation;** he has covered me with the **robe of righteousness.**"*
>
> Isaiah 61:10

However, the testimonies of these pictograms validate the significance of God's signet ring assignment and establish a firm scriptural foundation from the earliest pages of Genesis that without the shedding of blood, there is no forgiveness of sins (Hebrews 9:22). They also declare that salvation and righteousness is not achieved through works but through repentance and faith in the unconditional love of our awesome God!

Study Questions For Discussion

- I said in the Prologue that I believed God's words in Genesis 3:16 – 19 were redemptive, not punitive. Do you agree? What do you base your decision on?
- If you agreed with me, how would you answer the person who says God must judge sin?
  - o How does God's judgment express His **unconditional love**? (John 3:16 – 17)
- It is said that all of Adam's descendants "FELL" when he disobeyed the Lord. Paul seems to be affirming that conclusion when he writes, *"For as in Adam all die, so also in Christ shall all be made alive"*.
  - o What does Paul mean by writing – *"as in Adam ... so in Christ ...?"* (1 Corinthians 15:22).
  - o Does Ezekiel 18:20 bring any additional understanding?
- What do you believe changed Adam's mood from blaming the Lord and his wife to praising her as the mother of their descendants?
  - o Has that ever happened to you?
  - o As a husband and father? As a wife and mother?
- What part does an altar of sacrifice play in repentance?
- If God formed your body in your mother's womb, did **your life** begin at conception?
  - o If not, when were you made by God?
  - o Does Genesis 1:26 – 27; Jeremiah 1:5; Galatians 1:15 provide any answers?
  - o Both Jeremiah and Paul were consecrated and called before they were born. Does that mean God also consecrated and called you before you were born?
  - o Does Romans 8:28 – 30 provide any clarity?
  - o God placed Jeremiah and Paul at a certain time and place in history for His glory. Did God also place you at this time and in your location in history for His Glory?
- God made Eve's body so that she could bear children. Why

did God use a different word when He "made" her?

- o Was that difference more than giving her different reproductive organs?
- o Was her soul also different?
- o Do female animals relate differently than male animals?
- o Are those differences purely physical or are their souls also different?
- o You are a spirit being living in a body of flesh that is energized by your soul. Why is it important to know that God made all three – body, soul and spirit – as either male or female?
- o And why is it important to understand that God knew you as a spirit being BEFORE He formed you in your mother's womb?
- Why is it critical for the father to play an active role in raising his children?
  - o How is a child's **anger** related to "Where is my father?"
  - o Does a consuming focus on his job contribute to this issue?
  - o How can that anger be remedied?
  - o Can the father's love overcome a child's anger?
- Verse 3:20 ended with a Pey (⬤). What value does this mark have for you?
- Were you surprised to learn that the garments of skin were priestly garments?
  - o Both David and Isaiah say that God clothes us in the priestly robes of salvation and righteousness. Paul calls us to *"put on the Lord Jesus Christ"* (Galatians 3:27). How does that bring us salvation and righteousness?

CHAPTER 32

Genesis 3:22 – 24
Like One Of Us

"Then the Lord God said, "Behold, the man has become like one of us in knowing good and evil. Now, lest he reach out his hand and take also of the tree of life and eat, and live forever—" therefore the Lord God sent him out from the garden of Eden to work the ground from which he was taken. He drove out the man, and at the east of the garden of Eden he placed the cherubim and a flaming sword that turned every way to guard the way to the tree of life."

(Genesis 3:22 – 24)

PROLOGUE

Once again, these verses can be interpreted as either redemptive or punitive. On the one hand, disobedience has consequence. But our awesome God is always motivated by His unconditional love. So, our consequences are always couched in His steadfast love – His mercy.

Sent – Ⅲ ℓ ⱳ. This word reveals God's motivation when He expelled Adam from the garden. "Sent" should more accurately be translated as "consume / constrain (ⱳ) his authority (ℓ) – allow him to go – with restrictions (Ⅲ)." Jeremiah 40:1 – 5 gives us a window into this aspect of God's merciful care. Jerusalem had just fallen to its enemies:

"The captain of the guard took Jeremiah and said to him, "... Now, behold, I release you today from the chains on your hands. If it seems good to you to come with me to Babylon, come, and I will look after you well, ... Or go wherever you think it right to go" So the captain of the guard gave him an allowance of food and a present, and let him go (Ⅲ ረ W)."

Drove – WꞨ𐤉. The pride (𐤉) of the man (Ꞩ) is destroyed (W). If God's actions had been punitive, the description of their expulsion would likely have been expressed **only** by "drove" – a word often reserved for Israel's enemies – instead of including "sent."

"He drove out (WꞨ𐤉) nations before them; he apportioned them for a possession and settled the tribes of Israel in their tents."

(Psalm 78:55)

To work the ground

There were significant differences between Genesis 2:15 and 3:23:

2:15: Work (∪ ꟻ ● ረ) and
Keep (Ⴤ Ꞩ ᵐᵐ W ረ) the garden
3:23: Work (∪ Ⴤ ꟻ ● ረ) the ground

Initially, Adam not only worked the garden but also kept it through the blessing and guidance he received from the Kingdom of Heaven. Ⴤ Ꞩ ᵐᵐ W ረ had given Adam (Ꞩ) the authority (ረ) to destroy (W) the chaos (ᵐᵐ) he faced and establish order in a way (the first protocol) that brought praise (Ⴤ) to the Lord. But that focus changed in 3:23.

Notice that is present in 3:23 but is missing in 2:15. Earlier, Adam had not been **anchored** to his work in the garden so that it interfered with his relationships with the Lord and his wife. In my last chapter, I wrote of the importance of the father's role in the family and that **anger**, fed by the sense of "where is my father?", is reflected in the children.

I showed that one of the primary reasons for the passionate hostility ( ) exhibited in children is the anchor ( ) that disproportionately binds the father ( ) to his work ( ). This predicament is rooted in the definition of work in 3:23: – The yoke that controls ( ) the father's perception ( ) of his house ( ) as being excessively anchored ( ) to the door ( ) – the way to his work. He perceives that his value to those in his family is anchored to his commitment to his work. Verse 3:23 states Adam now perceived that his value was anchored to his commitment to his work.

God sent ( ) Adam from the garden with certain constraints to **work** the ground. He did not give Adam the authority to **keep** it because Adam had broken his yoked relationship. He had become *"like one of us knowing ( ) good and evil."*

"Knowing" in 3:7 ( ) meant their work ( ) was guided by what came in through the door ( ) of their eye ( ) – their physical senses. Now, in 3:22, Adam was yoked ( ) to that regimen and it had become his reality ( ).

Genesis 3:7 states that as soon as their eyes were opened, they sewed fig leaves into loincloths. The urgency of that moment had circumvented any decision to wait on the Lord for an answer. Now, as Adam prepared to leave the garden, he likely realized he would face a host of new issues that would be much more demanding than covering his loins. And with his new perspective of reality, he would be even less likely to wait on the Lord.

It is understandable that they were reluctant to leave the garden. The Bible says God drove Adam out *"lest he reach out his hand and take also of the tree of life and eat."* Adam's action would have repeated his wife's earlier activity and would be even more consequential – he would live forever.

There was a more basic reason for their expulsion

I said earlier that Adam and his wife had eaten from the tree of life before their eyes were opened. This tree with its twelve manner of fruit enabled them to live forever as long as they did not disobey the Lord. The underlying reason they were no longer allowed to enjoy its fruit was because they had become like God knowing good and evil.

Living by Faith in the Garden

I am asserting that the only way our first parents could stay in the garden was to live by faith. Before their eyes were opened, Adam and his wife perceived their environment the same way God viewed it. The Lord spoke of this perspective when He asked Samuel to anoint one of the sons of Jesse:

> *"Samuel looked on Eliab and thought, 'Surely the LORD'S anointed is before him.' But the LORD said to Samuel, 'Do not look on his appearance or on the height of his stature, because I have rejected him. **For the LORD sees not as man sees: man looks on the outward appearance, but the LORD looks on the heart'"** (1 Samuel 16:6 – 7).

God's Perspective: An Example

When the Lord brought creatures to Adam to see what he would name them, Adam did not make his assessment based on their **outward appearance** but on their unseen character that was also evident to God.

One of those creatures was the serpent in Genesis 3:1. We might look at the name "serpent" and conclude this creature was a snake simply because our dictionaries provide that definition even though the Bible says it was a beast of the field and not a creeping thing. Furthermore, the letters in "Serpent" say nothing about the actual character of this animal. The letters only give us the ability to pronounce the word and to find its meaning in a lexicon.

But the pictograms (**Wℼ ﬩**) give us an unseen window into its character: a fence (**ℼ**) between new life (**﬩**) and other herbivores that wanted to eat (**W**) the new life (vegetation). Little wonder that Adam would have chosen it as a guard animal in his garden.

A Second Example

When God brought the woman to Adam, he exclaimed,
> *"This at last is bone of my bones and flesh of my flesh; she shall be called Woman, because she was taken out of Man."*

"Woman" and "Man" reveal very little about the excitement Adam expressed in this verse. However, the pictograms reveal their unseen character as **Wᵬ** (fire) which also connected them with God as a consuming fire.

A Third Example

When the Lord described two of the trees in the garden, He

did not provide any identifying characteristics that would allow us to select them from a horticultural catalogue or their fruit at a grocery store. In addition, God never referred to the fruit of the trees, only to the trees themselves as a complete expression of their essence. He only revealed their function – their unseen character.

Later, when the woman examined the tree of the knowledge of good and evil, her analysis also focused on the "tree," not its fruit. And her assessment said nothing about its outward appearance. Her visual evaluation concluded that *the **tree** was **good** for food and that it was to be desired to make one **wise***, evaluations that further clarified the tree's essential properties?

Living by Sight in the Garden

When their eyes were opened, Adam and his wife no longer "saw" their situation the same way God perceived it. Their discernment of each other and their garden had changed dramatically.

> *"Then the eyes of both were opened, and they knew (*☉Ⴎ⅄*) that they were naked. And they sewed fig leaves together and made themselves loincloths."*

For the first time since they were married, this "knowing" motivated them to analyze their physical differences, conclude their own differences were inadequate, and hastily sew fig leaves from the garden into loincloths.

Notice that their new perception brought such urgency **to do something** that they didn't seek the Lord as they had always done before. It also suggests that Adam continued to discover more of his own inadequacies, and would likely try to alleviate them with anything that might help reduce the stress of working in his new hostile environment after he left the garden.

The Tree of Life

We are accustomed to equating the tree of life with the life gained by a yoked relationship with our Lord and Savior. In Chapter Seventeen, I carefully examined the tree of life and discovered that the Hebrew word for life was precisely the same as the word for life in Genesis 2:7. It referred to the physical life enjoyed by Adam and the other creatures God had made:

> *"Then the Lord God formed the man of dust from the ground and breathed into his nostrils the breath of life, and the man became a living (Ψ ⊐⅃Ⅲ) creature."*

If the fig leaves in the garden had helped cover their nakedness, the tree of life might also give Adam some measure of relief from working the ground. There was only one problem. The tree of life had helped sustain them while they were living in the Kingdom of Heaven. After their eyes were opened, if they tried to clothe their inadequacies with the "benefits" from eating its twelve different fruits, they would be extending their physical existence in the kingdom of this world – a solution quite apart from God's will for them.

Eve had been tricked by the serpent into believing that becoming like God knowing good and evil would bring them closer to the Father they both loved. Now, if they were allowed to continue living in the garden, they would be tempted to sustain their wretched life in the kingdom of this world by eating the fruit from the tree of life instead of seeking the Lord for a way out.

The harsh reality of working the ground was not punishment. Jesus said in His parable of the prodigal son that the Father gave the son his inheritance and let him go ($\mathbf{I\!I\!I}\ \ell\ \mathsf{W}$). But the father did so, hoping that his son would one day examine his awful circumstance, compare it with the life his Father's servants enjoyed and return home with a penitent heart. Jesus said the father saw his son a long way off and ran to meet him. There were no words of condemnation, only shouts of joy that his son who was dead was now alive (Luke 15:11 – 25).

Our awesome Father has never wavered in His loving commitment toward His sons and daughters. That commitment began with Adam and Eve and will extend throughout all the ages to come.

SUMMARY

My dad taught me a valuable lesson about the consequences of my actions. We were building a new barn on our farm at the time. He put a board in front of me and asked me to drive several nails into it. After I had finished, he asked me to pull the nails out of the board. Then he asked me to pull the holes out of the board. The nails were gone. But I could never restore the board to its original condition.

Once their eyes were opened, Adam and Eve could never again see their world the same way. Innocence was gone and Satan thought mankind would be forever trapped in the kingdom of this world. For us, it is impossible to pull the holes out of our boards. But not with God! With God, all things are possible! His arm is not shortened that He cannot save. The Holy Spirit did not inspire the first two chapters of Genesis only to show us what we lost and could never attain.

If you feel that your future is filled with thorns, thistles or debilitating pain, the Lord has the same solution for you as He had for our first parents. The first protocol still works! And we don't have to face it alone. Jesus, the last Adam, fulfilled that way of life, living every day doing only what He saw His Father doing. He took all our nails and allowed them to be fastened to His cross to set us free from their consequences.

Jesus died for us, sacrificing His life so we could appropriate His Life. Then His Father raised Him from the grave and enthroned Him above every name that is named. And now Jesus lives to intercede for us as only He can. His words ring out across the ages,

> *"Come to me all who labor and are heavy laden, and I will give you rest. Take my yoke upon you and learn from me. For I am gentle and lowly in heart, and you will find rest for you souls. For my yoke is easy and my burden is light"* (Matthew 11:28 – 29).

Study Questions For Discussion

- I said that Genesis 3:22 – 24 could be interpreted as either redemptive or punitive. What is your position?
  - o Can redemption deal with consequences?
- I said that "God Sent" could more accurately be translated as "God let Adam go with certain constraints." I supported the definition of "sent" with an example from Jeremiah. Does that example soften "sent" or would you rather perceive "drove" as a punitive action?
  - o How do you reconcile "sent" with "drove?"
- Why didn't Adam have the authority to KEEP the ground he was working?
  - o Where do we get our authority from?
- I associated the anchor symbol (Ϯ) in the word for work in 3:23 with a child's anger generated by a father's lack of physical, emotional and spiritual involvement with his family. One of the roles of the father is to work to support his family. How can a disproportionate commitment to his work isolate him from his family?
  - o How does walking by sight vs. walking by faith color his commitment?
  - o ☉Ʊ꜀ says that a man's work is guided by what comes in through his physical senses. Why does this perception often generate an urgent response to the situation?
- Why do we feel we have to **do** something **NOW**?
  - o Does the urgent need to address the problem shorten or eliminate our commitment to wait on the Lord for His solution?
- How often have you faced this inner conflict?
  - o How does "rest" redirect our focus?
- When did God solve the issues we are facing?
- Why did the Lord take away their access to the tree of life?
  - o How would they have lived if they continued to have

access?

- o Would allowing them continued access to the tree of life be like making the pig pen more agreeable to the prodigal son?
- Revelation 2:7 says, *"He who has an ear, let him hear what the Spirit says to the churches. To the one who conquers I will grant to eat of the tree of life, which is in the paradise of God."* I said in this chapter that Adam and Eve needed to live by faith in the garden in order to eat from the tree of life. This text says God will grant us to eat of the tree of life Under what conditions do we have access?
- o Why do we need to have an ear to hear?
- o What must we conquer in order to have access?
- o Where is the paradise of God? (Luke 23:42 – 43)
- o How many churches is the Spirit talking to?
- o Is the Spirit talking to us today or is this promise for later when our Messiah returns?
- o Can we access the tree of life **today**?
- Our actions have consequences. No matter what we do, we can never pull the "holes out of our boards" even if we are successful in removing the nails that caused them. But with God, all things are possible. Why is faith and obedience our only path to return to a yoked relationship with our awesome God and to His merciful, unconditional love?
- o Have you made a commitment to His Son Jesus Christ as your Lord and Savior?

CHAPTER 33

Genesis 4:1 – 2
A Brother Named Vanity

"Now Adam knew Eve his wife, and she conceived and bore Cain, saying, 'I have gotten a man with the help of the Lord.' And again, she bore his brother Abel. Now Abel was a keeper of sheep, and Cain a worker of the ground."

(Genesis 4:1 – 2)

PROLOGUE

Cherubim and a flaming sword now guarded the way to the tree of life. In a few years, with no man to care for it, the garden would be decimated by opportunistic animals, thorns and thistles. And without God's support, the trees would eventually succumb to the encroaching savanna. Adam could look forward to endless days of sweat and toil, and Eve could only wonder what the realities of childbearing would bring.

But chapter four does not begin with pessimistic desperation. Instead, we witness the new life of their son Cain bursting on the scene as a hope for their future. In this episode, I will endeavor to reveal the dynamics of this family and the relationships that will set the stage for the rest of Genesis chapter four.

Before and After Comparisons

Genesis 2:24 established an essential foundation for all future marriages:

"Therefore, a man shall leave his father and his mother and hold fast to his wife, and they shall become one flesh."

The Lord had put Adam in the garden to work and keep it. But his destiny would not be fully manifested without a helper. When God brought his help mate to him, Adam said,

"She shall be called Woman (ᴪШᎧ),
because she was taken
out of Man (ШᗒᎧ)."

With this proclamation, Adam commited himself to work (ᗒ) in the fire (ШᎧ) of their relationship, developing her character (ШᎧ) into an offering of praise (ᴪ). It would take sacrifice and a reliance on the Lord to unite their personalities into a union of one flesh that could fully reflect being made in the image and likeness of God (See Chapter Eleven where I explain "Image" and "Likeness"). This work would also take priority over his work (ᎠШᎧᏝ) in the garden as pointed out in my previous chapter by the lack of an anchor (ᴵ) in its pictographic definition.

Comparing Genesis 2:24 to 4:1

There are several important differences between these two passages. **First**, the participants in 2:24 were specified as Man (ШᗒᎧ) and Woman (ᴪШᎧ) indicating that they largely related to each other through their eyes of faith. But now, after their eyes were opened, verse 4:1 named them as Adam and Eve – the monikers of their physical bodies. This suggests that they related to each other more at their **soul** level – who they were as perceived through their physical senses.

Next, their original union was described as "hold fast" (ᎧᏝᎠ) meaning the Man entered the door (Ꭴ) of the

Woman's tent (ᗰ) during her cycle (⊖). This relationship was necessary in order for their union to become one FLESH and reflect the likeness of God. This physical and emotional bonding would progress over time as they became one in spirit, soul and body.

However, verse 4:1 says that Adam knew (⊖Ս⤳) his wife Eve – the same kind of knowing they experienced when their eyes were opened. Moreover, this text indicates that knowing his wife resulted in her conception – a one-time action, not a process over time to become one flesh. So, Adam's intimate activity (⤳) was likely soul-motivated through his physical senses (⊖)."

While it could be said that Adam was still "working" on their relationship, working in the fire to become one flesh and to reflect the likeness of God in their marriage may have been superseded by their physical and emotional desires for intimacy. Relating to each other in union with the Lord had been at least partially replaced by their **soul** desires for each other.

You may be wondering why "holding fast" did not produce children before the eyes of our first parents were opened. The answer is found in Jeremiah 1:5:

> *"Before I formed you in the womb, I knew you,*
> *and before you were born, I consecrated you; I*
> *appointed you a prophet to the nations."*

God knew (⊖Ս⤳) Jeremiah before he was born indicating that God had made him as a spirit being before **he** was conceived. Our awesome God has complete control over this entire process. The Lord made Cain and Abel as spirit beings before He formed their bodies in Eve's womb. God chose when these two brothers would be born, when and where Jeremiah would be born, and when and where you and I would be born. As parents, we participate in the birth of our children. But God alone is the Author of their life.

The Birth of Cain and Abel

"Eve ... bore Cain, saying, "I have gotten a man with the help of the Lord."

Cain – ⟨ᕐᒡᒣᴏ⟩. His name meant that her cycle (ᴏ) had produced (ᒡᒣ) new life (ᕐ).

Gotten – ᒡᒣ✝ᒡᒣ ᕐᴏ. From her cycle (ᴏ), new life (ᕐ) had been produced (ᒡᒣ) as a sign (✝) of the help she received from the arm (ᒡᒣ) of the Lord.

Eve's name for him may have reflected, not just their joy in his birth, but a hope that Cain would be the one who would bruise the head of the serpent (3:15) and put an end to their miserable existence. I say this because a child's name in the Bible often reflected the aspirations of the parents at the time of birth. Since Eve named their son instead of her husband, it may also indicate that she was still more sensitive to God's leading than Adam. Our first parents were at least nine months into their ordeal outside the garden, and the hope of a fulfillment of God's promise could have loomed large. However, they could only wait to see what would happen as Cain grew up.

"And again, she bore his brother Abel (ᒪ ᗡ᰸)."

In addition to the lack of fanfare over Abel's birth, they chose a name for him that seems puzzling – Vanity. This word has come to mean a person who is self-centered and has excessive confidence in his own capabilities. But according to Wikipedia, before the 14th century, it did not have such narcissistic overtones and merely meant "Futility" which reflects its biblical definition. If you read the book of Ecclesiastes, the preacher shares this gloomy assessment of his world:

"Vanity ($\mathit{l} \cup \Upsilon$) of vanities, says the Preacher, vanity ($\mathit{l} \cup \Upsilon$) of vanities! All is vanity ($\mathit{l} \cup \Upsilon$). What does man gain by all the toil at which he toils under the sun? A generation goes, and a generation comes, but the earth remains forever. The sun rises, and the sun goes down, and hastens to the place where it rises. The wind blows to the south and goes around to the north; around and around goes the wind, and on its circuits the wind returns. All streams run to the sea, but the sea is not full; to the place where the streams flow, there they flow again. All things are full of weariness; a man cannot utter it; the eye is not satisfied with seeing, nor the ear filled with hearing."
(Ecclesiastes 1: 2 – 8)

Substituting Abel's name for the Preacher's assessment provides a glimpse of the hopelessness they must have felt by the time this boy was born. Hope that Cain would be their salvation faded as he grew older. And by the time Eve bore Abel, all things must have seemed full of weariness and chasing the wind. Gone was the exuberance that another son was born into the family.

There's More

Let's take another look at verse two:

"And again, she bore his brother Abel. Now Abel was a keeper of sheep, and Cain a worker

of the ground."

I struggled for a long time trying to understand why Abel's name was listed first ahead of his older brother. Abel's name means "Behold (Ψ), the tent ($\square$) of a shepherd ($\mathcal{l}$)." How could the life of a shepherd be eventually equated in scripture with a **futile** lifestyle? More importantly, what meaning did Adam associate to $\mathcal{l} \square \Psi$ when his son was named?

The English word "Now" should more accurately be "And" (KJV) since the three clauses in verse two are all connected by Υ (a tent peg). It links Abel's birth and name to what he did ("keeper" is the same Hebrew word for a shepherd) in juxtaposition to what Cain did (a worker of the ground). Apparently, this close association between Abel and his eventual occupation was more important than maintaining his birth order. Why was this association important and why would it be contrasted with Cain's vocation?

Genesis 3:21 says that animals were sacrificed. So, a supply of animals would have been necessary to support repeated sacrifices. Initially, Adam might have hunted sheep for the sacrifice until he and Cain could shepherd a small flock. But, as soon as Cain was old enough to watch their sheep by himself, he likely relieved his dad so Adam could devote full-time to farming. Finally, Abel replaced Cain as the family shepherd so Cain could join his dad.

But this scenario still does not completely answer why their second-born son was named "Vanity" well before he assumed the role of a shepherd. I wondered whether Abel's name had more significance to Adam than just a manifestation of his frustration with his circumstance.

Remember that the ground had been cursed because of Adam.

He now faced working the ground by the sweat of his brow in order to feed his family. However, he may have felt that keeping sheep would not be as reliant as what the ground could bring forth even though it did not require the same horticultural skills he already possessed..

The stress of relying solely on farming for their livelihood could be lessened through a shepherding lifestyle change. Adam's farming skills could still create small patches of grain and vegetables around a base camp even as sheep and goats were shepherded by his children in the nearby grasslands of the savanna. I am asserting that the Lord, in a gesture of His unconditional love, instituted this form of sacrificial system so Adam could experience how shepherding might work for them.

But his new shepherding experience left Adam with a choice: adopt a lifestyle that would eventually become the norm for the children of Israel or cling to a way of life that he was more familiar with. Farming anchored him to a location while shepherds moved with their flocks. Keeping the sheep also meant Adam's security would be less dependent on his own skills and more dependent on the Lord for His direction and blessing. Would Adam view shepherding as a disruption to his already-hectic schedule? Or would he see it as an opportunity to transition to a way of life that was less dependent on working the ground?

His initial decision to add the phrase "neither shall you touch it" to God's command meant that Adam had not trusted God enough to ensure his wife's obedience to the injunction without this supplement. He had also enlisted the serpent to further constrain his perception of her motives. Even before their eyes were opened, his flared nostrils had indicated his frustration that she didn't see things his way. And afterwards, his efforts to blame the Lord for his predicament pointed to a growing suspicion that God did not have his best interests at heart.

Even though Adam repented for his disobedience and became a priest in his family, the need for further sacrifices (4:4) meant that the challenges to his security (3:17 - 19) could have renewed his feelings of doubt and fear.

It is not uncommon to denigrate a way of life as unimportant especially when a person's lifestyle is challenged. So, it seems reasonable to assume that Adam could have rejected shepherding as a **futile vocation for him** since he felt so committed to working the ground. Even though keeping the sheep was necessary to support their ongoing sacrifices, Adam did not perceive it as a viable alternative to farming because his ambivalent posture kept him from trusting his Father enough to help him overcome the curse of the ground.

What About Abel?

Abel was Cain's brother ($\Upsilon \, \lrcorner \, \text{Ⅲ} \, \delta$) meaning he was a strong (δ) fence (Ⅲ) working ($\lrcorner$) to keep Cain anchored (Υ) during these trying times. Since their brother relationship was obvious, its inclusion in the text may also mean that Abel was more secure and independent than Cain. As the first-born son, Cain pleased his father by following Adam's commitment to work the ground.

I believe Adam chose $\ell \, \text{⅊} \, \Upsilon$ as a name for his second son because he recognized that by the time Abel was old enough, shepherding would consume more of Adam's time than either he or Cain could afford. He also felt it would be better for the younger brother to take on this rather menial occupation so that Adam and Cain could work the ground.

However, by the time Abel could assume this role, the prolonged hardships from toiling day after day to eke out a living had likely taken a toll on attitudes toward shepherding. Both Adam and Cain had tended sheep when the flock was small and, compared to farming, shepherding appeared to consist of little more than leading the sheep to pasture and watching them graze. Little wonder that a growing animosity might have colored Cain's opinion of his younger brother particularly if Cain was intimidated by Abel.

SUMMARY

The children of Israel had been relegated to the land of Goshen because of the Egyptian antipathy for shepherds. David was the youngest in his family and cared for the sheep. His standing in the family was so inconsequential that when Samuel asked that Jesse's family join him for a feast, David was not invited. It was only after Samuel asked if Jesse had another son that David was summoned. Later, when Jesse sent David to inquire about his brother's welfare when they were fighting Goliath and the Philistines, they upbraided him for leaving his sheep.

There was an ancient dislike for a job that had little noble standing. And yet, the giants among Israel's leaders have all been shepherds: Abraham, Jacob, Moses and David. Abel did not accept an easy life path any more than these four men of God. "Keeping the sheep" made Abel more dependent upon the Lord and took special courage. It must have been difficult choosing to fulfill his Name, live in a tent and risk a growing antagonism from his brother. Abel chose to follow the still small voice of the Lord no matter the cost.

Study Questions For Discussion

- How do you compare the relationship differences between Genesis 2:24 and 4:1?
- Do you consider the relationship defined by 2:24 as foundational to a marriage?
  - How can a husband "work in the fire?"
  - How can a wife participate in the fire with their husband?
  - How can a couple focus on becoming "one flesh?"
  - Does "flesh" focus on their physical relationship?
- Is "flesh" a carnal or a holy component of a marriage?
  - Why is it important for a couple to become "one flesh?"
  - Why is their physical and emotional bonding necessary in order for the couple to became one in spirit, soul and body?
  - How is that focus different from having a family?
  - What can happen if the marriage is not founded on Genesis 2:24?
- Why didn't Adam and his wife have children shortly after they were married in 2:24?
  - Does your life begin at conception?
  - If not, what does begin at conception?
  - When do you become a viable person?
  - From God's perspective?
  - From a biological perspective?
- Were you surprised that Adam named his second son "Vanity?"
- Even though shepherds were maligned, many of Israel's greatest leaders began as shepherds. What does this revelation mean to you?
  - Does this revelation change the way you perceive those who are maligned in our society?
- Were you surprised by the definition of a brother?
  - If you are a brother or sister, does this perspective

influence your family relationships?

o If you are a parent, how does this knowledge help you raise your children?

CHAPTER 34

Genesis 4:3 – 7
Sin Crouching At The Door

"In the course of time Cain brought to the LORD an offering of the fruit of the ground, and Abel also brought of the firstborn of his flock and of their fat portions. And the LORD had regard for Abel and his offering, but for Cain and his offering he had no regard. So, Cain was very angry, and his face fell. The LORD said to Cain, 'Why are you angry, and why has your face fallen? If you do well, will you not be accepted? And if you do not do well, sin is crouching at the door. Its desire is contrary to you, but you must rule over it.'"

(Genesis 4:3 – 7)

PROLOGUE

The loving hand of the Lord was shaping Abel's life as a shepherd as it later molded Abraham, Jacob, Moses and David. His willingness to follow the Lord's encouraging guidance built a growing confidence in his character together with a realization that the blessings of this new lifestyle were overcoming the curse of the ground. Unfortunately, that curse continued to frustrate Cain who doggedly clung to the works of his hands for his security. Each time these two met, the disparity of their demeanor made Cain more uncomfortable. And his vexation only increased whenever Abel tried to keep his brother's disposition anchored during Cain's many discouraging disappointments.

Background

Initially, God placed Adam in the garden to work and keep it. Each day was an adventure walking with the Lord and witnessing how He was able to overcome even the most difficult situations. But eventually, the Lord wanted to raise Adam's relational experience to a higher level. Even though Adam was satisfied with his yoked commitment and his calling as a farmer, the Lord knew he would be alone until he was united with his help mate.

God's unconditional love did not force Adam to agree to this new relationship. But, by readily embracing this opportunity, Adam experienced the joy of a spirit, soul and body union with his bride. However, relating to his wife was orders of magnitude more challenging than facing the demands of the garden. Their essential character reflected God's character as a consuming fire. And bringing two firebrands together required an exceptional commitment from Adam to work in that fire so that their marriage would reflect God's image and likeness.

It also meant a shift in his primary attention from the daily concerns of the garden to his ongoing obligations in their marriage. Both involved "work" but "working in the fire" demanded greater dedication. The rewards for operating at this higher level of trust and obedience could only be achieved if Adam kept his priorities clear: God, wife, garden.

But at some point, Adam felt that his relationship with the Lord would be jeopardized if his wife did not agree with his procedures for working the garden. Earlier, when only he and the Lord faced the pressures of the garden, he had no difficulty obeying God's injunction. Now, he believed his relationship with the Lord was contingent on his wife's adherence to the commandment as he interpreted it.

Remember, his helper (𐤍𐤟𐤏) had eyes to see (𐤏) that he was not as aware of, and she wielded a sword / cudgel (𐤟) that he didn't have. He was challenged to relate to her head-to-head (𐤍) and should have realized that her perspectives were complementary to his, not competitive. Neither viewpoint was complete by itself. She would not see everything his way any more than he would see everything her way. But by combining their 𐤏 and 𐤟 anointings, they would be far less likely to be drawn away from their relationship with the Lord or each other.

Unfortunately, instead of seeking the Lord for an answer to his marital impasse, Adam chose to "enhance" God's commandment hoping her commitment to the Lord would keep her away from the tree. Instead of recognizing that their disagreement signaled his inability to cope and ask the Lord for guidance, he chose to rely on his own understanding for managing the garden. His actions highlighted the reversal of his priorities – garden, wife, God – and indicated that Adam was beginning to exchange his relationship with the Lord through the first protocol with his reliance on himself through the second protocol.

God shared His redemptive revelation to Adam (3:17 – 19) to help him see that by filtering his commitment to the Lord and his wife through his dedication to the garden, he had disobeyed the very command he wanted to uphold and had exchanged the light of the Kingdom of God for the darkness of the kingdom of this world.

Furthermore, as long as he focused on his adherence to working the ground, he would remain a servant of its cursed environment. Even Cain's participation could not alleviate the pain, the back-breaking toil or the thorns and thistles. Adam and his family would only be redeemed by repenting of this allegiance and seeking first the Kingdom of God and His righteousness.

An Alternative Lifestyle

Once again, God offered a way to raise Adam's relational experience to a higher level by giving him the chance to reconsider his way of life and embrace an alternative lifestyle that was not dependent on working the ground. Unfortunately, this time Adam (ᵐᵐ𝐔𝒪), whose name was derived from the ground (𝚼ᵐᵐ𝐔𝒪), could not extricate himself from his familiarity with and adherence to farming. And since Cain decided to work with his dad, Adam's disdain for Abel's lifestyle must have influenced his eldest son.

The Offerings

With this background in mind, let's look at the offerings Cain and Abel made to the Lord.

> "In the course of time Cain brought to the LORD an offering of the fruit of the ground, and Abel also brought of the firstborn of his flock and of their fat portions. And the LORD had regard for Abel and his offering, but for Cain and his offering he had no regard."

- Their offerings (𝚼𝚻𝚻 𝟝ᵐᵐ) were defined elsewhere in the Torah as grain offerings;
  - o A food offering for the priests (A portion was often burnt)
  - o It could also accompany the sin offering of animals such as bulls, rams and lambs;
- Cain brought the fruit of the ground as an offering to the Lord;

- Abel brought the firstborn from his flock and from their fat portions;
  - o "flock" is a collective name for animals like sheep and goats;
  - o Both sheep and goats were well-adapted to life on the savanna where grass and bushes grew without the need for Abel to cultivate the ground;
  - o The Lord had regard for Abel and his offering; but,
  - o for Cain and his offering, He had no regard.

Course – ⌐⊖ᴡ. Many (ᴡ) cycles (⊖) hooked (⌐) or held fast. In Genesis 6:13, God said to Noah that He would end (⌐⊖) all flesh. In Genesis 8:6, ⌐⊖ signaled the end of a forty-day period. And in Daniel 8:17, God withheld understanding of the vision saying it was for the time of the end (⌐⊖). Since ⌐⊖ signals the termination of a cycle, ⌐⊖ᴡ must indicate the end of multiple cycles.

Time – ᴡﾗ⅃ᴡﾗ⅃. The basic word in this phrase is ᴡ Ƴ ﾗ⅃: the symbols for "Day" from Genesis 1:5. Repeating them emphasizes their significance as a span of time. Taken together, "in the course of time" represents the conclusion of a span of time marked by the end of multiple cycles.

The first-born of Abel's flock was born in the early spring during the annual birthing season. So, Abel's sacrifice took place in the spring or early summer and marked the end of many previous offerings. It may also signal that after Abel was killed, these brother-ceremonies ceased.

Brought vs Brought – ⋔⅃⊃ﾗ⅃ (Cain)

vs ⋔ﾗ⅃⊃ＹＹ (Abel)

⋔⅃⊃ﾗ⅃ – Benner says that ⋔⅃⊃ means to fill a void or empty place[115]. So, Cain filled this void with an offering of the fruit of the ground produced by the strength of his arm (𐤉𐤋).

𐤅𐤏𐤁𐤋𐤀 – Benner says that 𐤁𐤋 indicates an empty hand that desired to be filled; an introduction for an entreaty or request; a void inside oneself (𐤁) that desired to be filled[116]. So, Abel's offering began with praise (𐤅) and was offered as an entreaty. He came to the Lord with an empty hand and asked the Lord to fill (𐤋) his request – to fill a void inside himself (𐤁𐤋). This action sounds similar to how his father had originally brought requests to the Lord (Chapter Twenty-One explains this first protocol from Genesis 2:25).

Fat Portions – 𐤅𐤅𐤁𐤋𐤌𐤌. 𐤁𐤋𐤌 is a Hebrew word for fat, the choicest part of the animal – separated (𐤌) by the shepherd (𐤋) for use in his tent (𐤁). The prefix (𐤌) says that there was ample fat on the animal to be sacrificed. And the suffixes indicate that the fat of the new lamb / kid (𐤅) was an offering of praise (𐤅). The specific inclusion of "fat portions" demonstrates that Abel's vocation as a shepherd was blessed by the Lord and that he was grateful for those blessings.

Regard vs No Regard – 𐤏𐤔𐤉 vs 𐤅𐤏𐤔 𐤁𐤋
First of all, the addition of 𐤉 means that the Lord was actively involved in regarding Abel's offering, but not so for the offering of Cain. This word literally means consume (𐤔) the eye (𐤏) – what the eye sees. In most of the other scriptural references, it is translated as "look" meaning to diligently give attention to / inspect / evaluate. We could say that the Lord personally paid close attention to Abel's sacrifice while glossing over Cain's offering.

There are other possible explanations. How did Cain know that the Lord had made such a distinction between them? Cain's response implies that this differentiation was so obvious that it enraged him enough to eventually kill his brother.

In this passage, God manifested Himself only as YHVH. Later, in Chapter Nineteen, three "men" approached Abraham as he sat at the door of his tent. All three were visible and one of them was YHVH. Perhaps, the Lord had made Himself visible to Cain and Abel as a "man" so that his actions and words were visibly and audibly apparent to both of them.

There Could Be More

In Genesis 25:18, YHVH made a covenant with Abram. The Bible says that Abram set up two altars, divided animal offerings between them but did not light a fire under these altars. Instead, Abram beheld a smoking fire pot and a flaming torch that passed between the pieces. In another passage, YHVH answered by fire when Elijah tested the prophets of Baal (1 Kings 18:38). So, "regard" (⊘W≻˩) could be rendered as: "The Lord, by the strength of His arm (≻˩), consumed (W) Abel's offering by fire as a visible (⊘) sign of His regard for it."

This passage does not say how the Lord revealed His intentions to Cain, and these possibilities I mentioned are only conjectural. But Cain's response makes it clear that by whatever means, the Lord's acknowledgement was so obvious that Cain erupted in hostile anger.

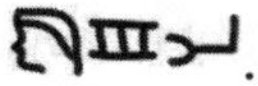

Angry – �গⅢ≻˩. This anger is not the same as the one mentioned earlier "Where is my father?" (Cain likely had a good relationship with his father.) Benner says that a person outside the wall will be exposed to the heat of the sun and will be hot[117] – the person (𝕹) is facing away from and is outside the fence / wall (Ⅲ) where he is exposed to the sun. This anger evoked strong passion (⊃⌐) and his face became hot.

Fell – Ƴ ℓ ⊙⌐ Ƴ . Not only did his face betray his anger, the first (Ƴ) shows that his fury was anchored on his brother whom he accosted (⊃⌐) verbally (⊙) venting his frustration and his authority (ℓ) as the elder brother, focusing / anchoring (Ƴ) his rage on Abel.

The Lord's Intervention

> *"The LORD said to Cain, 'Why are you angry, and why has your face fallen? If you do well, will you not be accepted? And if you do not do well, sin is crouching at the door. Its desire is contrary to you, but you must rule over it'"*

Let's step back for a moment and try to find a source for all this vitriol. Remember, that Cain was a spirit being living in a body that was activated by his soul. His soul's primary responsibility kept Cain's body physically alive. It was also motivated by what it perceived through Cain's physical senses to be good and pleasurable.

Cain had decided to work the ground with his father, resulting in a cascade of difficult circumstances that brought anything but good and pleasurable benefits. His soul could also perceive through the knowledge of good and evil that Abel's demeanor exuded a confidence that was almost totally lacking in Cain's mental attitude. This internal conflict eventually boiled over onto the only person Cain felt he could hate without irreparable consequences – not his father or the Lord, but his younger brother.

A Closer Look At 4:7 (Read from right to left)

Accepted   do-good   birth   Not

crouching   sin   at the door

do-good   not   Birth

⊔⊐⊕⊔† is derived from ⊔Y⊕ – the word for good associated with the tree of the knowledge of good and evil. ⊐⊔ replaced Y to emphasize that Cain perceived working (⊐⊔) the ground to be good; that he was actively pursuing a lifestyle that should produce "good" benefits.

The prefix ⊐⊔† means that the strength of his arm was totally dedicated to this pursuit. It is also linked to ᗰ♂, the word for "mother," meaning that he was actively "birthing" this effort – another indication of his commitment to this pursuit.

Cain wanted to achieve acceptance (†♂◄) by "doing good." Brown says that this word is associated with exaltation and dignity[118], blessings Cain desperately wanted and what may have led him to hate these same traits in his brother.

Notice this verse contrasts NOT [birthing "do-good"] with birthing [not "do-good"]. Furthermore, the first "not" is an emphatic configuration as compared to the second one. So, the Lord was asking Cain to reexamine his anger in light of his conviction that what he was doing was "good."

That is, the good Cain was striving to achieve by working the ground was reaping precisely the opposite: It was emphatically NOT "doing good" and if he continued, his misguided efforts would instead birth sin crouching at the door.

Door – . If Cain continued, he would be giving sin the authority () to enter through an opening () in his completed () fence () – the fence of security he had built around him because of his familiarity with working the ground.

Crouching – . Benner says that  represents the head of the house / tent[119]. So, sin would become Cain's master because it had the authority to enter his fence of protection.  also anchored sin's authority. Finally, sin would have a hook of desire () in Cain that would be hard for him to resist.

Sin – 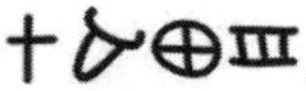. "Do well," "accepted," "door," "crouching," and "sin" all appear for the first time in this verse. Let's formulate a first-use, **pictographic** definition of "sin" because it undergirds so much of our interpretation of the rest of salvation history. Brown's definition[120] is the one I learned in seminary: Sin is "missing the mark." It was an archer's term saying that the arrow sinned when it didn't find its mark. There was no moral guilt or shame associated with the arrow. It did not become a "bad" or "evil" arrow. It simply missed the mark because the archer's aim was not accurate.

Strong supports this interpretation stating simply, "a primitive root meaning 'to miss,' 'to sin[121].'"

Benner agrees with this definition[122], but offers this explanation as an **abstract** meaning:

⊕Ⅲ – "Chords are used for binding as well as measuring. A chord is also used as a measuring device by placing knots incrementally. The chord is stretched between the object to be measured and the knots are counted. When shooting an arrow or other object at a target, the distance one misses is measured with a chord."

A fence (Ⅲ) surrounding (⊕) an enclosure can only be tangentially associated with a knotted chord used to measure distance. Further, measuring the distance of a miss would be more appropriate if the target was a long way off and the person was in some kind of competition or training exercise.

There is another archer's term that helps in this Greek explanation: parable – **para ballo** – to cast alongside. When a hunter shot at a moving animal like a deer and missed, the arrow **sinned** because it missed the dear. Since hunters carried only a few arrows at a time, retrieving lost arrows could extend the hunt. So, the hunter would ask his assistant to stand near the place where they thought the arrow had landed. Then he repeated his shooting motion with another arrow – the parable arrow – releasing it so that it followed the same trajectory as the first arrow. Only this time, his partner watched carefully where the parable arrow landed and searched alongside that location in the hope of retrieving the original arrow.

✝𝒷⊕Ⅲ. Seekins' analysis of the actual pictograms produced a different definition[123]: Sin is "the fence (Ⅲ) that surrounds (⊕) a person like a serpent strongly (𝒷)." The suffix symbol (✝) says the fence would not only surround Cain strongly but would surround him completely. This explanation is not abstract in any way. So, why do we prefer the Greek definition?

I shared earlier that the meanings of many Hebrew terms were derived much later from their corresponding words in the Septuagint and Aramaic documents. Here is Genesis 4:7 from the Septuagint translation:

οὐκ ἐὰν ὀρθῶς προσενέγκῃς, ὀρθῶς δὲ μὴ διέλῃς, **ἥμαρτες**; ἡσύχασον· πρὸς σὲ ἡ ἀποστροφὴ αὐτοῦ, καὶ σὺ ἄρξεις αὐτοῦ.

The highlighted word is **ἥμαρτες**. The noun form is αμαρτια from the verb αμαρτανω meaning "to miss the mark[124]". So, the Hebrew definition likely came from this Greek word.

Problems With This Interpretation

Why did Moses wait until Genesis 4:7 to introduce this term into the biblical literature? If it meant, "miss the mark," then obviously Adam **missed the mark** when he disobeyed the Lord, and Moses could have documented Adam failure with this word in chapter three.

Additionally, how could this term for sin apply to Cain in 4:7 and not to Adam in 3:17 – 19? That is, how could Cain miss the mark and not Adam? Using Seekins' definition, Cain had built a fence around himself, a sense of security gained from his familiarity with and his commitment to working the ground with his father. Cain sided with his dad that shepherding was akin to vanity because it seemed so unpredictable compared to the relative security of farming.

This attachment to the ground was especially strong for Adam who had known how blessed his earlier efforts were in the garden. Cain stubbornly clung to this agrarian lifestyle even though he could see shepherding was working for his younger brother. More importantly, he chose to walk by sight, trusting in the familiar patterns his dad espoused even though those patterns were not as applicable to farming on the savanna.

Before 3:17 – 19, Adam worked the ground as his God-chosen vocation. It was only after he disobeyed the Lord and was driven out of the garden that he had a choice between farming and shepherding. So, ✝ ☟ ⊕ Ⅲ would **not apply** to Adam **until after** he was evicted from the garden and had deliberately chosen to work the ground. He perceived it as a strong fence that surrounded him with a more secure way to provide for himself and his family.

Sin Separates

Cain's agrarian commitment was now a fence (Ⅲ) separating him from the Lord's alternative. It also seemed that the harder he tried to accomplish "good" results and provide pleasurable benefits for his soul, the more the curse of the ground worked against him, strangling (⊕) his efforts strongly (☟) like a serpent and completely (✝) frustrating him at every turn.

Sin's Relationship with Humility

According to Seekins, Sin is "the fence (Ⅲ) that surrounds (⊕) a person like a serpent strongly (☟)." He goes on to share that Humble (ⅢⱲ) means to destroy (Ⱳ) the wall (Ⅲ)[127]. So, sin is the fence of security we build around ourselves so we do not feel vulnerable. However, we can never build a wall that will give us security for all the future threats we will face. The Lord is the only One who "sees" tomorrow and can protect us. Moreover, when we take responsibility for our security, we willfully leave our yoked relationship in that area and step into the kingdom of this world, separating ourselves from the Lord. The only way back is through repentance, humbly confessing those areas of security we cling to.

Cain Must Rule Over Sin

> *"Its desire (*𐤕𐤔𐤅𐤒𐤕𐤅*) is contrary (*𐤀𐤋𐤉𐤊*) to you, but you must rule (*𐤕𐤌𐤔𐤋-𐤁𐤅*) over it.'"* (Genesis 4:7)

If Cain chose to continue emphatically NOT "doing good," instead of being accepted, he would birth sin crouching at the door. At that point, his only option was to rule over his soul's dislike for the cascade of arduous circumstances that yielded anything but good and pleasurable benefits. Let's see how sin's relationship with Cain was truly contrary to him.

Desire – 𐤕𐤔𐤅𐤒𐤕𐤅.
Sin's desire (𐤕𐤔𐤅𐤒𐤕) was anchored (𐤅) to Cain. That is, sin would completely (𐤕) consume (𐤔) his cycles (𐤒) of rage toward Abel and as such, his anger would be totally (𐤕) anchored (𐤅) to Abel.

Contrary – 𐤀𐤋𐤉𐤊. Sin will also be strongly (𐤀) yoked (𐤋) to Cain, working (𐤉) to conform (𐤊) him to its will.

Rule – 𐤕𐤌𐤔𐤋-𐤁𐤅. In order to overcome sin's overwhelming desire to conform Cain to its will, he must completely (𐤕) rule (𐤌𐤔𐤋) over sin anchored (𐤅) to his "tent" (𐤁) – his body activated by his soul. Since sin fed off Cain's episodes of rage toward his brother, he would be virtually powerless to rule over it because every time they met, his anger would be rekindled.

SUMMARY
Before we go on to the next chapter, I challenge you to reconsider the meaning of two very important words we use to

proclaim the Gospel: Evil and Sin.

Consider the Greek definitions found in Strong's Exhaustive Concordance, a popular reference for many pastors and serious laypersons:

Evil: hurtful, depraved, iniquitous, calamitous, vicious, malicious, bad, grievous, lewd, wicked[125]

Sin: Miss the mark, not share in the prize, offend, trespass[126]

Here are the pictographic definitions:

Evil – ⊙𝄐. A person (𝄐) guided by his sight (⊙).

Sin – ⌇⊕Ⅲ. The fence (Ⅲ) that surrounds a person like a serpent (⊕) strongly (⌇).

A person who is guided by his sight may be a very moral person but is still lost and in need of the Gospel. If we keep equating sin with evil character traits, we risk giving many people the excuse that they don't need salvation because they don't engage in "evil" activity.

Jesus' disciples were amazed when He told them how hard it was for a person like the rich, young ruler to enter the Kingdom of God. They thought this man was surely an exemplary example of a righteous person. But notice his words,

> "Good Teacher, what must I do to inherit eternal life?" Jesus replied, "Why do you call me good? No one is good except God alone."
> (Mark 10: 17 – 27)

Like Cain, this man was seeking what he thought was "Good." His riches had become his security just like Cain's farming regimen. He walked away sorrowful when Jesus asked him to exchange his security for an opportunity to become a disciple because he couldn't see how he could live without the fence of his wealth that surrounded him strongly. Our world is filled with people just like this young man who don't think the Gospel relates to them because of our definitions of evil and sin. Once again, the Hebrew definition:

- Evil is a person guided by his sight – by what **he believes** is his best course of action; and,
- Sin is our propensity to surround ourselves with strong fences like wealth, status , education, titles, etc., that make us feel more secure and less naked.

Study Questions For Discussion

- Has the Lord ever asked you to consider a less secure lifestyle so that you can rediscover the benefits of walking more closely with Him?
  - o What was your response?
  - o What was His motivation?
  - o What happened to your relationship with the Lord?
- Are there fences of security in your life?
  - o Are they shielding you from your dependency on the Lord?
  - o Are they shielding you from your relationship with your family and friends?
  - o Does your security control your life?
  - o Are you frustrated that this control is robbing you of good benefits?
- How are sin and humility related?
  - o Why is humility necessary?
  - o Can we ever achieve a closer walk with the Lord if we cling to sin – those elements we have added to our lives to make us feel more secure?
  - o ШШW means to bow down – to worship. Do you see an association between humility and worship in your life?
- How are evil and sin related?
  - o If sin is missing the mark and evil consists of immoral acts, do you feel you are not sinning because you do not live an immoral life?
  - o The Hebrew definition of evil is a man guided by his sight. How does this relate to your life?
  - o Can you be moral and still be guided by your sight?
  - o Is being moral enough?
  - o Why is it so hard to live a moral life?
- Can you always "hit the mark?"
- If you view bad habits (evil) as missing the mark (sin), can

you see why it is so hard to overcome bad habits?

  o Do your habits have a desire to conform you to their will?

  o What relationship does your security have with your habits?

• How do you feel about yourself when you miss the mark – again?

• Is anger a flag trying to alert you to change direction – to repent?

  o Has this chapter given you a fresh perspective on "sin" and "evil"? Explain?

CHAPTER 35

Genesis 4:8 – 9
My Brother's Keeper

"Cain spoke to Abel his brother. And when they were in the field, Cain rose up against his brother Abel and killed him. Then the Lord said to Cain, "Where is Abel your brother?" He said, "I do not know; am I my brother's keeper?"
(Genesis 4:8 – 9)

PROLOGUE

In the last chapter, the Lord asked Cain to examine why he was angry and face fallen. His actions were not achieving the "good" he hoped for, and if he continued, he would have to overcome sin that was crouching at his door. Perhaps as a result of his encounter with the Lord, he tried to rule over sin. Surely, he could find the mental and emotional strength to rise above this adversary and find a way to exist with his brother without further episodes of rage. Perhaps, if he faced his brother in the field while the presence of the Lord was still fresh in his mind, he could remain as a farmer and build a more compatible relationship with his brother Abel.

Spoke – 𐤓𐤌𐤁𐤉𐤅. The 𐤉 indicates that this verse is linked to the previous one and should more accurately be rendered: ***And** Cain spoke to Abel his brother.*" The 𐤁 also signifies that this verbal encounter was an intentional exchange. So, Cain's address to his brother was both deliberate and took place soon after his meeting with the Lord.

Cain To Abel – 𐤋 𐤅𐤘𐤉-𐤋 𐤃𐤔 𐤀𐤍𐤉. Their "brother" relationship was emphasized four times in these two verses. I am suggesting that 𐤋𐤃 (strongly yoked) further identified their familial ties. Perhaps, their encounter began in a somewhat amicable manner because Cain was trying, at least initially, to rule over sin "crouching at his door."

And When – 𐤌𐤕 𐤉 𐤉𐤅𐤉𐤘 𐤉𐤅𐤉𐤍. This is an unusual sentence structure. 𐤉𐤅𐤉 means "to exist" and was how the Lord defined His character to Moses in Exodus 3:14, "I AM WHO I AM." Moses used a form of this word 87 times between Genesis 1:2 and 12:16. But only here in verse eight is it used twice without any intervening word. I am asserting that this phrase sets the stage for the rest of the passage.

As you can see from the English translation above, the first term is ignored except for the connector 𐤉 (and). 𐤍𐤅𐤉𐤍 is a common variation of 𐤉𐤅𐤉, occurring 59 out of the 87 times, and is presented here without any added modifiers.

I discovered that this two-word configuration is unique at least in the first twelve chapters of Genesis. Translators are challenged to convert these terms in a way that makes sense to their readers. Most renderings largely ignore the first word. However, this pictographic style of writing gives us another plausible resolution.

Since the two words are located next to each other, I am suggesting that they described how Cain compared his own existence (𐤉𐤅𐤉) with that of his brother (𐤌𐤕 𐤉 𐤉𐤅𐤘). The second word is modified extensively to let us know that it is quite different from the first one.

$$\text{ᴍ†} \text{Y} \text{ﮩﺟﯼﺍﺍ} = \text{ﻟ} + \text{Yﮩﺟﻯﺍ} + \text{Y} + \text{ᴍ†}.$$

ﻟ – In the tent

Yﮩﺟﻯﺍ – Exists

Y – Anchored to

ᴍ† – Benner says that this word means "someone who is mature, whole, complete, full, undefiled, plain, upright."[128]

In The Field – Yﻟﺍﻟﺍ. We have encountered this word for field many times before. The prefix (ﻟ) declares that the meeting between these two brothers took place in the field – a place more compatible with Abel's lifestyle than Cain's.

When they met in the field, Cain could tell that his brother was in (ﻟ) his element, that as a shepherd (Yﮩﺟﻯﺍ), Abel had accepted (Y) the challenges of life on the savanna because his flock could easily adapt to the harsher environment without the need to cultivate the ground. And his shepherding mindset exuded a maturity (ᴍ†) that honored the conditions of the field as whole and complete for his flock without any appreciable modifications.

On the other hand, Cain perceived seemingly endless issues trying to work the ground that could only be overcome by the continuous, painful, sweat of his brow.

And Rose Up – ᴍﻩﮩﺟﺍ Y . Benner says that ᴍﻩ is a generic term "to rise up" and was originally applied to stalks of grain that stood upright[129]. (Y) indicates a definite connection between "in the field" and "rose up." Their meeting may have started out with the best of intentions. Abel may have tried to help his brother appreciate the advantages of "shepherding" because it didn't require cultivating the field. I am suggesting that Cain's frustration continued to mount as he tried to interpret what his brother was sharing in a way that would allow him to farm.

"Rose up" implies that Cain took some sort of aggressive stance against his brother. But its use in other places in the early chapters of Genesis does not support such an interpretation. For instance, in Genesis 6:18; 9:9, 11 and 17, it is rendered "establish" where God established (raised up) a covenant with Noah. In 13:17, God asked Abram to arise and walk through the land that he would be given. And again, in 17:7, 19 and 21, God established (raised up) a covenant with Abram.

However, if this word was originally associated with stalks of grain, it might indicate that Cain was arguing with his brother over how he could continue to farm – how could "stalks of grain stand upright" in the field without working the ground? The pictograms indicate that Cain's heated argument (𐤓𐤀) with Abel continued until sundown (𐤏) and escalated into chaos (𐤌).

Cain Against Abel – 𐤋 𐤁𐤅-𐤋 𐤀   𐤍𐤀-𐤏. This is precisely the same configuration as in the first part of this verse. However, in light of the pictographic interpretation of "rose up," this familial association became combative.

His Brother – 𐤉 𐤍𐤇𐤀. Cain's hostility (𐤍𐤀) was now totally anchored (𐤉) to his brother (𐤇𐤀).

And Killed Him - 𐤉𐤅𐤒𐤄𐤅𐤍𐤉. Benner says 𐤒𐤄 means to trample under foot – to kill[130]. The pictograms that precede and follow 𐤒𐤄 show just how frustrated and angry Cain became. His unrestrained wrath (𐤅𐤍𐤉) that

416   Back To The Garden

culminated in killing (𐤓𐤂) his brother was revealed (𐤅) and anchored (𐤉) to his brother.

> "Then (𐤉) the Lord said to Cain, 'Where is Abel your brother?'"

Even after this horrific deed, our awesome God reached out right away (𐤉) to Cain trying to restore a yoked relationship with him.

> "I do not know (𐤉𐤕𐤏𐤃𐤉); am I my brother's **keeper** (𐤓𐤌𐤔𐤅)?"

This verse offers several insights into the crescendo of lethal emotions that led to Abel's death. If we rely on an English translation, we might equate Cain's "keeper" with keeper in Genesis 4:2:

> "Now Abel was a **keeper** of sheep, and Cain a worker of the ground."

As such, we might assume that Cain refused to be the keeper of his brother in the same way Abel was a keeper (𐤅𐤏𐤉𐤓 – a shepherd) of sheep. However, "keeper" in 4:9 is the term from 2:15 and was the way Cain was trying to interpret Abel's lifestyle.

> "The Lord God took the man and put him in the garden of Eden to work it and **keep** (𐤓𐤌𐤔) it."

𐤏𐤅𐤉 was the term the serpent shared with Adam's wife at the beginning of Genesis chapter three and means a person's efforts (𐤉𐤃) are determined by what he perceives through the door ($\overline{U}$) of his eyes / his physical senses (⊜).

ᕁ†⊜Ū᠊ᕁ – The more Cain tried to identify (⊜Ū᠊ᕁ) with Abel's way of relating to the field as a shepherd (ᕼ⊜ᛝ𝕉) and to associate it with his way of working the ground (𝕉ᵐᴡ), the more frustrated and angry he became until he gave up (†) trying to work it out (᠊ᕁ) and killed his brother – his strong fence of support (Ⅲ𝒷) – in a fit of unbridled rage.

SUMMARY
God's warning in 4:7 had been fulfilled in Cain. Sin – Cain's insistence on clinging to his familiarity of working the ground – had won. As long as Cain viewed shepherding as vanity, he would portray himself as a victim and refuse to repent and accept his culpability.

Study Questions For Discussion

- Cain thought he could muster up enough emotional courage to face his brother and work out a way to incorporate Abel's shepherding lifestyle into his own. Why was this approach bound to fail?
  - o Do we justify our way of life because it is the way we have always lived?
  - o Has the Lord ever asked you to adopt a new way to live?
- Would this new lifestyle have made you depend more on the Lord?
- What happened?
- Why did the Lord ask you to make this adjustment?
  - o Why is perseverance important?
  - o Is it possible to "modify" habits so we can successfully manage them?
  - o How can the Lord help us break those habits?
  - o What must we do?
- Are "sibling rivalries" unusual in families?
  - o How did Abel try to help his brother?
  - o How did Cain respond to Abel's help?
- What part does unconditional love play in relationships?
  - o How can we love our enemies?

CHAPTER 36

Genesis 4:10 – 12
Redemption Offered

"And the LORD said, 'What have you done? The voice of your brother's blood is crying to me from the ground. And now you are cursed from the ground, which has opened its mouth to receive your brother's blood from your hand. When you work the ground, it shall no longer yield to you its strength. You shall be a fugitive and a wanderer on the earth.'"
(Genesis 4:10 - 12)

PROLOGUE

We can dismiss Cain as the first casualty of sin. We can also view this text as God's judgment on Cain for killing his brother. So, why have I titled this chapter "Redemption Offered"? From the very first verse in the Torah, I have been convinced that God's motivation for everything is His **unconditional love**. All too often, we misinterpret His love chase after the lost as judgment instead of His loving discipline meant to elicit repentance.

> *"For I desire steadfast love and not sacrifice, the knowledge of God rather than burnt offerings"* (Hosea 6:6).

> *"The Lord is patient toward you, not wishing that any should perish, but that all should*

reach repentance" (2 Peter 3:9).

> *"Those whom I love, I reprove and discipline,*
> *so be zealous and repent"* (Revelations 3:19).

We do an incalculable disservice to the Gospel if we do not extend a similar level of compassion and forgiveness to the hard-to-love. Jesus said,

> *"You have heard that it was said, 'You shall love your neighbor and hate your enemy.' But I say to you, 'Love your enemies and pray for those who persecute you, **so that you may be sons of your Father** who is in heaven'."*
> (Matthew 5:44 – 45)

It is my desire to reveal to you the steadfast loving heart of the Lord toward Cain even though He knew Cain would ultimately turn and walk away (1 John 3:12, Jude 1:11).

Cain's Motivation

I am suggesting that Abel's death was not premeditated. "Brother" is found six times in four verses, and since the text reveals Cain's perspective, he must have been wrestling with his **strongly yoked relationship** with his brother and how he could **keep** his brother's lifestyle in the same way he **kept** his farm. I am asserting that Cain killed his brother in a fit of unbridled rage only after he could no longer reconcile his frustration.

"What have you **Done?**" – ✝⤴︎⦚⦚. ⤴︎⦚⦚ is found in many verses in Genesis chapter one and is translated as "made." It is the same word for "What is this that you have **done**?" in Genesis 3:13. The ✝ adds finality to the action.

Your brother's **Blood** – ᴟᴟⴵ. Both Adam (ᴟᴟⴵ𖤚) and

Ground (ᗱᗰ⊓ᗝ) are based on this word. Its inclusion says that Cain did more than beat or strangle his brother to death.

Crying from the ground – ᗰᒣᒧᗱᗝ⌐. Benner says

this word means to cry or call out loudly for help[131]. *"Your brother's blood is crying to me from the ground,"* could be a euphemistic way of saying, *"You killed your brother by shedding his blood."*

However, there is another plausible explanation: When God formed Adam's body out of the dust of the ground, He breathed His Soul into Adam's body that became a living soul. Adam's soul was responsible for keeping Adam's body alive and healthy. Leviticus 17:11 tells us how the soul accomplished it:

> *"For the life (ᗯ◯⌐) of the flesh (ᗭᒣᗱ)
> is in the blood (ᗰ⊓), and I have given it for
> you on the altar to make atonement for your
> souls (ᗯ◯⌐), for it is the blood (ᗰ⊓) that
> makes atonement by the life (ᗯ◯⌐)."*

Soul – ᗯ◯⌐. Life (⌐) is sustained by what the mouth

(◯) consumes (ᗯ). (The mouth includes the nose.)

Flesh – ᗭᒣᗱ. The tent (ᗱ) that supports (ᒣ) the man

(ᗭ).

This verse illustrates how the soul brings life to the flesh through the blood, transporting oxygen, water and nutrients that were consumed by the mouth.

What happens when we die? Ecclesiastes 3:21 and 12:6 – 7

say,

> *"Who knows whether the spirit (* Ⅲ Y ᔐ *) of man goes upward and the spirit (* Ⅲ Y ᔐ *) of the beast goes down into the earth?"*

> *"Before the silver cord is snapped, or the golden bowl is broken, or the pitcher is shattered at the fountain, or the wheel broken at the cistern, and the dust returns to the earth as it was, and the spirit (* Ⅲ Y ᔐ *) returns to God who gave it."*

In Ecclesiastes 3:21, Solomon used the same term for the spirit that goes upward from man and the spirit from beasts that goes down into the earth. Beasts only have a body and a soul. So, his association of the spirits of man with beasts indicates that he was talking about man's spirit soul. Because of that association, I assert that when we die, our soul also returns to God Who gave it.

Returning to Genesis 4:10

Ecclesiastes 12:6 does not include homicidal death. Abel's "dust" – his body – was forcibly separated from his soul by Cain's hostile action. I suggest that before Abel's soul returned to God Who gave it, it cried loudly to the Lord from the ground saying it was no longer able to bring life to Abel's flesh because Cain had spilled Abel's blood on the ground.

Opened – Y † ↾ ◯ . The ground (Y ᵐ ∪ ⌀) opened its mouth (◯), pulling the blood toward it (↾) completely (†) in praise (Y) to God. We might conclude that this is another euphemistic way of saying, *"Abel's blood was spilled on the ground."* I will assert that Y elicits a more profound meaning and explains why I called it "praise" to God.

Receive – † Ⅲ ⊕ ∠ . The ground had the authority (∠) to recycle (⊕) Abel's blood, separating it (Ⅲ) completely (†) from Abel. The ground was given authority to receive Abel's blood by the Lord when Abel's soul cried out from the ground. Its intercession would bring praise to the Father because of the obedient life and martyrdom of Abel.

Yield Strength – Ψ Ⅲ Υ Ⱳ – † † . The two symbols († †) are linked to the next word and declare that the yielding would now be terminated.

Strength – Ψ Ⅲ Υ Ⱳ . Brenner says Ⅲ Ⱳ means the hand (Ⱳ) raised as a wall (Ⅲ) indicating a hand that corrects or chastises. The word with Υ placed between its two symbols represents strength, might or power because the person has become anchored to the benefits (Ψ) of the correction[132]. Taken together, these two words mean that Cain had not responded to correction, and God's strength would no longer be available for him to work the ground.

Another Alternative Lifestyle

By clinging to farming to provide his security, Cain continued to reject his yoked relationship with the Lord that enabled him to work the ground. Killing his brother revealed to everyone just how committed he was to doing things his way. Even though he knew the Lord blessed his brother, he could not let go and trust the Lord to take care of him.

In addition, Cain was likely overcome with guilt and shame for killing his brother, not to mention the growing resentment from his parents for murdering their son. For his sake, the Lord decided it was time for a change or his life would spiral further out of control.

> *"You shall be a fugitive and a wanderer on the earth."*

Neither of these options were related to farming or shepherding. They would allow Cain to start fresh without the guilt and shame associated with working the ground or his negative mental image of shepherding as a vain lifestyle. If he humbled himself and trusted the Lord to take care of him as he ventured into this new way of life, his yoked relationship would be restored.

Fugitive – ⌾ ꕯ. As a farmer, he could plant seeds and count on his skills to produce new life (ꕯ) from his efforts. Now, he would have to rely on the Lord to show him (⌾) where that new life (ꕯ) would come from. (We will see in the next chapter how these pictograms were reversed in Cain's reply to the Lord.)

Wanderer – ᴜ ꕯ. Both words start with a quest to find new life (ꕯ). As a fugitive, if he relied only on his sight (physical senses) to guide him, he would risk seeing any new promise of life (ꕯ) leave through the same door (ᴜ) that it entered.

SUMMARY

Perhaps Cain had spent countless evenings listening to his mom and dad reminisce over their "golden age" in the garden, and longed to recapture their paradise. But with each passing year, as that dream looked more and more elusive, he might have grown resentful that Abel's life seemed blessed by comparison.

Their spring sacrifice was the last straw when what had only appeared to be favor became obvious to everyone in the family. Cain was blind to God's unconditional love and the benefits of His manifest presence that was building another kind of paradise for his brother. He couldn't see that God's favor was not about blessing an occupation – shepherding vs farming. It was about blessing their obedience, trust and devotion to Him.

Abel had also heard some of those stories around a campfire. But the ones that likely stimulated his curiosity explained how Adam didn't rely on his own understanding or resources when tackling difficult situations. In every instance, the Lord had always revealed ways to succeed without shame or fear. It even seemed like God sometimes allowed them to encounter perilous circumstances to show them just how trustworthy and faithful He was.

For Abel, their parent's recollections brought hope that no matter what he faced as a shepherd, he could trust the Lord's love to provide security and a path to success. But for Cain, those same recollections only brought a greater determination to achieve the level of success his parents had attained while they were in the garden. Instead of embracing the challenges of a more intimate dependency upon the Lord for his security, he retreated – like his dad – into the security that he knew and could more easily control.

Now, he had to confront the reality of losing control of everything he held dear and being thrust into a hunter-gatherer existence where uncertainty and danger looming around every corner. Would he look at these new options as his redemption? Would he view them as an opportunity to conquer the terrifying fear welling up in his mind and heart by learning that the Lord would never leave him or forsake him? Or would he see himself as a victim being stripped naked and cast out into the unknown as punishment for killing his brother?

Study Questions For Discussion

- It may seem easier to leave the hard-to-love alone precisely because they are hard to love. Jesus calls us to have His compassion for them. There are two sides to this coin: the person who is hard to love and the compassionate person. It is said that those who are hurting, hurt others. When these hurting persons lash out at you, they expect you to hit back and walk away. What happens when you don't lash out but stay connected to their pain?
  - o Does it give you a greater appreciation for what they are going through?
  - o Does it build more character in you?
  - o Do you have a deeper sense of accomplishment as you see both of you changing?
- The world is going through a major upheaval and many people are wondering how they can survive. Some long to return to the normalcy they once knew. Cain and his father struggled every day to make a living. Are you feeling the same way?
  - o Are you redoubling your efforts to regroup and recapture what you once had?
  - o How does the pictographic definition of sin relate to your effort to build areas of security around you?
  - o Does the pictographic definition of humility provide a path for your recovery?
  - o Are you crying out to God because He doesn't appear to be listening to you?
  - o Are you open to trust the One Who made the heavens and the earth to take care of you even when it seems hopeless?
  - o Can you look at your circumstances that say with Paul, *"All things work together for good to those who love God and are called according to His purpose?"*

- o If you have small children – even infants – when you look at them in your arms, do you expect them to carry their own weight and provide for the family?
- Or do you know you will take care of their needs even before your own needs are met?
  - o God is our Father and He loves you immeasurably more than you can ever love your own children who trust you to care for them. He only asks that you come to Him as a little child, to seek a personal relationship with Him and He will move heaven and earth to meet all your needs out of the riches of His storehouse in Christ Jesus!
- Are you willing to listen for His still, small voice to lovingly nudge you into a new and what may appear to be, a perilous adventure? The world is changing and many are seizing once-in-a-lifetime opportunities. It may look to you like the Lord is guiding you to a place of wandering. He only asks you to launch out with Him on His adventure one step at a time. He loves you and will never leave you or forsake you. Will you place your trust in Him as your Lord?
- Were you surprised that the Lord ministered to Cain face to face even after Cain killed his brother?
  - o Jesus called Abel righteous in Matthew 23:35. The Apostle John wrote that we should not be like Cain who was of the evil one (1 John 3:12). Since the Lord ministered to Cain face to face, what does this say about the Lord's willingness to minister to you the same way?
  - o Adam and his family expected to walk with the Lord face to face. Do our expectations have anything to do with how the Lord reveals Himself to us?

CHAPTER 37

Genesis 4:13 – 16
Redemption Rejected

"Cain said to the LORD, 'My punishment is greater than I can bear. Behold, you have driven me today away from the ground, and from your face I shall be hidden. I shall be a fugitive and a wanderer on the earth, and whoever finds me will kill me.' Then the LORD said to him, 'Not so! If anyone kills Cain, vengeance shall be taken on him sevenfold.' And the LORD put a mark on Cain, lest any who found him should attack him. Then Cain went away from the presence of the LORD and settled in the land of Nod, east of Eden." (Genesis 4:13 – 16)

PROLOGUE

This English translation of Cain's reply to the Lord does not adequately reveal what was going on in his heart. I said in the previous chapter that Cain would likely see himself as a victim being punished by the Lord for killing his brother. Before we consider the witness of the pictograms in this passage, we need to take another look at Cain's perspective of himself.

Like his father and brother, Cain had a choice to live in one of two kingdoms: The Kingdom of Heaven or the kingdom of this world. In the Kingdom of Heaven, he would walk by faith yoked with the Lord Who loved him unconditionally and only wanted him to succeed in everything he did without shame or fear. As such, he would experience God's grace and abundant blessing. He would also be a blessing to others, sharing freely as the Lord blessed him.

> *"But love your enemies, and do good, and lend, expecting nothing in return, and your reward will be great, and* **you will be sons of the Most High, for he is kind to the ungrateful and the evil. Be merciful, even as your Father is merciful.** *Judge not, and you will not be judged; condemn not, and you will not be condemned; forgive, and you will be forgiven; give, and it will be given to you. Good measure, pressed down, shaken together, running over, will be put into your lap.* **For with the measure you use, it will be measured back to you."**
>
> (Luke 6:35 – 38)

However, in the kingdom of this world, Cain would walk by sight under the control of the prince of this world who only wanted to steal, kill and destroy both him and everything he attempted to accomplish. To live in this domain was cursed in that he was strongly anchored to himself (ℵ ‍𝐘 ℵ𝔟) instead of to the Lord and would have to rely on his own resources and understanding to supply his needs. As such, he would cling to everything he had and was familiar with out of fear that there was no other source he could rely on.

> *"For no good tree bears bad fruit, nor again does a bad tree bear good fruit, for each tree is known by its own fruit. For figs are not gathered from thornbushes, nor are grapes picked from a bramble bush.* **The good person out of the good treasure of his heart produces good, and the evil person out of his evil treasure**

produces evil, for out of the abundance of the heart his mouth speaks" (Luke 6:43 – 45).

I have said previously that we need to interpret the words of the New Testament in light of their associated pictographic terms in the Torah. The pictograms for "good" are ⌂ Υ ⊕ – baskets (⊕) of blessings the Lord anchors (Υ) to the person's house / domain / tent / body (⌂). So, out of the good treasure of his heart (out of the baskets of blessings from the Lord), the good person produces good – he produces baskets of blessing, mercy and forgiveness to everyone.

The pictographic word for "evil" is ⦿⟁ – a person (⟁) guided by his sight (⦿). So, out of the evil treasure of his heart (being guided by his sight and not by the Lord), the evil person produces evil – he "sees" the motives of others to be like his own, that they too, are guided by their sight and not by faith. So, it was out of the abundance of Cain's heart – from his perception (⦿) of his brother's and God's motives – that he replied to the Lord.

Cain did not perceive (⦿) that Abel was anything more than his younger brother who had chosen shepherding over farming. He could not see God's anointing or the blessings his brother enjoyed living in obedience, perhaps because his father had named him "Vanity." Cain's perspective of his brother was further clarified in Genesis 12:2 – 3:

> *"And I will make of you a great nation, and I will bless you and make your name great, so that you will be a blessing. I will bless those who bless you, and him who dishonors you I will curse, and in you all the families of the earth shall be blessed."*

4:13-16 Redemption Rejected   433

Those who blessed Abram were responding to him through the lens of his relationship with God in the Kingdom of Heaven. In turn, the Lord blessed and filled their heart with good treasure: *"good measure, pressed down, shaken together, running over."*

There are two different words for curse, and the ESV translates the first one correctly as "dishonors." It actually means to hold Abram in light esteem – to "see" Abram as similar in honor to themselves without any acknowledgement that he was a child of the King and anointed by God.

This verse indicates that anyone who **dishonored** Abram was actually giving little credence to God or His covenant with Abram. They were living in the kingdom of this world and were perceiving () Abram's life and motives to be like their own. The second portion of this verse literally says, "Those who dishonor you are cursed" – they are living in the cursed kingdom of this world. **Let me make this point perfectly clear:** God was not cursing them. They chose to live in the cursed kingdom of this world following the prince of the power of the air (Ephesians 2:1 – 2).

By **dishonoring** his brother, Cain was fencing himself off from the One Who was blessing Abel and Who yearned to bless him as well. Please understand that God was not against farming. Cain's choice was not about which profession received God's blessing. Repentance and obedience were the keys to a yoked relationship with **the One Who also knew how to restore Cain's relationship with the ground**. The Lord only asked Cain to *"take His yoke upon him – a yoke that was easy and its burden was light."*

With this prologue as a background to Cain's perception of himself, his brother and the Lord, let's examine the relevant pictograms in this passage.

> *"Cain said to the LORD, 'My punishment is greater than I can bear. Behold, you have driven me today away from the ground, and from your face I shall be hidden. I shall be a fugitive and a wanderer on the earth, and whoever finds me will kill me.'"*

Punishment – ⊐ ﬥ ﬗ ⊙. ⊐ at the beginning of a word usually means that the work is being done by the person speaking. But since this symbol is at the end, it indicates that Cain perceived his "punishment" was the work of the Lord.

ﬥ ﬗ ⊙ is the Hebrew word for **"iniquity"** and is found 218 times in the Hebrew Bible. My Olive Tree Bible App says the Hebrew definition for iniquity is a person who is perverse / evil / depraved / guilty or punished for iniquity. Its New Testament definition is a person who is unjust / unrighteous or one who violates the law. We could look at these Olive Tree definitions and paint Cain as a perverse, depraved, evil, guilty person.

But the pictographic meaning is much simpler: A person's perception (⊙) is anchored (ﬗ) to new life (ﬥ). Since this is the **first use** of "iniquity" in the Bible, we need to take a closer look at it. Cain chose to work the ground with his father. There are six verses in the Torah that address the iniquitous relationship between a father and his children.

Four of them contain the phrase, *"**visiting** the iniquity of the fathers upon the children unto the third and fourth generation."* Exodus 20:5 and Deuteronomy 5:9 append the phrase "of them that hate me." And Exodus 34:7 and Numbers 14:18 declare that God forgives iniquity *"but he will by **no means**"* *clear the guilty.* " Let's briefly examine the words I have high-lighted.

Visiting – ᚢ ⊖ Y ○. Benner says it means oversee, over-seer, oversight[135]. (Joseph was made overseer of Potiphar's house in Egypt.) What the overseeing person says (○), an-chors / determines (Y) the cycles (⊖) of the person who is going in and out (ᚢ) – his daily activities – while he is under supervision. Because of their close occupational ties, Adam likely oversaw Cain's development as a farmer working the ground.

Hate – ᚥ Ⴟ ᚎ ᚎ ᒪ. Benner say its root word is ᚎ ᚎ – a thorn (ᚎ) plant (ᚎ) which is avoided / hated[136]. This kind of hate strongly (Ⴟ) works (ᚥ) against the authority (ᒪ) of the Lord. For Adam and Cain, their difficulty trying to work the ground that produced more thorns and thistles than fruitful produce may have elicited a growing animosity toward the Lord and toward Cain's sibling.

By no means clear the guilty – Ψ ⊖ ᚎ ᚥ Ⴟ Y ᒪ Ψ ⊖ ᚎ. Benner says Ψ ⊖ ᚎ signifies the innocence of an infant[189]. Infants are the new life (ᚎ) produced by the cycles (⊖) of their mother that brings praise (Ψ) to her and to the Lord. Ⴟ Y ᒪ is the Hebrew word for "not." So, this phrase literally means "innocence not innocence." There are other Hebrew words for guilty but were not used here. This phrase emphasizes innocence **transitioning** to not-innocence and may explain the corrupting influence the iniquity of the fa-ther (Adam) has on his children (Cain) that prejudices them toward the Lord and others who are perceived to be different (like Abel).

Punishment vs Iniquity

If I substitute "iniquity" for "punishment," Cain's reply reads:
"My iniquity is greater than I can bear."

Iniquity – ⟨ 𐤉 ⟨ 𐤏 ⟩. A person's perception (𐤏) is anchored (𐤉) to new life (⟨).

Greater – 𐤋 𐤉 𐤅 𐤆. Benner says this word means to magnify or be magnificent[133]. It was first used to describe the greater lights and the great sea creatures in Genesis 1:16 and 21 and indicates the magnitude of Cain's assessment.

Bear – 𐤏 𐤍 𐤔 𐤌. Much (𐤌) new life (𐤔) supported (𐤍) Cain strongly (𐤏). "Iniquity" and "bear" enter the Hebrew testament for the first time in this verse. In Genesis 7:17, 13:6 and 10, "bear" meant to lift up or support.

Behold – 𐤍 𐤄. A man standing in awe (𐤄) as he perceives new life (𐤍). This is the first time it was uttered by a person. All previous times, it was part of God's proclamation. Here is its **first use** in Genesis 1:29,

> *"And God said, 'Behold, I have given you every plant yielding seed that is on the face of all the earth, and every tree with seed in its fruit. You shall have them for food.'"*

Note: The first use of Behold in 1:29 was 𐤄 𐤍 𐤄. So, there was no awe (𐤄) resulting from the fruit of the ground – only Cain's amazement (𐤄) that it (𐤍) was being taken from him.

Verse 1:29 reflects God's work during Day Three when He brought forth vegetation from the earth. Genesis 1:11 reads,

> *"And God said, 'Let the earth sprout vegetation, plants yielding seed, and fruit trees bear-*

4:13-16 Redemption Rejected   437

*ing fruit in which is their seed, each according
to its kind, on the earth.'"*

I said earlier that this progression defined a **vegetation life
cycle**:
seed -> sprout -> yielding -> seed

So, the first time "Behold" entered the biblical literature, it
declared that this vegetation life cycle would provide food for
Adam. And Adam "beheld" its fulfillment later as he worked
and kept the ground in the Garden of Eden (Genesis 2:15).

The words for "iniquity", "bear" and "behold" all contain the
pictogram (⟨) which depicts a sprout emerging from the
ground from a seed. It is the **visualization** of Genesis 1:11,
*"Let the **earth sprout vegetation.**"*

Driven – ✝ᴡᴧ⁊. Benner says **ᴡᴧ⁊** means "cast
out." He explains that the land around a city was inhabited
by a lower class of people – outcasts. It was also pasture land
suitable for raising the flocks of the city[134]. The ✝ adds finality to being cast out.

I contend that Cain spoke this word because he believed the
Lord had driven him away from the ground, thereby relegating him to a lower class of person – an outcast – more like
how he perceived his younger brother, the shepherd his father
had named "Vanity."

Let's redefine "iniquity," "bear" and "behold" in this more re-
stricted manner:
Iniquity – ⟨ Υ ☻. Cain's discernment (☻) of a **reliable
source of food** was **anchored** (Υ) to **his ability** to work the
ground where he could perpetuate the vegetation life cycle

represented by a sprout (⟨) coming out of the ground.

Bear – ⟨glyphs⟩. The multitude (ᴟᴟ) of sprouts (⟨) Cain managed to coax from the ground by the sweat of his brow were the **food source he relied on** as his primary (⟨) support (⟨).

Behold – ⟨glyphs⟩. Cain stood in amazement (Ψ) that the Lord was separating him **from his ability** to work the ground and **produce a reliable source of food** (⟨).

Adam's iniquity had indeed been visited upon Cain

Adam's (ᴟᴜ⟨) close identification with working the ground (Ψᴟᴜ⟨) had precipitated his transition from innocence to not-innocence coloring his relationship with the Lord and with his wife. And, by naming Abel "vanity," Adam revealed his lack of respect for his son's occupation or for the way the Lord blessed him. Adam's "oversight" of his eldest son may also have fueled Cain's demeanor towards the Lord as well as his hostile attitude with respect to Abel's decision to "work the ground" **as a shepherd** or to God's continued favor toward his brother.

There's More

We read in Genesis 4:1 – 2,

> *"Now Adam knew Eve his wife, and she conceived and bore Cain, saying, "I have gotten a man with the help of the LORD.' And again, she bore his brother Abel."*

Notice that these two verses say that Eve **bore** both Cain and Abel. Unlike Genesis 4:25, they do not say she also named them. I contend that Adam **named** both of his sons. We know that Abel's name meant "Vanity." But let's take a closer look at Cain's name.

Gotten – ⨼✝⨼⟩☉. The root word is Ⲩ⟩☉ and my Olive Tree Bible App says that "Cain" sounds like the Hebrew for "gotten." This word is found later in Genesis 14:19, 22; 25:10 and 33:19 and signifies something that is a possession of the one speaking. So, Eve said that Cain was her "possession" from the Lord.

However, this definition for Cain's name pales in comparison to the pictographic meaning of "gotten," especially in light of what we have learned about Adam's iniquitous relationship with his first-born son: **Gotten** – Cain's daily cycles (☉) managing the vegetation life cycle (⟩) on their farm would be worked (⨼) in a totally dedicated manner (✝) by the strength of Cain's arm (⨼).

Cain – ⟩⨼☉. Cain's name is a manifestation of this regimen: His daily cycles (☉) worked (⨼) the vegetation life cycle (⟩).

I assert that Adam named both of his sons to predestine how each one would support him as they grew up. For Cain, his father's **oversight** (∪☉Ⲩ◯) was constant because they labored together. Adam supervised (◯) Cain's work anchoring (Ⲩ) every aspect of his daily routine (☉) so that his farming methods – his daily going in and out (∪) – met with his father's approval.

On the other hand, Cain assigned Abel to shepherd their fledgling flock in order to supply sacrifices to the Lord and clothing for themselves. Since Adam had tended sheep early on, he considered it vanity – a vocation not nearly as demanding or as worthy as working the ground. Furthermore, Abel could take over this rather menial task at a much younger age.

Adam's distain for shepherding meant that he likely believed it didn't need much oversight. And since Abel would live with their growing flocks as they moved from pasture to pasture, his constant dependence on the Lord far outweighed his father's influence.

Returning to Cain's reply to the Lord
"Behold, you have driven me today away from the ground"

The Lord did not drive Cain away from the ground. His own choice not to repent but to remain in the kingdom of this world was separating him from the ground so that it no longer yielded its strength. "**Driven**" was first used in Genesis 3:23 – 24:
*"Therefore, the LORD God sent him out from the garden of Eden to work the ground from which he was taken. He **drove out** the man (Adam), and at the east of the garden of Eden he placed the cherubim and a flaming sword that turned every way to guard the way to the tree of life."*

Initially, God cursed the ground for Adam's sake. Because He loved them, the Lord wanted them to realize the contrast between working the ground in the Garden and working the ground in the kingdom of this world. Like the pig pens for the prodigal son, their Father wanted them to "work the ground from which Adam was taken" just long enough to realize how much God loved them and desired to redeem their situation.

But instead of seeking God for His way to overcome this looming chaos in their lives, Adam must have held back because the Lord had to drive them out of the garden and forcibly block their return. This experience must have created an indelible memory of rejection in Adam. He felt inexorably tied to the ground and was blind to any other way to provide for his family. Even though it would now take long hours of sweat and toil to eke out a living from thorns and thistles, it was still "working the ground!" Anything else was rejected as "vanity."

Adam's oversight of Cain's training as a farmer must have burned this determination into his son because it was reflected in the way Cain couched his response to the Lord – a way that mirrored his father's devastating sense of rejection – *"you have driven me today away from the ground."*

> *"And from your face I shall be **hidden**."*

Adam's iniquitous relationship with Cain was also keeping his son from recognizing that the Lord had not hidden Himself from Cain. Even after Abel was murdered, the Lord still sought Cain out face to face. But the fear that had gripped his father shortly after he ate the fruit was also part of Adam's legacy urging Cain to hide himself as well.

> *"I shall be a **fugitive** and a **wanderer** on the earth"*

Cain's fatalistic acceptance of these two lifestyles indicates that, like his father, he would have to find a way to survive using his own resources even though there would be no way to work the ground under these circumstances.

Unfortunately, he could not see their redemptive opportunities. First, being a fugitive and a wanderer would separate him from the influence of his father and make him much more reliant on the Lord – a separation that had freed Abel to pursue a shepherd's life. Secondly, this kind of hunter-gatherer society could forge closer ties with those in his new family group because they would have to rely on each other – unlike his long-distance association with Able.

> *"and whoever finds me will kill me.'*

If you were wondering who these people were, remember that Adam's family was the only source of human procreation. The Bible only records that Adam and Eve bore three children by the end of Genesis, chapter four. However, verse 17 says *"Cain knew his wife."* Our first parents, their children and grandchildren continued to bear children even though they were not recorded in Genesis.

I propose that Abel did not shepherd his flocks alone but was assisted by some of his brothers, his children and his brothers' children. Cain's reference to "whoever finds me" suggests that he may never have personally visited Abel's clan. However, his fear tells me he believed their motives would mirror his own in a similar situation and that as soon as they found out he had killed their leader, they would surely avenge Abel's death.

> *"Then the LORD said to him, 'Not so! If anyone kills Cain, vengeance shall be taken on him sevenfold.'"*

The Lord's reply challenged Cain conclusion and underscored His love chase after Adam's eldest son. Instead of agreeing that He was driving Cain from the ground and hiding His face from him – an action that reflected Cain's estimation of God's motives – the Lord assured Cain of His commitment to protect him. A sevenfold vengeance would be meted out on anyone killing Cain.

Cain had tried to overcome sin crouching at his door and had failed miserably. Now, before the Lord assured Cain of His protection in spite of what he had just done, He spoke one word translated as "Not so!" that may have extended yet another opportunity for Cain to reassess his entrenched evaluation of God's motives.

Not so! – ꗞ This word is only found in four other places in the Torah: Genesis 30:15b, Exodus 6:6a and Numbers 16:11, 20:12. The phrase "Not so!" comes from the Septuagint translation. In these other instances, our Bibles translate it as "Then" or "Therefore." Referring to this specific verse, Brown says, it is an **idiom**. "In reply to an objection, to state the ground upon which the answer is made. *Therefore –* this being so – whoso killeth Cain ..."[139].

Let's see what the pictographic interpretation might reveal. First of all, this word also contains ꗞ which played a significant role in "iniquity," "bear" and "behold." **In those instances,** ꗞ represented the vegetation life cycle. ꗞ stands for cover, allow or conform, and ꗞ represents control and authority. I am postulating that the Lord began His reply by stating "I have the authority (ꗞ) to conform (ꗞ) your management of the vegetation life cycle (ꗞ)."

I share this interpretation as a conjecture. I mentioned earlier that God was never against farming. He was only against Cain's commitment to living in the kingdom of this world under the heavy hand of its prince.

Living as a fugitive and a wanderer on earth would separate him from the continuous oversight of his father as they

444   Back To The Garden

worked the ground together. But his farming skills could still be employed wherever he lived. However, those farming (ⸯ) skills would have to conform (Ⱳ) to the authority (⸦) of the Lord in order to be successful.

Our awesome God could see the life Cain would lead if he continued "by the sweat of his brow" as well as the iniquitous endowment he would pass on from his father to the third and fourth generation.

Better to offer salvation to Cain than to spurn him and watch the trail of misery that would follow! Perhaps these two manifestations of unconditional love might open the eyes of Cain's heart to leave his "pig pen" existence, repent and seek the embrace of his Father Who wanted to save him to the uttermost.

> *"And the LORD put a mark on Cain, lest any who found him should attack him."*

In Genesis chapter one, Day Two, I shared a pattern of how God worked His will: "God said" then "God made." So, this verse is what the Lord MADE – putting a mark on Cain – in response to what He SAID: *"Not so! If anyone kills Cain, vengeance shall be taken on him sevenfold."*

Put – ᴹ ⸯ ⸰. The same word is from Genesis 2:8 when the Lord put Adam in the garden. This word comes from ᴹ⸰ⸯ and means that God built a "thorn-bush" fence (ⸯ) around Cain capable of thwarting (⸰) any attempt by those (ᴹ) who wanted to attack him.

Mark – ✝ Ⲩ ⸲. ✝ ⸲ indicated to a Hebrew reader that what followed was the focus of the subject of the pictographic sentence. For example, in Genesis 1:1, it was placed right before the heaven and again before the earth to signify that Elohim and His Son were focused on / were dedicated to the task of making the heaven and the earth. The addition of Υ between these two symbols anchored the focus and commitment of the Lord to fulfill His promise of protection to Cain. In other words, the Lord took personal responsibility for Cain's welfare and would act on his behalf if anyone tried to attack him.

Lest – ᴚ†𝘓ᗡ𝘓 . Benner says this word means the attempted effort (the attack) would come to nothing[140].

Attack – †Υ𝕌Ψ . First used here, Benner's definition: to crush, wound, strike or slaughter[141].

This "mark" was nothing short of the fear of the Lord that surrounded Cain like a thorn-bush "sheepfold-like" fence. God's declaration warned everyone that Cain's death would be avenged seven-fold. Furthermore, Cain need not fear death since any attempt to attack him in this manner would come to nothing because the Lord would personally intervene.

Who Were His Would-Be Attackers?

I submit that Cain was afraid of reprisals from Abel's clan. However, like their leader, these shepherds were likely much more in tune with the Spirit and the will of the Lord than either Cain, his father or the other members of his clan. The Bible is replete with examples where the Spirit of the Lord went ahead of a person to prepare his way. I am convinced that Abel's extended family would have been sensitive to God's "mark" on Cain and would not have attacked him.

> *"Then Cain went away from the presence (face)*
> *of the LORD and settled in the land of Nod,*
> *east of Eden."*

Redemption Rejected

Unfortunately, Cain could not overcome the fear he felt standing in the presence of the Lord. Like his dad that fateful day in the Garden, he only wanted to hide from the One Who had offered him so much. The iniquitous influence of his father had blinded him to the blessings that had been extended to Abel and were now being offered to him. But, instead of a roadmap of redemption, Cain could only see the Lord's words as "his punishment for killing his brother" and it was more than he could bear.

Went away – 𒀱 𐎟 𒌋. Benner says this word means to go or come out of something[242]. Its first use was in Genesis 1:11 - 12,

> *"And God said, And God said, "Let the earth sprout vegetation, plants yielding seed, and fruit trees bearing fruit in which is their seed, each according to its kind, on the earth." And it was so. The earth **brought forth** vegetation, plants yielding seed according to their own kinds, and trees bearing fruit in which is their seed, each according to its kind."*

The pictograms that **brought forth** the very vegetation (𐎟) Cain had worked so hard to grow were now describing his departure as he **went away** from the face of the Lord and the new life (𐎟) He offered.

Settled – 𒌋𐎟𒌍. By the strength of his arm (𒌋), Cain consumed (𐎟) – dwelled in – his tent (𒌍). This word describes people who dwell in tents (Genesis 4:20).

In the land of Nod – 𒌍 𐎟 𐎟. In the land of wandering – where Cain wandered as a tent-dweller. It is the same word as wanderer in 4:12 and 14.

I said earlier that the Lord offered to help Cain apply his farming skills to grow vegetation after he became a hunter-gatherer. However, those skills would have to conform to the authority of the Lord in order to be successful. Unfortunately, when Cain went out from the presence of the Lord, his departure separated him from the Lord's authority to guide him in a manner that would conform his expertise to his new situation. As a result, every effort to apply his skills to bring forth crops (‫ו‬) eluded him because it was anchored (‫ז‬) to the way he had been taught by his father – the going in and out (‫ח‬) of his supervised daily activities.

SUMMARY

The reason the word iniquity is found 218 time in the Hebrew Bible is because it is such an insidious taskmaster. Chances are, you have felt it does not apply to you or to your friends or family because you have identified iniquitous behavior with a person who is perverse, evil, depraved, unjust, unrighteous or one who violates the law in a perverse manner.

Where are you on this iniquitous journey from innocence to not-innocence? Please understand that God is not against working for a living. But our occupation can blind us to the reality that the Lord is the underlying source that supplies all our needs. The world today is in such a turmoil that many find themselves out of work or so severely compromised that they are filled with anxiety and are wandering in a land of uncertainty. Cain rejected God's offer of help and protection because he could not believe that the Lord could forgive him or reveal a solution that could supply all his needs.

When your security is compromised or even destroyed, where do you turn for help? Do you pray that God will restore your security to the way it was? God forgives iniquity. But He will by no means clear the guilty – those who have transitioned from innocence to not-innocence – and will no longer seek God for ways to resolve their chaos.

Do you blame God for your predicament? Don't make Cain's mistake! God loves you and only wants you to rest in the security and protection of His constant care.

Study Questions For Discussion

- Why is it important to remember that we live in one of only two kingdoms: The Kingdom of Heaven or the kingdom of this world?
- Are your definitions of evil, sin and iniquity blinding you to how they apply to your life?
- Iniquity anchors you to solutions that are totally dependent on your own resources and abilities. Do you see a connection to the pictographic representation of a person living a cursed life (ᔐᔑᔐᔑ)?
- Are you a son or daughter of the Most High (Luke 6:35 – 38)?
- Out of the abundance of the heart, the mouth speaks. What are the treasures your mouth speaks?
- Hurting people hurt others. Cain expected others to avenge Abel's death because that was how he would have responded in a similar situation. Are there people like Cain in your life? They likely believe you will respond to them with anger or worse. The Lord wants to redeem them just

like He desired reconciliation for Cain. Could a kind, thoughtful or loving word from you be the tool the Holy Spirit uses to remove the veil from the eyes of their heart?

- Iniquity is an insidious taskmaster. Do you see yourself caught in its web?
  o As a father?
  o As a son or daughter
  o Is there a way to break this generational curse?
- Do you feel the Lord is "driving you away" or hiding His Face from you because of something you have done or said?
  o Is there anything that could separate you from the unconditional love of Elohim that His Son Jesus Christ did not reconcile through His death on the cross on your behalf?
  o What is the only request God asks of you so you can know He has forgiven you and you are a child of the King?
- Do you feel like you are a fugitive and a wanderer?
  o Can you see that God may be shutting doors that are no longer fruitful in order to open other doors so He can put into your lap, good measure, pressed down, shaken together and running over?
- Do you really believe that all things work together for good to them that love God and who are called according to His purpose (Romans 8:28)?
  o Do you love God?
  o Cain never discovered God's call and purpose. What is your call and purpose?
- What was the mark the Lord put on Cain to protect him?
  o Does He have the same care and commitment for you?
  o Do you believe that, as your loving Father, He wants to protect and care for you even more than you want to love, protect and care for your infant child?

CHAPTER
38

Genesis 4:17 – 24
Cain Built A City

"Cain knew his wife, and she conceived and bore Enoch. When he built a city, he called the name of the city after the name of his son, Enoch" (Genesis 4:17).

PROLOGUE

There is one word in the last chapter that I did not define and it highlights the futility of everything Cain will try to accomplish in this chapter:

*"Cain went away from the **FACE** of the Lord and settled in the land of Nod east of Eden."*

The Face of the Lord – ᎧᎧᎧᎧ ᎧᎧᎧᎧ.
In Psalm 23:1, David said, *"The Lord (ᎧᎧᎧᎧ) is my shepherd."* Cain couldn't appreciate the shepherding role the Lord played in Abel's life. The pictograms for "face" indicate that the mouth (Ꭷ) of the Lord (ᎧᎧᎧᎧ) is the source of all new life (Ꭷ) for everyone including Cain. The word for face was preceded by Ꭷ assuring Cain that the words from the Lord's mouth were able to shepherd (Ꭷ) him and retrain him so he could continue working the ground as he settled in the land of Nod.

The Lord offered to shepherd Cain so that he could successfully cultivate the ground in his new hunter-gatherer environment. However, instead of asking for guidance from the Source of the New Life he desperately sought, he tried to employ his own skills in the land of Nod (⊔ 𐤉 𐤅). As a result, every effort to grow crops (𐤅) eluded him because his experience was anchored (𐤉) to the way he had been taught by his father – the going in and out (⊔) of Adam's supervised daily activities.

> *"Cain knew his wife, and she conceived and bore Enoch"* (Genesis 4:17).

Adam's iniquity extended to his children to the third and the fourth generation and would be passed on to Cain's son Enoch unless either Adam or Cain sought forgiveness and restoration from the Lord.

Enoch – � 𐤉 𐤅 �III. Benner says ⟋ 𐤅 �III means to dedicate or be dedicated – to begin something new or to be experienced with something[146]. Like Cain's relationship with his father, Enoch was dedicated to his dad, desiring to become experienced in working the ground in the same manner as his father.

Let's briefly examine the pictographic meaning of Enoch's name. Enoch's iniquitous inheritance meant that Cain carefully constrained (�III) the way Enoch learned to manage the life cycle vegetation (𐤅) he produced by anchoring (𐤉) Enoch's training to his own so that it conformed (⟋) to the way Cain was taught by his father. Unfortunately, what had worked marginally for Cain and Adam did not work at all in this hunter-gatherer environment. Instead of seeking guidance from the Lord, Cain decided to build a city that reflected the name (**the character**) of his son Enoch.

> *"When he **built a city**, he called the name of the city after the name of his son, Enoch"*

Built – ᕐ ᛌ ᛏ ᗯ. This city would reflect Enoch's character by establishing a domain (ᗯ) specifically anchored (ᛏ) to the constrained (�) and conformed (ᗯ) way Enoch was trained, a way that would hopefully yield a praise-worthy (ᕐ) life cycle of vegetation (ᛌ).

Cain's fear that Abel's clan might seek revenge likely meant that Cain also had an extended family who followed him into the land of Nod. But even with this extra help, Cain had been unable to successfully work the ground as long as they lived as wandering nomads. Perhaps Cain's goal could be achieved if a tribal center was established in a specific location where numerous individuals could live and work together.

City – ᛉ᛫ᗒᗴ. See (ᗴ) the working (ᗒ) man (ᛉ). This is the first use of this word and it fits well with how I have just described the city Cain was building for his son. It was a localized hub of activity where men (ᛉ) from Cain's clan worked (ᗒ) together under Cain's watchful eye (ᗴ).

There's More
ᛉ᛫ᗒᗴ are the first three pictograms for the "naked" protocol (ᛯᛯᛉ᛫ᗒᗴ) found in Genesis 3:7. When the eyes of Adam and his wife were opened and they encountered a growing (ᛯ) dilemma (ᛯ), they chose to work (ᗒ) out a solution (sewing fig leaf aprons) on their own (ᛉ). That this was not a long-term solution is evident from their subsequent fearful encounter with the Lord.

That protocol was contrasted with the one shared in Genesis

2:25 (Naked – ᴍᴠᴸᴍ Ⴤ ₪◉). Although Adam and his wife found themselves anchored (Ⴤ) to unmanageable problems (ᴹ), they did not try to work out solutions on their own. Instead, they sought the Lord to resolve their chaos (ᴹ) by the strength of His arm (ᴠᴸ). Those solutions were far superior because they did not result in either shame or fear.

Building a city may have achieved a measure of short-term security for Cain and his son. But, by perpetuating Adam's iniquitous legacy, the city did not promote the redemptive opportunities the Lord wanted for them. The Lord yearned to provide their security through a yoked relationship with them. He also desired to reconcile family members now separated by suspicion, vocation and distance, and to renew an appreciation for the intrinsic worth of every individual.

When Cain went away from the **FACE** of the Lord, he removed himself and his family from the Source of Life that could have redeemed them from the steady moral decline exemplified in the names of his progeny.

Irad – Ʊ₪ᴠᴸ◉. See (◉) the working (ᴠᴸ) man (₪) going in and out (Ʊ) of the door / gate of the city. Irad's name indicates that during his generation, their work (ᴠᴸ) was closely monitored (◉) by Cain and his son. (Notice that ₪ is facing / overseeing the door Ʊ in keeping with the iniquitous oversight portrayed by the word "visiting" in the last chapter).

Mehujael *"... and Irad fathered **Mehujael**, and **Mehujael** fathered ..."* What is not apparent by the spelling of this person's name in English can be seen in the pictographic progression from a child fathered by Irad to an adult fathering the next generation:

Mehujael (as a child) – $\ell \, \delta \, \rightharpoondown \, \Upsilon \, \text{III} \, \text{M}$. Many ($\text{M}$) fences ($\text{III}$) anchored ($\Upsilon$) to work ($\rightharpoondown$) strongly ($\delta$) controlled ($\ell$). The constraining influence of Adam's iniquitous relationship with his children deteriorated into more control through Irad's family. The fence (III) set up by Adam to constrain Cain ($\text{W} \, \Upsilon \, \text{?} \, \text{III}$) was now multiplied into many fences around Irad's young son. And the anchor (Υ) in Cain's name moved closer to the constraining fences strongly (δ) controlling (ℓ) Mehujael's work ($\rightharpoondown$).

Mehujael (as a father) – $\ell \, \delta \, \rightharpoondown \, \rightharpoondown \, \Upsilon \, \text{III} \, \text{M}$. Many ($\text{M}$) fences ($\text{III}$) working ($\rightharpoondown$) work ($\rightharpoondown$) strongly ($\delta$) controlled ($\ell$). The anchor ($\Upsilon$) was gone and was replaced by another layer of work ($\rightharpoondown$). Those familiar with layers of management may recognize that the city was growing and needed levels of control in order to sustain the iniquitous oversight.

$\Upsilon \, \text{III} \, \text{M}$ – Benner says this word is a battering ram – an instrument of war. $\text{III} \, \text{M}$ is the word for bone marrow. In order to obtain the marrow, the bone must be struck[148]. These three pictograms highlight the abusive environment Mehujael perpetuated as a management style by the time he fathered the next generation.

$\ell \, \delta \, \rightharpoondown$ – Yoked – the placing of a yoke on the shoulders to perform work[149]. This "yoked" relationship between father and son must be viewed in the context of an abusive management style.

Methushael – $\ell \, \delta \, \text{W} \, \Upsilon \, \dagger \, \text{M}$. $\dagger \, \text{M}$ is the word for man as mortal / mortality. $\mathcal{L}\,\mathcal{b}\mathbf{w}$ means that the mortality of Methushael's generation was consumed ($\mathbf{w}$) by the strong ($\mathcal{b}$) authority ($\mathcal{L}$) of his father's generation. The civility of the city kept spiraling downward.

Lamech – ᐇᴟᴧᴧᴧ $\mathcal{L}$. I couldn't help comparing this name with ᐇᴟ $\mathcal{L}$ ᴧᴧᴧ.

> *"And Melchizedek king (*ᐇᴟ $\mathcal{L}$ ᴧᴧᴧ*) of Salem brought out bread and wine."* (Genesis 14:18)

Melchizedek ruled with the all-sufficient (ᴧᴧᴧ) authority of a shepherd-king ($\mathcal{L}$), conforming (ᐇᴟ) his people to the ways of peace (Salem).

ᵞᐇᴟᴧᴧᴧ – Benner says this word means "Crushed – crushing by beating, wounding, slaughter, striking with blows."[149] Adding $\mathcal{L}$ at the front indicates the authority of a ruler or king. So, Lamech's name meant that he was a cruel tyrant ruling over the city with merciless brutality.

Took – ᵞ $\mathcal{L}$ ⁻ꛂ⊖ᒍ. Lamech took two wives. We may hold up monogamy as a preferred marital relationship. But having more than one wife was not uncommon, especially among rulers and men of means. What is unusual about this conjugal arrangement is the two last pictograms ᵞ $\mathcal{L}$. These two wives were anchored (ᵞ) to Lamech's ruthless authority ($\mathcal{L}$).

Adah – ᵞᴂ⊖. See (⊖) the door (ᴂ). To witness a place, time or event that occurs repeatedly[150]. We will see Lamech call on his wives to bear witness to his grim proclamations.

> *"Adah bore Jabal; he was the father of those*

who dwell in tents and have livestock."

Jabal – ⟨ℓ⟩ ⟨□⟩ ⟨⊐⟩. His children worked (⊐⟩) livestock dwelling in tents (□) as shepherds (ℓ). So, Jabal's clan dwelled in the land of Nod, living in tents working their livestock as shepherds. Like Abel, Jabal had been named by his father when he was born to adopt the "vanity" lifestyle in order to provide livestock products for the city.

Although they were likely perceived by Lamech as having little social value, living in tents and following their grazing herds would have separated them from Lamech's constant oversight. And like Abel, they would have been much more likely to seek guidance from the **face of their Shepherd**.

Livestock – Ψ ⟨⟩ ⊝ ⩘. This is its first use. Many (⩘) cycles (⊝) of new life (⟨⟩) yielding praise (Ψ). For livestock, the cycles of new life point to the annual kidding and lambing cycles. Many such cycles yield the blessings of wealth. Benner says this word means to gather or acquire livestock or property as a measure of wealth[156]. Once they were out from under the iniquitous constrains of the city, they likely relied more on the guidance from their Shepherd who blessed them with the security and wealth of His new life (⟨⟩).

Jubal – ℓ □ Ψ ⊐. Jubal was also named by his father Lamech. The anchor (Ψ) pictogram in Jubal's name is the only difference between the two brothers and means that Jubal's children were not tent dwellers that moved with the herds. They were anchored to one place – the city.

Benner says ℓ □ signifies "coming to nothing"[152] – a tent / a person's body (□) under someone else's control (ℓ). ⊐ in front of $\mathcal{L}$ 𐤋 indicates his work, as well as the work of his children, came to nothing.

Play – $\mathsf{1} \mathsf{O} \mathsf{t}$. "Play" is an unusual translation of this word. In the other instances in the Torah, it means to seize or take hold of something by force. (See Genesis 39:12; Numbers 5:13, 31:27; Deuteronomy 9:17, 20:19 and 22:28.) Brown says it can be translated as "to lay hold of."[153] It was likely translated in this manner because of the two words that follow used elsewhere to define musical instruments.

However, "play" seems weak since there would be little reason to lay hold of a harp, seizing it by force. So, let's take another look at the word for "lyre" in light of Cain's motivation.

Lyre – 𐤍 𐤑 𐤅 𐤔. Conform (𐤔) the vegetation life cycle (𐤅) by anchoring it (𐤑) to the person (𐤍). Benner says 𐤍 𐤅 means that the person is preparing the ground by plowing[154].

Pipe – 𐤋 𐤅 𐤑 𐤏. This is another reference to a musical instrument. It is only found here in the Torah. The three other verses in scripture allude to some type of flute (Psalms 150:4; and Job 21:12, 30:31). Once again, let's look at these pictograms in the context of this passage.

Benner says 𐤋 𐤅 can refer to the high arch of a person's back when digging[155]. The first two pictograms add merit to this translation: The person's attention (𐤏) was anchored (𐤑) to his high-arched-back posture necessary for cultivating the sod around the city. Taken together with the meaning of the previous word "lyre", Jubal's family prepared the ground around the city cultivating it by hand, utilizing their own strenuous, "high arched back" efforts. Unfortunately, as

Jubal's name implies, their sweat and toil came to nothing.

Zillah – ⅄ ℓ ⌐. Benner says ℓ ⌐ is a shadow / a place of shadows, and ⅄ ℓ ⌐ is a roast which becomes dark when cooked[151]. This could mean that Zillah either had a darker complexion or perhaps her personality was "roasted" by her husband's abrasive demeanor keeping her in the submissive shadows of their relationship.

> *"Zillah also bore Tubal-Cain; he was the forger of all instruments of bronze and iron."*
> (Genesis 4:22)

Tubal-Cain – ⊃⌐◉ ℓ⊔⅄†. There is only one pictographic difference between Jubal's name (ℓ⊔⅄⊃⌐) and the "Tubal" portion of this name. † replaced ⊃⌐. Jubal's manual work (⊃⌐) had not been able to sustain a reliable harvest for the city. Tubal-Cain developed a more successful / complete (†) way to work the ground, replacing manual labor with forged implements that could facilitate the vegetation life cycle from plowing to harvest.

Forger – W⊕ℓ. Benner says W⊕ means hammering – shaping by hammering[157]. It also defines the person doing the hammering – the forger.

All Instruments – W⊡Ⅱ−ℓ⊎. We have seen ℓ⊎ before. It means to conform to the staff or to tame. A forger conforms – tames – what he hammers to his will. Benner says W⊡Ⅱ means to scratch[158]. A plow – the instrument the forger has made – scratches a furrow in the soil. He can also forge instruments that help harvest, thresh and transport the crops to the city.

Bronze – ✝ᏔᏆ ᛞ. Bronze is an alloy making it an un-likely metal for this period. However, there is another inter-pretation for this word. Benner says ᏔᏆ ᛞ means to di-vine – to learn something through divination or enchantment. It is also a word for brazen, fetters, chains and filthiness[159]. Since there is no indication that Tubal-Cain sought guidance from the Lord, he may have received revelation for his forging skills through divination.

Iron – Ꮭ Ꮐ ᏁᏗ. This is the word for the metal "iron." However, its pictograms yield another interpretation. Tubal-Cain, as an adult son (ᏁᏗ), forged harvesting tools called cudgels (Ꮐ) to help laborers manage (Ꮭ) their harvest.

In some indigenous cultures today, plows, wagons, harvesting and threshing tools are still made of wood, hardened in some cases by fire. May I suggest that "forge," "bronze," and "iron" were terms that provided an antediluvian framework for fu-ture terminology when metallurgy was more advanced.

I submit that Tubal-Cain "forged" wood by burning it in a con-trolled environment to harden it[160]. Using this "tamed" wood, he fashioned a number of tools like primitive plows, wagons / sledges, cudgels and threshing implements to help laborers manage a more sustainable harvest for the city.

"The sister of Tubal-Cain was Naamah."

Naamah – ᎩᎷᎤ ᛞ. Benner says her name means to be sweet / pleasant / beauty / delight / pleasures / delicacy[161]. The insertion of her name as Tubal-Cain's sister likely means that his breakthrough efforts were successful in improving the physical life of those who lived and worked in and around the city. Unfortunately, this economic prosperity did not translate into the kind of relational tolerance and sensitivity to each other that the Lord desired for them.

> *"Lamech said to his wives: 'Adah and Zillah, hear my voice; you wives of Lamech, listen to what I say: I have killed a man for wounding me, a young man for striking me. If Cain's revenge is sevenfold, then Lamech's is seventy-sevenfold'"* (Genesis 4:23 – 24).

Hear – ꟽꙨꟽꟽ. This word means "hear and obey" and came as a warning to all who were listening.

Listen – ꟽ ꟾ ꟿ ꟿ. These pictograms depict an intense (ꟿ) battle (ꟿ) over the city's vegetation life cycle (ꟾ). Lamech was boasting to his wives about his victories to maintain control over the city's food source.

Wounding – ꟾꙨꟾꙨꟿ. Benner indicates that Lamech was wounded by being smashed[163].

Striking – ꟾꟿꟿꙩꟿꟿ. Benner suggests that Lamech was struck with ropes after his wrists were bound[164]. This unsuccessful coup attempt was met with severe retribution: a merciless, seventy-seven-fold revenge that purged his adversaries.

SUMMARY

This cycle of violence began when Cain became very angry that the Lord had paid attention to Abel's sacrifice but not his own. He wanted God's approval "his way" – a self-serving strategy Cain continued to espouse through one devastating failure after another.

The iniquity of his father cast a long shadow over Adam's off-spring, and even though Cain's namesake – Tubal-Cain – may have brought a degree of prosperity to their city, its relational makeup still reflected Cain's hostility toward Abel.

Through it all, the Lord continued His love chase after them. When Jabal's clan broke free from the suffocating constraints of the city by adopting a more nomadic lifestyle, their closer reliance on the Lord brought His blessing of livestock wealth. It is hard to imagine that his brother Jubal or Lamech were not aware of this disparity. It may have been the motivation for the coup led by others associated with the city against Lamech that he put down so ruthlessly.

There was another sign of the Lord's grace toward Adam and Cain I believe is overlooked. Within five generations after Cain went away from the face of the Lord, the city he founded with his son Enoch was governed by a diabolical tyrant. During those same five generations through Adam's son Seth, Enoch walked with the Lord for 300 years and he was not for God took him.

Could that generational "coincidence" have been another call to Cain and to his son Enoch that God loved them and yearned to bless them as He did with Jabal's extended family – that Cain's son Enoch could also have walked with God as the other Enoch had done.

Study Questions For Discussion

- The face of the Lord is the source of new life for all of us. What is your mental image of the face of the Lord?
  - What is the new life that proceeds out of the Lord's mouth?
  - Is that new life what He speaks / reveals to you?
  - Jesus said, *"Man does not live by bread alone but by every Rhema word that proceeds out of the mouth of God."* Cain sought "new life" through farming that could produce "bread" to sustain his life. What is your source of new life?
  - When you pray, are you only asking the Lord for a solution that will yield a physical source of new life for you or for a Rhema source of new life?
  - Jesus' words *"live by bread alone"* means that both are necessary. Which one are you seeking first? (Matthew 6:33)
- You may feel that you are living in the land of Nod. Enoch's name meant that he was dedicated to the ways of Cain. As you face the turmoil of your *"land of Nod,"* are you praying that the Lord will restore your life to the way that is more secure for you or are you asking Him for a new way to bring forth His new life in you?
- Were you surprised by the pictographic meaning of the "city"?
- Are you "building" a "city" in an attempt to make your life more secure?
  - Do your efforts reflect the protocol shared in Genesis 2:25 or 3:7?
  - Do the fruits of your efforts remind you of the life of Jabal or Jubal?
- Tubal-Cain appears to have discovered forging skills in one lifetime that took later generations thousands of years to perfect. Did the pictograms for "forge," "bronze" and

"iron" shed a different perspective on his work?

o Even though his accomplishments helped sustain the city's food source, did it also promote peace the way Melchizedek ruled in Salem?

o Do the pictographic meanings of "lyre" and "pipe" shed new insights into the city's predicament?

o Can economic prosperity promote peace? Explain.

o If prosperity only yields peace for a favored few, does it move those less favored to seek something better like the apparent coup attempt during the reign of Lamech?

o Do you see in the way Lamech mercilessly crushed this coup, a response of how those in power in the kingdom of this world respond to anyone who resists them?

o They ruled by fear. Can this type of oversight ever yield true peace for everyone?

o The Lord continued to love them unconditionally. How does He want to work through us to continue His love chase?

o Which Enoch do you want to emulate? (Genesis 4:17; 5:13)

CHAPTER 39

Genesis 4:25 – 26
A Pattern For Worship

"And Adam knew his wife again, and she bore a son and called his name Seth, for she said, 'God has appointed for me another offspring instead of Abel, for Cain killed him.' To Seth also a son was born, and he called his name Enosh. At that time people began to call upon the name of the LORD" (Genesis 4:25 - 26).

PROLOGUE

Verse twenty-six has a single, isolated Pey (◯) affixed to it. As you can see from Appendix B, this is the only such assignment to verses in chapter four. Because of its importance, we will examine these last two verses very closely.

Adam knew his wife again

The word "again" does not mean that Seth was their third child. Cain's wife was likely his sister or niece, and the people he thought might avenge Abel's death were also his relatives. "Again" means that Adam's lineage going forward would progress through Seth.

Adam's wife called the name of their son Seth. However, Genesis 5:3 states that Adam named Seth. It is likely that Adam named both Cain and Abel. So, what motivated him to agree to this collaboration with his wife?

Analyze The Anger

In order to better understand what eventually motivated him to consider her suggestion, I want to step back briefly and compare Adam's initial anger toward his wife with Cain's anger toward his brother. Even though Adam's unrecorded anger must have occurred before the first verse of Genesis chapter three, I will start with Cain's situation since it explicitly illustrates anger's corrupting influence.

> *"And the LORD had regard for Abel and his offering, but for Cain and his offering he had no regard. So **Cain was very angry, and his face fell**. The LORD said to Cain, 'Why are you angry, and why has your face fallen? If you do well, will you not be accepted? And if you do not do well, sin is crouching at the door. Its desire is contrary to you, but you must rule over it'"* (Genesis 4:4 – 7).

Cain was convinced that his offering should be regarded by the Lord. If neither offering had been accepted, I am sure Cain would not have been so angry. But when the Lord made it obvious that Abel's sacrifice was preferred, instead of asking the Lord how he could "do well and be accepted," he became very angry and sullen.

The Lord reminded Cain that there was a path he could take in order to "do well and be accepted." But if he continued to dwell on his anger toward his brother, sin was "crouching at his door." Sin would be strongly yoked to Cain through his anger and would work to conform him to its will. He must rule over it in order to overcome sin's desire to control his life.

At that point, Cain had a choice: to ask the Lord how to rule over this adversary, or to try to control his anger on his own. Sin († ⩘⊕Ⅲ) was defined as Cain's fence (Ⅲ) – his reliance on working the ground for his security – that surrounded (⊕) him strongly (⩘) and completely (†). That security had produced his offering. It must have **infuriated** him that his sweat and toil to overcome the thorns and thistles of the ground was "not doing well" while the comparative "vanity" offering of his brother had been regarded as "doing well."

Adam's Flared Nostrils

According to the pictographic definitions of words spoken by the serpent and Adam's wife in the opening verses of chapter three, the serpent had asked the woman why Adam had been so frustrated with her attitude about eating fruit from the trees in the garden that his nostrils were still flared in anger during his conversation later with the serpent.

Her defensive response indicated she saw her role in their marriage as relational support for her husband and not as a co-laborer in the garden. The Lord had told Adam that it was not good for him to be alone; that he needed a helper fit for him. His helper (ⴻ⨅ⴗ ⊙) would see things from a different perspective (⊙) and would harvest opportunities (ⴗ) he might be unaware of.

Their ability to work together would be complementary **only** as long as Adam honored his helper's opinions and participation as worthy of his sincere consideration – as his equal (ⴻ⨅). Unfortunately, when it came to the garden, Adam must have insisted that she adhere to his way of working and keeping the garden or else **she** might inadvertently pick fruit from the tree of the knowledge of good and evil and endanger **his** relationship with the Lord.

As I shared earlier, his wife's perspective addressed their three-fold union with God. Her destiny supported her husband by **working and keeping** their marriage covenant strong. Adam's destiny focused on **working and keeping** the garden in accordance with God's work orders for him. Neither one was sufficient by itself. But instead of taking their differences to the Lord to seek a comprehensive solution, Adam chose to insist on his viewpoint.

The way he saw it, her role was much easier than his. After all, she didn't have to "**work the ground**" like he did. All she had to do was harvest produce from the garden. He had to tend and keep it. At some point, he became so frustrated with her "refusal" to restrict her perspective of her destiny to his perspective of his destiny that he "enhanced" God's injunction to not even touch the tree.

Adam's anger toward his wife was provoked by the same anger Cain experienced toward his brother – an anger that would become generational. Both saw their role as being more essential than the "vanity" role of the other person. Both saw the fruit of their labor as critical for obtaining God's favor. Both saw the fruit of the other's lifestyle as jeopardizing their own security.

Neither Adam nor Cain could understand how the destiny of the other person could be complementary and not contradictory. Instead of seeking God to open their eyes to see the other person in a more inclusive manner, they both became angry and took steps to force the other person to comply with their wills.

Adam's security had been associated with his yoked relationship with the Lord and with his obedience to follow God's guidance to work the ground and produce its abundance. At some point, the Lord wanted to raise Adam's relational "work" **up a level:**

  from his yoked relationship with the Lord working the ground,

    to his yoked relationship with the Lord AND with his wife who supported him working the ground.

It was not good for Adam to remain in his initial relationship because he would be unable to experience the joy of marriage and family. But this new conjugal arrangement would also mean that they were now yoked together as a three-fold chord with the Lord. It would not take long before their different perspectives and abilities would bring potential conflict UNLESS they saw those "differences" as added benefits the Lord was revealing to them through their commitment to each other and to Him.

The Lord brought his wife into Adam's life at a point where he was stable enough in his relationship with the garden that he could benefit from this new three-fold union. There was no disagreement or misunderstanding that could not be overcome through the protocol outlined in Genesis 2:25. And just as the Lord continued to reason with Cain even after Cain killed his brother, there was no chaos Adam and his wife would face – not even disobedience – that was too intractable for God to redeem through humbling themselves.

Anger and frustration were flags for both Adam and Cain that their security rested more in their own ability to provide for themselves than in their trust that the Lord would supply all their needs. He had created the heaven and the earth and could see the end from the beginning. So, He alone could reveal truly comprehensive solutions that would yield no shame or fear. He also had the resources to achieve those solutions.

Cain's dialogue with the Lord revealed his propensity to cling to his OWN security as *"sin crouching at the door."* **Both** Cain and Adam had to rule over sin. Otherwise, its desire would be strongly yoked to their **anger**, controlling them to take matters into their own hands instead of seeking the Lord for answers. **Sin** was the fence of security **both** had built around themselves strongly and completely.

The Lord asked Cain to consider his anger as a flag and said if he did good, he would be accepted just like his brother Abel. But in order to do that, Cain had to be willing to learn why the Lord was blessing Abel. As I said earlier, the Lord was not against farming. He just wanted Cain – and Adam – to rely on Him as their source of security and blessing.

Instead of rebelling against his father's wishes, Abel had accepted the more perilous life of a shepherd and trusted the Lord to guide him as his Shepherd. When Cain revealed his fear that he would be killed if he became a wanderer as Abel had, the Lord offered to retrain him so he could still make use of his agricultural skills in the land of Nod. But instead of asking for that guidance, Cain went away from the face of the Lord.

For Adam, instead of confessing to his wife that "touching the fruit" was his idea and ask the Lord for a solution to this dilemma that seemed to be growing by the minute, he kept his involvement a secret, took the fruit from her hand and ate it. By taking matters into his own hands, he jeopardized the very relationships he had tried so hard to protect.

After their eyes were opened as a result of Adam's disobedience, the Lord asked him, *"Who told you that you were naked? Did you eat of the tree I commanded you not to eat?"* But instead of admitting his disobedience, he chose to blame the wife the Lord had given him.

Even after cursing Adam's relationship with the ground so that it yielded thorns and thistles, and even after driving him from the garden, Adam still clung to working the ground for his security, contemptuously labeling Abel's vocation as "vanity."

Adam had elevated sin to the next level: direct disobedience – his transgression of God's commandment. Later, he elevated sin to yet another level – iniquity – when he began to train Cain and convince him that working the ground brought more security for them than trusting the Lord.

Earlier, Adam's solution "don't touch it" had turn into a crisis. Much later, Adam must have been mortified that his iniquitous oversight of Cain had propelled his oldest son to kill his brother. Imagine how devastating that tragedy must have been for Adam and Eve! Yet, even then, the Lord did not pull back but continued to offer His forgiveness and grace.

I am asserting that Adam finally "turned away" from his iniquitous oversight. The Torah says that the Lord forgives iniquity (Exodus 34:7 and Numbers 14:18). Adam had originally been unwilling to listen to his wife. But now, they both were living with Abel's tragic death at the hands of their first-born. As a result, Adam must have humbled himself, repented and seriously considered his helper's name suggestion.

There's More

> "Now Adam knew Eve (𐤅𐤅𐤏) his wife (𐤀𐤔𐤕𐤅), and she conceived and bore Cain, saying, 'I have **gotten** a man with the help of the **LORD**'" (Genesis 4:1).

> "And Adam knew his wife (𐤀𐤔𐤕𐤅)

*again, and she bore a son and called his name Seth (✝ W), for she said, 'God has **appointed** (✝ W) for me another offspring instead of Abel, for Cain killed him'"* (Genesis 4:25).

In both 4:1 and 4:25, it is Eve who acknowledged God's support during the birth of her sons.

Appointed – ✝ W. This word was also Seth's name – ✝ W – and adds considerable meaning to their circumstance at the time of Seth's birth. We first encountered this word imbedded in Genesis 3:15 where it was closely associated with the term "offspring":

> *"I will put (ｌ✝ ⅃W⏌𝜕) enmity (Ɏ�ゝ𝜕) between you and the woman, and between your offspring and her offspring; he shall bruise your head, and you shall bruise his heel."*

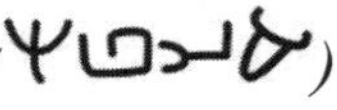

In Chapter Twenty-Eight, I shared that God's enmity was the father's (⏌Ɒ𝜕) hostility (ゝ⃕) toward the enemy of the woman's offspring. I also shared that the sign (✝) represented the work (ゝ⃕) of the serpent and his seed that would be strongly (𝜕) destroyed (W) by her seed. He would bruise the head of the serpent while the serpent and its offspring would bruise his heel.

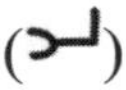

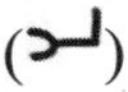

Since Seth's pictograms and the word for offspring are found in 3:15 and 4:25, I will suggest that the meaning of his pictograms carries over into verse 4:25. Adam's anger had degenerated into his iniquitous oversight of Cain which was fueled by the seed of the "serpent." The only way the work (ゝ⃕) of this sign (✝) could be destroyed (W) would be through Adam's enmity (Ɏ⏌Ɒゝ𝜕) – his hostility toward what his iniquity had done in his "tent." By humbling himself and seeking the face of the Lord, he could find forgiveness and mercy, and see his domain – his tent – healed and his yoked relationship with Elohim restored.

Seth's Name Related to the Woman

In verses 4:1 and 4:25, the pictograms for "woman (ᵞⱲᏏ)" also contain Seth's name (ᵞ⁄†Ⱳ⁄Ꮣ). I propose that the Lord was opening Eve's eyes early on to see how her husband's behavior was being adversely influenced by the seed of the serpent. Perhaps, she had even suggested a different name for their first-born. Now in 4:25, having witnessed the devastating murder of Abel at the hands of Cain, Adam was ready to change.

There's More

Elohim had appointed (†Ⱳ) her another offspring in place of Abel. And this mother-son relationship would be linked across the rest of the Hebrew testament. Permit me to explain.

When Abraham brought his son Isaac to the foot of the mountain the Lord had shown him, he said this in Genesis 22:5.

> *"Then Abraham said to his young men, "Stay here with the donkey; I and the boy will go over there and **worship** and come again to you.'"*

We rejoice at these words of faith for they reveal an unwavering commitment between Abraham, his son Isaac and the Lord. But there is another mystery that is largely overlooked in his declaration:

> *"I and the boy will go over there and **WORSHIP**..."*

This is the first time "**worship**" appears in the sacred text and the pictograms for this word reveal a Seth - Eve commitment.

Worship – ΨΥ𝕏†W. Notice that this word for worship is a combination of Seth (†W) and Eve (Life – ΨΥ𝕏. So, Seth's name joined with Eve's name expresses Worship.

Abraham's Journey Of Faith

We also point to Genesis 15:6 as a watershed event in Abram's life of faith.

"And he believed the LORD, and he counted it to him as righteousness."

The Lord had shared His word to Abram in a vision that He was Abram's shield and that his reward would be very great. But Abram rather despondently replied that these rewards would be of little value because he was childless and his servant would inherit the rewards. We know the storyline how God asked Abram to step outside his tent and try to count the stars: *"So shall your offspring be."*

When Isaac was born miraculously, he represented Abraham's legacy – those "stars" past counting who would forever establish Abraham's name. Why then did the Lord test Abraham by asking him to sacrifice Isaac before his son was old enough to carry on his father's name? Adam had clung to his ability to work the ground not only for his own security but also as a way to extend his legacy to the third and fourth generation through his iniquitous training of his son Cain.

In contrast, Abraham believed his **true legacy** was anchored in God's faithfulness to fulfill His promise that "in Isaac shall your seed be blessed" even if he sacrificed Isaac's life in obedience to the Lord. His actions demonstrated the pictograms for worship (ΨΥ𝕏†W): Consume / destroy (W) the sign (†). Abraham sacrificed his own **desire** to cling to Isaac and his future offspring as his legacy, and instead he affirmed God's will be done over his own will.

Praise Followed Sacrifice

By sacrificing (𝐖) his desire (🕇) to retain his legacy, he received his son back alive (𝚿 𝚼 𝗠).

> *"Do not lay your hand on the boy or do anything to him, for now I know that you fear God, seeing you have not withheld your son, your only son, from me"* (Genesis 22:12).

Can you imagine the joy, praise and gratitude that swept over Abraham and Isaac as they took the constraints off Isaac and replaced him on the altar with the ram caught in the thicket?

The Dimensions Of Worship

Abraham had walked with the Lord for many years by the time of his test in Genesis chapter 22. He too had confronted the flags of fear, disappointment and worry and had found that the Lord was faithful in every situation. So, when he was challenged to sacrifice his son, he obeyed without question and demonstrated that exchanging his will for God's will would always yield a greater reward.

Joshua provides another example of worship. His biggest obstacle to entering the Promised Land was the fortified city of Jericho. He had sent spies ahead to check out their defenses. Forty years earlier, there had been giants in the land that terrified most of the scouts Moses had sent. Now, the wall around the city was virtually impenetrable and its warriors were the best in Canaan. Even though the Holy Spirit had stricken the inhabitants with fear, I am sure Joshua was pondering as they marched toward the city how he was going to defeat this foe and enter the land God had promised them.

Try to identify with Joshua's situation as they approached Jericho. He was the leader of the children of Israel and this was their first major test. His "army" was a rag-tag band, cobbled together from the children of slaves who had never faced such a daunting foe. Would they turn tail and run from the best fighting force in the region? What possible military strategy could he muster that would bring victory in the face of such overwhelming odds?

> *"When Joshua was by Jericho, he lifted up his eyes and looked, and behold, a man was standing before him with his drawn sword in his hand. And Joshua went to him and said to him, 'Are you for us, or for our adversaries?' And he said, 'No; but I am the commander of the army of the LORD. Now I have come.'* **And Joshua fell on his face to the earth** *and worshiped and said to him, 'What does my lord say to his servant?' And the commander of the LORD'S army said to Joshua, 'Take off your sandals from your feet, for the place where you are standing is holy.' And Joshua did so."*
>
> (Joshua 5:13 – 15)

As they approached Jericho, a man stood before Joshua with a drawn sword. Could he have been an advanced scout from Jericho? *"Are you for us or for our adversaries?"* Can you hear the fearful concern in Joshua's voice? But then the man spoke, *"No, but I am the commander of the army of the LORD. Now I have come."*

Now suddenly, everything had changed. This "man" had come as a commander – not of Joshua's "army" but of the army of the LORD! Why did Joshua fall on his face to the earth? This commander didn't come without a battle plan or with insufficient warriors to achieve victory! All those hasty contingencies swirling around Joshua's head were immediately sacrificed in a gesture of supreme humility and repentance that he had struggled to come up with his own battle plan instead of trusting the LORD Who had already delivered them from the most powerful and ruthless dictator on earth when they had no army at all.

In order to drive home this reality, the commander then said to Joshua, *"Take off your sandals from your feet, for the place where you are standing is holy."* Those same words had been spoken to Moses at the burning bush before he faced Pharaoh. Now, Joshua was facing Jericho, and the place where he was standing was declared just as holy with the presence of the LORD.

Sin (✝ ⟩⟩ ⊕ �🏛) is a fence of our resources that we construct to bring us security and victory. When this man showed up, Joshua's initial question revealed that he was working on a battle strategy.

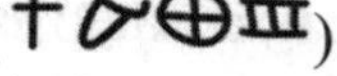

One of the words for humility (🏛W)[127] indicates that we must destroy (W) this fence (🏛) – to reject our solutions – in order to truly seek the Lord for His solution. His ways are always higher than our ways as was evident in the commander's battle plan. If we do not acknowledge that our solutions are inadequate, we will try to convince the Lord to follow our ways. By falling on his face to the ground, Joshua humbled himself and abandoned his battle strategy and worshipped (Ψ Υ 🏛 ✝ W): By destroying (W) his battle plan (✝), he achieved victory (Ψ Υ 🏛) for Israel.

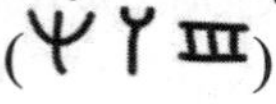

Praise Followed Sacrifice
"So the people shouted, and the trumpets were

blown. As soon as the people heard the sound of the trumpet, the people shouted a great shout, and the wall fell down flat, so that the people went up into the city, every man straight before him, and they captured the city" (Joshua 6:20).

For six days, they had marched once around Jericho. Now, on the seventh day – their Sabbath day of rest – they marched around it seven times in accordance with the battle plan from the commander of the Lord's army. Still, nothing changed. The wall was still as imposing as ever and Jericho's sentries on the wall still seemed invincible.

Yet, at Joshua's command, the priests blew their shofars and the people shouted a great shout. Then to their utter amazement, that same wall with its soldiers stationed on every position suddenly fell down flat! Can you imagine the rush of exhilaration this rag-tag army must have felt as they ran over the flattened wall and straight into the city that was now in total panic? Those initial shouts now turned into shouts of praise and joy for the faithfulness of their Lord and Savior and His awesome victory.

Adam's Journey

Adam had named both Cain and Abel in order to control his future as he saw it. Cain would help him work the ground and Abel would take care of the livestock so he and Cain could spend all of their time farming. But walking by sight had once again gone devastatingly wrong.

But this time, instead of blaming God for his predicament, he must have realized that the pictograms (✝ W) hidden in his wife's name were a sign to sacrifice (W) his iniquitous desire (✝) to control his own destiny and free himself (Ψ Υ Ⅲ) from its hold on him.

By affirming his wife's name for their son Seth, he demonstrated his willingness to humble himself, repent and seek the Lord's solution for his posterity. By doing so, he reclaimed his role as the hostile defender – his enmity – against the seed of the serpent who had already stolen, killed and destroyed the legacy of his initial offspring. He also restored his "tent" and achieved an even greater legacy of life through his renewed relationship with Elohim.

Biblical names share much more than a title to address or remember a person. They reveal the person's character as well as his potential destiny. We already saw that Seth's name defined a transition for Adam from death to life – from his iniquitous behavior, through a path of humility and repentance, to a redeemed, yoked relationship with Elohim. This transformation would continue through Seth's son Enosh.

Enosh – WΥ ⅃ꙮ. In Genesis 2:23, Adam declared that the helper God had brought to him would be called woman for she was taken out of man. The pictograms for man are **W⅃ꙮ** indicating that Adam was working (⅃) in the fire (**Wꙮ**). Enosh's name replaced ⅃ with Υ ⅃ declaring that Adam's "work" had been replaced with new life (⅃) through his sacrifice (**†W**), anchoring it (Υ) in the fire (**Wꙮ**) of his redeemed character. Instead of working (⅃) to control the course of his **legacy**, he relied on the LORD to anchor (Υ) that new life (⅃) into the character (**Wꙮ**) of Seth and Enosh.

How do I know?

Adam had lived 130 years before Seth was born, and Genesis 5:3 says,

> "... he fathered a son in his own likeness, after his image, and named him Seth."

The book of the generations of Adam would begin with Seth and the sacrifice his son represented, yielding the potential of new life to those who followed. Verse 5:3 offers a window into Adam's transformation. Both Cain and Abel had been **fathered** in Adam's likeness. That is, Adam passed on his physical genes to them as well as to Seth. But only God makes us as spirit beings **IN** His image. So, it was not until Adam was yoked with Elohim that the Lord teamed with him to father Seth's image **AFTER** Adam's own image.

Praise Followed Sacrifice

"At that time people began to call upon the name of the LORD."

At that time – 𐤓 𐤏. Benner says this word indicates a strong (𐤏) harvest (𐤓) time[165].

People – 𐤅 𐤉 𐤅 𐤏. This is Enosh's name. The KJV also uses a generic term "man" in this verse. My Olive Tree Bible Study App says that "Enosh" can mean "mortal," "man" or "person" when used in a more generic sense. This is definitely the case in Psalm 8:5, 90:3; 2 Chronicles 14:10 and Job 7:17. However, by rendering it here generically, these biblical editions are saying that when Enosh was born, Adam's offspring (people) began to call on the name of the Lord.

While I don't discount that Adam's offspring began to call on the name of the Lord after the birth of Seth's son, this generic interpretation hides some of the significance of Enosh's name[166]. Let's look at the rest of this verse.

Began – 𐤋 𐤇 𐤉 𐤅. Praise (𐤅) is anchored (𐤉) to the fence (𐤇) – the protection – of the shepherd (𐤋).

Call – I said in Chapter Seven that God set up a three-step pattern in Day Two: God **said**, God **made**, God **called**. Following this pattern, let's expand the pictographic meaning of verse 4:26.

After Adam humbled himself and sacrificed his propensity to determine his own destiny (Adam working in the fire), he gained a new perspective of his wife, family and posterity as revealed in Enosh's name (𐤅𐤉𐤅𐤍𐤀). New life (𐤍) was now anchored (𐤅) to his character (𐤅𐤀) through the renewal of his yoked relationship with the Lord. Adam and his family reaped a strong (𐤀) harvest (𐤐) time calling on the name of the Lord as they sought His solutions to the challenges they faced.

In response to their requests, the Lord (𐤋) put the revelation of His will into their mouths. Next, they **proclaimed** His Word by faith believing that the Lord saw it as completed before He revealed it to them. Then, God **made** visible what was yet unseen by fulfilling His Word to them. Finally, when what was unseen became seen, they **called** on the name of the Lord. That is, they bore witness to what the Lord **had done** by the power of His Name. And their praise (𐤉) was anchored (𐤉) to the fence (𐤇) of their Shepherd's (𐤋) security and abundance.

SUMMARY

This pattern of worship (𐤉 𐤉 𐤇 𐤕 𐤅) forms the foundation for salvation history beginning here in Genesis and extending into the New Testament. Permit me to share some examples:

The Passover

Just before Israel was to be delivered, the Lord told Moses that He would judge Egypt by killing all the firstborn of both creatures and man. Believers were to slaughter a lamb and spread its blood on the doorposts and lentil of the house where they were living. They were to roast the flesh of the lamb and eat all of it by morning. Anything left was to be burned. The blood of the lamb was a sign to the Lord and He would pass over their homes and keep them safe from death. By morning, Pharoah and the Egyptians would urge them to leave and would give them much wealth as they departed. Only those who believed Moses and obeyed the Lord's instructions would be saved.

By consuming (**W**) the covenant sign (**✝**) – the lamb that was slain – their firstborn would be granted life (**Ψ Υ ፹**). After they left Egypt, crossed the Red Sea and watched as the Lord vanquished the armies of Pharoah, Miriam led all the women with dancing, singing praise to the Lord for His marvelous **deliverance** (Exodus 15:19 – 21).

> *"For when the horses of Pharaoh with his chariots and his horsemen went into the sea, the LORD brought back the waters of the sea upon them, but the people of Israel walked on dry ground in the midst of the sea. Then Miriam the prophetess, the sister of Aaron, took a tambourine in her hand, and all the women went out after her with tambourines and dancing. And Miriam sang to them:*
>> *Sing to the LORD, for he has triumphed gloriously; the horse and his rider he has thrown into the sea.'"*

Jesus Our Savior and Messiah

> *"Have this mind among yourselves, which is yours in Christ Jesus, who, though he was in the form of God, did not count equality with God a thing to be grasped, but emptied himself,*

by taking the form of a servant, being born in the likeness of men. And being found in human form, he humbled himself by becoming obedient to the point of death, even death on a cross. Therefore, God has highly exalted him and bestowed on him the name that is above every name, so that at the name of Jesus every knee should bow, in heaven and on earth and under the earth, and every tongue confess that Jesus Christ is Lord, to the glory of God the Father."
(Philippians 2:5 – 11)

Jesus demonstrated in His Own Person the Worship pattern outlined in this chapter. Unlike Adam and Cain, though Jesus was in the form of God, He did not count His equality with God a thing to be grasped. Instead of clinging to His eternal relationship with His Father, He emptied Himself of these awesome qualities by taking the form of a servant, being born in the likeness of men. Yet even then, He humbled Himself by becoming obedient unto death – even death (**W**) on a cross (**ϯ**). Therefore, God raised Him from the dead, exalting Him with everlasting life (**Ψ Υ Ⲙ**) on the third day and bestowing on Him the name that is above every name, that at the name of Jesus, every knee shall bow in heaven and on earth and under the earth and every tongue confess that Jesus Christ is Lord to the glory of God the Father.

Jesus is our Model

*"Therefore, since we are surrounded by so great a cloud of witnesses, let us also lay aside (**W**) every weight, and sin which clings so closely (**ϯ**), and let us run with endurance the race that is set before us, looking to Jesus, the founder and perfecter of our faith, who **for the***

joy that was set before him endured the cross, despising the shame, and is seated (ᛉ ᚤ ꘌ) at the right hand of the throne of God."

(Hebrews 12:1 – 2)

A Pattern For Our Worship

*"For if you live according to the flesh you will die (man walking by sight), but if by the Spirit you put to **death** (ᛃ) the **deeds** (✝) of the body, you will **live** (ᛉ ᚤ ꘌ). For all who are led by the Spirit of God are sons of God."*

(Romans 8:13 – 14)

*"I appeal to you therefore, brothers, by the mercies of God, to present (ᛃ) your bodies as a living sacrifice (✝), holy and acceptable to God, which is your **spiritual worship**. Do not be conformed to this world, but be transformed (ᛉ ᚤ ꘌ) by the renewal of your mind, that by testing you may discern what is the will of God, what is good and acceptable and perfect."*

(Romans 12:1 – 2)

Jesus – God's Lamb That Was Slain

"Truly, truly, I say to you, unless you eat the flesh of the Son of Man and drink his blood, you have no life in you. Whoever feeds (ᛃ) on my flesh (✝) and drinks (ᛃ) my blood (✝) has eternal life (ᛉ ᚤ ꘌ), and I will raise him up on the last day. For my flesh is true food, and my blood is true drink. Whoever feeds on my flesh and drinks my blood abides in me, and I in him. As the living Father sent me, and I

*live because of the Father, so whoever feeds on me, he also will live because of me. This is the bread that came down from heaven, not like the bread the fathers ate, and died. Whoever **feeds** (W) on this **bread** (✝) will **live forever** (Ψ Υ Ⅲ)"* (John 6:53 – 58).

*"Now as they were eating, Jesus took bread, and after blessing it broke it and gave it to the disciples, and said, 'Take, **eat** (W); this is my **body** (✝).' And he took a cup, and when he had given thanks he gave it to them, saying, '**Drink** of it (W), all of you, for this is **my blood of the covenant** (✝), which is poured out for many **for the forgiveness of sins** (Ψ Υ Ⅲ). I tell you I will not drink again of this fruit of the vine until that day when I drink it new with you in my Father's kingdom'"* (Matthew 26:26 – 29).

When you consume (W) the cross (✝) – accept Jesus as your Savior and Lord – you receive the forgiveness of all your sins and obtain His eternal life (Ψ Υ Ⅲ). If you haven't asked Jesus to be your Lord and Savior, I encourage you to make that commitment now and worship Him.

Study Questions For Discussion

- Were you surprised to discover that the word for Abraham's worship was a melding of Seth's name and Eve's name?
- Why was worship so important to Abraham?
- Why is worship so important to your relationship with God?
- How can worship change your perspective of your situation?
- How can worship redeem your relationships with your family, friends, enemies?
- What part does worship play in your relationship with sin?
  - o How do the flags of fear, anger, worry and anxiety help you pinpoint areas in your life where you are trusting your own abilities to take care of your needs?
  - o Do you believe that the Lord can actually meet all your needs and give you His peace in the midst of the chaos and uncertainty you are facing today?
- What role did Eve play in helping Adam grapple with Abel's death?
  - o How did the Lord reveal a potential solution to her?
  - o Did she see the "problem" before Adam did?
  - o Why did she wait until her husband was willing to collaborate on Seth's name?
  - o Would Adam have listened to her if she had insisted that he see things her way?
- When the Lord brings people into your life that see things differently than you do, how do you respond?
  - o Do you insist on your way, capitulate or try to compromise?
  - o Is there a better way than any of these options?
  - o Why are God' ways always higher than our ways?
  - o When you consider your next steps, how do they reflect your ways vs His Ways?
  - o How does worship contribute to achieving His ways?

- Why is praise and thanksgiving so important to worship?
- Were you surprised that *"Calling on the name of the Lord"* meant a lot more than just asking Him to help you with your problems?
    - o When you face trials of many kinds does the "urgency" of the situation play a part in your response to it?
    - o If your situation was solved before the foundation of the world, is it really a crisis when you face it or does the Lord want you to perceive it by faith as already completed?
    - o How does resting in His finished work relate to worship and calling on the name of the Lord?
    - o How does worship relate to His peace that surpasses all understanding?
    - o Will you trust the Holy Spirit to lead you into situations where you can *"Call on the name of the Lord"* as a testimony of praise for what the Lord has done for you?
    - o Will you trust the Holy Spirit to lead you into all truth?
    - o Will you deny yourself (W) – your will – take up your cross (┼) – obey His guidance – and follow Jesus Christ as your Lord and Savior? He is the Way, the Truth and the Life (Ψ Y Ш). He is worthy of our worship!

CHAPTER 40

Epilogue

PROLOGUE

I did not glean the majority of the insights for this book from Bible school, seminary or from other resources I have acquired over the years. Like Joshua, in order to be successful, I meditated early every morning in prayer seeking inspiration for each verse from the Holy Spirit **Who is present right now** when these events in Genesis took place. It has been an amazing and humbling journey of discovery over the last twenty-one months – revelations that only scratch the surface of these treasures.

This book is my offering to you. It is much more than a commentary on the first four chapters of Genesis. I pray that it will equip you with the pictographic tools you need to explore and meditate on the Hebrew Testament the way Joshua and David did laying a more secure foundation for your understanding of both the Old and New Testaments. These new capabilities will help embolden you to achieve victory over the unprecedented challenges we face as we prepare the Messiah's Bride for His soon return.

This epilogue summarizes two subjects that were originally spread over several chapters, and concludes with a call to action that will bring us "back to the garden:"
- The two protocols revealed in Genesis 2:25 and 3:7;
- A brief reexamination of "The Fall;" and,
- A call to both Jewish and Gentile believers in Yeshua

Hamashiach to prepare for the next and greatest awakening!

Two Protocols
These two protocols define two ways of living and are enshrined in the pictograms of two English words for NAKED in Genesis 2:25 and 3:7.

The First Protocol: Naked – ᴹᴅᴶᴹ Ƴ ꟼᴓ. The
first portion of this protocol reveals (ᴓ) a man (ꟼ) anchored (Ƴ) to chaos (ᴹ) – some issue / problem / trial he does not know how to solve with his own ingenuity and resources. The anchor implies that this situation is both immediate and unavoidable. It might be as seemingly insignificant as when to take the next step in a project or as formidable as the sudden loss of a job or the news of a devastating illness.

The secret of this protocol is understanding that God's ways and His thoughts are **always** higher than ours. Moreover, He is a **loving Father** Who will not allow us to face any situation until we are able to confront it successfully with His help. In fact, He has led us by His Holy Spirit to face this immediate and unavoidable chaos in order to show us that He is not only capable of solving our problem but has already done so **before** we became anchored to it.

He only asks that we trust and obey Him. He has blessed us to be fruitful (Genesis 1:28) and He never works alone (Amos 3:7). Moreover, He always follows the pattern He established in Day two to overcome our chaos – God said, God made, God called. Our part in our yoked relationship is to seek His Rhema instructions (what God **says** to us) recognizing that His way will **always be superior** to our "solutions." Then by faith, we **proclaim / call** what He reveals to us with our mouth believing that what is yet unseen has already been accomplished (what God **has made** to destroy our chaos). Because our loving Father sees the end from the beginning, He always reveals a Rhema Word solution that answers all of our issues: both the current ones we see and the future ones we don't see. So, we don't encounter shame or fear as we move forward.

The last two pictograms for this protocol are ᴍ⌐ᴶ. These two symbols reveal God's final role in our yoked relationship with Him to solve this issue:

- First, He leads us by His Holy Spirit to face our dilemma only when He knows we are capable of victory through Him;
- Then, He waits expectantly for our request to reveal His Rhema Word;
- Next, He puts His Word (His solution) in our mouth – a solution we cannot achieve with our own abilities and resources; and,
- He listens for our call proclaiming what He has already done by the strength of His arm (⌐ᴶ) to destroy our chaos (ᴹ) and establish His order.

The Second Protocol: Naked – ᴹᴹᴍ⌐ᴶ⊙. This protocol reveals (⊙) a working (⌐ᴶ) man (⌐ᴺ) dealing with chaos (ᴹ) added to more chaos (ᴹ). The difference between this protocol and the first one is its focus (⊙) on the person **WORKING** (⌐ᴶ) on the issue he (⌐ᴺ) is facing with **his own solutions** – problems that appear to him to be growing more complex (ᴹᴹᴍ) in spite of his efforts to solve them.

Notice that the ⌐ᴶ symbol has moved from after the first ᴹ to before the person (⌐ᴺ). Instead of seeking God's solution and the strength of His arm to completely overcome the perceived crisis, the person has decided to solve his dilemma with his own resources and skill. The problem with this approach is that the person is guided by the chaos he currently sees and is unaware of how his solution will play out in the future.

Two Protocols
Two Kingdoms
Both Are Unseen

There are only two kingdoms: the Kingdom of Heaven and the kingdom of this world. The first offers a yoked relationship with our Father through His Son in the power of His Holy Spirit. Our loving Father will only allow us to encounter circumstances that will result in our victory and His glory. His way yields life in all its fullness. But in order to live in His Kingdom, we must not rely on our own understanding, our resources or our solutions, and instead, follow Him by faith.

The kingdom of this world is aptly named. Because it is unseen, we could assume when we are guided by what we see that we are in control of our own destiny. But this is an illusion. There is **no third kingdom** where we are the master of our own domain. The kingdom of this world is ruled by the prince of this world whose **only goal** is to steal, kill and destroy. He delights in leading us into situations that overwhelm us and leave us defeated or worse.

> *"And you were dead in the trespasses and sins in which you once walked, following the course of this world, **following the prince of the power of the air, the spirit that is now at work** in the sons of disobedience"* (Ephesians 2:1 – 2).

Our Father didn't want us to exercise the knowledge (✝☻ᘮ) of good and evil because that knowledge comes through the door (ᘮ) of our sight (☻) and, therefore, we perceive it as reality (✝). It also gives us the ability to compare what we perceive as good or evil instead of trusting the Lord to bless us with His goodness. When Adam and his wife gained the knowledge of good and evil, they could only see their immediate circumstances. So, they compared their individual differences with each other, concluded their own differences were not as good as those of their spouse, and sewed fig leaves together to cover their uniqueness.

After Adam disobeyed the Lord and ate the fruit of the tree, their eyes were opened to yet another kind of knowing – the one the serpent said was how God knew good and evil,

> *"For God knows* (⌐ ⊔ ⊃⌐) *that when you eat of it your eyes will be opened, and you will be like God, knowing good and evil... Then the eyes of both were opened, and they knew* (⌐ ⊔ ⊃⌐) *that they were naked* (⌐ ⊔ ⊃⌐ ⌐). *And they sewed fig leaves together and made themselves loincloths."*
>
> (Genesis 3:5, 7)

The arm of God (⊃⌐) is guided by what comes in through the door (⊔) of **His sight** (⌐). Since He alone sees (⌐) the end from the beginning, His evaluation is always complete because He has considered all eventualities. However, for Adam and his wife, when they evaluated their differences, they were limited to their current observations and felt compelled to **DO** (⊃⌐) something **NOW**. They sewed fig leaves into loin clothes to "correct" the perceived reality that was coming in through the door (⊔) of their sight (⌐) so they would feel more secure in each other's presence.

Here are some of the indicators that we are living in the kingdom of this world and are operating with the second protocol:
• There is an urgency to **DO** something **NOW** based on our

perception of the circumstances we are facing;

- Our solution focuses much more on the crisis at hand than on destroying the authority that is anchoring the chaos to us; (Review the pictographic meaning of Shalom)
- What we **DO** is largely based on **our own abilities and resources**;
- Our solution is rarely enough to take care of all the issues and restore order; and,
- Our solution is often fraught with shame and fear – flags that signal our solution is not providing the remedy we had hoped for.

Our awesome God completed all the work (ユ) necessary to establish His Kingdom on the Seventh Day and then He rested from all His work. He calls us to REST in His finished work through our walk of faith yoked with Him. All work (ユ) we do as we walk by sight bears witness that we **do not believe** the Lord is finished, and is the reason we cannot please God unless we walk by faith.

Reexamining the Fall

> *"Therefore, just as sin came into the world through one man, and death through sin, and so death spread to all men because all sinned— for sin indeed was in the world before the law was given, but sin is not counted where there is no law. Yet death reigned from Adam to Moses, even over those whose sinning was not like the transgression of Adam, who was a type of the one who was to come"* (Romans 5:12 – 14).

Paul's words seem to imply that through Adam's single transgression – what we call his original sin – all mankind has been corrupted by that one act of disobedience. Many of our Bibles even mark this event by labeling Genesis chapter three as

"The Fall." However, the conviction that all mankind has been corrupted because of Adam's disobedience must be weighed against another relevant scripture.

The Lord asked Ezekiel to confront an errant proverb that speaks directly to this issue.

> *"The word of the LORD came to me: 'What do you mean by repeating this proverb concerning the land of Israel,* **"The fathers have eaten sour grapes, and the children's teeth are set on edge'?** *As I live, declares the Lord GOD,* **this proverb shall no more be used by you in Israel.** *Behold, all souls are mine; the soul of the father as well as the soul of the son is mine* ... **The soul who sins shall die. The son shall not suffer for the iniquity of the father,** *nor the father suffer for the iniquity of the son.'"*
> (Ezekiel 18:1 – 5; 20)

This proverb implied that the penalties for the sins of the father were subsequently meted out on his children. But God declared **by His life** that this proverb *"shall no more be used.* **The soul who sins shall die. The son shall not suffer for the iniquity of the father** *..."*

So, Cain did not die because of Adam's sins – and by extension – we do not die for Adam's sins either. We all die as a consequence of **our own sins** which gives a more accurate context to Paul's phrase, *"and so death spread to all men **because all sinned.**"*

A Call to Jewish and Gentile Believers

> *"Then the eleven disciples (μαθηταὶ) went away into Galilee, into a mountain where Jesus had appointed them. And when they saw him,*

they worshipped him: but some doubted. And Jesus came and spake unto them, saying, 'All power is given unto me in heaven and in earth.

Go ye therefore, and teach (μαθητεύσατε) all nations, baptizing them in the name of the Father, and of the Son, and of the Holy Ghost: Teaching them to observe all things whatsoever I have commanded you: and, lo, I am with you alway, even unto the end of the world. Amen.'"
(Matthew 28:18 – 20 KJV)

This passage, known as the Great Commission, was first led by a small group of Jewish believers in a remote enclave of the Roman empire. They were filled with the Holy Spirit and with fire to go into all the world and spread the glorious truth of the Gospel of how God had reconciled the world to Himself through the death and resurrection of His Son Jesus the Messiah.

The King James Bible was originally printed in 1611 and remains one of the most popular editions of the Bible. Nowhere was its influence more pronounced than in the great missionary movements that followed its printing. Unfortunately, several words and phrases in its Great Commission did not reflect the underlining Greek **in the context of its Jewish roots**.

"Go ye therefore, and teach all nations."

Go ye therefore – πορευθέντες. I can forgive these translators for wanting to elevate the importance of this word into a clarion call to spread the Gospel to the whole world. But this word is not a command. It is a **participle**. Moreover, it is a **passive** participle as is this same word in Mark 16:15. Jesus was calling them to go into all the world based on His authority **as they were led and empowered** by the Holy Spirit.

Here is Luke's version of the Great Commission:

> *"Then he opened their minds to understand the Scriptures, and said to them, 'Thus it is written, that the Christ should suffer and on the third day rise from the dead, and that repentance for the forgiveness of sins should be proclaimed in his name to all* **nations** *(ἔθνη), beginning from Jerusalem. You are witnesses of these things. And behold, I am sending the promise of my Father upon you. But* **stay in the city** *until you are clothed with power from on high'."*
>
> (Luke 24:45 – 49)

> ***"And while staying with them he ordered them not to depart from Jerusalem, but to wait for the promise of the Father,*** *which, he said,* *"you heard from me; for John baptized with water, but* ***you will be baptized with the Holy Spirit not many days from now... But you will receive power when the Holy Spirit has come upon you, and you will be my witnesses in Jerusalem and in all Judea and Samaria, and to the end of the earth"*** (Acts 1:4 – 5, 8).

They were not to depart from Jerusalem – to go out on their own – until they had received the promise of the Father. The Holy Spirit would baptize them with His power as He led them to be their Messiah's witnesses in Jerusalem and in all Judea and Samaria and to the end of the earth.

Teach – μαθητεύσατε. This word is the **imperative command** in this sentence and should be translated "Disciple." These men had been Jesus' disciples during His earthly ministry and were now being commanded to repeat His mentoring method by discipling their converts.

"Teach" is an unfortunate translation. Missionaries have gone "into all the world" establishing Bible schools, seminaries, colleges and universities sincerely believing that what they were doing fulfilled the Great Commission. Tremendous benefits were obtained through these efforts training their converts to:

> *"Study to shew thyself approved unto God,*
> *a workman that needeth not to be ashamed,*
> *rightly dividing the word of truth."*
>
> (2 Timothy 2:15 KJV)

But there is a distinct difference between discipling in Jesus' day and teaching during and after the reign of King James VI of England. In some instances, these institutions were set up to ensure that their graduates "rightly divided the word of truth" along denominational lines, wrongly dividing the Church into religious camps that were at times hostile to each other.

All nations – πάντα ἔθνη. While ἔθνη can be interpreted as "nations," its meaning to these disciples was much deeper. The children of Israel were translated into Greek as the λαός and the Gentiles were translated as ἔθνος. Jesus was commanding his disciples to "Disciple all Gentiles" as He had discipled them. While it was possible to teach all nations in the style of King James VI, it was not possible for "nations" to be mentored in the same way Jesus discipled them. So, a more accurate translation of this phrase would be, "disciple all Gentiles / all your Gentile converts."

> *"baptizing them in the name of the Father, and*
> *of the Son, and of the Holy Ghost."*

This clause defines the first portion of the content the Eleven were to follow to disciple their Gentile converts. Unfortunately, over the centuries, it has been largely reduced to an ecclesiastical pronouncement made over converts as they are being baptized with water.

Baptizing – βαπτίζοντες. The word means "to immerse" and has divided denominations for centuries because it was interpreted as dictating how water baptism should be administered.

In – εἰς. Although this preposition was derived from the Greek word ἐν, it carries a slightly different meaning. If you picture a circle, ἐν (in) describes a location inside the circle. However, εἰς defines a movement from outside the circle **into** the circle, and is more accurately translated as "into."

The Name[167] – ὄνομα. We learned earlier that Name (𝙼𝙬) in Hebrew is much more than an identifier. It describes the character of the person named – his ability to destroy (𝙬) chaos (𝙼) and restore order. This is why Jesus' name is above all names because He alone was able to destroy sin, death and disease on the cross, delivering us from the power of darkness by the authority of His Name. Here is a translation of this phrase in an expanded version:

"**Immersing** them (your Gentile converts)
- **into the character of the Father** as He is revealed through the door of His Son (𝕹𝖑𝖀 – "The Word" Genesis 15:1) in the Torah, the Prophets and the Writings;
- **into the character of the Son as Messiah** who was foretold in the Hebrew Scriptures and Who revealed Himself to you His Jewish disciples; and,
- **into the character of the Holy Spirit**, revealed in the oracles of God, Who will guide you into all truth and empower you to proclaim the Gospel everywhere He leads you."

Epilogue

499

This emphasis was absolutely necessary because their Gentile converts would have little if any true comprehension of the character of Elohim as revealed in the oracles that He had entrusted to the Jews. Nor did they possess any real knowledge of a Savior as their Lord and Messiah as revealed in Hebrew Scripture and understood by Jesus' disciples. Finally, the Gentile world was awash with demonic spirits that had for centuries inspired false prophets and priests to proclaim allegiance to a myriad of pagan gods.

If their mission was to succeed among the Gentiles, their message and witness had to be firmly rooted in the knowledge of Israel's God and in a personal, yoked relationship with Him through His Son Jesus the Messiah in the power of His Holy Spirit. Any compromise would blunt the effectiveness of the Gospel.

> *"Teaching them to observe all things whatsoever I have commanded you"*

This clause defines the second portion of the content the Eleven were to follow when discipling their Gentile converts.

The first great awakening

The first century saw explosive growth in the Church under the guidance of the Holy Spirit and the Jewish disciples who were trained by their Messiah. But after the fall of Jerusalem in 70 AD, the Church gradually began to see itself as the new Israel and moved away from its Jewish roots.

The same Septuagint translation that allowed the Gospel to be spread across the entire Roman Empire because everyone spoke Greek also brought with it several challenges to teach Gentiles to observe all things that the disciples had been taught. As I shared earlier, the **Greek meaning** of words like "evil" and "sin" gradually replaced their foundational **Hebrew meaning** as the Church became more Hellenistic.

The second great awakening

By the time of the Reformation, leaders like Martin Luther felt that the Jews had relinquished their role in God's Kingdom because they had crucified Jesus. The Hebrew Testament was portrayed as a shadow of the New Testament, and the leaders of the Protestant Reformation focused on salvation by faith in Jesus Christ as revealed in the New Testament. Their ministry immersed Gentile converts into the character of Jesus Christ the Son of God and revitalized the mission of the Church. But they were unable to lift up Jesus as the Jewish Messiah because this foundation had largely been abandoned.

The third great awakening

The Welch revivals and those at Azusa Street in California, immersed the Church into the character of the Holy Spirit and spread rapidly across the globe. However, this association focused largely on the Spirit's ministry in the book of Acts.

The next great awakening

Now, over a hundred years later, many of us are restless for another awakening – one that will immerse the world into the character of the Father and also ignite the fire of the Holy Spirit to immerse us into the character of Jesus as the Messiah. But this can only happen with a resurgence of Jewish believers in Yeshua Hamashiach. Jesus foretold the fall of Jerusalem and its key role at the end of the age:

> *"For there will be great distress upon the earth and wrath against this people (λαῷ). They will fall by the edge of the sword and be led captive among all nations, and **Jerusalem** will be trampled underfoot by the Gentiles, until the* ***times of the Gentiles (ἐθνῶν) are fulfilled****...*

*Now when these things begin to take place,
straighten up and raise your heads, because
your redemption is drawing near"'"* (Luke
21:23 – 24, 28).

The Great Commission to the Gentiles (ἔθνος) began in Jerusalem, and the times (plural) of the Gentiles being fulfilled
will also be signaled by the end of the occupation of Jerusalem
by the Gentiles. Jesus was speaking to His Jewish disciples,
and ended by stating that when they (His Jewish disciples)
saw these things begin to happen, to straighten up and raise
their heads (take a prominent role) because these events signaled that their redemption (and ours) was drawing near.

One only has to read books by rabbis Jonathan Kahn and Ja-
son Sobel to catch a glimpse of the enormous richness of the
glorious inheritance that is available to them to share with us
because they are "native branches" grafted into the vine and
are fed by its roots.

> *"For if you believed **Moses**, you would believe
> me; for **he wrote of me**"* (John 5:46).

> *"Yes, to this day whenever **Moses is read** a veil
> lies over their hearts. But when one turns to the
> Lord, the veil is removed. Now the Lord is the
> Spirit, and where the Spirit of the Lord is, there
> is freedom. And we all, with unveiled face, be-
> holding the glory of the Lord, are being trans-
> formed into the same image from one degree of
> glory to another. For this comes from the Lord
> who is the Spirit"* (2 Corinthians 3:15 – 18).

Even though Jesus said that Moses wrote about Him, Paul
knew from his rabbinic training that any evidence of Jesus as

God's Messianic Son was not obvious in the Torah. For him, it was only when a person repented and turned to the Lord and beheld the glory of His unveiled face in the Gospel that the Holy Spirit transformed him from one degree of glory to another.

This book is my small contribution to the unveiling of the Torah especially for our Jewish brothers and sisters. The Holy Spirit has led me daily through the pictograms of the first four chapters of Genesis to provide tools for the **Jews first and also for the Gentiles** (Romans 1:16) so **we all** can explore the amazing Hebrew Testament under the guidance of the Lord Who is Spirit. By doing so, we will also bring to light new and vital nuggets of God's revelation to the New Testament that have for centuries been buried under clouds of mystery and tradition.

IT IS TIME!

Many of us believe that the events of Israel's 1967 six-day war and the acknowledgement of its sovereignty over Jerusalem by the US and other Gentile nations in 2017, signaled at least the beginning of the **times of the Gentiles** being fulfilled. **It is now time** for Messianic Jews in Israel and across the world to recognize, affirm and proclaim Elohim's Messianic Son in the Torah. They hold the keys to immerse us Gentiles into the awesome character of the Father, the saving character of the Lord Jesus Christ as our Messiah, and the abiding character of the Holy Spirit. **Together, united as one new man through the cross** (Ephesians 2:15), under their inspired leadership, the Great Commission will be fulfilled, and **we will all witness** an outpouring of the Holy Spirit and an end-time harvest that is unprecedented.

The original Jewish disciples of Jesus the Messiah handed the baton to us and we Gentiles have relayed it forward during the last two thousand years. The **anchor runner** in a relay race is chosen as the most capable member of the team to finish the race. Now, it is time for God's chosen Jewish anchor runners to grasp the baton and **team with us** to carry it across the finish line to victory.

SUMMARY

Our awesome Father is bringing us back to first principles. That is, He is bringing us back to the model His Son established when Jesus sent His Jewish disciples to disciple the Gentiles during the first great awakening. Elohim is also calling us "back to the garden" to be clothed with the glory of His first covenant – the marriage covenant – that will be fully revealed at the marriage supper of the Lamb in the new heaven and the new earth in the holy city of the new Jerusalem!

> *"Therefore, since we are surrounded by so great a cloud of witnesses, let us also lay aside every weight, and sin which clings so closely, **and let us run with endurance the race that is set before us, looking to Jesus (our Messiah)**, the founder and perfecter of our faith, who for the joy that was set before him endured the cross, despising the shame, and is seated at the right hand of the throne of God."*
>
> (Hebrews 12:1 – 2)

> *"Now to him who is able to keep you from stumbling and to present you blameless before the presence of his glory with great joy, to the only God, our Savior, through Jesus Christ our Lord, be glory, majesty, dominion, and authority, before all time and now and forever. Amen."*
>
> (Jude 1:24)

END NOTES

1. As you read the current Hebrew alphabet in my texts, you will notice that I do not use the proper characters for several letters that change shape if they are placed at the end of a word. I apologize for this unfortunate situation. But I do not have a Hebrew character set in my computer that allows me to use the final symbols for כ, מ, נ, פ, צ.

2. <u>Gesenius' Hebrew And Chaldee Lexicon to the Old Testament Scriptures</u>, Samuel Prideaux Tregelles, © 1893 John Wiley & Sons, pp. DCCLI – DCCLIII (Hereafter referred to as Gesenius Lexicon). Dr. William Gesenius published a Lexicon between 1810 and 1842.

3. <u>Gesenius' Hebrew Grammer</u>, 2nd English Edition by A.E Cowley, © 1909, Oxford Press. (Hereafter referred to as Gesenius Grammar). This grammar was originally written in German in 1813 (from the German preface.) German, like Greek and English, requires a formal language structure containing the various part of speech in order to make the sentence understandable. Gesenius' lexicon and grammar became definitive textbooks for students like me.

4. The following books are the sources I have used for the information about the Ancient Hebrew pictograms: <u>Hebrew Word Pictures</u>, Frank T. Seekins, McMillen Publishing Company, New York, NY © 1989 / © 2012 Frank Seekins, (Hereafter referred to as Seekins). Dr. Seekins is the modern founder and leading expert on Hebrew word pictures. <u>Ancient Hebrew Lexicon of the Bible</u>, Jeff A. Benner, Virtual Bookworm.com Publishing Inc., © 2005. (Hereafter referred to as Benner). Jeff Benner is the founder of the Ancient Hebrew Research Center.

5. Benner, pp. 72 – 73.

6. Ibid., p. 102.
7. Ibid., p. 289.
8. Ibid., pp. 63 – 64.
9. Ibid., p. 345.
10. Ibid. pp. 104 – 105.
11. Ibid., p. 186. The Hebrew characters in this word are נשא not נסא. But the second character has a dot over the left side of the ש instead of the right side. So, it is equated with the letter ס instead of ש and its meaning is equivalent to ס.
12. Ibid., p. 443.
13. Ibid., pp. 55 – 56.
14. Ibid., pp. 58 – 59.
15. Ibid., p. 141.
16. Ibid., p. 250.
17. A job order refers to the job posting or requisition. Once a candidate has been selected and the terms of the assignment (e.g., start and end dates, hourly billing rate) have been mutually agreed to by the hiring manager and the supplier, the job order becomes a work order. A work order is specific to that worker(s) and that job. It includes an agreed-upon hourly billing rate, cost allocation, length of assignment, and other elements used to track that specific combination of persons and positions. Revisions to the assignment, such as extension of the assignment or changes in the costing, require a work order revision. (See https://hr.harvard.edu/faq/what -difference-between- job-order-and-work-order)
18. Seekins, P. 163.
19. Ibid., P. 187.
20. Gesenius Lexicon, pp. CCCXL – CCCXLI.
21. Strong's Exhaustive Concordance, James Strong, Crusade Bible Publishers, originally published in 1890. I purchased this publication while in seminary. (Hereafter referred to as Strong.), p. 48 of the Hebrew dictionary.
22. A Hebrew and English Lexicon of the Old Testament

based on the lexicon of William Gesenius, Francis Brown, S. R. Driver, and Charles Briggs, Oxford at the Clarendon Press, © 1968, p. 298, Section C, 2d. (Hereafter referred to as Brown.)

23. Strong, page 35 of the Greek Dictionary.
24. A Greek-English Lexicon of the New Testament, William Arndt and F. Wilbur Gingrich, The University of Chicago Press, © 1957, p. 346, segment 1. (Hereafter referred to as Arndt and Gingrich.)
25. Benner, p. 55. Benner says ᴍᵕ is the Hebrew word for mother. When animal hides were boiled in water, the residue that floated to the top was sticky and was used for glue – strong water. So, a mother is the glue that binds the family together. And what is the unique role of a mother in the family? She BIRTHS new life (children) into the family. So, the pictograms for SAID mean that God by His own work (by the strength of His arm) birthed (spoke) from His head (His mouth) LIGHT into existence. Put more generally, the words that God speaks BIRTH what He says into existence.
26. Ibid., p. 449.
27. Ibid., pp. 284 – 287.
28. https://en.wikipedia.org/wiki/Age_of_Enlightenment; https://en.wikipedia.org/wiki/Biblical_criticism; https://en.wikipedia.org/wiki/Biblical_minimalism
29. Ibid., pp. 98 – 99.
30. Ibid., p. 328.
31. Genesis 15:12 (שמש),17; 19:23; 28:11, 32:32; 37:9 (sun, moon and stars)
32. Even though מאור is singular, the English Standard Version translated this one Hebrew word as "heavenly lights" to more closely associate it with its use in Day Four.
33. Exodus 25:6, 27:20, 35:8, 35:14, 35:28, 39:37; Leviticus 24:2; Numbers 4:9, 4:16.

34. https://www.space.com/18090-alpha-centauri-nearest-star-system.html
35. Benner, pp. 60 – 61.
36. The Gospel In Ancient Hebrew, Frank T. Seekins, www.LivingWordPictures.com, © 1996 / © 2018 Frank Seekins, (Hereafter referred to as Seekins-2), p. 26.
37. Benner, p. 122.
38. Seekins-2, p. 47.
39. Benner, p. 425.
40. Ibid., p. 94.
41.  means "conform () to the son ()." God blessed Adam as male and female by deliberately () conforming them to His Son.
42. Benner, p. 255.
43. Ibid., pp. 168 – 169.
44. Ibid., p. 352.
45. Ibid., p. 257.
46. Ibid., pp. 28 – 29. Here is what Benner says about the meaning of these two letters. (I am not implying that their meaning indicates why they were chosen. Others more knowledgeable than myself can make that determination).  – "This pictogram portrays speaking or blowing taken from the functions of the mouth as well the edge of something from the lips or mouth."  – "This letter can stand for a shield. Thorn bushes were used by shepherds to build a wall or shield to enclose their flocks during the night, protecting them from predators. Another meaning: to grab hold as a thorn is a seed that clings to hair and clothing."
47. Ibid., p. 146.
48. Ibid., pp. 159 – 160.
49. Seekins, pp. 171, 216.
50. Benner, pp. 432 – 433.
51. Since there are no verbs (or verb tenses) in a picture book (or in the Hebrew pictographic text), I translated

†ᗯᗯ as "resting" to denote how Joshua might have perceived Elohim on that "page."

52. This is another reason why translating ᗷᗉᗡ as a verb is problematic.

53. I am reminded of Romans 8:29, *"For those whom he foreknew he also predestined to be conformed to the image of his Son, in order that he might be the firstborn among many brothers."*

54. Hebrews 11:17 – 19.

55. Gesenius Grammar, p. 108, Section 33.e לוֹ means "to him – to himself."

56. The Israel Bible, edited by Rabbi Tuly Weisz. The Israel Bible was produced by Israel365 in cooperation with Teach for Israel and is used with permission from Teach for Israel. All rights reserved. First edition 2018, printed and bound in Jerusalem, Israel.

57. שמומ is found in Genesis 1:1 and 1:8. שמומ (like אלהימ) has a "plural" ending. Since verse eight is best translated as a singular word (heaven), the "plural" ending can be viewed as either a qualitative or a quantitative attribute.

58. Benner, p. 54.

59. Brown, p. 41. See also Deuteronomy 11:18, 1 Kings 8:59, 10:8, 22:23; 2 Kings 1:13; Jeremiah 31:21; Ezra 2:65; Nehemiah 6:14. (oath/covenant/strongly yoked) In some instances, the translation "these" seemed forced and in other instances, no translation was given. In every instance a translation of "oath," "covenant," or "strongly yoked" fit equally well or better.

60. It may be pointed out that †ᗯᗯ is preceded by a ᗍ in Genesis 2:2 indicating that it is a verb while in Exodus 16:23, it stands alone indicating that it is a noun. I have two issues with this interpretation: **First**, ᗷᗉᗡ stands alone as the second word in

Genesis 1:1. If † ᗯᗯ is a noun because it stands alone, then ᗷᑎᗯ should not translated as a verb. **Second**, ᗷᑎ⊖ is translated as a verb (called) twice in Genesis 1:5. It is preceded by a ᗒᒐ when God called the light "day." But it is not preceded by a ᗒᒐ when God called the darkness "night." (I explained why in Chapter five.) Since both instances of ᗷᑎ⊖ are translated as verbs, ᗒᒐ must not be a verb/noun indicator.

61. Gesenius Grammar, p. 12. This grammar distinguishes two periods of Hebrew script: those written down to the end of the Babylonian exile, and those written afterwards. The pictographic writings that existed before this exile were converted into the Hebrew script we are familiar with today.

62. Ibid., pp. 19 – 20.

63. From Vulgate.org.

64. יהוה is the most sacred Name for God for orthodox Jews and underscores their belief and ours that God is One (Mark 12:29). According to <u>The Israel Bible</u>, orthodox believers recite Deuteronomy 6:4 twice a day. Both "YHVH Elohim" and "YHVH" alone are translated as "Hashem" but pronounced verbally as "Adonai" which is the Aramaic word for "Lord."

65. <u>The New American Study Bible</u>, Oxford University Press, Inc., © 1990, pp. 45 – 50.

66. Benner, p. 385.

67. Seekins, p. 167.

68. Ibid., p. 162.

69. Ibid., p. 399.

70. Ibid, p. 156.

71. Ibid., p. 188.

72. Benner, p. 374.

73. Ibid., p. 62.

74. Ibid., p. 417.

75. Ibid., pp. 214 – 215.
76. Seekins, pp. 184, 225.
77. Brown, p. 475.
78. Strong, definition number 5920 in its Hebrew dictionary.
79. Seekins, p. 143.
80. Benner, p. 216.
81. Brown, p. 736.
82. Benner, p. 32.
83. The Hebrew word for "said" in Genesis 3:1 is the same one used to describe God's conversation with Adam in Genesis 3:9 and 11 – אמר a word we first analyzed when God **said**, "Let there be light."
84. Benner, p. 68.
85. Ibid., pp. 445 – 446.
86. Ibid., p. 195.
87. Ibid., p. 461.
88. Ibid., p. 223.
89. Ibid., p. 57. See Genesis 13:13; 18:23,24; and 40:16 for other examples.
90. Taken from the Complete Word Study Bible found on my Olive Tree Bible App, version 6.5.5, © 1998 - 2020 for Ephesians 4:26.
91. Benner, p. 335.
92. Ibid., pp. 52, 100.
93. Ibid., p. 212.
94. Ibid., p. 391.
95. Ibid., p. 221.
96. The Israel Bible, p. 12. See Endnote 56 for more information about this Bible.
97. https://en.wikipedia.org/wiki/Etesian
98. Benner, pp. 244 – 245.
99. Ibid., p. 117.

100. The only difference between its use in Genesis 3:9 (אֵיֶּכָּה) and in the other examples I am sharing (אֵיכָה) is in the diacritical marks used to facilitate the pronunciation of the Masoretic Hebrew character set that were developed in the Middle Ages. Since no such marks were used on pictograms and since all of the authors of the texts given in the other examples used pictograms, I can only assume that the pictograms in all these texts were the same. (According to a word search in the ESV <u>Hebrew/ Greek English Interlinear Bible</u> in my online Olive Tree App, Genesis 3:9 is the only instance where אֵיכָה is found with these particular diacritical marks. This pattern follows the Septuagint translation: Genesis 3:9 is translated as ποῦ - "Where?" - Deuteronomy 1:12; 7:17; 32:30 are translated as πῶς "How?")

101. Benner, pp. 142 – 143.

102. Ibid., p. 253.

103. For instance, in Genesis 2:23, *"Bone from my bone and flesh from my flesh"* is signified by a ᗐᒐ at the end of the second words for bone and flesh. So, Adam was declaring that his bone and his flesh were active participants in the making of the woman.

104. Benner, p. 165.

105. See Luke 7:36 - 50; John 13:5 – 11 for New Testament examples of this action.

106. Even though the pictograms for these two words are essentially the same, we owe the selection of different words to the Septuagint scholars. In ᛗᒐᒐᛗ Υ ᑫᓇᕼ 2:25, was translated by γυμνοι – naked. However, they translated ᛗ Υ ᑫᓇᕼ by φρονιμωτατος – an entirely different word meaning "wise."

107. Benner, p. 51.

108. Ibid., p. 283.

109. Ibid., p. 268.

110. Ibid., pp. 408 – 409.

111. Ibid., pp. 283 – 284.

112. Ibid., p. 97.

113. Seekins, pp. 112, 143; Benner pp. 51 – 52; Brown p. 33. ⌍⌁⌀ – Exodus 23:22; ⌍⌁⌀ – Exodus 15:6; ⌍⌁⌀ – Genesis 3:15.

114. Brown, p. 509. The more common Hebrew word for garment is ＋ ＼ Ｙ ＋ Ш. Notice the change of position of the Ｙ in the more common word – ＋ Ｙ ＼ ＋ Ш.

115. Benner, p. 62.

116. Ibid., p. 65.

117. Ibid., p. 130.

118. Brown, p. 673.

119. Benner, p. 253.

120. Brown, pp. 306 – 308.

121. Strong (2398), p. 38 in the Hebrew section.

122. Benner, p. 120.

123. Seekins, p. 208.

124. Arndt and Gingrich, p.41.

125. Strong, p. 10 in the Greek section.

126. Ibid., p. 59 in the Greek section.

127. Seekins, p. 173.

128. Benner, p. 291.

129. Ibid., p. 245.

130. Ibid., pp. 255-256.

131. Ibid., p. 428.

132. Ibid., p. 145.

133. Ibid., p. 313.

134. Ibid., p. 318.

135. Ibid, p. 418.

136. Ibid., p. 200.

137. Ibid., p. 189.

138. Ibid., pp. 258 – 259.

139. Brown, p. 487.

140. Benner, pp. 66 – 68.

141. Ibid., pp. 184 – 185.

142. Ibid., p. 229.
143. Ibid., p. 459.
144. Ibid., p. 105.
145. Ibid., pp. 206 – 207.
146. Ibid., p. 337.
147. Ibid., p. 167.
148. Ibid., p. 55.
149. Ibid., p. 184.
150. Ibid., p. 206.
151. Ibid., pp. 233 – 234.
152. Ibid., p. 66.
153. Brown, p. 1074.
154. Benner, p. 190.
155. Ibid., p. 77.
156. Ibid., pp. 246 – 247.
157. Ibid., p. 302.
158. Ibid., pp. 343 – 344.
159. Ibid., p. 377.
160. According to Wikipedia (https://en.wikipedia.org/wiki/Fire_hardening), "Fire hardening was first developed by primitive humans at least 400,000 years ago—long before flint or stone points."
161. Benner, p. 381.
162. Ibid., p. 256.
163. Ibid., p. 418.
164. Ibid., p. 330.
165. Ibid., pp. 52 – 53.
166. The Septuagint translation for Genesis 4:26 does not generalize Enosh's name: *"And Seth had a son, and he called his name Enos: he hoped to call on the name of the Lord God."*
167. ὄνομα is a singular noun and is modified by three genitive phrases *"of the Father and of the Son and of the Holy Ghost."* It is the only Biblical reference I know that explicitly defines the trinity.

APPENDIX
A

Each two-letter Hebrew word in this list is followed by a new word that concatenates an aleph (א) to the end of the original word. As you can see, the added Aleph intensifies, broadens and builds upon the meaning of the original Hebrew word. (I limited the examples to four pages.)

These words were taken from <u>Ancient Hebrew Lexicon of the Bible</u> by Jeff A. Benner, 2005.

Both Benner and Dr. Frank T. Seekins, Hebrew <u>Word Pictures</u>, 2012, have devoted many years to relating the early pictograms to the current Hebrew characters and words to help undergird the meaning of the scripture inspired by the Holy Spirit.

(Sorry, my computer's Hebrew character set does not include final symbols for כ, מ, נ, פ, צ)

אש	Press down strongly (rubbing a stick on a board to start a fire) / Fire
אשא	Foundation – what is firmly pressed down
את	Plow – An oxen moving toward a mark
אתא	Destination – Arriving at a mark
בד	Alone / Apart / Separated
בדא	A separation from the truth / To invent a false account or story

| בז | Spoils – What is removed from a house |
| בזא | A division of what is plundered |

| בל | Flow / Nothing |
| בלא | A stream / Old – A flowing away of life |

| בנ | Tent panel (Panels are added to the tent to expand it) – (young) Son (Sons are added) |
| בנא | Build / Build up / Repair / Building / Children |

| בקע | Fissure |
| בקעא | Plain / valley |

| בר | Feed / Grain – A house of heads, (mature) Son / Clean / Pure |
| ברא | To fill / Fatten / Create / Make |

| גב | Arch (of the back when digging) |
| גבא | Dig / Cistern |

| גז | Shear / Fleece |
| גזא | Stump – A sheared off tree |

| גי | High / Pride |
| גיא | Valley / The high walls of a valley |

| גמ | Gather (around the watering well) |
| גמא | Drink / Reed that grows (gathers) near the water |

| דב | Rest / Slow |
| דבא | Rest / Strength |

| דכ | Mortar / Crush (back and forth action) in a bowl |
| דכא | Break by beating it |

| הל | Shine / Star |
| הלא | Distant – A distant sight that is looked toward |

| זר | Spread out / Span |
| זרא | Vomit / Something spread out |

| חב | Hide / Bosom |
| חבא | A place of hiding / Refuge |

| חג | Feast / Circle – An outside gathering (Dancing in a circle) |
| חגא | Terror / A spinning around in fear |

| חז | See / Perceive |
| חזא | Behold / Look / Prophecy |

| חט | Measure with a chord |
| חטא | Sin – When an arrow misses, the miss is measured by a chord |

| חי | Live / Stomach |
| חיא | Alive / Quicken / Life |

| חל | Bore / Hole / Pain (Drill a hole with a tool) |
| חלא | Sick / Disease – A spinning or piercing pain |

| חמ | Heat / To separate / Father-in-Law |
| חמא | Cheese (Separated from milk) / Fury (An intense heat from anger) |

| חפ | Cover / Innocent |
| הפא | Cover (Something that is covered and hidden) |

| חר | Burn (Burnt from the sun or from anger) |
| חרא | Dung (A manure pile creates heat) |

טל	Scatter / Dew
טלא	Spots (A covering of color or spots)

כל	Vessel / Complete / Whole
כלא	Restrain / Prison

כס	Cover / Cup / Seat
כסא	Appoint / Appointed (To be set in place) / Seat

כר	Dig / Bowl / Hollow
כרא	Prepare – Prepare a banquet or feast

לא	Nothing / No
לאא	Worthless / An idol (A god without power)

לל	Howl / Night
ללא	Loop (When night comes, the sky is rolled up like a scroll)

מח	Strike / Marrow (Liquid inside) / Fat (Of the marrow)
מחא	Strike (Strike the bone to break it and release the fat inside)

מל	Speak / Word / Continue
מלא	Fill / First fruits / Full / Lord (The one who speaks and is full of authority)

מנ	Firm / Kind / Sure
מנא	Count or number a set of things

מצ	Squeeze / Strong
מצא	Find (In the sense of squeezing something out of a hidden place)

APPENDIX
B

This appendix documents where single Hebrew letters / symbols (⟨symbol⟩ or ⟨symbol⟩) were positioned at the end of "sentences." Here is an example from Genesis 1:5:

⌓	⊓Ⅲᴍ	ᴍꙨ⅃	Ꙙⵁⵃ	⅃ꙨꙨ⅃	Ɣ	ⵁꙘⵁ
first	**day**	**morning**	**there was**	**and**		**evening**

This appendix does not attempt to explain **why** these two symbols were placed in particular locations. It only indicates **that** the symbols were placed at specific locations. Although I am only interested in the table entries from the initial chapters of Genesis, I extended the table through the end of Genesis so you can see that this process was not limited to the beginning of the Torah.

Text Symbol   Scripture

Text	Symbol	Scripture
1:5	⟨symbol⟩	And there was evening and there was morning, the first day.
1:8	⟨symbol⟩	And there was evening and there was morning, the second day.
1:13	⟨symbol⟩	And there was evening and there was morning, the third day.
1:19	⟨symbol⟩	And there was evening and there was morning, the fourth day.
1:23	⟨symbol⟩	And there was evening and there was morning, the fifth day.
1:31	⟨symbol⟩	And there was evening and there was morning, the six day.

2:3	⬯	So God blessed the seventh day and made it holy, because on it God rested from all his work that he had done in creation.
3:15	⟨	I will put enmity between you and the woman, and between your offspring and her offspring; he shall bruise your head, and you shall bruise his heel."
3:21	⬯	And the Lord God made for Adam and for his wife garments of skins and clothed them.
3:24	⟨	He drove out the man, and at the east of the garden of Eden he placed the cherubim and a flaming sword that turned every way to guard the way to the tree of life.
4:26	⬯	To Seth also a son was born, and he called his name Enosh. At that time people began to call upon the name of the Lord.
5:2	⟨	Male and female he created them, and he blessed them and named them Man when they were created.
5:5	⟨	Thus all the days that Adam lived were 930 years, and he died.
5:8	⟨	Thus all the days of Seth were 912 years, and he died.
5:11	⟨	Thus all the days of Enosh were 905 years, and he died.
5:14	⟨	Thus all the days of Kenan were 910 years, and he died.
5:17	⟨	Thus all the days of Mahalalel were 895 years, and he died.
5:20	⬯	Thus all the days of Jared were 962 years, and he died. (Father of Enoch)
5:24	⬯	Enoch walked with God, and he was not, for God took him.

5:27	○	Thus all the days of Methuselah were 969 years, and he died. (Son-Enoch)
5:31	◄	Thus all the days of Lamech were 777 years, and he died.
6:4	○	The Nephilim were the mighty men who were of old, the men of renown.
6:8	○	But Noah found favor in the eyes of the Lord.
6:12	◄	the earth was corrupt in God's sight, and the earth was filled with violence.
6:22	◄	Noah did this; he did all that God commanded him.
8:14	◄	In the second month, on the twenty-seventh day of the month, the earth had dried out.
9:7	◄	be fruitful and multiply, increase greatly on the earth and multiply in it.
9:17	○	God said to Noah, "This is the sign of the covenant that I have established between me and all flesh that is on the earth."
9:29	○	All the days of Noah were 950 years, and he died.
10:14	◄	Pathrusim, Casluhim (from whom the Philistines came), and Caphtorim.
10:20	◄	These are the sons of Ham, by their clans, their languages, their lands, and their nations.
10:32	○	These are the clans of the sons of Noah, according to their genealogies, in their nations, and from these the nations spread abroad on the earth after the flood.
11:9	○	Therefore its name was called Babel, because there the Lord confused the language of all the earth. And from there the Lord dispersed them over the face of all the earth.

11:11	✦	And Shem lived after he fathered Arpachshad 500 years . . .
11:13	✦	And Arpachshad lived after he fathered Shelah 403 years . . .
11:15	✦	And Shelah lived after he fathered Eber 403 years . . .
11:17	✦	And Eber lived after he fathered Peleg 430 years . . .
11:19	✦	And Peleg lived after he fathered Reu 209 years . . .
11:21	✦	And Reu lived after he fathered Serug 207 years . . .
11:23	✦	And Serug lived after he fathered Nahor 200 years . . .
11:25	✦	And Nahor lived after he fathered Terah 119 years . . .
11:32	✦	The days of Terah were 205 years, and Terah died in Haran.
12:9	◯	And Abram journeyed on, still going toward the Negeb.
13:18	◯	So Abram moved his tent and came and settled by the oaks of Mamre, which are at Hebron, and there he built an altar to the Lord.
14:24	✦	I will take nothing but what the young men have eaten, and the share of the men who went with me. Let Aner, Eshcol, and Mamre take their share."
15:21	✦	the Amorites, the Canaanites, the Girgashites and the Jebusites.
16:16	✦	Abram was eighty-six years old when Hagar bore Ishmael to Abram.

17:14	◄	Any uncircumcised male who is not circumcised in the flesh of his foreskin shall be cut off from his people; he has broken my covenant.
17:27	○	And all the men of his house, those born in the house and those bought with money from a foreigner, were circumcised with him.
19:38	◄	The younger also bore a son and called his name Ben-ammi. He is the father of the Ammonites to this day.
20:18	◄	For the Lord had closed all the wombs of the house of Abimelech because of Sarah, Abraham's wife.
21:21	○	He lived in the wilderness of Paran, and his mother took a wife for him from the land of Egypt.
21:34	○	And Abraham sojourned many days in the land of the Philistines.
22:19	○	So Abraham returned to his young men, and they arose and went together to Beersheba. And Abraham lived at Beersheba.
22:24	◄	Moreover, his concubine, whose name was Reumah, bore Tebah, Gaham, Tahash, and Maacah.
23:20	◄	The field and the cave that is in it were made over to Abraham as property for a burying place by the Hittites.
24:67	○	Then Isaac brought her into the tent of Sarah his mother and took Rebekah, and she became his wife, and he loved her. So Isaac was comforted after his mother's death.
25:11	◄	After the death of Abraham, God blessed Isaac his son.

25:18	⬭	They settled from Havilah to Shur, which is opposite Egypt in the direction of Assyria. He settled over against all his kinsmen.Ishmaelites settled from Havilah to Shur, which is opposite Egypt
25:34	◀	Then Jacob gave Esau bread and lentil stew, and he ate and drank an1:5d rose and went his way. Thus Esau despised his birthright.
26:33	◀	He called it Shibah; therefore the name of the city is Beersheba to this day.
26:35	◀	and Esau's wives made life bitter for Isaac and Rebekah.
28:9	◀	Esau went to Ishmael and took as his wife, besides the wives he had, Mahalath the daughter of Ishmael, Abraham's son, the sister of Nebaioth.
32:3	⬭	And Jacob sent messengers before him to Esau his brother in the land of Seir, the country of Edom
33:17	◀	But Jacob journeyed to Succoth, and built himself a house and made booths for his livestock.
33:20	◀	There he erected an altar and called it El-Elohe-Israel.
34:31	⬭	But they said, "Should he treat our sister like a prostitute?"
35:8	⬭	And Deborah, Rebekah's nurse, died, and she was buried under an oak below Bethel. So he called its name Allon-bacuth.
35:29	⬭	And Isaac breathed his last, and he died and was gathered to his people, old and full of days. And his sons Esau and Jacob buried him.
36:19	◀	These are the sons of Esau (that is, Edom), and these are their chiefs.

36:30	⬯	Dishon, Ezer, and Dishan; these are the chiefs of the Horites, chief by chief in the land of Seir.
36:43	⬯	Magdiel, and Iram; these are the chiefs of Edom (that is, Esau, the father of Edom), according to their dwelling places in the land of their possession.
37:36	⬯	Meanwhile the Midianites had sold him in Egypt to Potiphar, an officer of Pharaoh, the captain of the guard.
38:30	⌇	Afterward his brother came out with the scarlet thread on his hand, and his name was called Zerah.
39:23	⌇	The keeper of the prison paid no attention to anything that was in Joseph's charge, because the Lord was with him. And whatever he did, the Lord made it succeed.
40:23	⬯	Yet the chief cupbearer did not remember Joseph, but forgot him.
44:17	⬯	But he said, "Far be it from me that I should do so! Only the man in whose hand the cup was found shall be my servant. But as for you, go up in peace to your father."
46:7	⌇	his sons, and his sons' sons with him, his daughters, and his sons' daughters. All his offspring he brought with him into Egypt.
46:27	⬯	And the sons of Joseph, who were born to him in Egypt, were two. All the persons of the house of Jacob who came into Egypt were seventy.
47:31	⬯	And he said, "Swear to me"; and he swore to him. Then Israel bowed himself upon the head of his bed.

48:22	⌀	Moreover, I have given to you rather than to your brothers one mountain slope that I took from the hand of the Amorites with my sword and with my bow."
49:4	⌀	Unstable as water, you shall not have preeminence, because you went up to your father's bed; then you defiled it—he went up to my couch!
49:7	⟨	Cursed be their anger, for it is fierce, and their wrath, for it is cruel! I will divide them in Jacob and scatter them in Israel.
49:12	⌀	His eyes are darker than wine, and his teeth whiter than milk.
49:13	⟨	Zebulun shall dwell at the shore of the sea; he shall become a haven for ships, and his border shall be at Sidon.
49:15	⟨	He saw that a resting place was good, and that the land was pleasant, so he bowed his shoulder to bear, and became a servant at forced labor.
49:19	⟨	"Raiders shall raid Gad, but he shall raid at their heels.
49:20	⟨	"Asher's food shall be rich, and he shall yield royal delicacies.
49:21	⟨	"Naphtali is a doe let loose that bears beautiful fawns.
49:26	⌀	The blessings of your father are mighty beyond the blessings of my parents, up to the bounties of the everlasting hills. May they be on the head of Joseph, and on the brow of him who was set apart from his brothers.

This process continued in the Torah and the rest of the Hebrew Testament.

APPENDIX
C

Each two-letter Hebrew word in this list is followed by a new word that concatenates a Hey (ה) to the end of the original word. As you can see, the added Hey intensifies, broadens and builds upon the emotional content of the original Hebrew word in most cases.

These words were taken from <u>Ancient Hebrew Lexicon of the Bible</u> by Jeff A. Benner, 2005. There were many more two-letter Hebrew words ending in Hey than in Alpha. So, I limited the number of entries to four pages – the same as in Appendix A.

(Sorry, my computer's Hebrew character set does not include final symbols for כ, מ, נ, פ, צ.)

אב Father
אבה Desire of the father

אה A sigh
אהה Screaming out of pain

או Desire
אוה Longing

אז A specific time (harvest time)
אזה Kindle / hot

אי Place
איה Where

אל	An ox in the yoke / Strongly yoked
אלה	Oath / Curse / Swear
אמ	Bind / Glue / Mother
אמה	Bondwoman / Terror
אנ	Strong seed / A male searching out a female to reproduce / Produce
אנה	Seeking out of another to meet / The arrival of another
את	Plow mark / Moving toward a mark
אתה	Arrive / You – as one who has arrived
בז	Spoils, A house attacked / plundered
בזה	Despise, To despise what is now worthless
בל	Flow, Nothing, To come to nothing
בלה	Terror, A flowing away of life / strength / function
בנ	Son, New life in the tent / house.
בנה	Build a building, home, family – make children
בר	Adult Son, Grain
ברה	Eat, Meat, Covenant
גא	High
גאה	Pride
גב	Lift, Arch of the back when lifting
גבה	Something that is lifted up high
גו	Back – the middle part of the body
גוה	Lift, High – something that is lifted up high

גז	Sheer, Fleece – The sheering of sheep for their wool
גזה	Sheer

גן	Garden / A gathering of seeds often surrounded by a wall
גנה	Garden

גר	Sojourn / Traveler / Fear
גרה	The cud chewed by a clean animal

דד	A woman's breasts / Passion / Love
דדה	The grace and beauty of the breasts

דכ	Crush / Mortar / Crush seeds into powder
דכה	Bruise / Wounded

דל	Door / a Poor or weak person
הדל	a Lifting out of the well / Draw / Enough / Lifted

דמ	Blood
דמה	Likeness / Compare

דע	See / Knowledge
דעה	Knowledge

הו	Sigh
הוה	Exist / Breath

הי	a Sigh / Disaster
היה	Breath / Exist

המ	Roar / Sea
המה	Roar / Abundant

הנ	Look / Here
הנה	Behold / Here
הר	High / Hill
הרה	Pregnant
זכ	Belt
זכה	Pure / Without impurities
זנ	Harvest / Mattock
זנה	Whore / Whoredom / Commit fornication
חד	Unite / Unity
חדה	Join
חז	See / Vision – Beyond physical sight
חזה	Perceive / Light / Behold / Prophecy
חי	Live / Stomach
חיה	Lively – Having the vigor of life
חכ	Stick / Palate / the Roof of the Mouth
חכה	Stick to the roof of the mouth
חל	Bore / Hole / Pain – drill a hole
חלה	Cake – As perforated
חמ	Heat / Cheese / to Separate
חמה	the Sun – The source of heat
חק	Inscribe / Custom
חקה	Inscribe / Carve / Print
חת	· Break / Fear
חתה	Seize - To break down causing great fear

APPENDIX D

I wanted to compare the Hebrew and Septuagint texts for the verses in Genesis that contained the words "the generations of" to better understand why the first word in 2:4 was translated as "these" as is found in virtually all the translations of this word combination.

As you can see below, Genesis 5:1 is the only text in Genesis that writes a different Hebrew word at the beginning of this phrase. That word is correctly translated as "This." However, it is used for the meaning of אלה in all the other verses.

Notice that the Septuagint translation of 2:4 contains the word "book" even though that word is missing from the Hebrew text. It is also missing from all the other instances except 5:1 – the same Hebrew text whose first word is also different.

It seems obvious that the Septuagint scholars used the first word in 5:1 to translate אלה in 2:4 because they also included "book" in that verse even though it is missing from the Hebrew. 2:4 is the only verse that speaks of generations other than human ones.

Perhaps the Septuagint scholars had such a hard time understanding how the heavens and the earth could have generations that they could added "book" to the sentence making it more comprehensible.

Genesis 2:4 from the Hebrew text:

אלה תולדות השמים והארץ

(These) are the generations of the heavens and the earth.

Genesis 2:4 from the Septuagint edition:

αυτη η βιβλος γενεσεως ουρανου και γης

This is the book of the generation of heaven and earth

Genesis 5:1 from the Hebrew text:

זה ספר תולדת אדם

This is the book of the generations of Adam

Genesis 5:1 from the Septuagint edition:

αυτη η βιβλος γενεσεως ανθρωπων

This is the book of the generation of "men" / Man

Genesis 6:9 Hebrew text:

אלה תולדות נוח

(These) are the generations of Noah

Genesis 6:9 Septuagint edition:

αυται δε αι γενεσεις νωε

And these are the generations of Noah

Genesis 10:1 Hebrew text:

ואלה תולדות בני־נוח

(These) are the generations of the sons of Noah

Genesis 10:1 Septuagint edition:

αυται δε αι γενεσεις των υιων νωε

These are the generations of the sons of Noah

Genesis 11:10 Hebrew text:

אלה תולדות שמ

(These) are the generations of Shem

Genesis 11:10 Septuagint edition:

και αυται αι γενεσεις σημ

And these are the generations of Shem

Genesis 11:27 Hebrew text:

ואלה תולדות תרח

(These) are the generations of Tera

Genesis 11:27 Septuagint edition:

αυται δε αι γενεσεις θαρα

These are the generations of Terah

Genesis 25:12 Hebrew text:

ואלה תולדות ישמעאל

(These) are the generations of Ishmael

Genesis 25:12 Septuagint edition:

αυται δε αι γενεσεις ισμαηλ

These are the generations of Ishmael

Genesis 25:19 Hebrew text:

ואלה תולדות יצחק

(These) are the generations of Isaac

Genesis 25:19 Septuagint edition:

και αυται αι γενεσεις ισαακ

These are the generations of Isaac

Genesis 36:1 Hebrew text:

ואלה תולדות עשו

(These) are the generations of Esau

Genesis 36:1 Septuagint edition:

αυται δε αι γενεσεις ησαυ

These are the generations of Esau

Genesis 36:9 Hebrew text:

ואלה תולדות עשו

(These) are the generations of Esau

Genesis 36:9 Septuagint edition:

αυται δε αι γενεσεις ησαυ

These are the generations of Esau

Genesis 37:2 Hebrew text:

אלה תולדות יעקב

(These) are the generations of Jacob

Genesis 37:2 Septuagint edition:

αυται δε αι γενεσεις ιακωβ

These are the generations of Jacob

Table of the Ancient Hebrew Alphabet

א		Aleph	An Ox, A Leader, Strength, Power, First
ב	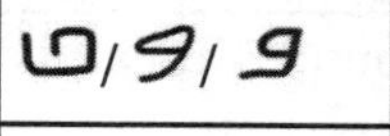	Bet	A Tent, House, Body, Family, Inside, "In"
ג	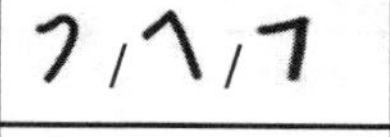	Gimel	Foot, Camel, Lift Up, Benefit, Self Will or Pride
ד	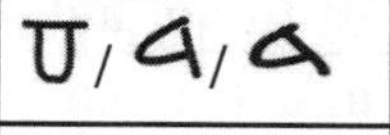	Dalet	Tent Door, A Path, Way, Movement In and Out
ה	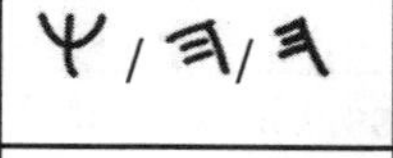	Hey	Lo!, Behold, Show, Reveal, Praise, Awe, "The"
ו	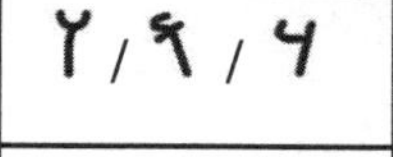	Vuv	Tent Peg, Hook, Nail, Join Together, "And"
ז	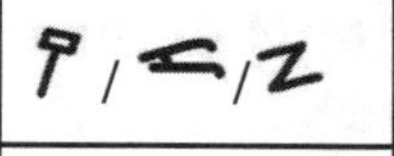	Zayin	Cudgel, Weapon, Sword, To Pierce, To Cut
ח		Chet	Fence, Wall, Separate, Cut Off, Protect
ט		Thet	Surround, Twist, Coil, A Basket, A Snake
י	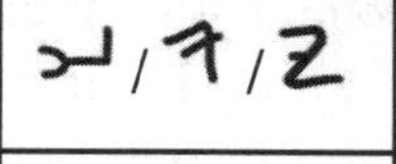	Yood	Hand, Work, Strength of My Arm, A Deed Done
כ		Kaph	Palm, Cover, Allow, Conform To My Palm, Open
ל		Lamed	Shepherd Staff, Control, Authority, "To," "Toward"
מ	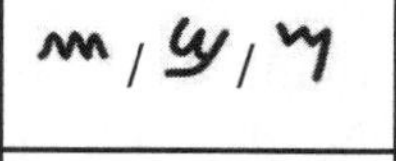	Mem	Water, Chaos, Mighty, Many, "From," "Than"
נ	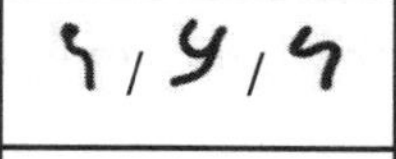	Noon	A Sprout, New Life, To Spread, Continue, Action
ס	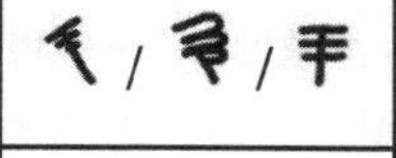	Samech	A Thorn, A Support, A Shield, Protect, Assist, Prop
ע	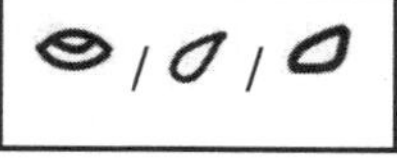	Ayin	An Eye, See, Experience, Understand

פ	ⵔ / ⵕ / ⵖ	Pey	A Mouth, To Speak, An Opening, The Beginning
צ	ⵀ / ⵁ / ⵂ	Tsade	A Hook, Pull Toward, Desire, Trouble, Ambush
ק	ⵃ / ⵄ / ⵅ	Qoof	Cycle, Surround, Sun at the Horizon, After
ר	ⵆ / ⵇ / ⵈ	Resh	A Head, A Person, First, Highest / Most Important
ש	W / ⵉ / ⵊ	Sheen	Teeth, Consume, Devour, Destroy
ת	+ / ⵋ / ⵌ	Tav	A Sign, Cross, Covenant, Finish, Complete

Converting Hebrew Characters Into Pictograms

Convert the characters in the Hebrew word you are studying from their representation in column one into their corresponding pictograms in column two. Then, determine the meaning of this word by meditating on the basic definition of each symbol in column four together with each symbol's position in the word and the word's position in the verse. When you meditate, ask the Holy Spirit to lead you into the meaning He inspired for this verse. Believe that He will guide you through prayer and your meditation (John 16:13 – 15).

Example: ברא House (ⵔ) Heads (ⵆ) First (ⵀ). Either a grain of wheat or a first-born adult son.

A grain of wheat: Think of a mature wheat plant. At the top of the stalk is a cluster of grains in the wheat heads – a house of heads. When a grain is planted, it creates the next generation of wheat.

A first-born adult son: Think of a first-born adult son who is one of the sons in his father's house – a house of heads. When the son leaves home, he creates the next generation of his father's family.